By the Grace of the Sea

By the Grace

A Woman's Solo Odyssey

AROUND THE WORLD

Pat Henry

INTERNATIONAL MARINE / McGRAW-HILL

Camden, Maine • New York • Chicago • San Francisco • Lisbon • London • Madrid
Mexico City • Milan • New Delhi • San Juan • Seoul • Singapore • Sydney • Toronto

The **McGraw·Hill** Companies

Visit us at: www.internationalmarine.com

10 9 8 7 6 5 4 3 2 1 DOC
Copyright © 2003 Pat Henry
All rights reserved. The name "International Marine" and the
International Marine logo are trademarks of The McGraw-Hill
Companies. Printed in the United States of America.

Library of Congress Cataloging-in-Publication Data
Henry, Pat, 1941–
    By the grace of the sea : a woman's solo odyssey around the
world / Pat Henry.
            p.   cm.
    ISBN 0-07-135527-8 (hardcover : alk. paper)
    1. Henry, Pat, 1941– —Journeys. 2. Southern Cross (Sailboat).
    3. Voyages around the world. 4. Sailing, Single-handed. I. Title.
    G440.H495 H46 2002
    910.4′1—dc21   2002006319

To Aileen Tobiassen Stuber

HER COURAGE,

FAITH,

AND COMPASSION

GAVE ME MINE

Contents

Preface

By the *Grace of the Sea* is more than a sailing story of my eight-year journey on board *Southern Cross*. To understand the drive and motives behind it I had to examine those moments from childhood, marriage, motherhood, career, and life that propelled me to the edge of a chasm and pushed me out of Acapulco on May 4, 1989. It took an inner journey as well to reach the other side.

Revealing the threads, treasures, refuse, and rubble of my life meant including those who shared it. Some will wish I had not told all that I did and others may wish I had said more, but I chose from among life's fragments those that defined the woman who left Acapulco and those en route that left an indelible impression and tilted the course of my life.

The people and boats found in *Grace* are real, but some identities and descriptions have been changed. Most of those mentioned contributed to my life and this journey in significant ways. Writing about them is one way to express my debt of gratitude. Even those who might seem to have been a negative influence gave me a lesson in life and an opportunity to better know myself. I thank them, too.

There are letters throughout the following pages. None are literal copies, but some reflect closely the nature and content of real letters. Others I wish I had written. They carry the thoughts and emotions of the moment that I failed to put down and send. Those for whom they were intended may only now know my feelings.

Within the following story are entries from the logs of *SC*. They reflect the conditions on board that shaped a day of struggle against harsh forces or one of tranquillity. They are written in the common language of a ship's log. The date follows international conventions (like the U.S. military) of day, month, and year in ascending order. Time is based on the twenty-four-hour clock used around the world without A.M. or P.M. Sometimes it is local time and at others it is Zulu time, which we also know as Greenwich Mean Time (GMT), the time at the prime meridian, 0 degrees of longitude, which runs from pole to pole through Greenwich, England. My location is shown in degrees of latitude and longitude with the hemisphere indicated. *SC*'s course is expressed in magnetic degrees, not in true, as I steered to the compass reading, which varies across the surface of Earth with the pull of the magnetic poles. Distances are given in nautical miles and speeds in nautical miles per hour, the universal measurement of sea and air travel. A nautical mile—the distance along the curve of the earth—is slightly longer than a statute or land mile, which is the chord of the curve. This difference makes a knot slightly faster than a mile per hour. Sea, wind, and current directions are by the marks of a compass rose, the card inside a compass showing NNE (north-northeast), S, NW , SSW , and so on. Wind and sea read as the direction they are coming from and current in the direction it is flowing toward. These are the hard-edged details that ruled my days and nights at sea.

At the end of my voyage my mother pressed me to write the story of my travels. It seemed a simple thing to her, a journalism graduate. I resisted, considered a coauthor, and finally agreed to the task. Armed with materials gathered over eight years and a contract with International Marine/McGraw-Hill, I began. Three months later, after ninety pages were finished, my editor wrote back that he liked the first three paragraphs. Writing this story seemed far beyond my capabilities, but it was too late to back out. Jumping on *Southern Cross* and sailing away was not a solution this time. As in the trip itself, I would go ahead word-by-word and page-by-page until it was finished.

I stumbled, groping for threads not of the outer journey but of the inner process that had changed me. I sought inspiration and direction from the bookshelf in my studio in Puerto Vallarta, Mexico, starting with Christopher Vogler's *The Writer's Journey*. Not only did the story begin to take form, but also an understanding of my life. Vogler approached story analysis and telling through the universally recognized form of myth. Using the symbolic parallels he found with human life unlocked a path to understanding and provided focus and structure to my writing.

I began again, consuming books I had collected: Maureen Murdock's *The Heroine's Journey: Woman's Quest for Wholeness*; Joseph Campbell's *The Hero with a Thousand Faces*; Clarissa Pinkola Estés's *Women Who Run with the Wolves: Myths and Stories of the Wild Woman Archetype*; Caroline M. Myss's *Anatomy of the Spirit: The Seven Stages of Power and Healing*; Arnold Mindell's *The Shaman's Body: A New Shamanism for Transforming Health, Relationships, and Community*; Michael J. Harner's *The Way of the Shaman: A Guide to Power and Healing*; Gregg Levoy's *Callings: Finding and Following an Authentic Life*; John Broomfield's *Other Ways of Knowing: Recharting Our Future with Ageless Widsom*; Linda Schierse Leonard's *The Wounded Woman: Healing the Father-Daughter Relationship*; Ted Andrews's *Animal-Speak: The Spiritual and Magical Powers of Creatures Great and Small*; and Shakti Gawain's *Creative Visualization*. Each book set me on another path back through my life, then forward to question where I was going and why.

I dug deeper into the layers revealed en route. Words sprang from insights and the following story emerged. It took both the physical journey of sailing and the spiritual journey of writing about it to bring peace.

Above all else this is a story of affirmation, of the power of grace, of listening to dreams that wait to be followed.

Puerto Vallarta, Mexico
June, 2002

_____ *for Pat Henry, who sailed the world alone*

IF THE MOON, IF YOU DANCE

I.

Draw a line across paper,
pale blue, slip inside
and you are a woman
   alone, sailing
where none have gone
before, you are
   simply woman
      on a journey
within thoughts of wind,
   sea and anchors.

Often anchors: ponderous weights
only the sea can bend. Fears
of being touched or not enough,
of getting what you want or losing
what you never knew you had.
About being without home, adrift,
sure the hand that extends for miles
is a reef off shore. Afraid. That you are not
today's woman: proud, able to do as man.
That striking a pose for his chiseling gaze

still feels so natural. You journey (sure
others feel you abandon) to ask
ancient stones about the sea, how it
rounds the edges of pride, you wander
in search of the missing Mother
　at the Oracle of Delphi
　　to tell you of your life.

11.

It is time you believe in
at first and not the moon
as you draw who you are
on the horizon and wait
for minutes to take you there.
Time. You study her face and hands
in a mirror. You point
(with fingers that feel
how you snatch at seconds)
to barbel lines around eyes
afraid the world is flat and that
　dreams sail over the edge.

As you wait to cross the line of time
when everything reverses,
the faces of sister, of parent
and brother, of child at every age
ripple across the water. You reach
to touch the years you have missed
and everyone, even you,
　disappears.

Then it happens. You see the moon
for the first time, and yourself
an ebb and flow of reason and spirit,
of engine and sail. Dolphins leave
the linear wake at the bow
to leap one quarter-note then another.
Even the wind feels jazzed. You hear

the music, the call of strings, the response
of a flute, the syncopated breach
of a baleen whale, you sigh
with an ancient knowing: you
   once belonged
      to the sea.

iii.

If you dance.
If you've ever swept the hair from your neck,
let the pluck and the moan of bouzouki strings
cause your bones to swoon with wave, if you've ever
been in love, ever swallowed the breath of another
and tasted the sweet absence of time, ever straddled
the border of country or state and imagined
your body a breeze across line and space
where Walls fall, where West meets East,
where sea brushes sky, if you've ever heard a voice
whose notes kiss your mind like silk
on naked skin, whose prayer prompts hairs
to lift your arms and you know you can fly
with the angels, wing-and-wing,
   then you know
      the wind.

SARAH ZALE

Prologue

CHAOS AND STICKY TROPICAL AIR SURROUND ME IN the tiny cabin of *Southern Cross*, my 31-foot sailboat, as I face my fears and my dreams. In the morning I shall leave the comfort and familiarity of this harbor at Acapulco, Mexico—my home of the past two weeks—to sail across three thousand empty ocean miles alone.

Lists strewn across the drop-down table show what I have finished, but also the number of projects that shuffled to the bottom of the pile again and again and still wait. I've run out of time, money, and know-how. It is now three days into the North Pacific hurricane season, and the calendar is breathing down my neck. Each day's delay raises the risk of encountering a storm at sea.

Over every counter and seat tumbles the harvest of last-minute errands: fresh produce, exotic medical supplies, clean laundry, charts, and a final stack of mail. My passport sits on top of the clutter, along with a visa for the Polynesian Islands of the South Pacific newly issued from the French Embassy in Mexico City. The photo inside shows someone I no longer recognize: a self-controlled woman in a fashionable business hairdo and elegant suit jacket, her smile more of gritted teeth than joy. Tonight the one-square-foot mirror in the head, my tiny bathroom, flashes back a tanned grinning face, a short natural haircut, and the crew neckline of a white T-shirt.

The strains of Pat Metheny's "Watercolors" slide through air scented with lemon oil from freshly polished bulkheads: sounds and smells that trigger memories of my left-behind life in Santa Cruz, California. There were Friday afternoons when I returned from the office to the lemony perfume of my just-cleaned little bungalow. There were Monday evenings when I was a faithful at the local jazz club. In that small concert space, I could almost reach out and touch the likes of Mose Allison and Lew Tabackin.

Once memory's door opens, more reminders crawl out to coax me back home: the scent of jasmine from my vest-pocket backyard by the yacht harbor—I always kept a fresh sprig next to my bed; the familiar feel of tiny rooms filled with the artwork of friends; the sounds of surf crashing against the breakwater and sea lions calling to mates on the rocks, lulling me to sleep; the feel of salt-laden fog in the summer as I walked the beach with tiny sandpipers racing ahead.

Scattered around my cabin are mementos from family and friends, each one carrying the touch of someone dear. Orange yarn baskets nestle down above my bunk, ready for the small treasures I will collect along the journey ahead. My younger daughter, Terri, made them for me when she was in grade school. They sit as empty as my heart, waiting for us to bridge twenty-two years of separation and become close again. When she was eight she chose to live with her father. Since then we have shared letters and visits but never the relationship I envisioned when I first held her in my arms. The yarn baskets have survived almost a quarter century of upheaval and transition. I hope their maker is as strong.

My grandmother's tomahawk is tucked behind my place at the table. I claim some of the same adventurous spirit that pushed her, in her early twenties, out of Iowa, alone on horseback, to stake her claim and build her tarpaper shack in the Sioux country of South Dakota.

My older daughter Tamara's gift of a small shell cradling an air fern is just visible in a cubbyhole across from my table. She has a strain of the Earth Mother in her veins and cannot bear to see me go without something alive and growing for me to nurture and to nurture me—to take me out of my self-containment.

A long, white gull's feather from my friend Shane pokes out from a crevice above the chart table. She picked it up the day of our last stroll on the beach. Shane knew me almost as well as I know myself, if bodies give away our deepest secrets. Every week when I visited her small studio for a massage, she unlocked mystery after mystery with probing fingers that searched out the hidden pain, stored anger, and old fears of a lifetime.

I taped my friend Kitty's handmade postcard to the galley wall. The crazy collage of rubber-stamped images diverts and delights me while I fix meals and do dishes. Down the center, three turbaned swamis stare out from a blue background. On both sides of each head a brown hand points to a red moon nesting one star. It says to me: "It's all a matter of chance whether we go right or left, but the end is the same."

A two-and-a-half-foot long, spindly, dry stick is Velcroed at one end to the wall by my seat at the table. The Abnaki Indians of Maine and the Maritime Provinces used these to forecast the weather. If wind is on the way, it curves up; if the wind is abating, it curves down. My brother, Stu, sent it to guide me around the storms ahead. His humor comes tucked in with every gift and letter, a sly, dry wit from our mother with his own light sprinkling of Illinois "corn."

Long soaks in a steamy bathtub are the hallmark of Libby, my sister. She sent a container of Paloma Picasso bath powder, ensuring a little luxury to follow my cold saltwater bucket baths on long ocean passages. It is safely wedged in the small medicine cabinet in the head. The archaeology of my life can be found in layers of different scents: Royal Secret perfume takes me back to the mid-1960s and weekends skiing in northern Illinois; Dalton recalls life with Lars, my former husband the banker, in the mid-1970s, and Paloma Picasso is from the 1980s business life I am leaving behind. The sense of smell, it is said, has more power to evoke memories than any other.

My mother gave me a small edition of the New Testament full of her annotations, hoping I would someday open the cover and find the joy and peace it brought to her stormy life. In her mid-sixties she found a husband who shares her view of the world and the purpose of life. Her old pains and trials are only fading memories, lost behind her newfound happiness.

Sitting on a shelf is a wood carving my grandfather made of a swordfish jumping from a curling wave. He was the kindest, most gentle person I ever knew and my favorite companion between the ages of five and seven, when his love and attention softened the absence of a real father. Only after he died at eighty-two did I realize what I had let slip away in the years when I had been too full of myself and my own interests to listen to his lessons. To the end he remained a strong, tall vibrant man, testing himself and trying new things, like building his first violin at eighty even though he could not play one.

I have one small treasure from my father, a man who exists only in fleeting images and barely captured memories. I saw him twenty times in my life, between ages fourteen and thirty-four. I don't yet know how to measure his absence. I always pretended it didn't matter. He once gave a speech in Australia and brought me two black opals cut from the same rock; I designed a ring and had it made. It's the only piece of him I own.

More than three hundred books fill every leftover space. Some I treasure and cannot live without: *A Room of One's Own*, *The Color Purple*, *West with the Night*, and Elizabeth Barrett Browning's *Sonnets from the Portuguese*. Others I always thought I should read: *When the Cathedrals Were White*, *Kindergarten Chats*, *Great Adventures in Small Boats*, *Androgyny*, and *Walden*. Others have moved from shelf to shelf, house to house, waiting to be read: *The Brothers Karamazov*, *Babbitt*, *20,000 Leagues under the Sea* and *Moby-Dick*. There are recipe books, how-to-fix-it books, health, travel, and some books for soul-searching during the long, private days ahead.

From my Santa Cruz home I have brought reminders of pleasurable times and comforts from the life left behind. My stovetop espresso maker, down pillow, and good cotton sheets—fixtures from the beginnings and ends of days, moments to celebrate with ritual and renewal. I no longer have my early morning breakfasts at the butcher block table by the front window, reading the paper and watching the morning sky change color over the masts in the harbor below; nor can I take the long walk on the tide-washed sand that offered, each morning, an unblemished expanse for fresh footprints, free of regrets. Now I take my coffee to the cockpit and curl up to watch a foreign harbor awaken, anticipating the gift of another day in my strange new life.

The overhead of *Southern Cross*'s cozy cabin gleams white, shiny, and clean; plump, sea-green cushions with tiny flecks of pink soften the inside of my cocoon. Every other home I created was black and white with strong primary accents. This time my soul called for something peaceful. Hand-embroidered throw pillows, brass kerosene lanterns, nautical gear, and teak-and-holly flooring give the feeling of warmth and safety, security and home.

The names of the islands and villages at the end of my passage swim into focus. I am torn between dreams of far-off places and the safety of this one. If this were my first transoceanic sail, I don't know if I could do it alone. But I have sailed almost forty thousand miles on other people's boats and about two thousand coastal miles solo on this one. I think I know what will happen out there.

The lists on the cabin table are my safety net. All my life, since at least the age of ten, I have made endless lists of everything. My mother thought it funny when she once found a list of the lists I needed to make. For me they were keys that might open any door; later, they were an attempt to bring order and structure to an ambitious life. Now, at forty-eight, I trust my lists to keep me safe. I have addressed the potential dangers in one headed "Situations to Deal With: Fire, Capsize, Holing, Grounding, Overboard, Dismasting" . . . all the worst possible scenarios I could imagine. I read what I could about each, but the resulting gear lists were formidable and beyond my budget. Avoiding these situations looks like my only option. I carry only the basics for survival and safety and hope I never have to use them.

I finish stowing and organizing, getting the cabin ready for sea, then pull out my typewriter for one last job. My mother keeps asking why I am making this trip. She was born and raised in South Dakota and has lived all her adult life in central Illinois. She has never traveled to see the world. How can she understand my love for the sea, for foreign places, and my hunger for more in life? But that is only a piece of the story. I still have not shared with her the nightmare of the last two years. Now it is time, before I set sail.

I face the blank sheet and listen to the minutes ticking away on the bulk-head clock. The words toss back and forth in my mind. None of them look pretty. A scolding Greek chorus pops unbidden into my imagination, fingers wagging, offering a running judgment on my life: "Failure, incompetent, too big for her shoes, always setting her marks too high, she got what she deserved . . . "

In 1987 TWT, the textile import company I started in 1982 in answer to the twin dictates of wanderlust and the need for an occupation, began to fail. In five years we had grown from one to twenty-two employees in two divisions: home fashion textiles and high-performance industrial fabrics. From 1984 on, while I directed product development and marketing, Kelly, our CFO, handled finance, accounting, and staff. The company breathed its last in early 1988, leaving me broke and emotionally spent. In the midst of the rubble I faced my shortcomings with shame. Mom knows of the failure, but I have lacked the courage to divulge the whole story. The magnitude of my poor judgment reached far beyond anything she can imagine, including the involvement of my former husband Lars.

Each of her letters for the past seven months has begun, "I don't under-stand why you're making this trip or why you're going alone." At first I brushed her off with descriptions of a life in Mexico on board *Southern Cross*, then talk of a trip through the South Pacific to New Zealand, and finally this spring with the dream of a full circumnavigation. Each time I have attributed these plans to my love of sailing and seeing the world, but I have never spoken of my real reason. Harry Stern, an old school friend, has finally brought things to a head by suggesting to my mother that my going off in a sailboat alone is tantamount to a "death wish."

Dear Mom,

Southern Cross and I are finally ready for our first major ocean crossing. I'll leave in the morning and should arrive in Nuku Hiva in about thirty days. That's the first of the Marquesas Islands en route to Tahiti.

You're right; there's more to the story behind this trip, but it is certainly not the death wish Harry suggested. In fact, it's the opposite. I hope it will restore a sense of self-esteem and purpose after the disastrous end of TWT. This is the rest of the story.

In 1986 our debt reached $3 million with the last loan Lars wrote for us as our banking officer at his savings and loan. He told Kelly and me we should apply for $500,000 for a real estate project he wanted us to pursue—a project having nothing to do with our textile business—then without consulting us he wrote the loan for $1.7 million. The balance was to go for projects he had lined up under his own sideline company.

Kelly and I both balked at first. It didn't feel right to either of us, but Lars emphatically assured us that everything was fine. The loan committee had approved it all. We signed the papers, including the personal guarantees they required from us as CEO and CFO. What a joke. Neither of us had anything to back up such amounts, and we were positive they knew that. We had submitted accurate financial statements and projections to the committee. Lars explained it was just a matter of form. We assumed that if they were willing to loan us the money based on our documentation, everything must be fine.

A year later, while I was in Korea scrambling to get our fire-retardant products back on line, Kelly got a call from our bank saying that the FBI had requested all our records. You can imagine the emotions that call produced.

But it was only the beginning of the nightmare. Before long the FBI called to tell Kelly there were signed documents in our files they knew we'd never seen. "The signatures were forged," they said.

Next we got word from a legal firm in San Francisco claiming they had a connection inside the grand jury judge's chambers—the judge was the wife of someone in the firm. They reported that an indictment was in the pipeline for me and recommended that I not go home that night. Eventually we found their claims were groundless—there was never a threat against me—but meanwhile the fear and uncertainty ate at my soul.

FSLIC, the government insurance program for savings and loans, took over Lars's institution and eventually sued most of the officers, TWT, and many other clients. Each bank officer including Lars sued every other one, and each of them filed against us. Countersuits were our only defense.

We became a part of the California savings-and-loan debacle of 1988. Many of the officers of our institution went to prison, including Lars. I can only tell you that Kelly and I made very poor decisions, and we failed to listen to our inner voices. We did nothing illegal and never set out to deceive anyone, but these facts do little to take away the tainted feeling I carry.

In the aftermath, each day I looked at the want ads and could only see what I couldn't do. If I had failed at running my own business, if I had made such poor decisions in my dealings, who would want to hire me for a position of any responsibility? With each ad I imagined the interview and the reaction to my failure. Day after day I closed the paper and took my morning walk instead of sending out résumés.

All my life, my reaction to roadblocks has been to keep going—in a new direction, maybe, but with no less energy. This time it's different; I don't have the energy, and I don't know the direction. This trip is my answer. I hope in the months or years ahead I can find what I have lost—the ability to see myself with pride. I hope in time to forgive myself and accept the path I chose for the lessons it offered.

With a heart full of love for your compassion and understanding,

Pat

I roll another sheet of paper into the typewriter as thoughts of Kitty stroll through my mind. I remember her as she looked the day we met in 1974 at San José State University. Two weeks into the semester—my first as an assistant professor in interior design—Kitty appeared to take my advanced design class.

Blond, statuesque, a bit patrician, and six feet tall (she prefers to say 5 feet, 11¹⁵⁄₁₆ inches), Kitty looked down 8 inches at me, announcing that she was enrolling in my class. A trip to Yugoslavia had detained her, she said. Her performance on that first project ended my concern over the time she'd missed. Kit went on to become the best student I ever taught, adding a degree in Interior Design to her Stanford degree in journalism. Later she earned a master of fine arts from San Francisco Art Institute.

Our student-teacher relationship gradually evolved to one of friends who worked, traveled, and once even lived together. She became a full-time artist and art teacher, leaving her interior design profession behind in the early 1980s. Her reputation as a sculptor and painter grew as she entered juried shows, held her own exhibitions, and found galleries to represent her in Atlanta and San Francisco.

Now our roles are reversing. I am the student, timidly seeking my own path to become an artist.

Dear Kitty,

It is my last night in Mexico. Tomorrow the great adventure begins as I head to the South Pacific—the land of Paul Gauguin. Mexico's mainland has brought some surprising developments in my life. By the time I arrived at Puerto Vallarta in February, I was broke. For six months every penny had gone into *Southern Cross*.

My solution to the problem—paint. It seemed the most logical choice: no problems with foreign authorities for violating my immigration status by taking a job, supplies and equipment would be easy to carry on board, and as an architect I had learned to draw. I counted on my fellow cruisers buying miniature art to decorate their boats and dismissed thoughts of the starving artists I knew and doubts about my artistic ability.

In 1955, Miss Stein, the art teacher at Bloomington High School, shrugged her shoulders and rolled her eyes when I showed her my sketches and asked if I should bother taking any art classes my sophomore year. The seeds of self-doubt she planted in that moment have never left.

After much procrastination, I gathered my courage and rowed my little rubber dinghy around the anchorage, boat-to-boat, asking if anyone was interested in seeing my miniature paintings of shells. Sometimes I was almost relieved when they sent me away without looking, but I sold enough to earn $270 in the first three weeks. The acceptance meant more than the money. Perhaps I have found a new direction.

I'm far from being an "artist." The little paintings are technically all right, but it will take more than that.

I'll write you next from Tahiti.

Much love,

Pat

After stowing the typewriter for sea travel at the bottom of the hanging locker, *SC*'s sixteen-inch-wide closet, I fix a cup of Stash Licorice Spice tea and sit in the cockpit, trying to settle my departure nerves. Voices reach across the water from a nearby boat like the murmur of fellow campers in the woods, only here the ghosts of masts tower above instead of sentinel trees. A guitar player strikes a few familiar notes, and voices join in on Joan Baez's "Plaisir d'Amour." The lyrics remind me of the short, joyous beginnings and long, painful endings in a lifetime of marriages and relationships. For me, at least for now, life is easier and safer alone.

Lights shining from the hillsides around the harbor suggest families and couples sharing life and love in safe homes, homes with four walls sheltering people whose neighbors won't sail away on the morning tide. Familiar sounds drift down, as they will every morning and evening to come: the clang of the cowbell announcing the garbage truck, the ringing bell of the man bringing bottles of filtered water, church bells, the sounds of buses running down the same streets day after day. Tomorrow night for them will be the same, and I will be gone, somewhere at sea.

By the Grace of the Sea

PART ONE

Acapulco to New Zealand

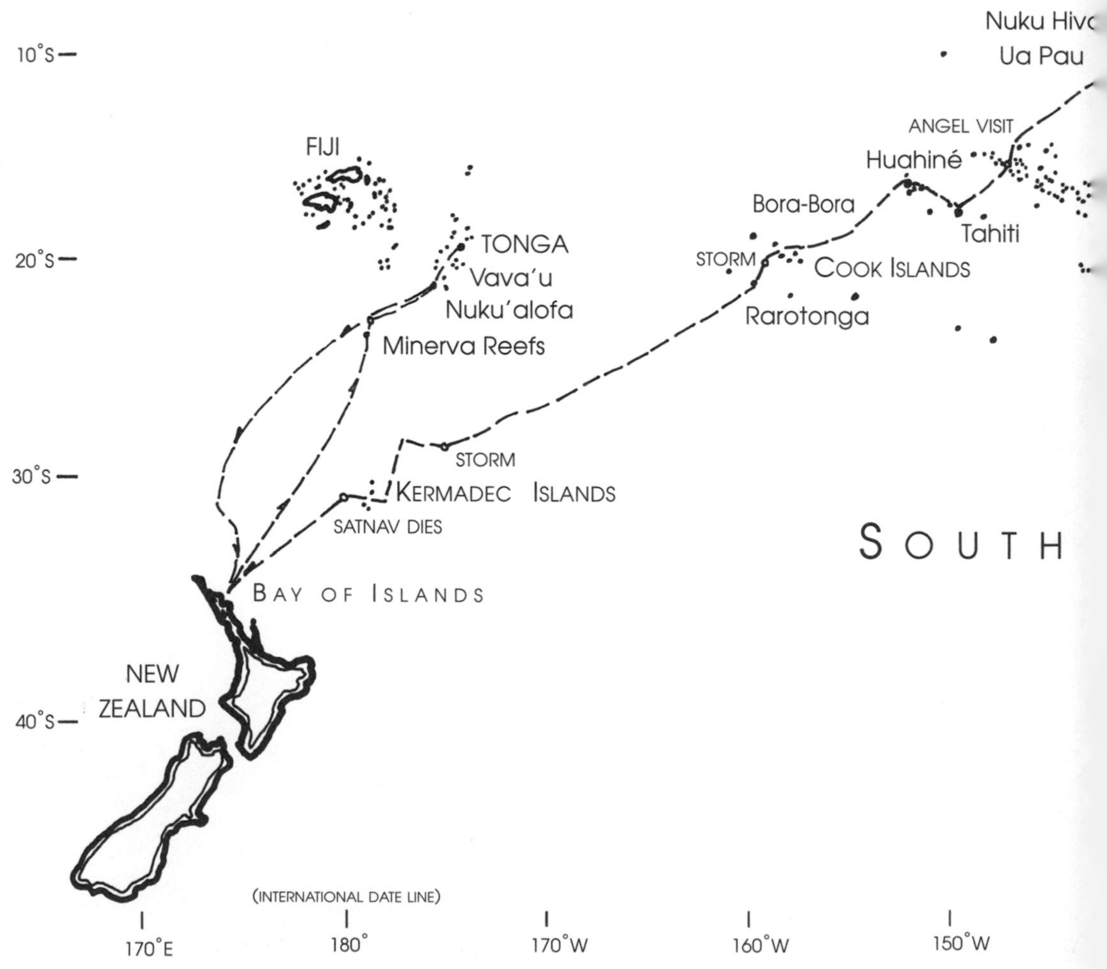

Nuku Hiv‹
• Ua Pau

10°S—

ANGEL VISIT

FIJI

Huahiné

Bora-Bora

TONGA
Tahiti

STORM
20°S—
Vava'u
COOK ISLANDS
Nuku'alofa
Minerva Reefs
Rarotonga

STORM

30°S—
KERMADEC ISLANDS
SATNAV DIES

SOUTH

BAY OF ISLANDS

NEW
ZEALAND
40°S—

(INTERNATIONAL DATE LINE)

170°E   180°   170°W   160°W   150°W

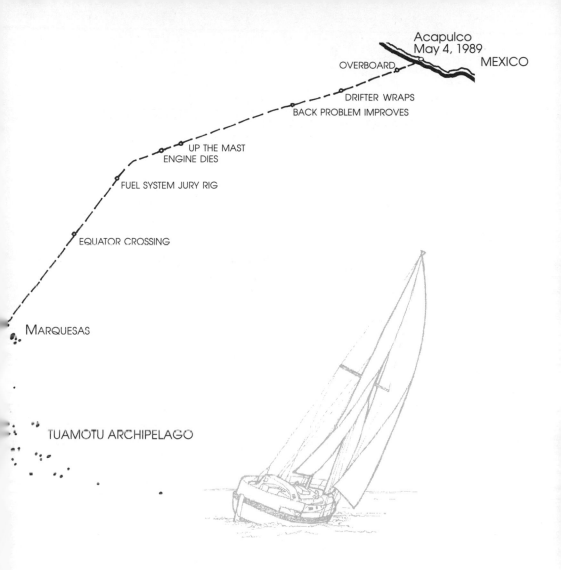

Acapulco
May 4, 1989
MEXICO

OVERBOARD

DRIFTER WRAPS
BACK PROBLEM IMPROVES

UP THE MAST
ENGINE DIES

FUEL SYSTEM JURY RIG

EQUATOR CROSSING

MARQUESAS

TUAMOTU ARCHIPELAGO

PACIFIC OCEAN

°W   130°W   120°W   110°W   100°W

SHIP'S DIARY: 0442 Local, 16°14′N/100°38′W, motorsailing at 5 knots with the main, steering 238M, light WSW wind, clear skies. Since departure at 1330 yesterday I've made 56 miles.

OF THE MORE THAN TWO HUNDRED CRUISING SAILBOATS arriving in Mexico in 1989, only a handful were turning southwest into the Pacific, sandwiching their departures between the South Pacific hurricane season ending in April and the one that had officially begun on May 1 in the North Pacific. And of that handful, only a few, like *Southern Cross*, had come to Acapulco for the large supermarkets and chandleries; the rest had already departed from points farther north.

The stragglers among a group en route to the Caribbean via the Panama Canal had waved good-bye as I circled past neighboring boats. For more than five months we had shared anchorages—down the coast from San Diego through Baja Mexico and the Mexican mainland—forming friendships almost instantly. A neighboring boat often greeted my arrival in an anchorage with a dinner invitation or a loaf of freshly baked bread, and by the end of the evening I knew them better than I had known most of my neighbors in Santa Cruz after eight years. Our shared experiences—of storms, broken gear, homesickness, and good news—and the help we offered each other—tools, know-how, charts, and a friendly ear—brought us together despite the knowledge that we would eventually part company.

Cathy Mackenzie, the Scottish veterinarian on board *Super Tramp*, remained behind to finish preparations for her sail north to Canada. She was the first woman singlehander I had met.

The rest of the anchorage considered the Mexican coast "home." Some had come south with plans to continue but found a place they liked. Others had run out of money, developed boat problems, or decided the boating life was not for them and were waiting for another dreamer searching for a boat to buy.

Waving friends off on long passages had become an accepted but still painful reality of my new life. For those with ham or single-sideband radio, the separation was gentler. They could keep in touch over thousands of miles, plan reunions at future ports of call, report problems, get advice, and through phone patches keep in contact with family back home. *Southern Cross* carried only a small Sony shortwave receiver to gather weather reports and news broadcasts via Voice of America and BBC, and listen to the progress of friends over the ham radio nets run by volunteers. I had no way to contact anyone more than 20 miles or so away. That was the limit of my VHF radio's range.

Before motoring out of the harbor the previous afternoon, I had finished preparing *Southern Cross* for the coming weeks under sail—tying fuel and water jugs, dinghy, and fenders securely to the lifelines, handrails, and rigging, topping off water and fuel tanks, replenishing food, ice, and bottled gas for cooking, and mailing letters. Below, the cabin was sea-ready, with dishes done and put away, extra sails stowed forward on the V-berth, charts and plotting sheets ready for use on the chart table, and every movable item stowed safely inside a locker.

After dinner, five hours offshore, I had seen two ships, confirming the anticipated presence of commercial traffic in the area. With the kitchen timer set at fifteen-minute increments—half the time it would take a ship doing the typical 18 knots to cover the distance from the horizon to *Southern Cross*—I dozed in the cockpit.

Now, through predawn air tinged with the scent of cilantro from last evening's vegetable stir fry, the glow from Acapulco's lights, fifty six miles behind, still defined the edge of the Earth above my wake. Ahead, the compass to the left of the companionway cast a pale red light over the cockpit, and from the right the blank screen of the knotmeter display stared back. Its malfunction usually indicated that a tiny creature had settled on the small paddle wheel on the bottom of *SC* and prevented the wheel from turning. The screen normally displayed *Southern Cross*'s speed and distance through the water— information I needed to gauge currents, navigate by dead reckoning, and tell if *SC* were carrying too much or too little sail for the wind.

Motoring forward and backward at full speed failed to dislodge the creature. I refused to go back to Acapulco and would not pull the mechanism out of the hull from inside. The manufacturer had provided a plug, but the thought of the ocean pouring into the boat through an inch-and-a-half hole, even for a second, terrified me. That left only one option—diving overboard to unfoul the impeller. A shiver ran down my back as I waited for sunrise and my impending baptism.

My subconscious replayed a scene from the movie *Overboard* in which Cliff Robertson watched helplessly from the water as the wind pulled the sails slowly up the rigging and his boat sailed away from him. I got up to tie all the sails to the boom and lifelines, secure the halyards, and find a line with which to tie myself to *Southern Cross*.

A well-known cruisers' story floated through my thoughts. Someone had found a boat in the middle of the ocean with the table set for dinner and no one on board. Later authorities pieced together the last moments of life: becalmed, the crew had decided to take a predinner dip from their high-free-board sailboat. Everyone jumped in together and then could find no way to climb back on board. Fingernail scratches showed in the gelcoat surface near the water. I hung *SC*'s small boarding ladder over the side and tied it securely to the rigging.

I squelched scenes from *Jaws* and looked hopefully, one more time, at the screen. It was still blank.

With a screwdriver in one hand and scrub brush in the other, wearing mask, snorkel, and the line tied around my waist, I backed down the ladder, took a deep breath, and slipped below like an astronaut floating into open space. An endless, featureless blue stretched in every direction. Drum rolls of apprehension pounded in my chest as I dove over and over, scrubbing the little wheel while darting 360-degree glances for danger. Finally finished, I rolled and played at the end of my tether for a moment, becoming one with the warm sea.

I climbed the ladder, turned on the engine, engaged the gear, and watched the numbers flash on the knot log screen. A smile spread across my face as I reached over to pat the deck. "*SC*, we're going to be all right."

That night I covered the narrow settee in the main cabin with a fresh white sheet, plumped up my pillow, and crawled in, savoring the delicious feel of cool cotton on bare skin. The moon swayed lazily above, visible through the open hatch. *Southern Cross* floated at the center of an immense black bowl studded with a million stars above and pulsing with life below.

A decade earlier, three years of voyaging on the trimaran *Windy* had shown me aspects of the life I was now entering. Over the next few days, in the absence of stimuli, everything would come into sharper focus. Sounds would magnify—the lap of the sea against the hull, the high-pitched call of dolphin, and changes in the wind piercing the quiet. By daylight, blue upon blue in varying shades would force my eyes to search for details in miles of sameness. The absence of smells would heighten each small scent. Sensors all over my body would awaken.

In 1981, after 35,000 miles on *Windy*, I moved ashore seeking a new home. Friends asked if it wasn't claustrophobic living on a boat "in that small space," but looking out one small window after another into tree limbs or neighboring walls felt like a jail cell to me. When I found a studio perched on a cliff in Santa Cruz with a view over the ocean and could see to the horizon again, I signed the lease and breathed deeply.

During the past year, memories of being at sea had pushed me through days in the boatyard working on *Southern Cross*. My body knew the rocking motion, the constant sway, the quick roll, and the need to brace instantly for the unexpected—one hand for me and one for the boat. Amid the turbulence of TWT's demise, I had craved the peace of the emptiness around me now. But nothing could have prepared me to be here alone nor told me what difficulties might lie ahead.

I closed my eyes, keeping one ear tuned for any unusual sound. In all those sailing miles on *Windy*, someone had kept a watch—twenty-four hours a day. Dangers lurked in the nighttime sea from big tankers and freight carriers moving at high speeds—often with no one at the helm and with their radar turned off—and from unexpected squalls, floating debris, other sailboats, or equipment failure. From books and conversations I knew that, once offshore, most singlehanders sleep at night. The odds are comfortably high against colliding with another vessel, and they assume the noise of changing weather conditions or equipment problems will rouse them. It is impossible to stay awake indefinitely. I made the same assumptions but wished my small budget could have included a radar—one with an alarm to notify me when anything approached.

With 120 miles of presumably empty sea between *Southern Cross* and land, on a windless night with the electric autopilot steering and the engine running, I sank into dreamless sleep. Every two hours or so the soft beep of the SatNav receiver announcing a new fix from orbiting satellites awoke me. I climbed to the cockpit, marveled at the sky, scanned the empty horizon, and returned below to plot the new position and go back to bed.

In the morning after breakfast, on the way up the stairs to the cockpit with a mug of coffee and *Gulliver's Travels*, I froze. The stern of a tanker mocked my assumptions. How closely and when had we passed? There was no way to know if she had crossed behind *SC*, or I had sailed in front of her. For the next forty hours I lived in the cockpit watching for ships that never came.

Three hundred miles out from Acapulco on May 8th, under sail in very light winds, I tracked a large cargo ship closing on a collision course. When she didn't answer my VHF call to ask if we would pass without a problem, I started the engine. She passed one mile off ten minutes later.

On May 9th, nearly four hundred miles offshore—no man's land—

another ship steamed dead ahead. Desperately needing sleep, I called to ask whether there would be more traffic in the area, but again there was no answer. She was the last encounter. Exhausted, I stretched out below and slept.

Peaceful days followed—in marked contrast to those of 18 months before. My only obligations were meals, a little navigation, maintenance, cleaning, and an occasional tweak of the sails, searching for more speed in the light winds. Then back to reading. Each night after dinner I doused a few buckets of salt water over my slowly browning body, dusted on a little Paloma Picasso, put on tights and a long-sleeved shirt, studied the familiar shapes in the emerging stars above, and returned to the settee.

Knowing I couldn't steer all the time, I carried two self-steering devices: an electric autopilot, which steered to an internal magnetic compass, and a non-electric wind vane controlled by changes in the direction of the wind. The autopilot consumed far too much electricity, and whenever the wind vane steered, *Southern Cross* made a wobbly line across the plotting sheets on which I recorded her progress. The Pathfinder vane had been one of *SC*'s selling points, but I had lacked the experience to evaluate the merits of its design. Either the wind vane was faulty, or there was too little wind to make it reliable, or I simply could not master it. A macramé of bungee cords to dampen the motion of the tiller and balance the helm grew steadily across the cockpit as I tried to control my course.

The line on the plotting sheets steadied whenever I engaged the autopilot, but only at the cost of precious battery power. I could recharge the batteries from a solar panel mounted on the stern rail and by running the engine, but conservation of water, fuel, and electricity was paramount. The fuel tank in the bottom of the hull held thirty-five gallons of diesel fuel, and the jerricans on deck another twenty—enough for 140 hours of engine time. With good weather, that might mean 630 miles of the more than 3,000 to Nuku Hiva.

SC's two water tanks contained fifty-five gallons, with twenty more in the water jugs on deck. That meant a gallon per day for drinking and cooking and one for a freshwater shower and shampoo once a week, with a safety margin. Nothing was allotted for laundry. My halfway-point celebration would include a clean sheet, and during warm days I abandoned clothes.

In the ghosting breeze I began to worry. At departure there had been enough fuel to get offshore and partway to the northeast trade winds, run the engine an hour a day for the batteries, use some to cross the doldrums around the equator and pick up the southeast trades in the Southern Hemisphere, and cover my arrival. In six days I had used the first allotment with no sign of the trades. Three miles away the horizon beckoned; I knew I could sail three miles. I wouldn't think about the miles on the other side.

These were the very conditions that had prompted me to lay out a sizable portion of my departure funds for a brand-new light-air sail—a radial head drifter that promised to respond to the lightest zephyr. But my first efforts at controlling this huge, bubbling piece of Dacron off the Baja coast, en route from Santa Cruz to Acapulco, had ended with a vow to keep it permanently stowed below. Now it was the only sail on board that could catch the light northeasterly breezes.

I tried flying it with and without the mainsail and with and without a downwind pole, looking for a winning combination. At 0730, as I brought the pole down to stow it, the boat rolled, the wind shifted and puffed, and the huge blue, white, and green spinnaker-like sail maypoled its way over and under itself, wrapping around the headstay in a hundred knots. At 1630, I finally dropped the last of the errant sail on deck and stuffed it through the forward hatch.

With the mainsail and 150 percent genoa catching a freshening northeasterly breeze, I collapsed below—dehydrated, hungry, close to heat exhaustion, and nursing a serious sunburn—once more swearing never to try *that* again.

That night, my eighth at sea, I tossed and rolled, hunting for a comfortable position. Tender, freshly burned skin made sleeping on my back impossible, and sciatica interfered with every other position.

The low back pain had first struck the previous November, immobilizing me as I built cabinets and installed heavy new marine batteries in Ventura, California. Off the Baja coast, it had brought me to my knees at every sail change.

Halfway across the Sea of Cortés, beam seas had tossed me backward across the cabin, smashing my spine against the chart table edge. The two pains merged at Isla Isabela. In San Blas, a hike through town meant alternating each ten minutes of walking with ten minutes prone on the nearest flat surface.

I nursed the pain down the mainland coast and into Banderas Bay to La Cruz de Huanacaxtle, a sleepy fishing village north of Puerto Vallarta. There, neighboring boaters told me of an acupuncturist ashore who sold pies.

In cool morning air I walked down bougainvillea-lined cobbled streets, asking for the pie lady. When I entered her open-air shop we went straight to a small, second-floor office graced with flowered curtains and incense. She diagnosed and treated me for classic sciatica.

An hour later, for the first time in three months, I was able to move pain-lessly. Then forty-eight hours passed, still without pain, and I returned for a second appointment. We pored over acupressure charts while she showed me how to keep the condition under control by working three points on each leg and ankle. In Acapulco, when the pressure points no longer responded and the pain returned, I assumed that hauling heavy jugs and supplies had triggered it again. Now I could no longer sit, stand, or lie down without pain shooting from my lower back to my left leg. I could barely remember what life was like without it. Friends had provided various medications, but the resultant nausea and drowsiness worried me.

As I sat in the cool cabin, a voice deep inside called clearly, "You just don't have enough nerve."

Nerve! Sciatic nerve. The realization hit. I was afraid but wouldn't admit it, even to myself. In the boatyard in San Francisco Bay, knowing I would turn right at Acapulco and head across the South Pacific, doubts had begun to surface about my ability to sail solo. Each time I suppressed them with reaffirmations of experience, knowledge, maturity, and good preparation, allowing no room for fear. But every time another point of no return approached, my body had known it and sought a way to make me stop by turning my back muscles into iron rods. In Acapulco they had made their final attempt to end the trip.

I massaged the long, rigid knots, leaning against corners of the boat. They twanged in protest. I rolled over hard limes, then a tennis ball, then the knuckles of my fists. When I stretched the next morning it felt as if a baseball bat had landed in the middle of my back. The tender muscles seized in a painful con-tortion. All day spasm followed spasm as the boat tossed in a lumpy beam sea.

Peace settled over *Southern Cross* that night. As I allowed my fears to surface, the pain gradually oozed from my body. Seas steadied into the regular lift and fall of downwind sailing. The soft *whoosh* of the Pacific murmured just inches from my ear.

I awoke the next morning with no pain, my internal rhythm matching that of the sea the way an Indian raga blends with the beat of a human heart. The trade winds had finally arrived, promising that the next day I would reach 3,000 solo miles since leaving Santa Cruz.

SHIP'S DIARY: 14 May 1989, 1426 Local, 12°15'N/112°02'W, sailing with the 150 and main wing-and-wing, steering 232M, winds ENE, 790 miles from Acapulco. Day Ten and there is a shift in the air.

My fears were not of death. I had passed that point in a storm on *Windy*. Three of us had battled 50-knot winds and 50-foot seas for three days wrapped silently in our fears, certain the end was inevitable. As the chaos around us subsided and the towering seas gave way to long rollers, we emerged from our private nightmares knowing we would make it. Every day since had been a bonus.

There were other, more insidious fears, however, like the fear of losing *Southern Cross* through lack of knowledge or vigilance. She was my home, my companion, and my responsibility. The "most severe possibility list" was still no more than items on a notepad. Over the chart table I posted step-by-step plans for abandoning the boat, including what supplies to take with me to augment the grab bag of emergency gear that remained packed and ready by the companionway. When I was tired, those fears merged into a larger, more nebulous one: the fear of failing to rise to an emergency, failing to solve the problems that undoubtedly lay ahead as well as behind—simply failing. Underscoring that nameless dread was the question of money. I didn't know what I would do if my paintings couldn't support me. For now I could only accept that uncertainty.

Good downwind days allowed time for letters, talking to family and friends as if they were sitting in the cabin. I pulled out an envelope of photos to make a collage of faces on the door to the head. Near the top of the bundle I found Mom and Stubby, my stepfather, smiling over their ninth-anniversary cake— September 17, 1988.

Gazing at her image, my first memory in life surfaced—I was a suntanned three-year-old drying dishes as my mother washed them in our tiny bungalow in Florida. We lived among other mothers and children, all waiting for husbands and fathers to return from the war in Europe and the Pacific. But when my father came back from New Guinea, the woman who would be his new wife came with him. Many years later I learned of the letters my mother and father had written. His had come first, requesting a divorce. Then Mom wrote letter after letter begging him to reconsider. He claimed never to have received those letters—not that it would have mattered. In the end, faced with the finality of his decision, she struck an agreement with him: in exchange for releasing her right to child support and alimony, he would never see me again. For Mom it left open the possibility that she could yet realize her dream of a "normal" family, free from stigma, with a new husband and "their" little girl. To the best of my knowledge, my father readily assented.

She sent me to my grandparents' home in Draper, South Dakota, and found work in Sioux Falls, two hundred miles away. Nine months later I joined her for six months . . . until she married my first stepfather in June 1947. He was a handsome young veteran who made us both laugh. She sent me back to Draper while they relocated in Iowa. I don't recall being told why they couldn't take me with them. Perhaps he wanted to experience marriage before fatherhood. Maybe they needed to establish themselves, to find work and a place to live. I haven't pressed Mom on these questions. The country then was full of people who were keeping up appearances while papering over the traumas of war. Looking back, maybe that was when I learned that pretending things were okay might make them so.

At seven I moved with my mother and stepfather to Jerseyville, Illinois. My last name was changed to match theirs; he became "Dad," and my mother had her "normal" family. No one in Jerseyville would have to know about the divorce. It would be our deepest, darkest secret, buried in the past. Fear of disappointing her sealed my lips.

My mother and I spent that summer gazing at clouds and turning them into stories. In the summer of 1949 my stepfather's new job as an advertising executive took us to Bloomington, Illinois, and a year later my grandparents followed us. Over the next three years, absorbed by childhood friends and school, I missed the changes that had begun. My mother stopped driving, though she and I had once traveled by car across the country during the war. In one small way after another her confidence was eroding.

In 1952 my stepfather's growing alcoholism finally penetrated the barrier she had erected to protect me. Now we had another secret together. His ad agency job vanished, and they bought a Laundromat with an apartment upstairs. We moved from a comfortable residential neighborhood to a busy commercial zone. Mom created a pleasant home in the ample three-bedroom quarters, but the noisy, truck-filled street and tiny backyard could not replace our former surroundings.

Cancer struck Mom the summer after my thirteenth birthday. First came the biopsy, then a radical mastectomy. Told little, and caught up in my own changing and confusing world, I understood nothing of the fear, terror, and worry she endured. Only her tenacious faith carried her through.

In her absence I ran the new business. Each morning, Monday through Saturday, I looked for my stepfather passed out somewhere in the building, opened the door at 7:00 A.M., waited on customers, ran the machines, worked with the other employees, and locked up at 7:00 P.M. He surfaced now and then when he was sufficiently sober, and sometimes when he wasn't. The two of us shared the apartment upstairs. He was no longer a parent, and I was no longer a child. Across town my mother recuperated at my grandparents' home.

With my income of $37 a week for seventy-two hours of work, I walked a perilous line that summer: too much money, no supervision, and the face and body of an eighteen-year-old. But I survived intact. In September I went back to school, and my mother came home.

By my fifteenth birthday, conditions were even more chaotic in the upstairs apartment. My mother and I lived in a nightmare of insecurity from my step-father's drinking bouts, never knowing if we would make it through the night without needing to escape his violent outbursts. One night he handed me a gun, begging me to shoot him and end the agony for all of us. I have no idea where the weapon came from or what demons drove him to such an edge.

I moved to my grandparents' house in May 1956 and that September married my high school sweetheart, Robert. He had just graduated; I was entering my junior year. We didn't tell our families. No one asked for proof of our ages or parental consent in the small town in Indiana where we said our vows before a minister, his wife, and a neighbor who came in from mowing his lawn. To Robert I promised "love and honor"; to myself, I was promising a peaceful home as soon as we were ready to live on our own. In December, in recognition of my stepfather's few months of sobriety, I moved back home for the holidays.

By the time we told our parents in January what our friends had known for several months, it was too late for the annulment my mother wanted to seek, too late to send me away to the father who had agreed never to see me. I was pregnant. "It's done and you can't change it," I taunted her as I packed my bags. Mom's dreams for my future lay crumpled on the floor between us: col-lege, a chance for success and happiness, a normal family of my own. What hope could there be for two children, sixteen and not quite nineteen, to make a solid marriage?

But she helped us make a home out of rooms we rented from Robert's grandparents. She found a way for me to finish my junior year at home with tutors. She never turned her back on me, never voiced her disappointment and shame. In October 1957 she welcomed her first grandchild with unrestrained love. She was there for me, as her parents had been for her.

Alone in SC's cabin, I looked again at the two contented faces above the cake. My mother had never lost her faith in the possibility of a happy mar-riage. That second smiling face in the photo was Herschel (Stubby) Stuber. Our families had known each other through the church for thirty years when he was widowed in 1978. The following year he proposed, pursuing my mother with gentle determination. After fourteen years alone she accepted slowly and hesitantly, with many prayers that she was making the right decision. She was sixty-six, and he seventy. At times I allowed the happiness I saw them sharing nurture hope that there still might be someone for me.

In 1957 Robert gave up his university studies and football scholarship at Illinois Wesleyan. He traded his part-time design job for full-time with the same employer, assuming the role of husband, breadwinner, and father-to-be. I left behind academics, swim team, school paper, debate team, and Spanish club to become a wife and prepare enthusiastically for motherhood—baking bread, sewing curtains, ironing starched white shirts, making cakes from scratch, and decorating our meager apartment on an almost invisible budget. Tamara arrived October 5th, three months before I turned seventeen.

The following spring, childhood friends dropped by full of plans for sum-mer trips to New England, bicycling through Europe, and college in the fall. I knew then that it was the chance to further my education that I would miss deeply. Soon after, the principal of my high school granted my request to return in the fall.

In September 1958, leaving Tamara with my mother from 8:00 to 3:30 and doing homework from 9:00 P.M. to 2:00 A.M., I began my senior year. When I earned a place in the National Honor Society, Robert refused to attend the ceremony—embarrassed at having a wife in high school. On graduation night I went with my mother and stepfather to receive the precious piece of paper. My mother wept with pride.

With a $2,000 inheritance I made the down payment on our first home in Stanford, Illinois, a town of four hundred and a good place for a young, grow-ing family. With lots of open space, it was inexpensive and neighborly. I was nineteen. Two months later, Tamara's sister, Terri, arrived. To friends our life appeared idyllic, but it was not. Robert had slipped by degrees from psycho-logical to physical abuse, dishonesty, and infidelity.

"I'm getting a divorce; I'm leaving," became a familiar threat, and I waited for him to do it. Unhappy as I was, I would not be the one to sever our fam-ily. Between flare-ups our lives went on as in most real families. I did my best to hide our arguments and unhappiness from the girls and hoped that they were experiencing a childhood in which nameless fears did not intrude.

One day Robert announced his desire to become a veterinarian. I took a secretarial job in an architectural firm, prepared to sell the house and move to married student housing. Terri was three and in a childcare center close to my office. Tamara was in first grade and with a neighbor after school. But Robert put off applying. His job improved. He waited. I loved my work, and we all welcomed the money. Robert changed his mind about going to college; we bought a home in Normal, near work for both of us.

The marriage spiraled downward in bickering and fighting. I wanted out. Robert's father begged me to try again for the sake of my daughters, and for eight months more I did. But by now the fifteen-year-old bride and the eighteen-year-old groom had grown irrevocably apart. My dream of a nurturing family was not one we could realize together. We both loved and cared for our girls, but not for each other.

Verbal attacks and accusations littered our evenings. I returned home from a women's bowling league one night to find my nightgown hanging outside the door. Because I was out "whoring around," he said, he needed to punish me. Then one night we attended a party at the home of an old friend of mine and her husband. We mingled, introducing ourselves and visiting with their other guests until, jealous over a perceived flirtation, Robert began kicking me when others couldn't see. "I saw my lawyer today. I'm filing for a divorce," he threatened. I longed for him to get it over with. I moved away from him to sit on the porch steps and began discussing a design project with some guests. He followed, then hit me hard across the head as everyone watched in shock. I got up, walked away, and never returned to our home with him again. Within two months the divorce was final, after nine years of marriage. I don't remember what I said to Tamara and Terri to explain what had happened and why. I hope I did it with compassion, respecting their love for him. He needed and wanted to be a part of their lives, and they needed that too.

Soon the same fears that must have assailed my mother at the prospect of raising a child alone hit me. I was making just $3,000 a year, though my job had expanded from secretarial duties to include some interior design responsibilities. By January 1966 I knew I must get an education if I were going to give my daughters any chance in life. From the beginning, work in the drafting room had attracted me. Four years could make me an interior designer, but in five I could become an architect. I called my mother at 2:00 A.M. with my plans. "Of course," she said, "I'll do all I can to help."

One Sunday that spring, as Robert dropped off the girls, he asked if I would consider getting back together with him. He was planning to propose to his secretary but first wanted to know my feelings. "If you're in love with her, why are you asking me this? Why are you getting married?"

"I need someone to iron my shirts and cook my meals," he replied.

In August I sold the house in Normal and bought a small trailer in Urbana, near the University of Illinois. The years that followed brought a constant struggle for space, time, and money, but I embraced every day, thirsting for knowledge to banish eight years of mental cobwebs. A part-time job, a small scholarship, and $25 a week of child support barely made ends meet. The girls and I stood in line mornings for the iron. We cooked, cleaned, and did laundry together. Monday evenings were theirs to plan— bowling, ice cream, a movie, pizza—a sacred commitment squeezed between examinations, papers, and design projects. I pinched pennies for special out-ings—a skiing weekend, their first airplane ride—and sought to enrich their lives with trips to the art museum, concerts, and outings to meet my profes-sors and see the homes they had designed. I enrolled in summer school and took heavy class loads, compressing a five-year program into four, so we could finish and get on with our lives.

Robert's court-established Sunday visits changed by mutual agreement to weekends and summers, to accommodate my study and work schedule. He and his new wife lived in the country with his parents. The girls loved their weekends in the open spaces, playing with the animals and their cousins next door, but dreaded the fifty-mile bus rides with strangers.

As the girls grew older, we needed more space. I sold the trailer, bought fur-niture, and moved to a two-bedroom apartment in December 1967. Two months later, Robert arrived unannounced to ask Tamara and Terri if they would like to live with him. Tamara was ten and a half and Terri almost eight. They agreed instantly. In shock, I ran out and drove away, unable to deal with the devastating pain of rejection.

When I could calm myself and return, he left. I asked my daughters to make a list of the reasons they wanted to leave. Both lists said, "So you will have more time to study. To spend more time with my grandparents. To take dance lessons. To have animals and be in the country." Their father had out-lined the benefits well, it seemed. He was building a new home next to his father's and planning to raise horses; against such prospects, I couldn't com-pete. Having grown up without knowing my own father, I could not stand in their way.

In June I watched as my two young daughters took their suitcases to their father's car, knowing they would not return at the end of the summer. I won-dered if they saw it as an ending or as a beginning. For me, it was the most painful experience of my life. After graduation I moved to Palo Alto, California, and at fourteen, after three visits, Tamara joined me and my second husband, Lars.

SHIP'S DIARY: 18 May 1989, 1245 Local, 09°58′N/119°30′W, sailing 5 knots under main and staysail in heavy seas. Bad squall early this morning.

A jolt from on deck pulled me outside—one more accidental jibe from the morning's heavy following sea. The wind vane's responses were too slow and inadequate. Each time it failed to hold the course, powerful quartering waves turned SC until the wind reached the backside of the main, causing it to shudder and snap as it strained against the preventer line that held it to leeward. I adjusted the lines and returned to my course. SC picked up her offwind rhythm once more, and I ducked back below.

Sorting through the stack of photos again, I found one from the past Christmas of Tamara and me on the beach in Cabo San Lucas. Even more than the eyes, cheeks, and noses, the smiles said we were mother and daughter. We both radiated an almost fierce determination and appetite for life, for good or for bad, coupled with an abundance of optimism.

In many ways Tamara approached life much as I had. She graduated from high school at sixteen, left home, and traveled for the summer around the States alone with her cat and guitar in her VW bug. I might have been able to stop her, but too many of my friends in the mid-1970s had lost their children by standing firm and rigid. I kept the door open for dialogue and my arms open for love, as my mother had for me. Tam followed her early passion for animals, earning a degree in zoology in 1979, then became a leaded-glass artist, creating windows for homes, churches, and Las Vegas casinos. At twenty-six she approached motherhood with equal intensity—dedicated to making her home and her child's welfare the center of her life. Gradually over the years we became friends and supporters as well as mother and daughter. She could say, with love and concern, "Mom, you should listen to how you talk to yourself. Don't say, 'That was a stupid thing to do,' or 'Don't be so dumb.' It builds a bad self-image."

Her smile in the photo was not just from seeing me. She had come with her fiancé to announce their wedding plans for the following August. There would be no money for me to fly from the South Pacific for the wedding; I prayed for a happy life for them and for my five-year-old grandson, Shawn. Both from my own childhood and from being the buffer between Lars and

Tamara, I knew that building new families from parts of old ones is not easy.

I stuck double-sided tape to the photo and mounted it on the door, then reached back into the pile. The next snapshot showed Shawn Bogdan-Myers at age three, his pug nose covered in freckles, nose-to-nose with my grandmother, Mildred Tobiassen, on her hundredth birthday. Their two profiles meshed like parts of a jigsaw puzzle. The photo told the story of ninety-seven years and five generations.

Grandma had round, rosy cheeks under a carefully coifed mound of snow-white curls, and her blue eyes twinkled above the sly little smile that had disarmed everyone. She had been loved and respected by old friends in Draper, where she staked her claim, opened a confectionery shop with her mother, married my grandfather, gave birth to my mother, and tended her garden with enough determination to overcome South Dakota's perpetual winds, drought, and grasshoppers. Grandma left mothering duties largely to her mother, Alice Hawkins, while she joined Grandpa at one of his enterprises—the general store, newspaper, or movie theater.

Grandma had another chance to try motherhood when, at five, I was sent to live in the house Grandpa had built. In the small town of 150 I found freedom to explore the forbidden dam south of town, visit the tepee village across the railroad tracks, climb to the roof of the two-story schoolhouse, and bloody the nose of a bully to the cheers of the old men along Main Street.

Grandma seemed unfazed by my exploits even when someone reported that I had gone alone to register for first grade one year early. The story caught up to Grandma when someone on the school board told her they were allowing the exemption in the face of my determination.

My memories from the two years with my grandparents are of carefree times. But when I replay life's old mental tapes, the voice I hear most often admonishing me is Grandma's: *If you start something, finish it. Don't get built up; you'll just be let down. You got yourself into this; you'll just have to get yourself out. Who do you think you are with your champagne tastes? Nothing's free in life. Don't be a naughty little girl; what will people think?*

When my grandparents followed us to Bloomington in 1950, their new backyard, stretching down through flower and vegetable gardens to Sugar Creek, became my private sanctuary. I could escape to a branch of the mulberry tree with a book or along the creek with a sack lunch, stalking visions of Nancy Drew mysteries around the next bend.

When she died in 1987, my grandmother left her legacy in boxes and trunks—photos from her days as a telephone operator, a clipping recognizing her as valedictorian of her class of three, lace-edged hankies and handmade bloomers from her trousseau, letters discussing the divorce of my mother and father, rattles from the snakes she killed clearing her land, gifts from the Sioux Indians who passed by her shack—including the tomahawk by my seat on *Southern Cross*—and jewelry made by her father before he abandoned her when she was three years old. As far as I know, she was the first child in our family to be raised by a single mother. But her feelings toward each of her family members, including her father, were buried with her. She was as austere as a South Dakota landscape in November. My mother had waited seventy-four years to hear her say, "I love you." It never happened.

Looking back into Grandma's eyes in the photo were those of my grandson Shawn. Though his parents could not commit to each other, they were both unequivocally committed to their son, and he was thriving. With our homes in Santa Cruz not far apart, Tamara, Shawn, and I were often together. He and I had become close buddies, going for walks on the beach and through the Santa Cruz marina, naming all the types of sailboats, reading stories, playing games. At four, he amazed me as he wondered aloud, "If you have four fifties, does that mean you have two hundred?" Just before his fifth birthday I left on *Southern Cross*. That good-bye had been, perhaps, the most difficult.

From the photos on the head door, my thoughts turned to the places and people, sights and sounds waiting beyond the horizon. I envisioned *Southern Cross* anchored off a small, palm-fringed beach in the South Pacific, with the hammock swinging on the bow; crossing the eastern Mediterranean to little Greek villages with tavernas where *bouzouki* music played every night and the dancing lasted till the early morning; or sailing through the Caribbean with coral gardens tempting me over the side. My mind's eye held images of every country gleaned from magazines, books, and movies. I wanted to hurry and to be everywhere at once.

SHIP'S DIARY: 20 May 1989, 0618 Local, 09°07′N/123°25′W, sailing in rain with overcast skies and sloppy high seas. A vicious squall at midnight. Should pass the halfway point at 0900—1,500 miles. 158 miles yesterday helped, but I got no sleep.

Each morning the batteries showed just 11.6 volts on the meter—technically dead. The morning sun began recharging the solar panel, but by early afternoon shadows from the sails and rigging reduced its effectiveness. One daily hour of running the engine was not enough for recharging, but I lacked the fuel to run it longer. I stopped listening to music and reading after dark. Even the masthead navigation light drew more power than I could afford to use. And below 11.8 volts the SatNav shut down.

I marked the midway point with a tin of butter cookies and a mug of mint tea and started a letter to Jim, the owner of *Windy*, my old sailing friend and teacher with twinkling blue eyes and an unruly mop of blond curls. I tucked myself into a corner of the settee, wedged against the table while *Southern Cross* surged and rolled in the tumbling seas, and hoped he would be able to decipher my scrawl.

We met at the end of my five-year marriage to Lars—a marriage that had dissolved not because we fought (we never did), or because we didn't care for each other (we did), or because he wasn't good to me. If anything he was too good—taking control of my life, my clothes, my dreams, and, years later, my business. Our marriage ended because he would no longer share physical intimacy . . . and he would not talk about it. We separated friends but no longer lovers.

Jim and I were teaching colleagues at San José State University in 1976. When I learned that he owned a fifty-foot trimaran, I took a week's worth of lessons in an eight-foot El Toro, devoured a how-to-sail book, and talked him into including Kitty and me in his crew of ten to Cabo San Lucas over Christmas break. From the moment we sailed under the Golden Gate Bridge that December night, I began a love affair with the ocean. Looking back at the city lights, I thought, "I could be sailing off any coast in the world if I had my own boat. Someday I will."

Dear Jim,

It may come as a surprise to you, but here I am alone in the middle of the Pacific Ocean. Thank you for all the miles of experience on *Windy*. They made this possible.

Last August 2nd I sold the harbor bungalow and bought my *Southern Cross* 31 on the same day, and five days later began two months of rebuilding and outfitting at Svenson's yard in Alameda on San Francisco Bay. She was a perfect blue-water cruiser—cutter rigged, with modified full keel, solid bulwarks, a sturdy bridge deck, oversized rigging, bronze portholes, and partially outfitted for long-distance sailing. As I rebuilt, serviced, installed, and caught up on deferred maintenance I learned every inch of her—an effort that will serve me well over the miles ahead.

Sometime during our years of sailing together, the first Transpac Singlehanded Race was run with no women entrants. The dream of being the first woman competitor caught my imagination. I wasn't worried about the passage or the challenges at sea, but I had nightmares about my arrival. They showed me approaching the finish line under full sail with television cameras capturing the details, then crashing through the spectator boats and landing on shore. If only boats had brakes instead of anchors to stop them.

In a hundred anchorages on *Windy*, you patiently taught both the techniques and the rationale of anchoring: how to choose a sheltered spot with sufficient swinging room; how to factor in future tide and weather changes; how to back down and set the hook; how much scope to put in the rode; and how to deal with a wide range of special circumstances. I approached *Southern Cross* convinced I knew what to do.

But after eight months of coastal sailing I've learned that anchoring *Windy* was like working on the deck of an aircraft carrier compared to *Southern Cross*. Some things change when you step off a big trimaran with mostly anchor line onto a small monohull with all chain.

On the California coast I avoided stopping anywhere without a dock. Then I faced my first wild, remote Mexican anchorage.

Motorsailing through the night from San Diego toward Todos Santos, the tiny island off Ensenada, I rehearsed the instructions in my sailing guide: anchor *Southern Cross*, quickly unpack the new rubber dinghy (for the first time), install the floorboards, inflate and launch it, and finally row a line ashore to tie the stern to a rock—all before the wind swings her to face the wrong direction.

Pastel morning light showed the postage stamp anchorage in a pretty cove with one boat already in the two-boat space. Too embarrassed to let them watch my debut performance, I sailed on to Ensenada, where the chart showed a large, roomy harbor.

The next morning I left for the San Benito Islands. I had dreamed for years of reliving our stop there on *Windy*. Since steering with the wind vane was still a mystery, for two days I fought the tiller to hold the course through churning swells. At dawn I saw the three islands, including the one where Kitty and I had hiked through the small fishing shack village and past the cemetery with beer bottle headstones. In my memory the islands enclosed a tight little bay where we easily rowed from one island to another. But in fact it was an open, exposed piece of water. I imagined the wind blowing my dinghy out the south side and on out to sea, with nothing to stop me. Disappointed in myself for lacking the courage, I abandoned my dream and stayed on board, feasting on lobster brought by two fishermen from the camp on shore and planning my departure for Cabo San Lucas the following morning.

After seven days with only eight hours of sleep, I arrived off the cape. The engine had plagued me with air bubbles all week, but I bled the lines and used it to enter under power. My exhaustion was so acute all I could think about was getting the anchor down and sleeping.

I passed out on the settee until a shout awoke me. Less than ten feet off my stern a frantic captain was yelling, "*Southern Cross*, you're dragging into me." Adrenaline pumped. I couldn't start the engine without bleeding it. To get out of trouble I had to retrieve the anchor and 160 feet of chain and raise sail, at the same time. And there were boats everywhere.

Hauling in chain by hand as fast as possible in forty feet of water, I lifted more than forty-five pounds with each pull while my neighbor held *SC* at bay with a boot hook. I raced from the foredeck back to the mast to raise the main. When it was partially up, I jumped to the bow again to pull in more chain. Operating only on instinct and fear, I finally got both the anchor and the sail up and turned back out to sea.

Neighbors passing in their dinghy asked if they could help. "Sure," I said, and one guy climbed on board. He sailed while I started the engine.

On the way back we talked about anchoring procedures for the singlehander with an all-chain anchor rode. Following his suggestions, this time I went to the bow while *SC* still had forward motion so I could drift back where I wanted to be. When I had enough chain on the bottom to hold the boat, I put the engine in reverse at slow revs. As I paid out chain, it laid in a straight line across the bottom—not in a heap. Then I revved up to set the hook. Down the coast to Acapulco I kept practicing and never again heard, "Hey, lady, I think you're dragging down on me." The only thing I hear after anchoring now is, "When we watched you running back and forth on deck alone, we wondered where your lazy husband was."

It's great to be back out here, even when I'm head down with a wrench in the bottom of the bilge or clinging to the top of the mast.

Fair winds and following seas,

Pat

The letter to Jim joined a small stack waiting to be mailed from Nuku Hiva, and I climbed out for a look at conditions.

The knot log hovered near 4.5; it would take the staysail to give *SC* more speed and a smoother ride. I buckled my harness and carried the sailbag forward, crouching between the lifelines and the cabin trunk. Then, tucked behind the mast for protection, I began hoisting. Partway up, the sail whipped back and forth, gave one final wrench, opening the snapshackle, and dropped to the deck, leaving the lost end of the halyard flying wildly overhead.

Retrieving the halyard meant climbing the mast—the very situation for which I had installed the mast steps. I clenched my teeth, stepped up onto the winch for the staysail halyard, and paused. Then my right foot found the headsail winch, and I pulled myself higher to reach the first step. The boat rolled; already, just six feet above the cabintop, the motion was more pronounced than it had been on deck. The higher I climbed, the wider the arc I described through space with each roll.

At the spreaders I wrapped my arms around and reached for the next set of steps. Twenty-seven empty feet beneath me the tiny deck squirmed in the heavy seas. Finally I recovered the halyard end, lowered it to the deck, and started my long descent. By the next morning only the bruises and a terse note in my log, "up the mast to retrieve staysail halyard," remained of the incident. Memories at sea are short.

Squalls came from every direction that afternoon, and *Southern Cross* wallowed along her path in the shifty conditions as sails slatted back and forth between the changes.

SHIP'S DIARY: 22 May 1989, 1520 Local, 07°46′N/125°28′W, sailing 212M in fluky winds. Total miles at noon—1,647. Batteries 11.5 volts this morning. Steering impossible. This is the doldrums.

At dawn the sky had been a mélange of all the clouds ever inventoried by meteorologists. I sailed in a small clear patch of hot, muggy air surrounded by thunderheads and lightning. One squall threatened, and I started the engine to move out of its path. For a few minutes the comforting roar of the diesel sounded from the compartment below. Then there was silence. The engine had died.

From everywhere else the air shook with noise. Sails slatted, deck hardware banged, glass bottles in lockers clanged, the stairs in the companionway creaked, jerricans stowed on deck thumped back and forth against the gunwale, and the sea gurgled in and out of the galley sink. I squeezed my hands over my ears, praying for wind.

In the morning—wanting to curl up and read, to go to sleep, to let someone else solve the engine problem—I braced against cabinets with my how-to-repair-diesel-engines book at hand as tools careened across the cabin. A few hours of instruction from Jim and time with the mechanic at the boatyard were all I had to augment the pressure of need and the author's detailed instructions.

Bleeding air from the system produced a continuous stream of bubbles instead of a clear stream of fuel. I changed the external filters, which had been new in Acapulco. More bubbles. I tightened every fitting, but the bubbles continued.

Starting at the fuel tank, I dismantled each component, checking and replacing it until I reached the lift pump on the engine. Everything was fine. I made a new gasket and remounted the pump. Going back to the tank, I started again, but still the golden bubbles ran.

Squalls filled the next day. The wind vanished, then returned from directly ahead. *SC* beat into stiff seas that found their way into the bilge through a vent on the bow and through the abandoned chain hawse and its replacement.

The sky hung overhead, solid gray and oppressive, and the sauna-like air clung. With no sun for solar power and no other way to charge the batteries, fixing the engine became the center of my life. As each new inspiration failed, a rash grew down my arms. Finally, trying to forget the health hazards of petroleum fumes, I siphoned diesel through the filters from a full jerrican to an empty one and lashed it to the top step of the companionway. With intravenous fuel feeding by gravity from there to the engine, I turned the key and heard the distinctive music of a functioning Yanmar. For four hours it fed the hungry batteries.

Three miles off, the Canadian tanker *Ford Rouge* passed, en route to the Panama Canal. I called. The radio operator from his high perch saw only empty ocean—my sails were invisible against the white caps. "You're out here all alone?" he asked. I drew out the conversation as long as possible, then signed off and let my mind replay our voices in the silence.

The batteries came up to 11.7 volts, not enough to power the masthead tricolor light. Yet, where there was one ship, there might be more. I lit the small kerosene anchor lamp and hung it in the rigging, knowing as I did so that a ship would be on top of me by the time they saw it.

In the soft glow of the kerosene cabin lights, I studied the newest addition to my growing family of photos on the door—an 8 by 10 black-and-white model pose of my younger daughter, Terri. Her upswept hair and tilted head lent a question mark to her partial smile. She looked poised and in control, just as she had at eighteen months when she hurried around the house closing drawers and doors and straightening throw rugs.

After leaving to live with her father, she never came to see me again. I wrote countless letters asking her to come to California for Christmas or a summer break, but something always held her back. When I visited my family in Illinois, Terri and I would have lunch and chat, but that was all.

I invited her for a vacation when she turned fifteen, a birthday trip across Canada by train. We saw the musical *Grease* in Toronto, the Bolshoi Ballet in Montréal, and laughed at the old men in Québec who tried to explain the difference between a pub, a tavern, and a brewery. The distinction was lost on us, since none of the three would serve dinner to an underage girl. We settled on pizza time after time, Terri ordering in her high school French. The trip ended and our relationship resumed the same pattern of distant and polite contact.

During one of our brief visits, when she was eighteen, I brought up the divorce, wanting to tell her why and how it had happened. From Tamara I knew that I was the villain of the story Robert told. I longed for Terri to know that my love for her had never faltered—that my mistakes, whatever they were, did not include abandoning my children. But she ran from the car crying without a word. I wished we could talk about the things I valued most: not possessions or image, not success, but compassion, courage, curiosity, honesty, passion for life, faithfulness to oneself. People had asked, "What do your daughters think of your trip?" I had no idea what Terri thought about anything. She seemed to me like a crystal box sealed with a small golden padlock to which I didn't have the key. Gaining access meant shattering the carefully crafted container.

At the end of the war, after my father had returned from New Guinea, he and his intended new wife took me out to dinner and gave me a pair of roller skates. I was four or five years old. It is my first memory of him, but all I can see when I search the fragments of that evening for a face, a feeling, or a smell are the roller skates.

When I was ten, my mother and stepfather sought an adoption to legalize the last name I had carried for three years. The choice was mine, but the weight of their persuasion hung over it. My father called to ask if this was what I wanted. Who was he? I didn't even have a face to put with the voice. Why not take the father who sat at the table with me every night instead of the stranger on the phone? I had no reason to say "no." The judge asked for my decision, and I answered "yes."

In 1955, a letter and a $50 check arrived at the apartment above the laundry. "Congratulations on graduating from junior high school. I'd like to see you. Can you come to Chicago?" The following month, Mom and I descended the grand lobby stairway at the Conrad Hilton Hotel. He waited below, as handsome as she had described—a solid, serious man, with my square jaw. Her knees shook. I think she still loved him. He had planned a lavish evening to charm both of us, but just sitting between my own parents was enough for me. I looked for signs passing between them, fantasizing that they might remarry. The next summer I made the trip alone.

My stepfather knew nothing of these visits. After the adoption, the subject of my father was never raised again. Nor did I ever tell my real father anything of the nightmares unfolding at home. Not wanting to hurt my father, to him I always referred to my stepfather as "Stu"—never "Dad."

My father accepted my early marriage without criticism and came to visit. When Tamara was born he brought my sister Libby with him—to introduce us. She was ten years old. He had divorced Libby's mother when her alcoholism became so severe he could no longer live with it. As he had put his former wife on a train he had turned to Libby. "Who do you want to stay with? Your mother or me?" Seven-year-old Libby chose him.

A few years later he moved to Minneapolis and married a third time. We visited back and forth several times during the years of my marriage to Robert. When I made the decision to go to college, I was certain of his encouragement and support. He believed an education was a precious thing. He had worked five jobs earning his degree during the Great Depression, and my mother had supported him through a master's degree.

Counting on the promise he had made to my mother after the adoption— "I will help Patty when it comes time for college"—I wrote asking for a loan of $8,000 over four years to fill the gaps in my budget. "You shouldn't have divorced Robert," he replied. "You got yourself into this; you'll just have to live with it. You should stay with your job and improve yourself for what you're already doing. I can't afford it; I'm saving for my old age." Libby was then in her freshman year at an exclusive girls' college. I responded in anger and pain, closing the door on our relationship. He wrote back, "The ball is in your court." I never answered.

By the time he reached out for reconciliation he had been named president of the Fortune 500 company he had served as director of sales and marketing.

Eighteen months had passed when an invitation arrived for a holiday with my girls at his lake cottage, and I went thinking he wanted a chance to say he was sorry. The subject never came up. I left feeling empty, but clinging to the fragile thread connecting us.

Eight years later, in 1975, my father died at fifty-nine, one year after retiring. We never discussed anything we held in our hearts. My uncle, his brother, once said he had confessed that "divorcing Aileen was the biggest mistake I ever made." It was only a small consolation for all that might have been. There was no picture of my father for the door.

Another photo surfaced—Libby and I on the bow of *Southern Cross* from the past Christmas, when she had come to Cabo San Lucas. In June 1968, I was in summer school at the University of Illinois and she had just transferred to the University of Minnesota. Over summer break we lived together for the first time—playing, dancing, philosophizing, and building a shared history.

We laughed at how lucky we were not to carry all the baggage of growing up together. In truth, I did carry some of that "baggage." I was jealous of the time and attention she appeared to get from our father. To me, hers seemed a life of privilege made possible by his financial support. I imagined, too, that he provided advice and encouragement and took an interest in her life—that he let her know he was proud of her and loved her. She was beautiful, thin, and had everything I thought I lacked—clothes, boyfriends, poise, popularity, intellect, and confidence—things that could blind me to what Libby had missed: a girlhood wrapped in maternal love.

After earning a graduate degree, Libby achieved national recognition as a lobbyist. In the late 1980s, with two marriages behind her, she chose to stay single; not having children was a decision she had made long before.

The small photo at the top of the door showed Stu, my brother, smiling from behind a gray beard at his desk. He was born in 1950, shortly before I turned ten. We called him Toby then, my mother's old nickname, rather than Stu Jr.

A trail of funny stories followed him through childhood. When the car door flew open as my grandfather pulled into the busy commercial street in front of the laundry, six-year-old Toby tumbled onto the pavement. Grandpa screeched to a halt and Toby climbed back in, commenting, "That's the first time I was in Oakland Avenue by myself." His offerings of grace at family meals were legendary. One rainy day it was, "Help us to follow in your footsteps, even though they're a little muddy today." While Mom hurried to finish preparing a meal, he began, "Thank you, dear Jesus, for the tomatoes, bread, and . . . is that all there is?" He was the comic relief in our lives, and grew up to be the man I most respected. A small-business owner, he made great sacrifices for his family, his employees, and his community, always with characteristic humor. I had never been able to find his honesty, kindness, and wisdom in a potential mate.

SHIP'S DIARY: 28 May 1989, 1140 Local, 05°25'N/127°54'W. Beam reaching/beating with the 130% genoa (150 needs repairs) at 210M. No sun and lots of squalls.

In four days I had drifted, beat, sailed wing-and-wing, and reached north, south, east, and west, three hundred miles or more, in a never-ending attempt to harness the fluky wind, but when I measured the "distance made good" I was only seventy miles closer to Nuku Hiva.

Seventy-five gallons of ocean sloshed below the cabin floor, trapped in a low section of the bilge ahead of the mast where there was no pump. That day I bailed cup by cup, sailed 23 miles toward Nuku Hiva, and made a batch of bran muffins.

The next morning, I put the kettle on to boil and prepared the cone and filter for the insulated carafe. Holding the kettle with one hand and the filter with the other, I tried to pour in rhythm with the swing of the gimballed stove. The boat lurched, the boiling contents landed on my hand, and the filter full of ground coffee and water fell behind the stove. As I slathered aloe vera on my burn, the spreading brown mess ran under the stove and down the cabinet front, then trickled across the cabin floor to mix with a puddle of diesel fuel where the cabin sole met the slope of the bilge.

At noon I fixed a lunch of vanilla pudding and canned peaches. SC lurched again, and the first container of dried pudding joined the diesel and coffee grounds on the floor.

The voltmeter showed 11.55. I set up the gravity feed system again to run the engine. But after four hours, the batteries were still too low for the SatNav to work; it shut itself down. I looked in horror at the electrical panel. Every light switch on the boat was turned on: the masthead light, spreader lights, and running lights—the largest power drains on board.

An angry voice challenged, "Why did you do a dumb thing like that?" It was me talking, but not to myself. The voice stopped short as I realized that if anyone had been there I would have blamed an innocent person. In the echoing silence, I confronted a view of myself I'd never seen before. "Why did you do that?" had been a recurring theme in my marriage to Robert. He always responded that he hadn't, and I always knew he had. Whether they were things worth fighting over was not a consideration. It would remain "unfinished business" until I could point a finger.

In the morning, I pumped all the fuel from the tank into jerricans as they danced across the tilting cabin floor. Then I lost track of the days siphoning diesel to run the engine, charging batteries, and making more mistakes. But they were sunny days with wind, and *SC*'s track hurried across the plotting sheets. The source of the air in the fuel line remained a mystery.

SHIP'S DIARY: 2 June 1989, 0700 Local, 00°00′/132°55′W. Steering 212M, light southeasterlies and sunny. My fifth time across the equator.

I celebrated with a hot shower, fixed a Kahlúa and cream with a splash for Neptune at sunset, then pulled out a clean sheet. In the warm, liquid air I stretched out watching the moonlight play across my photo door, its glow catching the last addition. Dan—the love of my life that seemed forever out of reach—smiled back at me. His shock of blond hair and the warm blue eyes surrounded by crinkled smile lines still raised my heart rate.

At forty-eight, I could trace our connections back thirty-nine years to childhood church functions, choir, and youth camp. Our paths had not crossed in seven years when he walked through the door of the office where I worked in June 1964. He was fresh from a year in Europe and full of *savoir faire*. To an Illinois girl he reeked of adventure and sophistication.

I was twenty-three, married and faithful, but the electricity between us ignited my every nerve ending. For the next fifteen months we existed as office friends, talking and laughing through coffee breaks. He fed me ideas about the world: philosophy, art, literature, politics, architecture, and life. I soaked them in through my pores and began to grow and change. My world opened out beyond my narrow borders. I read insatiably and questioned long-held assumptions.

In private moments after everyone was asleep, that final year of my unhappy marriage, I cried and dreamed of the impossible—to be Dan's partner in life. But he occupied a pedestal high out of reach. Even if I divorced my husband, it couldn't happen. To me he was a door to the world. To him I was someone to visit with at the office, nothing more.

Dan became engaged and announced a date for his wedding. I bought a gift, a small pewter vase—pure and elegant to fit my sense of him.

Three weeks before the wedding, Dan attended the party that precipitated the end of marriage for Robert and me. Though we barely exchanged a word, Robert sensed something between us that may have contributed to his jealous outburst. When I fled at 1:00 A.M. and did not return, Dan followed in his car. I got in. He drove, and I talked about my failing marriage. He revealed that he cared for me and had felt so all along. But we stayed at arm's length, neither of us willing to risk unleashing the intense emotion we both felt. Did he mention "love" that night? Later I wanted to think so but couldn't remember.

His wedding took place as planned, and his first child was born five months later. Only then did I guess at the difficulty of those three weeks for him. Our lives wove in and out over time. Sometimes years would pass before one of us called the other or our paths would cross—but only for a day. He was married, then we both were. He was in a serious relationship, then we both were, then I was married. Every relationship I tried to build lived in his shadow. And when a partnership began to waver I would imagine Dan walking through the door and watch to see whom I chose. My choice was always Dan. He ruled the kingdom of my imagination in a way no real lover ever could.

There were letters, the familiar handwriting on the envelope causing my heart to skip a beat. The last one had come before I left northern California in 1988. He was surprised to hear of my plans, concerned, and possibly a bit wistful— maybe because it meant an end to our occasional visits, or perhaps he wished he were going somewhere too. I turned from his photo to *SC*'s cabin and the world outside the companionway. Could he love this life as much as I did?

SHIP'S DIARY: 5 June 1989, 0944 Local, 03°54'S/136°04'W. Sailing with ESE winds, steering 211M, 400 miles to go! Had French toast for breakfast from the loaf of bread I baked yesterday.

The Voice of America broadcast on my Sony carried reports of a thousand dead at Tiananmen Square. Memories of May 1970 and Kent State University flooded the cabin. Pain and unity had exploded from campus to campus across the country. My mother responded from the university where she was working with anger at the students. "Mom, that could have been me. Shooting those students was wrong." Stony silence followed. To this day that conversation remained unfinished, politics an untouchable subject between us.

The Pacific Maritime Net opened with a report from *Kama Hele*, a single-hander named Emmett sailing south from San Diego. He was two days behind me, en route for Nuku Hiva. I longed to check in and chat for a moment, or to make a phone patch home to say, "Hello, I'm safe."

Over the previous few days *Southern Cross* had sailed in and out of squalls and fair weather while I tangled again with the big radial-head drifter and struggled to keep a charge in the batteries. Exhausted and worried about finances, I was trying to forget I had less than $400 for French Polynesia, trying to trust that something good would develop once I made landfall. The sun was out and *Southern Cross* made a 124-mile run, noon to noon.

That night as I lay in my berth, the music of a following sea whooshed by inches away, in rhythm with my breathing. A starlit sky drifted back and forth above the open hatch, and velvety air stroked my bare skin as small breezes moved down through the open companionway. I drifted to sleep knowing the wind vane was steering an almost perfect course.

In the morning dolphins played double Dutch in front of the bow, and I sang them a song. I could almost feel Nuku Hiva, less than three hundred miles away. The SatNav smirked at me. After 30,000 miles as the celestial navigator on board *Windy*, I knew I could navigate, but wondered if I could trust that machine.

En route to Hawaii in 1978, there had been six of us aboard *Windy*: myself, two women with no sailing experience who had joined the crew at the last minute, and three guys I had sailed with frequently along the West Coast.

Three days out from San Diego, as I thought about the crew's capabilities, a fantasy emerged in which everyone except me contracted bubonic plague, and I was left alone to find Hawaii. I demanded immediate lessons from our navigator, and he handed me a book with a title like "Celestial Navigation for the Complete Idiot." I studied, took sextant sights in the centuries-old tradition, and worked out positions. Eventually I graduated from simple sun sights to shooting the moon and stars. After several months my sights guided *Windy* as I took over the job of navigator.

This time, being alone was no fantasy. I pulled out my sextant to practice and confirm the SatNav readings, but *SC*'s tiny cockpit couldn't compare with the large, stable deck of a fifty-foot trimaran. With legs and back braced against seats and coamings, I tried to stabilize myself like a tripod. In a few moments my arm ached. The new sextant was too heavy. Sails and gear blocked my vision as *SC* swayed down the waves. She sank in a trough, then heeled away from the sun. I lost the shot again and again, then got one and started over.

In squalls with 15- to 30-knot winds, clouds, and three- to four-foot seas, I ended the day with two perfect positions, but they were 30 miles from the Sat-

Nav coordinates. In the morning I realized my error—the tables and calculations had changed when I crossed the equator. I began again.

The next day dawned in perfect peace and contentment with sunny, two-foot seas and the islands forty-eight hours away. I wanted to keep going, to sail on past them. Only the present moment existed. Yesterday could have been Acapulco. *Southern Cross* could bring the whole world to my feet. I felt blessed in the only place I wanted to be—at sea, on my way to somewhere.

The difficulties of the past thirty-four days had all been concrete and manageable. The challenges had come from skills and knowledge I lacked or failures of the boat and equipment. Mistakes had been obvious and feedback immediate. In contrast, the end of TWT and my business life had been unreal—a giant chessboard with a hundred possible moves obscured by a mist of dubious information.

SHIP'S DIARY: 8 June 1989, 1148 Local, 07°54'S/139°14'W, sailing at 217M. Nasty squalls with 20 to over 35 knots and 6- to 8-foot seas. At last a good sextant position just 1 mile from the SatNav.

At daybreak on June 9th, weather helm pulled *Southern Cross*, straining, into the wind toward the middle of the pass between two pale-blue islands, the first of the Marquesas Islands of French Polynesia—tiny specks I had stalked over thousands of empty ocean miles. One boat sailed out of Baie Taiohae, the main port, as I rounded the end of Nuku Hiva. A wide grin spread across my face. I had made it—no one had to tell me I had done a good job. Arrival itself was enough.

By nightfall SC was clean and livable, with covers on and sailing gear stowed, and I was ready for a real night of sleep in the V-berth—minus SatNav beeps and sail changes. But over the deep black of the nighttime bay, through the open hatch, and into my sleep—as if from the pages of Herman Melville's *Typee*—marched the incessant beat of jungle drums. I tossed and turned as shadowy figures darted through my dreams, behind trees, bows drawn.

The next morning's sunrise washed over a placid red-roofed village behind a palm-fringed beach backed by looming, jungle-shrouded volcanic crags. Cascades of bright tropical flowers—not warring natives—peeked through the dense foliage.

The dilapidated dinghy from a small French boat nearby arrived ankle deep in seawater and covered in patches and blobs of black goo. "I'm Phillipe. Would you like a ride to shore to check in and see the town?" He reached down to reinflate the dinghy, and one black patch of goo puffed up like a great phallus. Gathering papers, money, and shoes I waded in, thankful for a translator as well as the lift.

Once ashore, I expected easy entrance formalities with my visa properly stamped in Acapulco and the required $750 "security deposit" on escrow in the island's French bank. The latter was a gift from Chris Henry—she and my father had married when Libby was in junior high school. The authorities would use it to buy a ticket to the United States if they wanted to send me home. But the *gendarmerie* was closed until Monday. I stopped at the post office to telegraph Mom "happy birthday" and the news she was waiting to hear: "I made it."

Visions of fresh fruit and vegetables had filled my dreams day and night the last week at sea. In the two little shops at the center of town limp greens, shriveled apples, and slowly browning green grapes from New Zealand peered out through condensation on the refrigerator doors. The mangos, papayas, and fresh greens I longed for never left local gardens. Inhabitants of Taiohae enjoyed what they wanted of the abundant tropical produce and left the rest to decompose or feed the animals. Chickens ran wild, but no one hunted for the eggs they hid. Generous French government subsidies made selling produce and collecting eggs unnecessary. I paid $2.50 for eight floppy carrots, picked out a few small, shriveled apples at $1 each, and cringed at $4.40 for a dozen eggs.

Kama Hele arrived that afternoon, becoming the fourth singlehander out of the sixteen boats at anchor. For two weeks cruisers entered through the pass in the reef, until Taiohae Bay anchorage swelled to fifty foreign boats. Among them were many sailing companions from Mexico, our reunion more a product of wind and season than of chance. All around the world I would be reassured by the sight of familiar boats in foreign harbors. Long-distance sailors make a kaleidoscopic community, scattered and drawn back together by the influences of weather, politics, regulations, the need for supplies and companionship, or simply impulse and curiosity.

Interisland ferries crammed with passengers landed at the jetty daily, and each night more jungle drums staccatoed over the water while musicians and dancers rehearsed for the second grand Marquesan Festival of the Arts. On opening day, James Michener, author of *Tales of the South Pacific*, sailed in on a cruise ship tour, celebrating his return to the South Pacific. The next day six thousand islanders and guests enjoyed a free lunch—roasted pig from pits in the ground, mounds of salads, poi, and fruits all piled on banana leaves.

Near the market I jostled through a crowd of women in brightly colored cotton dresses and men and children in shorts and T-shirts who were devouring the mountains of island fare. Stalls nearby offered handmade tapa cloth and local carvings; I hunted for a birthday gift for Libby, planning to offer one of my miniature paintings in trade. But when I found the piece of tapa I wanted, the scowling artisan shook her head at each painting I showed her, eyeing instead my favorite small gold hoop earrings. At last I reluctantly agreed to the trade, and she beamed a smile of triumph as I handed them over.

Drumming and dancing competitions drew nightly crowds to the open-air performance area. By firelight immense island men stomped out a war dance across the dirt, their grass skirts swaying and the ground beneath them shaking at each impact. From deep in their bellies, threatening grunts kept beat with the drums. Melville had crept up this shore to such a scene 150 years before, but then the men weren't wearing swim trunks under their skirts, and there were no neat, orderly rows of spectators and no James Michener as guest of honor.

Each day I weighed my favorite entry until six dancers arrived from Easter Island and won my vote. They had seen the festival on Papeete television, caught the next plane, and asked to be included. Lacking costumes, they scavenged in the jungle for vines, leaves, and clay to decorate their bare bodies. Without musical instruments they gathered cowry shells to beat a rhythm. Their extemporized choreography came from the heart as they leapt on boulders and wove the natural surroundings into their dance. The crowd cheered enthusiastically, but the judges chose otherwise.

Before leaving Nuku Hiva, I had to repair *SC*'s fuel system. My jury-rigged gravity feed from the jug in the companionway to the engine was not a long-term solution. I had no money for a mechanic, but Emmett, from *Kama Hele*, agreed to trade his help for a miniature painting of his boat. His job in San Diego had been installing Yanmar engines. We pulled the fuel system apart, put it back together, and took it apart again several times. Suddenly, the engine started and continued running. Our suspicion centered on the Fram filtering system, but no absolute conclusion emerged.

From one of the other cruisers I learned that the manufacturer of my dinghy had issued a general recall for all their inflatable dinghies going to the South Pacific. Apparently the material from which they were made wouldn't last in the harsh glare of the tropics. I wrote asking for instructions to get a replacement.

But the "tender to" *Southern Cross*, known officially as *T/T Southern Cross*, suffered more than a recall in Nuku Hiva. While I ran errands ashore, she drifted over the stern line of a newly arrived vessel at the tall concrete commercial jetty where I had left her. When surge pulled the stern line taut, it flipped her upside down, submerging my sixteen-year-old, second-hand-but-reliable Johnson outboard motor. A $200 purchase in Cabo San Lucas, it hadn't been beautiful—it was covered in grease, the clamps securing it to the transom had no handles, the gearshift was a bent bolt, the case was battered and scarred, and the shear pin was a nail. Now it was past revival. I would be rowing to shore, but inflatable dinghies do not row well, especially when winds are up and anchorages are choppy.

The fifteen-year-old son on board a neighboring boat in the anchorage heard my lament about fresh produce and delivered Sunday dinner—a large piece of freshly caught mahimahi and a bag of *pamplemousse*. Thick pale yellow skin covered a huge grapefruit-like, juicy, sweet center. They had been a gift from a local family living in a nearby bay. Apparently not all the Nuku Hivans were as withdrawn and reticent as those in Taiohae. On trips into town and hikes out of the village, my smiles and greetings were seldom returned.

I looked south out of Taiohae Bay and felt the tug to sail on toward the next Marquesan island, cloud enshrouded Ua Pau, twenty-six miles away.

———————— JULY 1989

THE VISION SOUTH THROUGH THE PASS OUT OF TAIOHAE Bay had woven images in my daydreams of Camelot rising into the clouds, Rapunzel unwinding her long hair, and trumpeters sounding their horns from medieval turrets of stone. Tiny, six-mile-wide Ua Pau beckoned with lavender spires carved by nature and rising sheer out of the sea more than four thousand feet, disappearing into the clouds above. It was a setting to spawn ancient sailors' fairy stories of mermaids, giant sea mammals, and ghostly mariners.

The borrowed cruising guide I had consulted reported that the village of Haka Hetau had good water on shore and fresh vegetables from a garden above the village. But I had no detailed charts or coordinates to pinpoint the entry, only small, handmade sketches and large, scantily detailed charts covering hundreds of miles. Still, I had more information than the explorers who approached this island in the late 1700s. The familiar sense of adventure from my childhood hikes on Sugar Creek followed as I left Nuku Hiva with sails drawing in the late morning breeze.

Details grew clearer and Rapunzel vanished as the island drew near. On shore lay a small village with a red-roofed church fronted by a beach dotted with fishing boats. Frangipani trees cast a sweet perfume over the bay as the sun slid behind the mauve hills that cradled the bay in total silence. *Southern Cross* sat alone in a picture-perfect anchorage.

When I was twenty-two, searching for the source of my unhappiness as a partner in a marriage that was going nowhere but would take two more years to get there, I wrote a list of things that made me happy—to bring them into my life. The list had ten items, and every one of them involved being alone. "To drive long distances alone. To dance alone. To explore places alone. To listen to good, live music alone." I never knew how much I liked being alone until then. In this empty anchorage, I was contented.

Water was my primary reason for stopping here. Health officials in Nuku Hiva had reported liver flukes in the public water supply. I had emptied and cleaned the tanks, waiting to fill them for the sail to Tahiti. A sketch in the cruising guide showed a tap near a small jetty hidden behind a rocky outcropping. I studied the route as it passed around a large rock and out of view.

With empty jerricans and shopping bags on board, I rowed around to the landing site. Swells surged onto the rocky ledge that the guide labeled "jetty," sweeping the dinghy up and tossing it among ten dark-skinned children who were playing in the roiling water. They grabbed for the handholds while I leapt clear, heart racing.

We lifted the dinghy to higher ground. I was shaken and embarrassed, but safe, thanks to their help. They laughed and resumed their game. Through the village and up the steep hillside people smiled and nodded greetings. The less-traveled places always produced the best welcome. I climbed higher, looking for the vegetable garden and the priest who planted it.

My mouth watered at the sight of neat rows, already tasting the crunchy green beans, succulent sun-warm tomatoes, and other treats. Buying as much as I could keep fresh without ice, I hiked down, looking out over the bay, a South Pacific tropical paradise with my own boat anchored in the middle. It seemed like a dream.

I searched down narrow dirt streets in the village for fresh fruit and found two young girls with huge baskets of *pamplemousse* on their heads. "They're not for sale," they laughed, dark eyes dancing, then handed me an armful of fruit for free.

At the jetty, I filled the jerricans with ten gallons of pure water—eighty pounds—and hauled it to the landing. With help from the children, as the dinghy hit the water, I leapt aboard and rowed out over the surge.

Each trip to the hair-raising landing became more difficult as the tide rose up to my thighs. The children helped, one last time, amid laughter and farewell waves.

That evening, still savoring the fresh flavors of eggplant and tomatoes from dinner, I sat outside in the dark, bathed in air so perfect I couldn't tell where it ended and I began. In the morning I left for Tahiti via the Tuamotu Archipelago, known for centuries as the "Dangerous Islands" for their low atoll profiles—with the tallest landmark a coconut tree—and their surrounding reefs that stretch miles from shore, just below the surface.

For four days the trade winds built and backed from beam to broad reach. SC slid down long, rolling seas under clear skies punctuated with cloud puffs marking small islands. I thought about stopping at Rangiroa, but as I drew near my courage failed or good sense prevailed. Alone, without someone watching from aloft, I wouldn't risk the treacherous entry through the reef or the lagoon dotted with coral heads. Instead, I shaped a new course above Ahe and down the middle of the pass between Rangiroa and Arutua.

SHIP'S DIARY: 11 July 1989, 1244 Local, 14°04'S/145°59'W, sailing 224M dead downwind in 25 knots and 10-foot seas. I'll pass Ahe between 1900 and 2000 tonight.

The afternoon passed and night came, the miles slipping under SC's keel. Ahe dropped behind me. I slept in the cockpit, setting alarms to wake me every hour and a half to check my progress and the weather. At 0400 I set two alarms for 0530, when I would be poised at the top of the current-filled pass.

The 12-inch-wide cockpit seat, which was just long enough for my 5-foot 3½-inch body if I flexed my feet, made an uncomfortable bed, yet I slept through both alarms. At 0800 the brilliant sun brought me to my feet in panic. Tiny coconut trees fringed the horizon on my left. I plotted the last SatNav position—dead down the middle of the pass despite the currents and the often-unreliable wind vane.

SC's guardian angel had kept me on course while skeletons and treasures from many not-so-lucky mariners littered the seafloor below. A special bubble of protection seemed wrapped around this trip. I didn't expect to be "saved" from my mistakes, but time after time, when events were beyond my capabilities, a helping hand mysteriously showed up.

I had first become aware of SC's angel in December, as I sailed down the Baja California Mexican coast. I was hurrying to meet Tamara, Shawn, and

Libby for a family holiday. After seven days with only eight hours of sleep, the final night brought 35-knot winds and eight- to ten-foot seas, and sometime after midnight I gave up. With the mounting for the wind vane broken I had steered and changed sails in everything from calms to gales. My arms and shoulders refused to struggle with the heavy tiller any longer. My eyes gave up trying to focus on the compass numbers in the dim red light of the instrument. I stood up, walked away, and climbed down the companionway to fix a cup of instant soup. Turning to go back out, I discovered a six-foot-tall, golden-haired angel in white effortlessly steering the course to Cabo that I had been unable to hold. I watched and rested until dawn, then took the helm as she disappeared in the encroaching daylight.

Now, thankful for her help again, I said a small prayer that she would be in Papeete, Tahiti, too. I would be arriving in one of the most expensive ports in the world with only $3, and no bank account, credit cards, or magic source of funds.

Night descended with lightning attacking the horizon in all directions, but *Southern Cross* sailed in a pocket of clear air. At dawn, a rainbow arched overhead, one end touching the center of Papeete harbor.

Bastille Day 1989: Banners and flags from around the world fluttered in the morning breeze on boats packed sardine-tight along Papeete's main quay, waiting for the celebrations. Photos of this scene had fired the dreams of sailors—real and armchair—since the early 1930s. The visitors overflowed in a continuous line west, anchored bow and stern off the main beach. But the obvious lack of space in the center of town made little difference when I needed a place that was free; the city charged $9 per day for the quay and $4.50 for the beach.

Aboard a passing boat I spotted Erica Abt, a friend and fellow artist from Mexico days. She waved, and I followed her west down the long reef-lined channel, past the airport, and south to Maeva Beach, where we could anchor for free. To the west, beyond the protective reef, the famous peaks of Mooréa rose against a deep red-orange sunset. On shore, fancy resorts shared the beach with fishermen's shacks. Nets hung drying, and pirogues—like the dugout canoes that once so impressed Captain Cook with their speed and seaworthiness—were suspended upside down on stakes above pink water and below the blue and turquoise wooden huts. In the fading light sarong-clad, topless sirens gathered their beach gear from the rocks, pulled on blouses, and sauntered out to the bus stop.

The next morning Erica climbed into my dinghy dressed in a lavender skirt and lacy white top; I wore tan shorts and a cherry-red silk blouse. Together our colors sizzled. She carried several pairs of her hand-carved earrings in her bag, and in mine were a few small paintings and my $3. We both had packed lunches. When we caught the open-air "Le Truck" heading into town, I handed over one-third of my worldly wealth for the fare.

Reggae music playing overhead filled the spaces between passengers dressed in colors as bright as those covering the bus. Islanders with flowers tucked behind their ears sat facing stoically forward on the long benches that lined either side, while Erica and I babbled like tourists. Lush hillsides slid by in an explosion of colors, then, abruptly, the high-speed freeway ended on small city streets.

On foot again, we followed full, rich voices to a pink church near the beach and peeked over a sea of white straw hats like a bakery window of wedding cakes covered in flowers and ribbons to glimpse the source of *a cappella* hymns sung in an unfamiliar tongue. Along the waterfront, languorous, soft, chestnut-brown bodies molded to benches, hammocks, rocks, and trees, recovering from late-night parties.

Erica and I strolled down café-lined streets to a new open market. Inside, under towering pink arches, shafts of sunlight fell on a city block of fresh fruit, vegetables, fish, and flowers. A lady from Wisconsin asked where we were from and what we were doing in Papeete, then bought a small painting and earrings. We took ourselves out for dinner at Lou Pescadou for $6 each.

When the Bastille Day celebrations finally receded and the Papeete port captain recovered sufficiently to open his office, I waited on the doorstep to check in officially and look for waiting mail. On top of the stack perched a well-traveled letter from Libby, smothered in stamps and notes indicating a roundabout trip from Portland, Oregon, via Port-au-Prince, Haiti, to Papeete, Tahiti.

Clutching my bundle of letters, I ducked out of the hot sun on Boulevard Pomare into *L'epi d'or*, already my favorite quayside cafe, for *pain au raisin* and a cappuccino while I savored my mail. I tore into the touring blue envelope from Libby first. "I would like to come for a long visit over Christmas," she had written. "I can probably get six weeks off. Let me know where you'll be and when I should plan my trip. I need to know as soon as possible to get a cheap ticket."

Back on *Southern Cross* I pored over planning charts, the calendar, and sailing guidebooks, trying to forecast where I'd be in December. New Zealand, my destination for the next hurricane season, was nearly 2,300 miles away. I had only a little more than the $3 I had arrived with on Saturday. A hundred things could happen in the next five months, but Libby needed to know where and when to meet me.

I wrote back to say I'd be in New Zealand by December 4th, then turned to the urgent problem of making money. Foreigners work all over the world, of course, but often illegally. Legal jobs in Tahiti, as elsewhere, must be secured from outside the country. Only positions for which no local inhabitants qualify are offered, and those must be approved by immigration authorities before one's arrival. My visa prohibited employment. Working illegally could mean deportation, confiscation of *Southern Cross*, or both. I took the threat seriously. Packaging my miniatures, I left to make the rounds of the anchorage. Selling my paintings was illegal too, but at least doing so didn't take a job from a Tahitian, and the French have a soft spot for artists.

Later that week, I followed the small map on Henri Hui's tan business card, looking for his shop, Pacific Curios, on Rue A. Leboucher. A fellow cruiser in Acapulco had given me the card along with a letter of introduction to Henri. Three generations back, ancestors of the Huis had arrived from China, and the family had prospered. Now Henri, Lena, and their two children enjoyed their life amid a circle of Chinese-Tahitian friends—all well traveled and fluent in several languages.

Short, dark, and businesslike, but with a ready smile, Henri whisked me home for dinner, then in the weeks that followed to the Sunday market for shopping, home for more dinners, on tours of the island, and to the Gauguin Museum. He even did my laundry. But more important than all of this during those lean weeks were his family's friendship, concern, and interest.

Money dribbled in from paintings I sold on the streets and to fellow cruisers, but often I barely had enough to buy groceries. The Huis always arrived at *SC* with armloads of fruit from their yard. When I discovered that no one on the island sold block ice and that it would cost $40 to buy what I needed in cubes, their son's girlfriend, Natalie, made large containers of ice for me. The Hui family became real-life angels.

One day Henri called via VHF through the operator at the dive center on shore to say he was on his way to pick me up for another island tour. Outside wind screamed across the reef, and a two-foot chop in the anchorage pitched *SC* up and down, yanking the snubber rigid. If I rowed the half mile or more to shore, I would not be able to row back against the wind. I sent my regrets via the operator. Henri was disappointed when he arrived, unable to understand the limitations of boat life. It was the last invitation I received.

Their generosity had enriched my stay and introduced me to life on shore, but it had also created a hurdle for my pride. It was difficult to admit that sometimes I needed help. I kept a scorecard, and the Huis were too far ahead of me. It didn't occur to me that sharing in my trip might have been all the compensation they wanted.

Evenings, in the anchorage, the tropical Polynesian sky revolved around the Southern Cross constellation overhead while night breezes gently lifted cockpit awnings and spread the scent of frangipani. Cruisers gathered in small groups in one cushioned cockpit or another, sipping wine and comparing experiences en route while the fast drumbeat of a Tahitian *tamare* trailed out from the hotel lounge on shore. Some nights we made our own music, including bluegrass played by two professional musicians from the States on fiddle and banjo. They were traveling toward New Zealand on their 27-foot Bristol Channel Cutter, leaving hectic recording and concert schedules behind.

Joe and Kat Fern had arrived in Papeete before the crowds, mooring their boat, *Champagne*, on the quay in the center of town so Joe could get his newspaper and croissants minutes after his eyes opened. We met at a dinner gathering on board *Fair Winds* hosted by owners Barbara McGuire and Charles Rockwell, friends of mine since Cabo San Lucas. Joe had left behind a solid record of wins as a personal injury attorney in Los Angeles; Kathy had been CFO for a major clothing import company.

Kat dreamed of drawing and painting while they cruised the South Pacific, and it was that shared interest that drew me to their boat the next morning. She couldn't wait to show me the new book she had just purchased. I opened *Carnet de Croquis*, the reproduction of a watercolor sketchbook by Jacques Boullaire, and studied each page, mesmerized. His sketches unlocked something; through tears I looked at simple aspects of island life: people, their clothes, moods of sea and sky, details of plants and fish and boats captured in sensuous pencil strokes and splashed with sun-drenched color. With reverence I handed her book back.

After that, I sat for hours in cafés drawing people, or along roadsides capturing bungalows, churches, and plants. I saw through new eyes. I took my watercolors to the street, looking for scenes and people to paint: passersby with bags of baguettes; taxi drivers napping at their stand; young men snoozing on concrete benches in the shade; and old women playing cards on woven mats, breasts cascading over generous bellies and heads ringed with flower crowns. Next to my seat I propped up the tiny, framed paintings, and locals and tourists stopped to look and buy. One couple asked for larger pieces. By the next afternoon they had commissioned four for their new jewelry store.

With new confidence I moved my workplace back to *SC*, but the larger, 8-by 12-inch pieces of paper intimidated me with all that empty space. Working from photos and sketches, I laid on layer after layer of soft pastel colors, too nervous to put myself on the line with dashing strong colors and strokes. For nine days I hibernated, immersing myself in the work. Friends from neighboring boats stopped to see what I needed from shore. "Just a few bananas and a loaf of bread, thanks," I would say, and dash below. Young Mark and Helen Halburt, delivery crew on board a 65-foot Swan (named, appropriately, *Swan*) that was anchored nearby, adopted me. Daily, Helen dinghied over to *Southern Cross* to check on my progress and talk about technique. Her wildlife paintings hung in a gallery in town.

_____ SEPTEMBER 1989

I GATHERED THE FOUR FINISHED PIECES FOR DELIVERY to their purchasers, planning one stop on the way—the RevaReva Gallery. For two months the changing displays inside the gallery had given birth to dreams of an exhibition of my own someday. That evening, I burst with news for Kat, Helen, and Kitty.

Dearest Kitty,

You won't believe what just happened! RevaReva Gallery in Papeete offered me a one-woman show for March 9–16, 1990. It is so exciting and so scary at the same time. Am I good enough? Am I ready?

At 8 × 12 they say I need at least 50 pieces. How in the world can I finish all that, sail to New Zealand, and earn money to live on while I paint? I just said "yes" and will hope for the best. I'll shoot photos and gather sketches for material from here and the other islands (when I leave in two weeks).

I'll have six pieces to send back from Bora-Bora to pay for my air ticket in the spring. We drew an agreement covering all the details: invitations, publicity, reception, framing, percentages, etc. Hope I didn't forget anything.

What a boost for my confidence! This should either get the creative juices flowing or frighten them into hiding forever. So far my plan seems to be working; I've sold more than 60 miniatures since February and have made $1,100 here doing something I love.

Hope all is well with you and Peter. I'm looking forward to a letter in New Zealand.

Love and hugs,

Pat

P.S. Can't wait to introduce you to my friend Kat. That just tickles me—Kit and Kat. You'll love her. Another artist in the making.

After dashing off the note to Kitty, I dinghied over to look for Helen. When I pulled alongside *Swan*'s large, fancy Avon, *T/T Southern Cross* looked even more pathetic with her growing field of patches. The manufacturer hadn't responded yet.

With Mark's family in Canada and Helen's in New Zealand, we three had become a surrogate family. On August 12th, Helen had brought me a fresh batch of fudge and stayed to hold my hand while Tamara celebrated her wedding thousands of miles away. For nine months I had scanned every letter for details of the day I couldn't share in person, hoping to visualize it as clearly as if I'd been there.

On board I found Helen in the middle of dinner preparations, and she insisted I stay as she had on countless other evenings. She and Mark listened to my news and told of their plans to leave for Chile as soon as weather patterns improved. At 10:00, as I left for home, Helen handed me the familiar red-lidded plastic container. Dinners on *Swan* always ended with her care packages. Though he would never know it, the generous food budget alloted by *Swan*'s owner helped stretch my tiny budget a little further.

Over two months Helen, Mark, and I had exchanged meals, books, ideas, tools, know-how, and art critique and technique. I counted on our good-byes being eased somewhat by Helen's invitation to spend the Christmas holidays at her family's farm in Te Awamutu, New Zealand.

That week I attacked a list of departure preparations and shopped for the long passages to New Zealand: through the Societies, to Rarotonga in the

Cooks, and on to the Bay of Islands. In the maintenance schedule of the shop manual for my Yanmar diesel the directive to "adjust the intake and exhaust valve clearances at 1,000 hours" washed over me like a wave of doom. My budget would never go far enough to pay a mechanic for that job.

From the shop manual and my be-your-own-diesel-mechanic book, I listed the tools and supplies needed, considered the differences in the procedures recommended by my two sources, planned the project in minute steps, then took a break in the cockpit. I looked out at the boats around me, knowing that each of those captains had done this job. "If they can do it," I told myself, "you can too."

The next morning, with all the tools and supplies laid out like preparations in a surgery theater and dressed in engine room clothes—an ancient, holey T-shirt and cut-offs—I began. Two hours later I climbed back to the cockpit and approached the ignition key as if it were a stick of dynamite. My mind's eye slipped in a view of the entire engine shaking itself into a thousand pieces, exploding, throwing a valve through the side and billowing black smoke. I turned the key. It burst into life, running perfectly. Swelling to 6 feet 4 inches with pride and looking over the anchorage again, I knew we captains shared a deep, mysterious knowledge. I had joined their ranks.

With the cabin back in order, I cleaned up and went ashore to run errands, just a little bit proud of the grease lingering under my nails. At the dinghy dock, I ran into the owner and captain of a 45-foot ketch, a man who exuded capability and knowledge. Unable to be modest, I quickly told him, "Well, I finally bit the bullet and adjusted my valves today."

"You did? I wish I'd known that. I planned to hire someone to come do mine, so I could watch and learn how."

Mark strolled up as I headed down the path. "Hi, Mark. Well, I did those valves today. Sure glad to get that job off the list."

"You did? I've never actually tried that one myself. Always hired someone."

I walked on to the *Le Truck* stop with a lurking doubt tapping on my shoulder. Had I just been lucky that it worked?

A letter from Mom and Stubby waited at the Port Captain's office. They wanted to send money to Libby so she could buy me a long-distance radio as a Christmas present from them. Lib could bring it to New Zealand in December, if I sent the information telling her what to buy.

One Sunday before Emmett left Tahiti for Hawaii aboard *Kama Hele*, I offered breakfast in exchange for helping me sort through the options available to provide *Southern Cross* with offshore communications. The results: a ham radio would be cheaper than a single-sideband, and a manual tuner would work as well as an automatic one for less money. I had already installed an insulated backstay for an antenna during *SC*'s refit.

Emmett provided brands and models and a list of every supply needed to complete the installation and study for my license. News via the cruising grapevine said ham tests would be given in New Zealand while cruisers were there waiting out the coming hurricane season. By April, I could be on the airwaves with my family and sailing friends. Mom and Stubby could listen to my daily check-ins during crossings over a cheap shortwave receiver, and the assistance of a local ham operator would make it possible for us to chat for free via phone patches.

_____ OCTOBER 1989

NOVEMBER 1ST—THE BEGINNING OF HURRICANE SEAson in the South Pacific and the enforced departure deadline for all foreign boats in French Polynesia—loomed on the calendar. The French authorities did not want to spend money rescuing foreign boats and sailors in their waters. But the names of the other islands in the Society archipelago Mooréa, Huahiné, and Bora-Bora—danced in my dreams. They would be full of opportunities for photos and sketches for paintings. A small voice pleaded, "You should take a little time to play, too, after all this work." Having journeyed so far and approached so near, how could I sail by without stopping?

A week before my final trip ashore in Papeete, I checked out and collected my "security" deposit from the bank, using it to top off the fuel tanks, fill lockers with fresh provisions, restock maintenance and repair supplies, replace the cutless bearing on the propeller shaft, and pay a $190 mooring, dinghy-dock, and water fee at the resort on shore.

On October 10th, craggy Mooréa, just twelve miles west of Papeete, offered a lonely, empty anchorage. I hiked and sketched the shuttered, pastel wooden bungalows frosted with colonial gingerbread, the grass shack sarong shops, and hammocks sagging under soft round bottoms while their owners waited out afternoon rains. Under layers of night ginger and *tiare*, an odor of wet earth and molding vegetation saturated the air. But daily squalls and rough conditions on the reef in front of the Bali Hai Hotel depressed me.

I moved on to Huahiné, a reminder of the Papeete described in Michener's

Return to Paradise. The French Polynesian garden island 130 miles west of Tahiti answered my island fantasies. *Southern Cross* hung suspended between lavender-bottomed clouds above and drifts of rippled, white sand below; air and water dissolved into a seamless blend of blues and turquoises. Small wavelets brushed the powdered-sugar beach with a pale melon blush, while the jungle edged in red and yellow hibiscus, pure white frangipani, and kaleidoscopic croton crowded from behind.

Birds darted through twenty shades of waving green fronds. I lounged under *SC*'s green-and-white striped awning with a Robert Ludlum page-turner, then dozed off in sole possession of this bit of heaven. The sound of tumbling chain broke the afternoon peace as the 51-foot charter boat *Impetuous* anchored 50 feet away, her deck swarming with men.

The next morning, through sleepy, pre-coffee eyes, I saw eight naked male bodies framed in my porthole. Round little middle-aged potbellies glistened with soap bubbles as the men scrubbed each other. They giggled, laughed, and leapt over the side. At nine o'clock, when I left to hike, sketch, and shoot photos, my playful neighbors shouted an invitation to join them, but I waved and rowed past.

That night, strong rich voices blending with an unfamiliar stringed instrument snaked across the water. In the morning as I headed for shore, they offered a second invitation, and this time I stopped for coffee and the chance to see the mysterious instrument.

Every two years the eight business friends aboard *Impetuous* made their escape from Finland, Norway, and Germany. From the youngest, at forty-six, to the seventy-three-year-old who offered to sail with me as deckhand, they came to sail, play, sing songs, and swap stories—but not to do business. The youngest, Heikke, brought out his kantele, the traditional Finnish zither that had enchanted my dreams.

The crew of *Impetuous* welcomed me into their group, issuing invitations for dinner, breakfast, and more music. That evening a van picked us up for an elegant, dress-up dinner across the island at a new resort. In the morning we ate breakfast ashore and strolled among market tables sagging with fruit and vegetables from island farms, displays of baskets and flowers, and strings of freshly caught, shimmering fish. We watched the ferry from Tahiti spill out passengers and freight—ladies in bright patterned dresses, then machines, coils of rope, and cases of cans and bottles. That night we went to a late soiree, but we didn't go late enough. Our only companions were two dusky island men who eyed me with all my escorts, and one shady island lady in red satin skin who eyed all my escorts. We danced one dance to the two-piece band and were home, sound asleep, two hours before the islanders showed up to party the night away.

The next day their stay drew to a close. Early in the morning we had an impromptu art exhibition on board *SC*. They bought every piece, then emptied their galley lockers to restock my diminishing supplies and challenged me to a race to Tahaa, the island sharing Raiatéa's barrier reef.

Impetuous arrived one hour before *Southern Cross*, but they declared a tie since I had started one hour late. We toasted our success and snorkeled in the flamboyant coral gardens beneath our boats.

From my first evening with the crew of *Impetuous*, they had talked about their favorite restaurant, L'Hibiscus on Tahaa. They invited me to dinner there the night before they left. Lou, the owner, greeted us at the dock like long-lost relatives and escorted us through tamed jungle gardens to his thatched-roof dining room. As I cooled off with a vodka tonic, LaLa strolled in for introductions. A fully grown sow, she held court in the open-air restaurant like the former high-class madam and mayor Sally Stanford at her Valhalla in Sausalito. LaLa swayed from group to group, checking out each table, then stretched out on the cool floor of the bar.

Dinner was a perfect mix of French and island flavors prepared by Lou's dark-haired companion, Lolita. Our conversation ranged around the globe, mixing travel stories with memories. Heikki played his kantele, and songs filled the evening air. At 2:00 A.M. we said good night to Lou, Lolita, LaLa, and L'Hibiscus and floated back to our boats over still, star-studded water.

In my last view of the Huahiné Gang, *Impetuous* was circling *SC* while they serenaded me with the traditional German farewell song, "Muss i denn, Muss i denn . . ."

Below in the *Southern Cross* guest book, I found their message to me from Johann W. von Goethe:

> *"Zwischen heut und morgen*
> *ist eine kurze Frist*
> *drum lerne schnell besorgen*
> *da Du noch munter bist"*

which they translated as: "Between today and tomorrow is a short time. Therefore, learn swiftly while you are still healthy." Or in my vernacular, "Life's short—go for it."

I SAILED SOUTH AROUND TAHAA INTO MARINI ITI and found *Fair Winds* swinging at anchor, with Charles and Barbara on deck waving a welcome. After leaving Papeete they had secured the impossible—permission to stay in the small hurricane hole on the south end of Tahaa for the storm season. After hugs and greetings, they asked if I had listened to the news recently. "Do you know about the San Francisco earthquake? How is Tamara?" I had no answers; this was the first I'd heard of the October 17th disaster.

I soon learned from a Voice of America broadcast that Loma Prieta, three miles from my daughter's home, had been the epicenter. The news carried details of the damage to freeways in San Francisco and the pandemonium at Candlestick Park, where baseball's World Series was in progress, but little on effects in the Santa Cruz area. I felt powerless to help, so far from home with no money to travel or even to place a long-distance call. My mind chewed on the edges of the what-ifs.

Hoping for more information, I added the morning VOA transmission to my daily radio schedule. Afternoons I picked up the South Pacific weather broadcast from Arnold, a volunteer ham operator in Rarotonga. He gathered the latest forecasts from several government and commercial sources and distributed them to the cruising community scattered across the Pacific, from South America to Australia and north to Hawaii.

For two days Barbara's gourmet meals held me captive, until the lure of Bora-Bora's famous cloud-draped crags coaxed me away. Cool early-morning ghosting breezes pushed me out of Passe Paipai.

That evening *Southern Cross* moored off Bora-Bora's Hotel OaOa. Lounging in a rattan chair on the verandah, Jerry, the owner, chomped on his huge, smelly Cuban cigar. "You must be Henry. We've been expecting you." *SC* was the last boat of the season, and my waiting mail had made the introductions for me. I skimmed through the envelopes searching for news of Tamara, trying to convince myself that if something had happened, Mom would have sent a telegram. Again I considered making a phone call, wondering how much it would cost. The bill for the telegram from Nuku Hiva had been $25. I couldn't afford a call and wouldn't burden my family by calling collect. Days passed with no news, gradually reassuring me that Tamara and her family were all right. My Casio said "October 28." Only three days remained to buy provisions, do laundry, and leave.

Then the weather turned nasty. Cold front after cold front rolled through the islands. Arnold talked only of gale warnings and fronts. Five days slid by while I waited for a departure window and gained a new status . . . illegal.

Finally, it sounded like the bad weather might be ending. My expired visa and Libby's scheduled visit pulled me off the mooring Saturday, November 4th, bound for Rarotonga in the Cook Islands. By Sunday night *Southern Cross* was bowling along wing-and-wing in 12-foot seas, carrying her mainsail with all three reefs on one side and the small, high-cut jib on the other.

SHIP'S DIARY: 7 November 1989, 1206 Local, 19°25'S/156°08'W. Sailing straight west with triple-reefed main and staysail in seas up to 20 feet and 45-knot winds, 100% cloud cover.

Day by day the weather deteriorated, and the wind vane struggled to hold the downwind course. Images returned from the three-day storm that had once engulfed *Windy*, but this time I was alone. *SC* careened wildly down steep, mountainous waves. I hauled out a nylon anchor line and trailed it in a 200-foot warp off the stern to improve control. Still *Southern Cross* raced forward, tossing this way and that under only a tiny, backwinded storm staysail. As each thundering surge passed under *SC* she rose to the crest, and I glimpsed an endless chaos.

Thursday morning the wind lightened, circled the compass, and returned with increased fury. Rarotonga Radio reported 60 knots. Foam blew horizontally from the crests of 25-foot seas, wind and spray burning my eyes. Below, sounds magnified into nightmares; I returned outside.

SC's course ran between islands hidden from view by the towering seas. For eight hours the SatNav waited for a new position. At last it flashed on the screen; I was safely through.

That night the winds began dying. By morning only huge, sloppy seas remained. I faced myself in the mirror. "Who are you now?" I wondered. I was no longer the woman who had feared rejection in an interview eighteen months before. A gift of confidence had ridden the wings of the storm.

I wet a washcloth to wipe the salt from my face and wept at the feel of my own touch. For two days I had lived outside my body, doing what was needed to survive. The tears unlocked the tension and emotions I had buried to stay focused.

While I had battled my sea storm, the people of Berlin had begun tearing down the wall dividing East from West. The morning news on VOA reported a flood of humanity pouring through the opening.

Saturday morning I arrived in Rarotonga's tiny port to dry out, pick up mail, reprovision, and rest. Ready to depart Monday evening, I turned the key and the engine responded with silence. I sank to the settee and once more pulled out my how-to-be-your-own-diesel-mechanic book, this time to read about starter motors.

I felt as if huge bungee cords were holding me back from New Zealand, one mishap or delay after another pushing the scheduled reunion with my sister out of reach. Libby's plans were tied to an airplane ticket and vacation time, mine to weather, equipment, and the vagaries of a moody sea.

I diagnosed a bad solenoid, but that was the limit of my skill. In the morning, I contacted a mechanic from New Zealand who had spent his professional life as a ship's engineer and now worked in a nearby shop. A short, middle-aged guy with thin, graying hair, a sympathetic manner, and an air of competence, he arrived at *SC* wearing Wellingtons and a gray jumpsuit.

We took the starter motor and solenoid for shoreside testing and pulled up at the shop in his truck in time for "coffee break." Under the shadow of heavy machinery and greasy engine parts, the staff of huge Polynesians circled a low Formica coffee table, drinking mugs of tea and devouring eight-inch-thick sandwiches. Around layers of white bread and canned spaghetti, while the mechanic ran tests, they asked questions and shook their heads, listening to tales of my trip.

My mechanic and I climbed back in his truck to search the island for a new solenoid, but there was no match on Rarotonga. He settled for the closest facsimile and manufactured one to fit from parts of the old, broken solenoid and the new one—the Dr. Christiaan Barnard of marine engineers.

Inside the starter motor, wires contorted back on themselves over puddles of melted solder. He reshaped each one, cleaned out solder drips, reattached wires, and filed down excess material. Watching him work was teaching me more about approaching repairs than about the starter motor itself. After retightening the last machine screw he applied power, and the musical whir of a healthy motor filled the shop.

By Tuesday evening, with the engine humming, I departed Rarotonga—next stop New Zealand. Of the $330 I had possessed leaving Bora-Bora, $65 remained. The repair had cost $212, and $53 had gone for departure taxes, harbor fees, fresh provisions, and fuel, though not enough of the latter to fill the tanks. My watch now read "November 14," which left twenty days to cover 1,800 miles to keep my date with Lib. I set money worries aside and focused on getting to New Zealand.

Over the long haul, my speed had averaged 100 miles per day—dependable and comfortable. With exhilarating runs of 129, 147, and 133 miles, just one week out from Rarotonga I celebrated the halfway point of the passage. An on-time arrival looked more than just likely.

By noon that day, however, the stable, though wild, downwind conditions that had been propelling *SC* disappeared. Winds became fluky, and seas chaotic. The sails fought each other for balance as squalls raced past.

Sheltered by the high weather cloths surrounding the cockpit, I sat next to the open companionway, feeling secure and safe from the following seas. Then one wave taller than the others rose above the stern and broke aboard. It flew over the cockpit and through the companionway, flooding the galley and the cabin sole below. I scrambled to place the dropboards in the opening before another wave could cause more damage. Gallons of seawater covered the port side—stove, floor, sink, counter, and galley lockers. If *SC* had been on a port instead of a starboard tack, the charts, radio, and electronics across the cabin would have been swimming in salt water instead.

As my celebration day wore on, sailing conditions went over the edge, pitting optimism against fear. *SC* raced down waves on the ragged edge of control. Her theoretical maximum hull speed was 6.7 knots, yet the log showed constant readings above seven. I shortened sail to triple-reefed main and staysail, and still she raced on at seven. Finally, with only the tiny storm staysail flying, I hauled out the anchor line to rig another warp behind the stern.

I always celebrated halfway points on a passage and sometimes even quarters, one-thousand-mile marks, and changing hemispheres. Anything sufficed for a party at sea—even if it was just a glass of wine and some favorite music. But, exhausted as I was, today it was only a few tinned butter cookies.

Arnold confirmed the gale on his evening net, but not in my location. It reached farther than he realized.

I stretched out below, listening to the sea race one inch from my ear as *Southern Cross* tossed and twisted, screaming down wave fronts. My dreams built a wild anchorage in the middle of an overcast and gloomy ocean. The night crept by. A yellow-gray dawn emerged, and my depleted reserves screamed for sugar. I baked a batch of oatmeal cookies.

Outside the rigging howled and whined. Sounds like shotgun blasts shook the hull at each large wave that smashed into *SC*'s side or dropped her down its face. I pulled heavy foul-weather gear over tights and sweatshirt, climbed outside, closed the companionway, and watched the raging seas, amazed that *Southern Cross* could endure such a pounding. I didn't know whether I could.

The white-streaked backs of rumbling seas raced ahead, and from behind came the roar of a towering, hissing mass. I braced as it curled and tumbled over the stern, pouring into every opening in my foul-weather gear and running down my neck, back, and arms. The force of the impact shot the companionway hatch open, and seawater charged over the top of the dropboards and into the cabin. This time the cockpit was half full and draining too slowly. I grabbed a bucket and bailed before it could find its way below through the unsealed cockpit lockers. Installing the seals was still a job on the "to-do" list.

The wind built to 60 knots, and I watched until exhaustion, hunger, or fear forced me below. But never for long. The gale dropped and increased time after time as the day wore on, moving around the compass from east to north to west to south and back again to east. At times *Southern Cross* needed more sail to keep her moving forward against a headwind, and at other times she needed less as she tore down wave fronts before the wind. Each time I crawled forward to make the change. At last, as evening came, conditions eased to 30 knots.

Instead of cooking dinner, I brought in the warp. The towering seas, still 25 feet high, tossed *SC* back and forth as I hauled the anchor rope back on board. With tears running and muscles shaking I coiled and stowed the 200-foot line, then collapsed and slept below. *Southern Cross* needed more sail to stabilize her, but I was too tired to raise it.

Thursday morning, the 23rd, skies lightened, the wind returned, and I felt sick. I took Advil, Marizene, and then more Advil. What I really needed was food, not medicine, but nauseated and with my head in raging pain, anything but lying flat seemed impossible. At 1000 the wind disappeared completely, and the barometer dropped another 7 millibars. I braced for more bad weather. Squalls marched down in an unending line, some ferocious and some just carrying rain. *SC's* cabin felt like the inside of a Maytag washer. I no longer cared about sails, making headway, or what direction *SC* traveled. The feast for this Thanksgiving Day stayed stashed in a locker. I ate a can of cold rice pudding and thought about family and friends gathering in dry and happy groups, safe, laughing, eating turkey.

Arnold's afternoon weather report came through loud and clear. I waited for the evening net, longing for the comfort of voices I knew saying "Happy Thanksgiving" to one another and telling what they had for dinner. But now the airwaves carried only static through the lightning-filled sky outside. Once again, tears of exhaustion and frustration coursed down my face.

Friday brought light air with a thin layer of clouds. The bar dropped another 7 millibars.

Saturday at daybreak, the wind rose to more than 30 knots from the south-west, quickly forming steep, chaotic, 12-foot seas as the old easterly swell collided with newly developed southwesterly wind waves. I reefed the main and changed the jib, but the building gusts were still too much for the sail area I had set. I dropped in the third reef.

Within moments the main split 30 inches along a line of stitching holes left from a former batten pocket. Afraid I might lose the sail overboard in removing it from the mast and boom to take below for repairs, I decided to patch the tear in place. Other than going up the mast, I dreaded the cabintop more than any other location on the boat. It was an exposed and vulnerable perch, with only the swaying boom to grab.

Wedged between the boom and the cabintop handrail, I stitched and hung on for life while the boat lurched and salt spray and green water flew at me. By the time I tied the last knot on 70 inches of handsewn zigzags I was wet, cold, and shaking from tension. SC plunged, heeled, and bucked into the 12-foot seas.

The knot log hovered at 2.5, but the SatNav showed 0. In the strong winds I couldn't put up enough sail to drive her forward through the steep head seas. I added the engine at low rpms for additional power.

SHIP'S DIARY: 26 November 1989, 0840 Local, 29°38′S/177°38′W. Motorsailing with double-reefed main, jib, and staysail in southwesterlies at 16 to 24 knots. Seas are down somewhat but sloppy. Tacking for a 200M course made good.

By midday Sunday, horizontal rainbows floated over the sea and small, white clouds puffed ahead. Forty-four miles made good noon-to-noon, and I bellowed a made-up opera. I had thought I might spend the rest of my life east of the Kermadec Islands, consigned to oblivion between Tonga and New Zealand.

But my good mood didn't last long. For three more days, winds of 16 to 45 knots drove at the bow, brewing steep, short seas. *Southern Cross* crashed and banged first one way then the other, but not forward. On port tack she steered 240 degrees by the compass, but SatNav fixes showed her sideslipping on a course "over the ground" of 315. I couldn't rely on the compass or log to navigate between fixes. The wind stirred an incessant whine in the rigging, winding my nerves taut. I threw a plastic container across the cabin, breaking it, and in tears begged for it all to stop.

Time and again the erratic conditions forced me up on deck to adjust sails. Outside the crash of sea against hull, the scream of stressed rigging, and the howl of the unending wind were even worse. I pulled on salt-caked lines that stung my cracked hands while the relentless march of seas from New Zealand built layers of salt spray over my face.

Each surge forward brought *SC* up against a steep wall of water, stopped her short, then threw her over as the wind hit again. Cold water raced over the deck along the lee rail and found its way below. A puddle built on the floor by the settee, and I could not find its source.

Cursing myself for what I didn't know about sail handling or feared to do, and in total frustration, I used the engine on and off to gain distance forward. I had allotted no fuel for this extravagance, but without it I made little progress.

Mile by mile the line on the plotting sheet crawled toward Curtis Rock, the beginning of the Kermadecs. The sailing directions reported that Curtis and Cheeseman islets lay five miles south of their charted positions. I plotted their true locations, drew a reasonable circle of safety around them, and laid my course well outside the boundary.

SHIP'S DIARY: 28 November 1989, 0712 Local, 30°30'S/178°55'W sailing 285M in 40–45 knots with triple-reefed main and jib. Only 18 miles to the good yesterday.

In a dawn mist, Curtis Rock appeared just four miles off *SC*'s stern. A chill ran down my back. My wake seemed to pass right through the middle of the rock. How close had I sailed, and when?

As I turned to go below, the screen of the SatNav went blank. It had died.

I looked for sunlight between squalls that day and the next, shooting sights, plotting positions, and making mistakes—forgetting when I crossed the International Date Line that not only did the date change, but the calculations for deriving a position reversed. Gradually my rhythm returned, and the string of fixes fell into a slow, steady line.

Passing out of the Kermadec Islands felt like going through a wall. The barometer climbed 21 millibars. Even the air felt different. Seas flattened as the wind dropped all the way to zero. For four days *SC* barely moved. With no spare fuel I sat helplessly on calm, flat water.

Still disappointed in myself for not being able to point closer or make better progress during the four days of headwinds that had just ended, I pulled out every sailing book on board and read about sail trim, rig adjustments, and sail theory. It was information I should already have known. I tightened the backstay, sewed telltales on sails, and tweaked rigging. The next day, with just six knots of wind, I sailed a close reach at four knots.

SHIP'S DIARY: 4 December 1989, Local Noon, 31°53'S/178°18'E (by sun shot), steering 210M at 1.5 knots. Made 30 miles noon to noon—better than yesterday's 27 miles.

Marine life appeared—little sailing jellyfish, a whale blowing to port, and scores of big-eye tuna that were too smart to take my stainless steel leader.

Wet cushions and clothes—almost everything in the V-berth—covered the deck and hung from the rigging. Off the bow the radial-head drifter swayed from side to side in the two-knot breeze—I was desperate enough for progress to try it again. SC wandered back and forth across her course, following the sashaying sail. Only 285 miles to go, but today Libby would arrive in Opua. I worried what her reaction would be when she arrived and I wasn't there.

For several days I had tracked another New Zealand–bound boat over the evening net and watched her position gradually closing on mine. There was a tiny chance that we would be within VHF range the next day, and I could pass a message.

Libby had answered my question—"What would make your vacation absolutely perfect?"—saying she just wanted to get her morning coffee and newspaper on shore and relax. She sought nothing more exciting than a little boatwork—polishing or something—but I wanted to show her more of my new life than that. I envisioned sailing to the small islands around Opua and Russell to anchor for a day or two, visit, read, swim, and then head back to town to socialize and venture out again. Before she left we would make a voyage to Auckland to catch her return flight home. But in between I needed to squeeze in some work—pieces for the show in Papeete in March and some for money to live on in the meantime. Six weeks would be a long visit in such a tiny space, but we'd manage.

That night Arnold relayed bad news. A low-pressure system with full storm-force winds would pass over Opua tomorrow and reach me the following day. It sounded worse than any previous experience. I wasn't sure I could handle one more.

The next morning a clean, solid wind and a 3-foot sea made for good sailing under the radial-head drifter while I repaired the 130 percent genoa, dried more clothes and cushions, and traced the leaks that had surfaced during the preceding gales. I called *Suhaila*, the boat approaching *SC*, but got no response. Once more I wished that the new ham radio and the license to use it were already mine.

The morning of the 6th the wind moved back on the nose, bringing a new wave of despair and tears. I was twenty-two days out of Rarotonga on a passage that should have taken eighteen. By midnight the storm threat dissolved, and *SC* sat on a perfect mirror. Then gradually, a wind filled in from the south, and she slid over long, lazy 16-foot swells while I waited to take sun shots as she paused for a second on their tops.

On December 8th, New Zealand stretched across the horizon in front of me in the first glow of dawn. The sailing directions described Cape Brett, my target, as a headland fronted by a prominent rock. But almost the same description appeared for Cavelli Rocks and Cape Wiwiki, both northwest of Cape Brett. I waited for the sun and studied a headland with a rock in front through my binoculars.

A boxy, white Japanese car carrier came into view, and I called on VHF channel 16 for a position. Silence. I called again. No answer. They passed so close I read the writing on their stern and called them by name. Still nothing. At last a cherry red sun hung above the horizon, and I quickly shot a line of position while *SC* perched at the crest of a swell. *Southern Cross* sat somewhere on that line. When the water grew shallow enough to register on the depth sounder, I was certain the headland in front of me was Cape Brett. I eased the lines and sailed on.

As details of the coast came into focus, I realized that I had been fooled by Cavelli Rocks. The entrance to the Bay of Islands lay south, toward the wind. I hardened the sails and beat along the coast. After lunch I passed a message to Libby through Radio Russell. There for four days, she already knew everyone in town. They called, and the desk clerk pinned a note to her motel room door: "Your sister is here." I tacked back out to sea over the 16-foot swells, then back in to the coast, hour after hour.

At five o'clock I rounded Nine Pin Rock into the bay, delirious with joy and exhaustion. The evening breeze died, and I started the engine. It ran a few minutes, then stopped. Bleeding the fuel line didn't help. I gave up, raised sails, and searched for the leading marks to Opua. The chart showed them bearing 213 degrees, which I wrongly assumed to mean degrees magnetic, not true. There was an 18-degree variation between the two in the Bay of Islands. The shallow-water alarm sounded, and I knew that I was lost.

Through all of this the Opua harbormaster talked me in, welcoming me to New Zealand. Following his instructions, I ghosted on a whisper of a breeze toward Russell and Pahia. Then the wind disappeared completely. I suggested anchoring for the night where I was, since the engine wouldn't start. "Oh no, that won't do," he said. "I'll come tow you in." Arriving on his own sailboat with a fellow cruiser to help, he tied *Southern Cross* alongside. I rode into port between lush green hillsides bathed in the scent of lilacs in the southern spring, too glad to be there to be embarrassed by needing a tow.

Leaving *Southern Cross* at the dock, the harbormaster warned, "No visitors are allowed before Customs and Immigration come in the morning. Just have a good sleep, and eat up any of those eggs, cheese, or fresh things we'll confiscate tomorrow."

The officials arrived in the morning and cleared me in, leaving with a large black plastic bag of forbidden food. Then Libby called down from the center of a pile of duffel bags on the dock ten feet above. My carry-on-only sister handed down bags of gifts from Mom, art supplies, mail, boat gear, and the long-awaited radio. She followed the bags, and we hugged, glad to be together again.

Over coffee in the cockpit we rambled through the past year since our last visit in Cabo San Lucas. I told her of storms at sea and the coming exhibition. She brought stories from the recent Oregon legislative session, her success at getting an important bill passed, her life in Portland, the status of her on-and-off relationship, news of our cousins and friends—stories filled with her insightful humor. We planned the long-awaited coming weeks, including my need for time to earn some money. After clearing in I was down to $25.

Libby's duffel bags filled the cabin as we searched for empty space amid the clutter of a just-finished passage. She unearthed the package of mail Tamara had forwarded from the post office box in Santa Cruz. I sorted the cheery holiday envelopes from the business mail and opened one from my attorney. "Call collect. The judge handling all the TWT cases needs to talk to you." Over the next week I looked for a way to connect with the judge by phone. He was willing but unable to accept a collect call, and I didn't have the money to call him from the one pay phone in Opua. He only wanted to know that I really did not have $3 million with which to repay the bank. Eventually he accepted my attorney's word.

Libby and I whirled through a round of social gatherings at the Opua Sailing Club, as local residents and cruisers alike swept her into their midst for Wednesday potlucks and informal coffee visits in cockpits around the anchorage.

With new fuel filters, the Yanmar purred once again. Word of my miniature paintings spread around the harbor and brought small commissions, sales,
and a job painting the name on a local sportfishing boat. As money trickled
in I breathed a little easier.

Libby's intellect and wry humor spiced our days with laughter and good
conversation. She followed the news religiously and always found something
in the New Zealand morning papers to spark up our breakfast conversation.

"Oh, listen to this: A man was arrested in Auckland on suspicion of mur-
der. The police found him doing a stir-fry in his wok with some guy's genitals.
Sort of a cock-of-the-wok." We rolled with laughter while she hunted for
another item.

Instead of leisurely days in the islands, time flashed by in Opua or Russell.
At last I started the first piece for the Papeete show but couldn't find the time,
space, or peace necessary to make much progress.

Christmas Eve we joined other cruisers, including *Champagne*, for an onboard
potluck feast followed by the midnight service in Russell at the first church
built in New Zealand. On Christmas Day, with tree, turkey, and all the trim-
mings, the Opua Sailing Club hosted more than seventy cruisers who were
waiting out the South Pacific hurricane season. Finally we left for our New
Year's sail south to Auckland on the 30th. The first night we spent in Whanga-
mumu, enjoying dinner by kerosene lantern. It was the peaceful island anchorage I had dreamed of sharing. But as we sailed on to Auckland in company with
Champagne, underlying tensions between Libby and me broke into *SC*'s small
cabin.

In four weeks in confined quarters, habits, mannerisms, and conflicting
needs, which had grated on our nerves out of sight, surfaced. In Tutukaka, as
I worked on the painting, Libby cleaned on deck. When she tossed a bucket
of salt water that poured in through the undogged hatch above, ruining the
piece, I exploded; only two months remained to paint the fifty pieces. We tried
to surmount the friction, but personal worries absorbed us. Libby had found
a reminder in my cabin to do a monthly breast exam, and now she thought she
might have found something. We mentioned our private concerns in passing,
but neither of us drew the other inside for support.

When we arrived in Auckland, my sister paid for eleven days at West
Haven Marina and checked into a hotel in quaint, nearby Ponsonby to
enjoy the rest of her vacation. She shopped, lunched with Kat, and dropped
by *Southern Cross* a couple of times to say "hello."

I took my miniatures, a folding artist's chair, and painting materials to join the thousands gathered on the docks to welcome the arriving sailboats from the Whitbread Around-the-World Race. The air in the harbor crackled with brightly colored flags and pennants as one by one the boats pulled in to resounding cheers and formal welcomes. Auckland was a city of sailors, and their hearts went out to every boat. Lost from view at knee level in all the turmoil, I painted my little scenes around the quay: the first-to-arrive *Steinlager*, the cute blue tugboats, elegant *White Gull* from Belgium, and the old Customs House decorated with flags from around the world. But no one bought. The few who noticed stopped, smiled, and walked away.

Each day the crowds on the waterfront grew as more racers arrived. And each day, with less and less money, I painted and prayed for someone to buy one small piece of art. But I was invisible. No longer could I even stop for a cup of coffee. My determination sank into despair, in marked contrast to the surrounding festivities.

Small bright spots pushed their way through the gloom: an invitation from the builder to tour the Irish competitor in the race; an introduction to Dawn Riley, the capable, confident American sailor on board the all-women entry *Maiden*; an invitation from two strangers, Hermione Heywood and Leo Tattersfield, who noticed me walking to town from the marina, offered me a ride, and took me out to lunch; and watching New Zealanders reach into their pockets, collect money on street corners, and hold raffles to fund Russia's first entry in the race, *Fasizi*, when the sponsors backed out. Despite these moments, however, I slid steadily downward, first to a low point and then a frantic one.

My sister and I visited a few times, but only on the surface of our thoughts, like strangers. It would have been too hard to join her on her shopping trips, and, perhaps knowing that, she didn't ask. I had no money to go for lunch with her or share a taxi. Her vacation ended and she flew back to Oregon. In the two prepaid days I had remaining in the marina, I struggled to find a solution to my situation.

On Sunday evening, Dame Kiri Te Kanawa had scheduled a free concert for the people of Auckland. It was her gift to the city. I spent the afternoon making sketches for paintings in a charming Ponsonby neighborhood of late-nineteenth-century homes with picket fences and hydrangea, agapanthus, and hibiscus standing vividly against a clear blue sky.

Later, I walked across town to the park for a good seat on a grassy hillside dotted with picnic baskets and blankets. I painted while the crowd gathered— 140,000 people—for what the New Zealand press reported was the largest classical music concert in history. When people around me noticed and asked about the little painting, I prayed, "Please let someone buy it." But they just smiled and turned away, back to their conversations.

The music began and wrapped around me. Te Kanawa's voice—one of the most beautiful in the world of opera reached inside, melting the knot around my heart. Then, as the hours stretched past 10:00 P.M., I thought about the long walk home, and the magic moment slipped away.

Te Kanawa's rich, full tones wove through the air a mile or more from the concert and then from radios in windows open to the warm summer night as I walked alone toward the center of town. I picked up my pace through empty streets and drew in my body for the dark, lonely approach to the marina. On board *Southern Cross*, once again my financial dilemma filled every corner of my mind.

My usual bouncy start to each day had evaporated long before; I awoke the next morning already weighted with worry. If no one would buy my little paintings and taking a job was forbidden, with no money at all, what was I going to do halfway around the world? The solution had to lie in the Bay of Islands; Auckland was too expensive.

Steeling myself for a final day in town, I returned to the waterfront. Nothing had changed, only there were more boats and more people. I thought about the office where the owner of the blue tugboats worked. Gathering my things, I walked the half mile through the gay crowds, boosting myself with a lecture on how to make a sale, and entered the office as optimistically as I could, a smile firmly fixed in place.

The secretary exclaimed, "Oh, this is darling! Look, Fred, isn't that cute?"

I held my breath. He tipped his old wooden desk chair back to take a look. From behind a cigar his voice boomed out, "What would I want with a thing like that?"

I groped for the door. Legs shaking, I walked out and crossed the drawbridge back to the marina with tears streaming unabashedly. My last ray of hope had just been extinguished.

Seeing Bill and Sam Harrison ahead, I pulled together a little composure. They were Auckland residents and friends of Joe and Kat. I had done a design layout for their new electronics shop and a couple of miniatures in trade for their repairing the broken SatNav. "I'll be leaving in the morning," I told them. "You can drop me a note when the SatNav's ready." They asked how sales were going, and I had to be honest.

Sam offered, "I know they'd love your work in Devonport, across the bay. There are several galleries. I'll drive you over in the morning." Torn between the temptation to try one last time and the fear of one more humiliating rejection, despite knowing if I stayed another day I would have to pay the marina, I yielded to Sam's cajoling.

The next morning I dressed in something colorful with a jaunty scarf around my neck. Four galleries later, lower than ever, I arrived back at *Southern Cross*. Thanking Sam, I descended into the cabin. It was too late in the day to make the first anchorage at Kawau Island before dark. There were a thousand boats in the marina. Maybe no one would notice one small sailboat that overstayed its prepaid dock fee.

With everything ready for an early departure, I climbed into my bunk. The gray, wet dawn matched my mood in the morning. As I finished drying breakfast dishes the dreaded knock sounded through the hull.

A young woman from the marina office waited outside. "Excuse me, but you owe $11 for another day."

"I know, but I don't have any money. If you want my last $3, you can have it, but that's all the money I have in the whole world. I was just leaving now."

"Oh! Well . . . bring it to us next time you come."

I let out my breath in relief and finished getting ready. Reluctantly, I climbed into my clammy, lightweight foul-weather gear, backed out of the slip, and left for a gloomy sail north, retracing the New Year's passage south.

My mood sank lower in the gray, drizzly morass. As evening crept over the mist, I pulled into Bon Accord Harbour at Kawau. Looking in lockers didn't improve my outlook. There was no coffee, toilet paper, fruit, milk, butter, onions, fresh vegetables, peanut butter, bread, crackers, honey, or much else but some dried beans, rice, and a few cans of vegetables. I pulled something together for dinner and let depression push me into my bunk.

In the morning I left for Tutukaka. The sun broke through the barrier above but couldn't penetrate the mood on *Southern Cross*. While my mind scudded down dead ends searching for answers, the day inched by. Less than two months remained before the exhibition, and I had one partially finished but ruined painting. Survival in New Zealand meant painting pieces to sell in New Zealand, but after Auckland, how could I believe that would work? I sagged under hopelessness and loneliness, longing to talk to someone—Kitty or Kat, or Mom, or Tam—knowing one of them could help me find a way out. An under-the-table job in Russell or Opua, if I were lucky enough to find one, would pay three or four dollars an hour—not much compared with the $15 an hour I could earn by painting. But the comparison meant nothing if I couldn't make a sale.

A bitter aftertaste arose from Lib's visit—the taste of jealousy. I resented her freedom to spend money as she chose on clothes and furnishings, going out to eat, staying in a hotel. The extra money I had spent trying to make her visit enjoyable, the time I gave up to take her to Auckland and entertain her when I should have been painting—I resented it all. Why had I felt responsible for making her vacation everything she wanted it to be? How could she leave without offering a few dollars to help me sail back north? In my misery it seemed to me that she still had everything in life, as always. A shadow of doubt prodded at my self-interest when I considered that she might really have found a lump in her breast, but the weight of depression spiraled me back into my own gloom.

By late afternoon, my mood was black. I looked at the back of the boat and wondered if that was the answer. All my problems would disappear if I just stepped off. There would be peace. It would all be over. Nothing was worth the effort anymore. I had failed with TWT, failed at giving my daughters the life they deserved, failed as an artist, and now I couldn't even feed myself. I wept. My mind spun in circles, spiraling down, taking me into uncharted territory. Not one positive thing lay ahead. Positive Pat was someone from another lifetime, another world.

But then something inside pulled me back from the edge. I turned to find "God light" radiating from the setting sun; white and gold rays shot through brilliant peach, melon, and lavender clouds and filled the sky behind the entry to Tutukaka. I recoiled in horror from the dark corner I had just inhabited. The thought came over and over: If I had stepped off the boat, I would have missed this incredible sight. For the moment, that was enough to make me go on trying.

I slept peacefully and left Tutukaka in the morning for the last leg back to the Bay of Islands, a quiet, less complicated place where I would somehow work out my problems.

Rounding Cape Brett to enter the Bay of Islands, *Southern Cross* skimmed over flat cobalt seas on a perfect broad reach, one of the best moments of sailing in my life. Every cell in my body came alive. Lights along the shore sparkled a welcome from strangers' homes.

In Opua, a neighboring boat welcomed me back with lasagna, garlic bread, and a crisp salad. The next morning someone put out fresh plums and oranges at the sailing club. "Free, help yourself," the sign said. I spent my $3 on butter, bananas, and raisins, washed one load of laundry, and paid for a hot shower, then sailed four miles to Matauwhi Bay by tiny, nearby Russell. This would be my home until late May. On shore, I found a bright blue wheelbarrow full of free, freshly picked cabbages and helped myself to one.

The following morning fellow cruisers stopped by to order and prepay for miniature paintings. In the afternoon I collected a stack of mail at the post office, and envelope after envelope carried good news. Some even held money. The one with Dan's familiar handwriting included a deposit on a full-size painting. Another, from my cousin Linda, brought a gift of $200. By that evening, the total was nearly $350. I counted my blessings, not in money but in family and friends and in the eternal power of God I seldom acknowledged.

Never in the rest of the trip did I sink to such a low point, even when all I possessed was $3 again. Remembering the outcome from this moment of despair always gave me hope. My shoulders uncoiled just thinking how close I had come.

The main street through Russell ended at the boat club on Matauwhi Bay. Vibrant green hills, sprinkled with white frame houses and shot through with reds, yellows, pinks, and oranges from carefully tended flower beds, wrapped snugly around the shallow bay waters and rose into a brilliant blue sky capped by pure white clouds. These same clouds had greeted the first inhabitants, the Polynesian Maoris, who arrived a thousand years before and named the land below the Long White Cloud of Aotearoa. Over a small hill a few blocks away lay the center of the village. It, too, nestled between verdant hillsides with inviting homes and gardens facing out on the open, deeper waters of the Bay of Islands.

Flags from everywhere flew over the community of cruising boats anchored side by side with the local fleet of sailing and fishing vessels. Together they filled the cove by the clubhouse as night after night, all through January, the anchorage rang with the persistent sounds of Morse code dots and dashes—"Di dah, di di dah, di di"—until the small hours of the morning. Half the foreign boats in the Bay of Islands were preparing for the annual ham radio exams to be administered on March 2nd. Foreign cruisers wandered the streets, their minds fixed on obscure formulas and strange jargon memorized only long enough to pass the test for a general class ticket allowing them to talk to family and friends over a wide range of frequencies.

When I left Santa Cruz in 1988, I had assumed my family and I would write to stay in touch, but letters and gifts had begun disappearing from the mail as soon as I crossed the Mexican border. From Nuku Hiva I had sent a first-year's itinerary to family and friends that only Mom could understand. She had written so faithfully that if no letters awaited my arrival in a scheduled port I launched an unrelenting attack on the local post office for losing my mail. Phone calls were out of the question, but with the new radio and a license I could anticipate talking to family back home.

The first requirement to qualify for the March 2nd exams was a beginning-level novice ticket—requiring five words of Morse code per minute. It would allow me to talk over a limited range of frequencies, but none that could reach across the Pacific Ocean. I passed on February 12th and gathered hope for the big one.

Meanwhile, in town, I gained a circle of friends among the residents and a stack of miniature paintings of local scenes. Russell, one of the earliest colonial settlements in New Zealand, possessed several firsts. The first hotel, a waterfront watering hole with umbrellaed tables and vine-covered trellises; the first restaurant, a quaint, wooden structure with stained-glass windows and flower boxes; and the first church, by a hydrangea-filled cemetery. It was the church Libby and I had visited Christmas Eve. The scenes and the people possessed a sweetness, an innocence reminiscent of small U.S. towns as they were in the 1950s, or as we wish to remember them.

The piles of photos and sketches from French Polynesia gathered dust as I focused day after day on paintings that would sell in Russell. The dream of an exhibition in Papeete ended in a letter to the RevaReva Gallery conveying my regrets at canceling our plans.

The owners of the village wine shop invited me to display my work in front of their place for Waitangi Day celebrations in early February. "The streets will be full of visitors on Saturday," they said.

At the end of a good day, as I was clearing my display, one last couple approached: a tiny, 5-foot 1-inch woman with pixie dark hair and wide-open, snapping brown eyes, and her 6-foot 4-inch husband. They introduced themselves as Nina and Garry Knight, and I liked them both immediately. We fell easily into bantering conversation. It was obvious that she liked to laugh. After a short conference with Garry in Indo-Malay, which they had picked up in Indonesia where they met and married, she launched into a dinner invitation and, without waiting for my answer, went on with plans for our evening, "We'll go up to our place, have dinner, and come down for the big dance at the boat club." It was more a declaration than a question. In no time Garry was grilling steaks and tossing a salad for three at their weekend bungalow above Russell.

For most of my life I had dreamed of finding a dancing partner, someone who could make me look like Cyd Charisse. Someone to whirl and float with, gyrate and shimmy with, someone to soar with as, our bodies matched in perfect rhythm, we stole the dance floor and became a single graceful creature. But none of the men in my life, since I was ten and my stepfather taught me the rumba, even liked to dance, let alone turn it into an art form.

The old dream leapt to life again that night as we walked through the door of the rustic Russell Boat Club to be greeted by a rousing party. Beer and wine ran freely, and the 1960s style band coaxed even the shyest onto the floor. Streamers and balloons hung from rough rafters. The band perched in one corner while a freshly polished dance floor reflected the swirling crowd: guys in sailing shorts and girls in cotton summer dresses.

A tall, nice-looking man emerged from the crowd to say "hello." He was an acquaintance of Garry—his college roommate's brother. Garry introduced Fran to me, and he invited me to dance. And could he dance! He whirled me, spun, and dipped me. I floated through the evening. At the end, as the band packed up their instruments, we agreed to get together soon.

The following Saturday I readied *Southern Cross* for Fran's visit, tingling with anticipation. *SC* and I both looked our best, and an impressive snack waited on ice—a can of home-smoked salmon from Alaska, one of a gift of two I'd received in Rarotonga. The first can had made one of my few good meals during the stormy passage to New Zealand. The second I had saved for a special occasion.

In midafternoon he arrived on shore, and I picked him up in the dinghy. He brought a bottle of his homemade *fijoa* wine made from a fruit unique to New Zealand, with a flavor like figs. We chatted, testing the water. Away from the dance floor, the interest still survived. I brought out the cream cheese and special whole wheat crackers from the general store, then the *pièce de résistance*— the chilled can of mouthwatering salmon. But when I opened the top, the unmistakable aroma of beef stew arose. Stamped on the lid it said "Smoked Salmon," but the contents were pure Dinty Moore.

He smiled graciously, munching crackers with cream cheese and cold stew, and I was smitten. I wasn't looking for a romance, but then, why not? Nothing serious, I told myself, just someone to have fun with—and he danced!

My letters home favorably compared Fran to my grandpa—a kind and caring man, not like the stereotypical Kiwi man who seemed to possess the "sensitivities of a grapefruit." They carried stories of our weekend sails to small rocky coves on tree-covered islands, diving through the caves at Black Rocks, sharing intimate beach picnics with freshly caught lobster and fish smoked over glowing coals, and more divine dancing. I left out the accounts of memorable afternoons and nights of lovemaking. I gave in to the developing relationship and enjoyed it. At times I thought about staying in New Zealand forever, if we could play and dance together as we did then.

Between the good times I worked on the didahdiddies, as I had renamed the dots and dashes of Morse code. The Pike's Peak of ham—the speed we needed to pass the exam—was thirteen words per minute, but in mid-February we each hit a plateau at twelve. It took all my willpower and concentration to climb above that last word, but when March 2nd came, I tripped. That thirteen words a minute eluded me and several other cruisers. I contemplated using a phony call sign or cutting the magic wires to disable the blocking diodes. Then I could use the marine single-sideband frequencies, for which no test was required. Both options were illegal, but Mom and Stubby had given me the radio and I owed it to them to get on the air . . . whatever it took.

Meanwhile, no one in my family expressed interest in becoming our land-based intermediary—a ham operator to "meet" me on the airwaves and connect us via a phone line or pass a message. I cajoled and begged my grandson and brother. "Shawn, wouldn't you like to be the youngest ham in the United States?" "Stu, you'd love this. I can't imagine why you aren't already a ham; it's right up your alley." I even tried Stu's daughter, Nikki: "You'd meet lots of interesting people all around the world." But there were no takers.

Mom and Stubby bought a ham set so they could listen, but they didn't want to tackle a ham license after hearing two months of my complaints. Instead they hunted for a sympathetic operator to relay and do phone patches for us. Roxie Moss (NO9W), our radio angel, appeared.

The volunteer examiners offered us stragglers another chance at that little piece of paper, our ticket to the airwaves. I returned to the didahdiddies again, and this time I passed!

I sent my folks the good news and picked up several waiting letters. Tamara wrote to say I would be a grandmother again in September. I heard her excitement and joy, but also felt a note of sadness underneath her words, so subtle only her mother would notice. A letter from the manufacturer of *T/T Southern Cross* indicated that my information was incorrect. Their dinghies were in use everywhere, including Hawaii, with no problems. The last envelope was from the IRS—a bill for TWT taxes and penalties, addressed to me personally, for $62,823.53. I filed it to deal with later. I didn't have even $62 to send them.

Fran and I grabbed opportunities between his job teaching high school physical education and my painting and boat work to be together. Most of the things we did Fran planned and frequently changed at the last minute without consulting me, but I enjoyed his outings, his companionship, and the romance. His need to control things was a small irritant—only noticeable now and then.

Little stories slowly emerged from his lifetime of sailing the Bay of Islands—owning fourteen boats and sinking two of them. Evenings he worked with his son Vaughn to repair *Skitz*, the last boat he had sunk, and weekends we sailed *Southern Cross*. With repairs, help, and supplies nearby and a sailing partner who seemed to know what he was doing, I relaxed and enjoyed our excursions on the bay. To Fran, navigating these waters was as familiar as walking in the dark through his own cluttered home. He knew the shallows like the lines on the palm of his hand. *Southern Cross* often sat at anchor a stone's throw from rocks, in places I would never have ventured alone.

Our conversations eventually turned to his winter break between semesters. He suggested an offshore voyage, and a little seed took root. I needed another year in New Zealand to earn money, but a $12,000 tax penalty might be levied if *SC* stayed more than twelve months. The time would be up December 8, 1990—unless I sailed out of New Zealand waters and then returned, gaining a fresh start. Fran had never been offshore and wanted to learn about ocean passages. A trip to Tonga took form.

Fran was granted a one-month extension of his holiday, and I planned the projects needed to get *Southern Cross* ready. He offered to supply money and help with the work; I would contribute labor, offshore know-how, and the boat. The trip would give our relationship time to grow. I drifted in a dream with my Kiwi dancer and imagined it might last forever. It felt like love. We dove into the project: making plans, buying supplies, and working side by side from bow to stern.

Between trip preparations and having fun together, I painted miniatures for commissions and a local gallery and investigated job possibilities for the coming year. Of the priority jobs New Zealand Immigration was seeking foreigners to fill, I qualified for three—professor, teacher, and import-export marketer. I envisioned life in business suits again—meetings, negotiating, or navigating through school politics—and cringed. What I really wanted was to paint and get paid enough to do more than just cover daily expenses. *SC* needed new sails—main and genoa—repairs to the rubrail, an outboard, new propane tanks (the propane distributors refused to fill my old ones), galvanizing for the main anchor, a haulout to clean and repaint her fouled bottom, a new bobstay, and a host of other small things from top to bottom.

For months I had passed Peter Arnold's gallery in Russell without going in. He had his business on the first floor and his home above. Having learned that Peter normally hired someone to take care of sales while he traveled during the winter, I gathered all my courage one day and opened his door. Before I could say anything, he asked if I would like to run the gallery for five months starting at the end of July—exactly when we would return from Tonga.

I reeled, wondering if he had read my mind. He offered his apartment, his studio for my own work, one wall of the gallery on which to display my paintings, a 25 percent commission on sales of his black-and-white prints from pencil drawings, and payment to dash a little watercolor on some of the prints. I said "yes" immediately.

Fall drifted by. Fran and I dove, explored, danced, and worked on the boat. Each of us was too excited to ask what the other expected from the thousand-mile voyage. I never heard him say that if he didn't like it he would fly back, and he didn't hear me declare, "I don't want to make a solo return passage during winter storm season." We mended, repaired, painted, cleaned, shopped, and tested and tuned the rig. Fran moved my winter clothes and excess boat gear to his house and filled the empty spaces with his things. I unloaded more excess gear and donated it to *Skitz*. The air turned chilly, and warm island beaches beckoned.

Fran's son, a professional electrician, tackled the radio installation. Harry from *Whalesong*, one of the local ham pros, announced, "Your insulated backstay is a perfect Wyndham dipole." I never met another radio jock who knew what that was, but *Southern Cross* had one. Harry designed the installation in squiggles and notes that only Vaughn could decipher.

Another expert among the cruisers, Bob on *Armoral*, convinced me to install a 2- by 3-foot solid copper plate on the outside of the hull for a ground while *SC* was out of the water. He told Vaughn to silver solder a large bolt through the plate and ground the radio to it on the inside, but he couldn't tell me how to make the stiff copper plate—as flat as the medieval world—conform to *SC*'s voluptuously curved bottom. When Vaughn stepped back from the installation, the plate only touched the hull at the bolt, while its edges stuck out in every direction. Someone suggested 3M 5200, a magic goop (actually a polyurethane adhesive) that could bond anything to anything forever.

I lathered several tubes—at more than $20 each—on the copper and on *SC*, then wedged the plate against the hull with twenty-three pieces of wood.

After allowing twice the recommended curing time I gingerly removed the braces. *Boingggggg*—the copper sheet resumed its flat shape, dragging tendrils of semicured goop behind. Fran suggested using copper rivets. I prayed as he hammered twenty new holes below the waterline with more 5200 to seal them. It held.

I faired the surface around the edge and over the bolt with underwater epoxy, and Fran fiberglassed the perimeter. The recalcitrant sheet had met its match.

At last we left Opua with a chaos of unstored gear and provisions filling the cabin below. Had I been alone, I would have stayed to finish stowing. For Fran, the thrill of departure descended quickly into lethargy and complaints of seasickness, as he looked in vain for his sea legs. I cooked, changed sails, cleaned, read charts, and steered as always, except that now I also had to feed and tend to the moaning man in the cockpit.

The new radio joined my daily routine. I waited to sign on the roll call for the Pacific Maritime Mobile Net at 0430 Zulu (Greenwich Mean Time). Across the Pacific I had listened to their unique and often codified vocabulary: "I'm QRT; 88's and 73's, old man. There's a YL waiting to check in. I've got too much QRM here. What's her handle?" It was still a foreign language to me; I posted cheat sheets around the chart table. The first day, after two hours attempting to break through the unending patter, I gave up. On the second day I made it through and gave my report: "At 0200 Zulu *Southern Cross* was at 32 degrees 40 minutes South and 176 degrees 16 minutes East with a boat speed of 4 knots steering 030 Magnetic. Winds are 15 knots from the north-north-west and there's a 2-meter swell from the southeast with 1-meter wind waves from the northwest. Cloud cover's 70 percent and the bar's 29.98, down from yesterday. I have no traffic." They assigned my position for the following day's transmission and at the end of the net took a boat description and safety inventory of *SC*. I deferred answering the final question, "How many days do you want us to wait if you don't respond to our call, and who do we contact?" What if I were merely out of touch due to radio failure or low batteries? And to whom should I assign the terrible responsibility of initiating a search? Tamara? My mother? I couldn't decide, and the question remained unanswered.

Tony's morning ham net from New Zealand was much more informal and without a roll call. The first week out I spent hours braced by the radio, waiting to check in, catch a weather report from Dr. John, and listen for friends on both nets.

Roxie Moss and I arranged our first "sked" for the middle of the night on May 19th. At last I could hear, "Pat, this is Mom. . . . Over." We halted and stumbled, but talked to each other from halfway around the world.

It was clear that standing night watches would not be part of Fran's routine this trip. The settee, my sea berth, now held his inert body. The forward V-berth, as usual, was filled with sails and other gear. Between checks on deck, I tried to sleep on the main cabin floor as Fran's air mattress deflated and swallowed me. His wet clothes accumulated in heaps above the companionway, and wafting breezes carried smells of damp and mildewed cloth.

In *SC*'s tiny cabin where once we danced, our bodies in perfect rhythm, we now bumped and bristled at each other's touch and could find no common way to move. As the days went by I alternated between longing for the peace of solo days and hoping the soft tropical moon would undo the growing tensions. This trip was not following the script I had written.

On deck strange knots and unexpected gear appeared, while other things went missing. After a year of cruising, every item on *Southern Cross* had its place. Once I could have worked the deck blindfolded, but not now. The patterns and self-imposed rules I had developed in more than 45,000 sailing miles had kept *Southern Cross* and me safe, but Fran did things his own way or didn't do them at all. The excitement he had professed at learning about offshore sailing vanished in the reality of the open sea. He showed no interest in how I did things and why, but instead moaned in the cockpit and asked for yet another sandwich.

A wild wind tore us out of dreams one night. The anemometer hit 50 knots as I raced to take down excess sail and looked for the sail ties kept ready on the lifelines. They were stowed somewhere in the cockpit. In total darkness, I fumbled with odd knots in the reefing lines, losing precious time. The seas hurled walls of cold water at me while Fran stood aft, wondering what to do, his foul weather gear stowed below. More piles of sodden clothes joined the molding stack. I began a new list: gear lost overboard. Fran had secured the deck gear on one side but neglected the other, though it was supposed to be his job before departure.

We planned a stop at Minerva Reef South, then North, the two tiny reefs where countless sailors had met their grief between Tonga, Fiji, and New Zealand. They lurked just at the surface, wrapping around protected lagoons. At high tide only a handful of boulders were visible in the wide blue sea. Working our way around to the entrance, with Fran up the mast to guide us, we found flat, crystal-clear water inside. As the reef emerged from the falling tide, we strolled around giant clams with cobalt and turquoise lips tattooed in hieroglyphics, our shadows triggering fountains as they snapped their valves shut to frighten us away. Sharks drifted by while we snorkeled at the surface, and a deadly lionfish lured us down to see her Dior-like gown of red-, black-, and white-patterned fins enticing the unwary, like Salome with her seven veils.

The strange beauty of this anchorage surrounded completely by the sea was not reflected in the moods on board. We were snarling, hurt, and disillusioned. I dreamed of stopping again someday . . . alone.

We followed the daily nets as they reported weather problems for boats off Australia. Two women sailing alone were airlifted off their catamaran with injuries. An Australian helicopter rescue team dropped a life raft to another boat. Before returning to base for refueling, they watched while the crew climbed inside. We waited for further news, but no sign of the life raft, boat, or victims was found again. Closer to us, thirty-four containers were lost from a freighter between Fiji and New Zealand. For days the New Zealand military stalked the floating containers, awaiting permission to sink them and eliminate a navigational hazard. But permission never came, and the cluster gradually dispersed.

A young family whose engine came adrift from its bed when their boat dropped off a 20-foot wave near the Kermadec Islands called the net requesting a tow to New Zealand and finally asking for rescue by airlift. Calm voices, familiar with the expense, limitations, and dangers of sea rescues, patiently talked them down. The boat was safe; the people were only shaken up. They continued on to Tonga.

We carried on to Nuku'alofa and then Vava'u, a geologist's dream, with every stage in the evolution of South Pacific landforms represented inside one huge protecting reef. *SC* sailed down narrow channels hundreds of feet deep between black volcanic islands, worn around the bottom to look like giant mushrooms draped in jungle growth. We ventured over Disney-Technicolored reefs to slivers of silvery beach on atolls of emerging coral. Long ago the atolls were fringing reefs on volcanic islands of their own. Eventually the volcanoes subsided below the water's surface while the growing corals rose above it, creating low-lying islands that often surrounded a central lagoon. We followed romantic legends into submerged caves, looking for signs of the fabled lovers hidden there in the nineteenth century.

Champagne and *Fair Winds* arrived, inviting us to join them for dinners on shore, potlucks, and sailing excursions. But all the natural beauty and friends around us could not dispel the gloomy air surrounding *Southern Cross*. One evening Fran tied the dinghy to the stern, and in the morning it was gone—not stolen, just tied poorly. He found it five miles away. He visited another boat, and the dinghy wandered away from there as well. Such oversights from a lifetime sailor were beyond my understanding, but neither *Southern Cross* nor I could afford his irresponsibility.

On the return sail to Nuku'alofa, in order to preserve our night vision, I asked Fran to use only the red cabin light over the chart table during our night watches. He slept through his watch while we passed islands and reefs in traffic, then turned the cabin lights on in my face. After six weeks of building tension I finally exploded: "I'm the captain, and you will do what I say on board this vessel." I wanted and thought I deserved respect for my knowledge and my safe cruising miles, and *Southern Cross* deserved his respect as well. We agreed to return to New Zealand separately. Fran would fly back, and I would sail alone. Perhaps, I thought, back in his world, we could still be friends.

The Kiwis on Tony's Net adopted me as their special project for the return voyage. Dr. John gave me a personal weather report each time I checked in while winter gales passed north and south of me. The thirty-four lost shipping containers still floated awash over a wide area that I hoped was not on my path. At the end Dr. John breathed a sigh of relief, calling it a "storybook passage" with only one gale day of 45 knots.

As I sailed down the Bay of Islands in cold midnight air, so glad to be "home," a solid wall of fog pushed unnoticed at my back. When my anchor touched bottom in Opua, the thick gray mass settled all around, hiding even the bow. The margin of safety in this landfall was measured in a minute or two. In the next two weeks, five gales passed through packing winds over 55 knots.

Fran waited on the dock in the morning, not to welcome me back or ask about my passage, but to claim his stuff and some of mine and work out how much I owed him. Since most small boats charged crew members a daily rate of $15 to $40, I felt he should contribute something to cover expenses and the wear and tear to *Southern Cross*. After all, our offshore passage had turned into a private charter complete with captain, cook, and engineer. A rate of $15 seemed more than fair for that. I offered to repay the funds he had put out to help get *Southern Cross* ready. We agreed on a number and went our separate ways with my parting request: "Would you please bring back the things you took to your house from the boat? I need my winter clothes."

As I started the engine and let the docklines go to return to Russell, regret and sadness enveloped me. It was time, again, to mourn the end of another relationship. Why could I never learn? The man I had fallen for was fun, free-spirited, sensitive, considerate, and enjoyed the things I did. The man who had turned *Southern Cross* upside down was none of those things. Once again, it seemed, I had been blinded by romantic illusion. Perhaps he'd been blinded too. The sea had finally opened my eyes. I turned *Southern Cross* down the channel toward Russell, where a gallery job was waiting.

_____ JULY 1990

THE ANCHOR HAD BARELY DUG IN BEFORE I LEFT FOR town, halfway expecting to find that Peter, the gallery, and the job had disappeared. But at the sound of the brass bell on the door, he was as relieved to see me as I was him. "You made it back. Great. I'll be ready to leave in five days. Let's get started on your training."

At first I slept on board *SC* four or five nights per week to air her out and keep her company. At night I huddled under blankets, reading, with the oven lit for heat. Then a gale drove in, and I couldn't row to shore against the force of the wind to open the gallery. Four nights dropped to three, then two, and finally none. One land-based luxury after another crept into my routine. Hot morning showers . . . inside. A freezer and refrigerator. A washing machine. Sun-dried sheets from the backyard—a pleasant reminder of the years when my children were young. Television and a phone. I returned to *Southern Cross* less and less often.

I painted miniatures, and they walked out the door almost as fast as I put them on display. Week by week I filled an envelope marked "Fran" and another labeled "Projects on *Southern Cross*" from sales of my own work and commissions from Peter's.

I sent the gallery phone number to my family, and soon the calls began. Mom called to tell me Terri had become engaged. Lib phoned with the news that the lump she had discovered on board *Southern Cross* had turned out to be malignant. The tumor had been removed, and she would begin chemotherapy in the fall. Her one letter since our visit eight months before had indicated that the doctor thought there was no problem. "Please don't tell anyone," she requested. Concerned, I wrote back pressing for more information and wondering why she hadn't written sooner.

On September 17th Tamara's husband called to say she had given birth to a baby girl, Kira. "Mother and daughter are both fine." I sent a colorful handmade quilt, hoping it would last through her childhood and provide a connection to me. I longed to deliver it in person, to help out, and to meet my first granddaughter.

Each morning I opened "my" little shop, dusted and vacuumed, then sat in the small studio area in the bay window by the street to paint. As the late winter sun warmed the air I opened the window, and passersby stuck their heads inside to watch. Commissions came my way: a pencil drawing of a 1920s house in Devonport, a small painting of an old family farm, and a full-sized (12- by 16-inch) piece for Pan and Dean Miller showing their view of Russell and the bay from the home they had rented high on the hill above the center of town.

Pan and Dean stopped almost daily to watch the progress on their painting. A handsome couple in their mid-seventies, with snowy hair and a healthy glow of vitality, they had come from Florida to spend the winter. This was the first stop in Dean's lifelong dream to sell their home and see the world. Next would come winter in England, then a return in May to the house on the hill above town. One day they asked, "Would you like to use the car while we're gone?"

More commissions followed—of homes, gardens, gates, views—and I painted and sold my own larger scenes, too. Life was dishing out more bounty than I could imagine.

Fran's envelope filled quickly. I mailed half our agreed settlement, but he still held hostage in Kawakawa my winter clothes, extra boat gear, and tools. I needed my things and had no way to get them; he balked and stalled.

I wrote to Libby again and again to ask how she was doing, but she didn't answer.

The Millers left Russell in November. The use of their car brought a newfound mobility for social occasions and artwork. I showed my miniatures at an all-day art fair in Kirikiri, on the opposite side of the bay; traveled to sketch and shoot photos; and visited clients for commissions.

Dearest Kitty,

Thank you for the order for a painting of *Southern Cross.* I've picked a view that shows the old clapboard boating club and dinghy dock. Perhaps you'll smell the sweet spring buds on the flowering trees behind the anchorage.

The gallery opportunity is giving me a chance to become an "artist." Doing art everyday, all day long, seven days a week has made the difference. I don't think about it, I just keep doing it.

And from Peter's example I'm learning how to turn this into a business. The miniatures are still doing well, but when I painted the old church for the eighteenth time I thought there must be a better way. A fellow artist in town mentioned high-quality laser printing that's available in Auckland. It's fantastic. The inks are permanent and the resolution is high. Now I can paint a scene once and sell the same little piece over and over. Of course, the price is much less, making them even more popular. Limited-edition series from some of my larger pieces are also selling.

I'm working on a commission that is 18 by 24 inches. That feels like the largest piece of paper in the world. Moving up in size is pushing me to a new level. Someone told me I would never be a real artist until I expanded beyond the smaller format. It's true that something shifts as the scale of the piece increases.

Before heading back from Auckland, I stopped to pay the old bill at the marina. No one could find a record. It's amazing how far I've come from the desolation of last January, when nothing seemed possible.

Hugs to Peter and lots of love to you,

Pat

Art was the center of my life, but film society showings at the grade school, parties with local friends, and small dinners at the gallery filled the gaps between paintings. I had a community, a job, a home, and friends. There were hours spent with Nina and Garry at their bungalow above Russell. Garry cooked gourmet meals while Nina and I discussed art, Chinese pottery, travel, and her frogs. In Indonesia Nina had had a pet python, Monty. But New Zealand had no snakes and would not allow Monty to immigrate with the family. Nina donated him to the Singapore Zoo and took up pet frogs instead. Each trip from Auckland included a carrying case for Chocolate, a small brown frog, and his colorful companions in brilliant turquoise, gold, and lime green.

I wrote to Libby again and waited for an answer.

One morning a trim, athletic woman with short, dark wavy hair entered the gallery with the aid of a cane. "Hi, I'm Ornith Murphy. People tell me you sailed down here singlehanded from the States. I made the same trip a few years ago. After sailing back to Hawaii, I was hit crossing a busy street. They told me I'd never walk again. Now I'm looking at the possibility of going cruising again. It won't be solo though. I saw your boat and would love to go aboard, but I don't think I'm ready to climb up from the dinghy."

That evening we shared dinner at the gallery and our views on singlehanding, agreeing that our experience was much the same as that of the men who sailed alone. The sea didn't notice the difference when she dished out her storms.

I wrote Fran requesting an appointment to pay him the balance of what I owed and collect my things. He didn't answer. "I'm too busy," he responded when I saw him six weeks later.

Still there was no answer from Libby. Very worried, I finally wrote to our cousin Linda, a doctor, asking how Libby's treatments were going. At last Libby called . . . unhappy with me for breaking her trust.

Peter returned from his travels for Russell's summer season, and I moved back to *Southern Cross*. She wrapped herself around me in welcome, and I cried. I was home.

The five-month results of my tenure at the gallery were more than Peter dreamed . . . twice the amount from any previous year for the same period, not including my work. I left with commissions waiting to be done and paintings still on display. Now it would be my turn to pay him.

The week before Christmas I left for a small vacation around New Zealand's North Island: first to Auckland to visit Nina and Garry in their city home; then to the Coromandel Peninsula to see the artists' community there; and finally to accept Helen and Mark's fifteen-month-old invitation for Christmas at her parents' farm.

On Christmas Eve afternoon I rolled over a narrow, paved country road through hills of rich, green cornfields and past dairy herds on my way to a big holiday reunion. At last I climbed the winding driveway beside Gay Kerridge's brilliant flower beds, camellias, and her flock of goats. Mark and Helen descended on me. Gay and Richard, her parents, followed, and behind them Helen's brother, Rob, their sister, Ardell, and Ardell's children. I felt like a long-lost cousin being welcomed home.

The warm summer air hardly felt like Christmas to a Midwesterner. That didn't matter as we decorated a seven-foot pine tree with strung popcorn and treasured family ornaments. Covering all the time since Tahiti, Helen and I discussed her artwork, a new calendar she had produced, Mark's boatbuilding business and his wooden bowls turned from exotic woods, their delivery passage to Chile aboard *Swan*, and my travels, romance, and art.

The tree was knee-deep in bright packages Christmas morning as still more family arrived—another sister, Rachel, her husband, Mike, and their new baby. I had followed Helen's explicit instructions—"Don't bring any gifts, just something to share if you want"—and had come with an old-fashioned, homemade Christmas pudding that had hung on *Southern Cross* ripening for two months, a bottle of wine, a large bag of Kerikeri oranges, a gift for Gay, and one for Helen and Mark. When "Santa" began handing out gifts, package after package had my name on it. They were lovely, handmade things—sachets, a nightie, a tiny needlepoint strawberry, and chocolates.

Between chatter and laughter, we grazed our way through the day, leaving the seven-foot dining table only long enough to milk the goats. No animal before had ever cooperated with me, but I milked a goat on December 25, 1990. We returned through Gay's gardens of agapanthus, roses, and daises, following the aroma of baking turkey, as the last of the clan arrived by motorcycle. With crazy hats and popping "crackers," my Kiwi family began their traditional dinner with all fourteen present plus one. In the morning I loaded the car with another of Helen's care packages for the long road back to *Southern Cross*.

My own family wrote to me faithfully, prayed for my safety, worried about me, ran errands, and helped in ways too numerous to count, but the profound reassurance of hugs, smiles, and leisurely chatter around a dinner table with people who cared about one another had to be experienced in person.

Mornings began again with the cruisers net and VOA news. The January 15, 1991, deadline for Saddam Hussein to pull back from Kuwait passed, and on the 16th, Desert Storm began. My neighbor Bob on *Armoral*, a former Navy Seal, brought daily blow-by-blow accounts from the television at the Veterans' Club in town. He was amazed by the instantaneous live coverage and by the precision with which we placed our ammunition. It was horrifying to think that a generation of children could eat their Cheerios and watch people dying as if it were a movie.

A month slipped by with my paintbrush flying across the paper while I waited to hear of sales results at Peter's gallery. Then friends reported that Peter was dissuading customers from buying my work. They had gone in without mentioning that they knew me, and he began denigrating my art. The small gallery down the street that had carried my miniatures the year before now had their own artist making prints from local scenes. Across the street from Peter's, the Blue Penguin sold handmade crafts and clothing, not art, but the quality and presentation of their offerings were impeccable. I made an appointment with the owner, Dayle Howard.

Dayle loved my paintings immediately. She installed a display of framed prints high on one wall and cleared shelf space for a set of sixteen miniatures. We waited. Days crept by, then weeks. Hanging on the edge of discouragement, I stopped by once again almost a month after we had begun. There were sales, lots of sales. I turned back to waiting boat projects.

I hired help to remove the leaky rubrails for repair and rebedding, and more help to rebed the handrails. Then I tackled the rest alone—buying a new 2-horsepower Yamaha and an aluminum propane tank, replacing the lower after port shroud and the main cabin light, installing a voltmeter and manual override for the voltage regulator on the engine, regalvanizing the main anchor, and finishing a string of routine maintenance from the masthead down. Finally I patched the dinghy, but the matching red patches were too expensive, so I bought yellow, and she began to look like a clown.

After three days spent hunting for another air leak in the diesel, I called a local mechanic. In fifteen minutes he pulled out the culprit—a brittle compressible copper washer in the Fram filters—and taught me how to anneal copper.

The IRS sent another notice of the outstanding tax bill for TWT. It was not going to disappear, but the numbers had to be wrong. In 1988 our CPA had presented Kelly and me with totals for the corporate taxes for which we would be held personally responsible, and we had paid them in full with certified checks that July. Unfortunately I had no records on board—only the phone notes, nothing with signatures and no copies of the checks. I wrote my CPA for clarification. She responded that the records were all with the bookkeeper assigned to the job, the bookkeeper was no longer working with her office, and no further information was available. I filed this notice with the others.

Before I left Santa Cruz, all the creditors except the bank had been paid. Insurance claims for legal expenses already paid and potential ten-year income from the sale of our rights to the new U.S. representatives of the Japanese high-tech fabrics had been earmarked to cover any loose ends. Beyond that, the bones of TWT were out of my reach—physically, intellectually, and emotionally.

Over the year I had written repeatedly to my personal attorney. In 1988 he had insisted that I sign blank forms for bankruptcy protection, assuring me it was premature then, but when the time came he would file the claim. The only item of value I owned was *Southern Cross*, and I had filed for protection under the Homestead Act of California. As my home she was covered up to $30,000. At last word came. My attorney had not been disbarred, but his practice had been taken from him—a first, I was told, for the California Bar—and he had disappeared. Halfway around the world, with limited resources, I could do no more. The weight of it would follow me while attorneys battled out the various lawsuits wrapped around TWT and the failed savings and loan, and the IRS pursued their claims.

Helen wrote that Mike, the young husband of her sister Rachel, had been killed in a diving accident. Their despair drew me closer to this place as "family," friends, and village pulled the threads of connection tighter.

But *Southern Cross* also tugged at me. Other shores and anchorages waited to be explored. The old mainsail and 150 percent genoa showed the wear of fifteen years of sailing. Hand stitches marched across both of them in row after row. I discussed replacements with Simon Willis, the sailmaker in Kerikeri. He was a racer who also understood the needs of a cruising boat for durable, easy-to-handle sails. I made a deposit for a new main.

Below on *Southern Cross* something above the passage to the V-berth caught Simon's eye. Only two inches bridged the span at the top of the opening in the primary bulkhead, and the lower edge sagged by almost a quarter of an inch. He investigated the deck, compression post, and overhead. No cracks showed, but only half of the mast butt rested over the post. The balance bore down on the deck with no support below to carry the load except that two inches of bulkhead. "There's no way I'm going to make a new sail until you take care of this," he said. "I'll get the sail ready and hold it until you have the money to pay me, but first fix that sag."

He was right, and I knew it. I'd been eyeing the problem for some time without finding the cause. With the rigging loosened, the yard jacked up the deck and added a glued-and-screwed shoulder to transfer the load to the post. All the work was done with *SC* in the water, but still the charges wiped out the balance of my new-sail budget. I called Simon to let him know, then called Dayle to tell her that future payments for my prints would go directly to Simon until the bill for the new sail had been paid.

A neighbor of Nina and Garry spent a day helping me install a new silicon bronze rod bobstay and rebed the bowsprit. At day's end we peeled caulking compound off our hands, faces, and clothes, marveling at how close he had come to losing tools off the deck in the bouncy anchorage while I was wedged inside the chain locker below, tightening nuts. Back on shore, when I walked him to his car, he reached in and handed me a second aluminum propane tank. Each gift, each helping hand, bound me tighter to this community, but I knew they were all taking a small piece of this voyage for themselves.

Bob on *Armoral*, an extra-class ham himself, pushed me to go for my "extra" ticket. With it I could join the volunteers who provided the tests, repaying those who had helped me. Twenty-six words per minute was the Mount Everest of Morse code; I could never do that many didahdiddies. I did try for "advanced" level, which provided access to more frequencies but only required a technical test, and emerged with the call sign "KM6DR."

Waiting outside for their test results were Nancy and Patti from *Tethys*. Nancy had left Seattle in the fall of 1989 en route to Barcelona for the 1992 Olympics. Patti, a New Zealander, had recently joined the all-women crew.

Other long-distance women sailors arrived in the Bay of Islands. New Zealander Lynn Service, on *Kiwi Star*, had lost her first boat (a small, wooden lightweight racer) in a storm in Italy's Strait of Messina. She had stepped onto a rock as the boat dropped out from under her and the stove catapulted over her head. This time she was sailing in a steel hull. Margaret Hicks on *Anonymous Bay* spent one evening at the Opua Sailing Club sharing her stories and firm ideas on sailing. "No one should be out without an EPIRB with satellite links," she argued, but that was a luxury beyond *SC*'s budget.

Months had passed and still Fran had not returned my things. Finally I wrote to say the matter was closed, and he could keep my possessions in exchange for the balance of the money I owed him. That brought the dance to an end. I received a notice to appear before an arbitrator. She brought us to the same figure I had been waiting to pay since December, and my winter clothing and piles of boat gear at last came home.

As fall crept toward winter Tonga's beaches beckoned once again. This time I would sing and sail solo, dancing to my own rhythm.

Dearest Kitty,

I'm leaving shortly with ongoing income and a permanent connection to Russell. The Blue Penguin wants to continue carrying my work and wholesaling to other shops around the Bay and in Auckland. If I could do the same in nine other countries I could travel forever.

The focused time for painting this year has changed my work. Joe and Kat passed through Tahiti a few months ago and stopped by RevaReva Gallery. One of the pieces I left there had sold. Kat collected the money and the remaining paintings for me. Looking at them, I am shocked to see how far I've come. They lack depth and vibrancy and seem so amateurish. I'm embarrassed to think of the ones I sold in Papeete and vow to go back someday to paint replacements.

The brilliant light and color of New Zealand has brought depth, complexity, and detail to my work. And how will they look to me next year?

Congratulations on the Arts Commission Show. What wonderful exposure.

Much love and hugs to you both,

Pat

THE HURRICANE THREAT IN THE ISLANDS TO THE NORTH ended. Next would come fall and winter gales across the Tasman Sea from Australia. Cooler and cooler breezes tiptoed across the bay, nudging *Southern Cross*. It was time to leave. Sweaters crawled out of lockers and shorts sank below a stack of jeans. Greetings on the boat club dock and along Russell's main street now ended with, "Have a safe sail north," and "We'll miss you; you've become part of our town." Thoughts of staying still crept through my mind, but were quickly replaced by visions of places waiting for discovery—Tonga, Fiji, Indonesia, Egypt, and most of all the islands of Greece, drifting in their ancient sea of music and dancing.

I faxed a final departure schedule to Mom and gave her a time and number to call for one last chat before Roxie took over. We drew out the words to make them last. "I gave Tam this number, too. Wait a bit when we're through; she may be trying to reach you."

The phone rang again. I answered, and Tamara's tearful voice responded, choking back sobs. She and her husband had separated.

Dearest Daughter,

Your every letter this year has carried the spirit of your unhappiness between the lines. My heart aches for you and the children.

I keep wondering: if I had made different choices in my life could I have spared you this pain? If I had made a solid, happy marriage would I have given you a better chance? Do we share a legacy that will repeat and repeat? I pray this is not so and beg your forgiveness if it is.

The three saddest moments of the past two years have come from knowing that I did not have the money to be with you when you needed me. We have both paid a high price for my trip.

When Mom sent photos of your wedding to Tahiti, I cried for all the joy and promise carried in your hearts. Last fall when the wonderful news came of Kira's safe and healthy birth, I said a prayer of thanks and wanted to wrap my arms around the two of you and care for you both. Now, that little family is breaking up, and how I long to hold you, wipe the tears, build your confidence, and help smooth the path ahead.

After we hung up this morning memories rushed back from 1965, when I faced with fear the prospect of raising you and Terri on my own. I could not imagine how I would even provide a roof, let alone the richness of life I wanted for you. My first thought—I can't do it; they'll have to live with their father—lasted about one minute. You were more precious to me than anything. Somehow, I would find a way.

You will find a way, also. You are capable, smart, and loving; you have skills as a teacher, a stained-glass artist, a naturalist, and a zoologist. But it is your inner strength that will pull you through. It will be desperately lonely and very frightening, but you're not alone. Remember, you have a higher power to call on. You have an inner beauty that radiates. It will draw those who can help you heal. In time you will laugh, and sing, and play again.

Now is the time to grieve for the lost dreams and the emptiness. But when you are ready, put that aside, look in the mirror, and see the magic of Tamara. Know that you already have all that you need to make your life and your children's lives whatever you want them to be.

You have been my teacher and my friend many times. Turn those powers inward to heal your own pain, to release and forgive, and to go on. I am there in my heart, holding your hand.

Love,

Mom

Rowboats made their way from shore bearing gifts of jam, chutney, and fruitcakes. My evenings were filled with dinners and final conversations with friend after friend. Gifts of boat gear and assistance left reminders all around *Southern Cross* that New Zealanders understood and embraced sailors.

My purse no longer bulged with money, but *Southern Cross* had never been so ready for a passage. Every system was serviced, old problems were resolved, and there was new gear to make life easier and safer. Fifteen months on the Long White Cloud of Aotearoa had taught me to let go and trust Divine

Providence. I had arrived with little and was leaving rich with friends and a surrogate family, confident of making my way as an artist. Aboard were enough supplies for months of sailing.

Dayle and I had one last meeting to inventory the paintings I was leaving with her, discuss my itinerary and a new piece she had requested, and make plans for her to meet me in Fiji. She was keeping all but one print of each piece to sell—they would do best in the Bay of Islands where they had been painted. I looked longingly at the handmade cotton sweaters on display, memorizing the beautiful colors and promising myself to order one sometime when I had a good check coming from the Blue Penguin. Then Dayle came out of her office with a gift-wrapped package—a rose-colored sweater. We hugged, making promises of a great time in Fiji and success in our future business.

May 28th arrived, and the last hours unwound. Nina and Garry arrived early with the day's schedule planned. They had been my closest friends for more than a year. On every trip to Auckland for new prints I had stayed at their home, with the lower floor to myself. Mornings we had gathered in their sunny bedroom watching *Good Morning, America* from the States while we lingered over breakfast. And evenings we had cooked gourmet dinners and visited until yawns propelled us down the corridor to our rooms. Each time I had left an addition to their collection of my prints as a thank-you.

Garry carted the poor, old red dinghy with its yellow patches ashore to remove the array of sea creatures that had migrated to her bottom. I hadn't looked in months while the underwater neighborhood grew to four inches thick. The housekeeper in me was embarrassed to have anyone see the upside-down dinghy fully exposed. He tackled the job, still smiling, while Nina and I went to buy fresh fruit, vegetables, and blocks of ice.

At 2 o'clock Garry laid out a gourmet feast with fresh pasta and a bottle of Chardonnay. And at three I tied the last lines down on deck and let the mooring go in Matauwhi Bay as horns sounded from boats all around the anchorage. Friends waved good-bye, and *Southern Cross* and *Agathus* sailed together to Nine Pin Rock at the entry to the Bay of Islands. We shot photos of each other, waved, and watched until our sails became small flecks.

I turned away, looking northeast toward Tonga through a mist of tears, and began to dream of new adventures waiting at the end this passage.

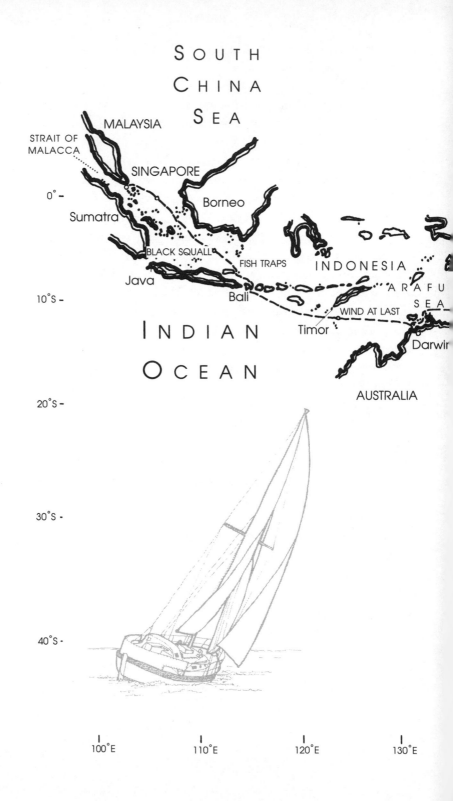

SOUTH
CHINA
SEA

MALAYSIA

STRAIT OF
MALACCA

SINGAPORE

Borneo

0° -

Sumatra

BLACK SQUALL

FISH TRAPS

INDONESIA

Java

ARAFU

SEA

10°S -

Bali

WIND AT LAST

Timor

Darwin

INDIAN

OCEAN

AUSTRALIA

20°S -

30°S -

40°S -

100°E   110°E   120°E   130°E

PART TWO

To

Singapore

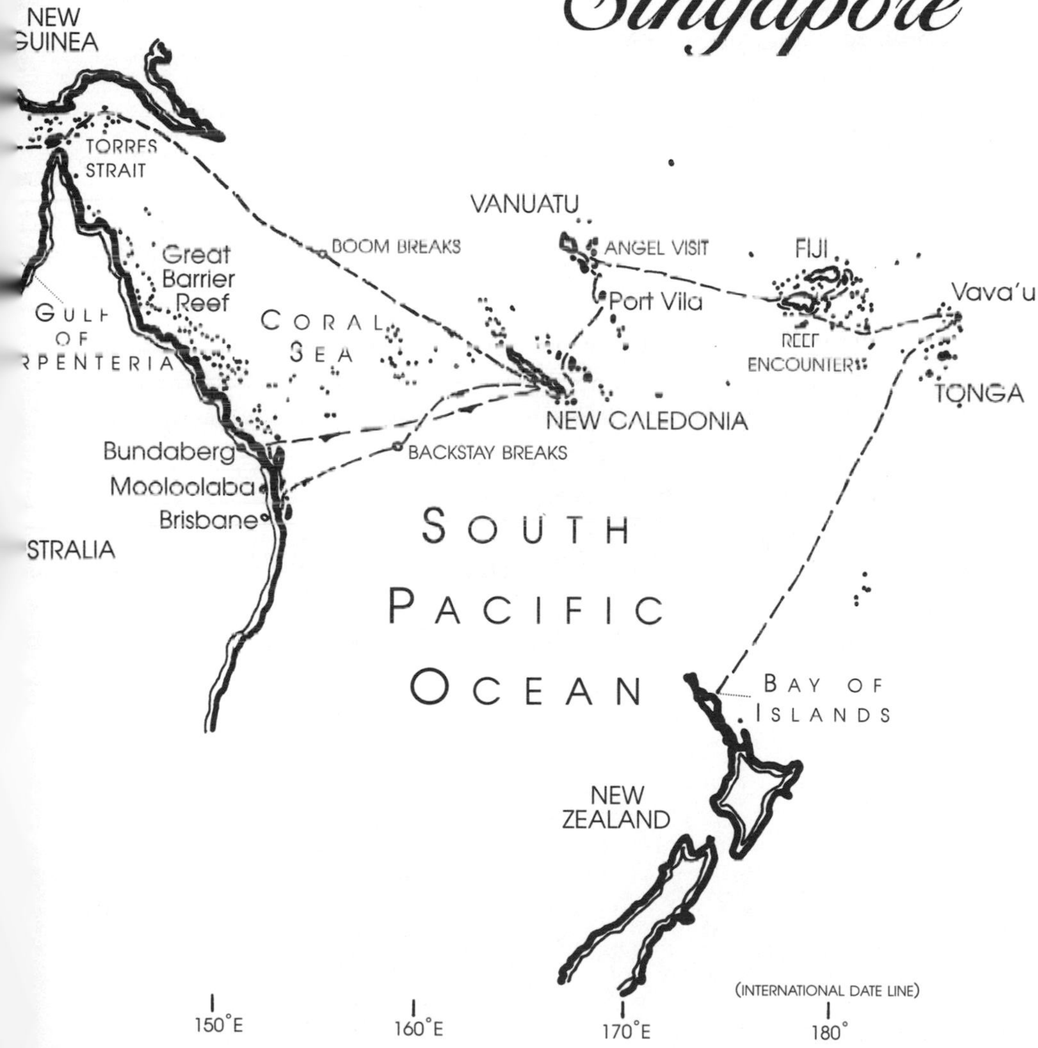

NEW
GUINEA

TORRES
STRAIT

Great
Barrier
Reef

GULF
OF
CARPENTERIA

AUSTRALIA

Bundaberg
Mooloolaba
Brisbane

BOOM BREAKS

CORAL
SEA

BACKSTAY BREAKS

VANUATU

ANGEL VISIT

Port Vila

NEW CALEDONIA

FIJI

Vava'u

REEF
ENCOUNTER

TONGA

SOUTH

PACIFIC

OCEAN

BAY OF
ISLANDS

NEW
ZEALAND

(INTERNATIONAL DATE LINE)

150°E   160°E   170°E   180°

Back at sea with *Southern Cross* aimed north-northeast, I checked in on the Pacific Maritime Mobile Net for the passage to Tonga. The friendly voice of one of the net volunteers welcomed me back like an old neighbor. "You'll be number five on the roll call." That meant there were four other singlehanders somewhere in the Pacific, since singlehanders came first on the list—four kindred spirits facing the ocean alone.

Ship's diary: 31 May 1991, 2000 Zulu, 30°18'S/178°06'E, course 020M, speed 5.2 knots, wind south at 10 knots, seas southerly at 2 feet, 15% cloud cover, bar 1021, steady. What a lazy trip; it feels like I'm at anchor.

I had read about passages where no one touched the sails for days on end, but until this voyage there had never yet been twenty-four hours without a sail change on *Southern Cross*. Now the days passed with nothing to do but keep radio "skeds," navigate, cook, eat, and read books. With the staysail sheeted hard to center, the wind vane even managed the steering in the light breeze. *Southern Cross* ghosted downwind while I vacationed.

The only problem in the first few days had surfaced May 30th when salt water puddled on the floor in front of the sink. I closed the through-hull and returned to Tom Clancy's *Cardinal in the Kremlin*, finding his paragraphs far more exciting than the inside of a galley cabinet.

Pleasant conditions carried through two more days, and I pulled out another book, enjoying this effortless slide across the Earth's surface. Memories from the year before, with Fran on board, kept surfacing. Going solo made absolute sense.

In 1988, when I was preparing to leave Santa Cruz, my ideas about crew had all come from encounters during the years on board *Windy*. Then, as now, the majority of the blue-water captains who didn't have permanent crew spent most of their time looking for people to help them get to the next port. When they found a willing body, they left the next day.

A fellow singlehander reported that, three days out of Acapulco, he had had to call a passing ship for help. His crew member was threatening to kill him. The ship sent over personnel with a straitjacket to remove the guy. Safety, privacy, peace, and space—alone on *Southern Cross*, I had them all.

I knew intimately what had been done, what had not been done, and the condition of each part of *Southern Cross*; my eyes and ears picked up the signals announcing potential problems. Another person on board might distract me from noticing a subtle warning sign. Besides, I savored the undiluted experience; my response to each sight, sound, event, or sensation came purely from within, undistorted and unalloyed by another's reactions.

The names of women singlehanded circumnavigators circled around in my mind. As I had sailed the Mexican coast in 1988, young Tania Aebi returned to New York, completing at age twenty the circumnavigation she had begun nearly three years before. If she had not given a ride for 63 miles to someone in the South Pacific, she would have been the first American woman and the youngest person to circle the globe alone.

In 1978, on board *Windy*, we had listened to news reports that New Zealander Naomi James had just completed the first singlehanded around-the-world voyage by a woman. I learned later that the *Guinness Book of World Records* gave that distinction instead to Krystyna Chojnowska-Liskiewwicz from Poland, who had finished her solo circumnavigation via the Panama Canal shortly ahead of Naomi.

Australian Kay Cottee made her epic voyage below the seven southern capes on *Blackmore's First Lady* in 1987–88, setting a number of records, including one for speed. Mom had read Kay's book, *First Lady*, recounting the eight-month trip and asked, "If you had a boat like Kay's could you do your trip in eight months instead of eight years?" But this trip would never be about going as fast as possible.

There was also Julia Hazel, who built her own 27-foot steel boat in Australia, then spent ten years circling the globe without an engine. And from the ranks of BOC Challenge solo around-the-world racers—themselves among the elite sailors of the world—incredible Isabelle Autissier stood out as one of the greatest, man or woman.

Tania, Naomi, Krystyna, Kay, Julia, and Isabelle all had done it alone. If I continued sailing solo the rest of the way around, I could join their tiny club. From what I knew, they were each younger than my fifty years. With the first, the fastest, and the youngest already taken I laughed and dubbed myself "The Oldest Woman Solo Circumnavigator."

For the past two years when most people met me and discovered that I was sailing alone, they had remarked, "I'll look for you in *Guinness*." I would just smile and shake my head. I was not trying to be great in any way, and I did not see myself as a great sailor. Maybe someday I would want to do one special thing to leave behind from my life—but as an artist or architect, not a sailor.

I woke up June 2nd determined to tackle the leaking sink. Three days doing dishes in a bucket was enough. The integral stainless steel studs that had held the sink in place had long since rusted away, leaving only caulking compound to secure it to the counter. That had been enough until Fran replaced the drainage system below—a Rube Goldberg array of elbows, nipples, and hose clamps—with a single length of stiff rubber hose. It would have been an improvement, but he had cut the hose too long and counted on the caulking to bond the sink to the counter. Now the sink sat half an inch higher than the counter, and water ran under the rim and into the drawers below. But far worse, the connection between the sink and the hose, just below sea level, leaked continuously whenever the one-and-a-half-inch through-hull valve was open.

I cut, shaped, glued, and screwed new framing inside the cabinet, cut a half-inch from the hose, tightened the sink-hose connection, recaulked the sink, weighted it down with my heavy steel toolbox while the caulking cured, then went back to the cockpit with Keri Hulme's *The Bone People*, marveling at the past week's weather.

Southern Cross was near the stretch of water where I had met the second of the two storms along my route to New Zealand eighteen months before. The boat Fran and I had heard calling for rescue after dropping 20 feet from a steep wave and dislodging their engine had been near here too. I slid down 18-inch seas, looking forward to seeing Tonga through new eyes . . . alone.

On the eighth day out from Russell the wind backed from south to east-southeast and increased. Overnight gusts rose to 30 knots from the east, and seas grew to six feet, becoming confused as the old southerly swell met the new easterly wind waves. The wind continued to back and increase, and I trimmed the sails tighter. At noon I dropped the first reef in the main and at 1600 lowered the staysail and added the second reef. At 2100 I bundled the genoa to the lifelines and raised the staysail, and by midnight *SC* carried only the staysail.

The following day the wind backed into the east-northeast and held steady at 25 to 30 knots, kicking up ten- to twelve-foot seas. Sheets of green water poured over the deck and I fought for easting, sails strapped in tight as *Southern Cross* punched into the wind and seas. The barometer had dropped 20 millibars in three and a half days. A solid mass of low, gray cloud cover pushed down from above. Then the wind backed even farther into the northeast and dropped to 12 knots. Rain-filled, muggy air hung a mood of gloom around the boat, and I tucked into a corner of the cockpit with André Brink's *A Dry White Season* the despair of South Africa in those times matching the atmosphere around me.

The low-pressure trough passed during the night and light west-southwest-erlies filled in behind it, moving *Southern Cross* toward the Vava'u group at the northern end of Tonga. By June 9th I was broad reaching at 7 knots down two- to three-foot seas, belting out a medley of old tunes as I headed for the anchorage at Neiafu, the main port for Vava'u. I was ready to wipe out every bad memory from the year before.

_____ JUNE 1991

LEGEND SAYS THAT MAUI, THE GREAT POLYNESIAN GOD, threw out his line to catch a fish and instead, after a great fight, pulled up the islands of Tonga. The Vava'u archipelago in the north comprises some fifty gems scattered across the sparkling sea inside the protection of a surrounding reef. From tiny, low-lying atoll islands of sand and palms to the sheer, 500-foot, jungle-covered volcanic cliffs of the main island, Vava'u, he created a perfect paradise with lush tropical fruits, coconut trees, and calm, bountiful waters to provide for his people.

Less touched by outside influence than the people of most South Pacific islands, Tonga's reticent, respectful, matriarchal society remained faithful to ancient customs. Visitors, foreign and local alike, were greeted with quiet nods and raised eyebrows. As the money sent home by male family members working abroad diminished, Maui's bounty had become even more important.

I checked in at Neiafu, the port of entry and government center for Vava'u, stocked up on fresh provisions and ice, and picked up my mail before leaving to explore quiet anchorages on nearby islands. With sixty boats from the annual northbound New Zealand regatta added to the regular cruising crowd, private coves were rare.

My brother, the inveterate fisherman, had asked again in his latest letter, "Have you caught a fish yet?"

"Bites don't count. You have to land them!" he reminded me, in response to my account of one that got away.

For two years I had towed a handline bought from retired cruisers. Various experts had offered their special techniques: "When you bring a fish on board, pour cheap whiskey in the gills"; advice: "You can't troll under 5 knots"; and sometimes even copies of their favorite lures, such as a piece of orange mesh onion bag or a beer can cut into strips on one end to look like a squid. I'd tried everything, but so far with little success.

As I left the fiord-like harbor of Neiafu and set a course for the narrow pass between fringing reefs, I paid out 200 feet of heavy monofilament line with a new lure from New Zealand, wound the end around a cleat, dropped the wooden handle in the cockpit seat, and forgot about it.

The morning sail was straight out of an advertisement for the Moorings charter company: 200-foot-deep underwater canyons beneath, and cool, green jungle tumbling down black volcanic hills on either side. "Come sail Tonga" could have been emblazoned overhead in the cerulean blue sky above *Southern Cross*. I skimmed the flat, protected waters, listening to one of the four copies of Vivaldi's *Four Seasons* my sister had given me. She kept forgetting that she had already sent one, so sent another.

As I rounded the top of Lape, minutes from the anchorage at Vaka'eitu, I remembered the fishing line. Something was bobbing on the surface behind me. Ten minutes later he was on board—a huge fish three and a half feet long, and already dead. In my excitement I could barely keep my mind on anchoring procedures.

My first fish! But I had no idea what to do with it. As I studied Maui's gift to me, a 50-foot Moorings charter boat arrived with three guys standing on the stern. "Do any of you know how to clean a fish?" I called.

A dubious, wrinkled-nose response came back, "What do you have?"

The tone changed quickly when I held it up and offered some for their dinner. In seconds they arrived in their dinghy, took a closer look, and confirmed that it was a king mackerel, a prize fish on the Chesapeake Bay where they lived. They requested knives, cutting board, and a large container.

Three minutes later eleven fat steaks sat on the cutting board, and the remains had been packaged for disposal. No scaling was required for the smooth-skinned fish I had caught. I handed over eight steaks and instructions for making *poisson cru* as they climbed into the dinghy and offered me an invitation for drinks at sunset.

Knowing they probably wouldn't try the delicious raw fish delicacy so popular in French Polynesia on their own, I fixed some to take along. It disappeared in minutes while we traded names, histories, and sailing stories. After years of sailing and traveling together the four couples shared an easy camaraderie that reached out to include me. The return on eight steaks from my first fish was a friendship with one of the couples that has continued ever since.

Heading back to Neiafu a few days later for more ice and produce, I mulled over a new idea. One of the charter boat guests wanted a miniature from Tonga. Perhaps other Moorings guests would be interested too. I stopped to sketch the rocky entrance at Swallow's cave and a colorful dugout canoe-load of women with umbrellas, mapping out a plan to present to Moorings.

The anchor had barely settled at Neiafu when Canadians John and Francine Stevens on *Baron Rouge* brought an invitation for dinner. More than most cruisers, they immersed themselves in the local life at each stop, quickly making friends on shore. John, who was infamous in cruising circles for his devilish humor, relayed his latest escapade.

He was a devout Catholic, which had endeared him to the nuns at the blue and white cathedral in Neiafu. The night before Easter, in the wee hours of the morning, John had crept into the nuns' chicken house carrying a large bag. He had stolen from nest to nest, shooing each sitting hen to remove and replace her cluster of eggs. When he finished, lavender, pink, blue, yellow, and green eggs had overflowed every nest.

Crawling silently back down the hillside to his waiting dinghy and stealthily rowing out to *Baron Rouge*, he joined Francine in the cockpit to wait. When the sun peeked above the bougainvillea-covered chicken house and spread across the boats below, they were rewarded by the squeals and giggles of the usually very reserved Tongan nuns. The sisters quickly pointed fingers in the right direction and loved John all the more.

The next day, with ice and fresh produce aboard, I left for more exploring—this time around Pangaimotu to the tiny island of Tapana.

From fifth grade on I had longed to play the flute. In Singapore on *Windy*, with a $100 flute, a $4.98 how-to-play book, and a teacher from the Singapore Symphony, I had made a beginning. Later, back in Santa Cruz, I had tried again with a new flute and a new teacher. But business eclipsed flute playing, and my flute waited in the case.

As *Southern Cross* had ranged the South Pacific, there had been moments that inspired me to try again. I had practiced scales, exercises, and the same beginning pieces over and over. Playing by ear and creating music lay beyond my imagination, but I dreamed of doing more . . . someday.

The center of action on Tapana was Maria's Paella Restaurant, a small beach establishment on the southern tip of the island a half-mile around the point from the anchorage. Mejias and Eduardo, the Spanish and Basque owners of Maria's, were former cruisers whose boat, *Rock and Blues*, still sat at anchor where it had come to rest three years before.

They had sailed in, built their grass shack, and proceeded to cook paella and make music. As word spread through the cruiser grapevine, people came. Most of their guests were yachties, since a boat was the only way to get there. They had hauled their VHF radio to shore and wired it into the twelve-volt electrical system at the restaurant. All day on channel 16, boats called in their reservations: "Maria's, Maria's. *Champagne* calling." "*Champagne*, this is Tapana, go ahead." "Three for dinner tonight." "Okay, see you at 7:30." And then another, "Maria's, Maria's. . . ."

With dinner dishes cleared, Eduardo took his place with his guitar and dove into some very righteous blues. Pepe, his brother, who had sailed in to Tapana one year later, took up percussion on a collection of unlikely homemade instruments dangling from a piece of driftwood. Then Cora, a German concert musician from the boat *Amber*, stepped in with her clarinet while her Polish husband Zdeneck took up his concertina. With tiny wire-rimmed glasses perched on the end of his nose, his eyes closed, he played as if he were in another world.

Mejias emerged from the kitchen, and the mood shifted as Eduardo launched into a flamenco and she danced to the front of the room. He really didn't like flamenco, but indulged her with a couple of numbers each evening. Then they shifted back to jazz, and Mejias whirled over to pick up her saxophone, newly acquired from a down-and-out French yachtie the week before.

She belted out the four notes she had mastered in her first week with a horn, and I was awed by her confidence and courage. Every cell in my body longed to join them—not to perform, but just to make music.

Soon it was time to return to Neiafu—the only commercial center in Vava'u—for more ice, veggies, and mail. I pulled up the anchor in the protected waters behind the island and sailed out into the fifteen-mile-wide lagoon that wrapped the entire archipelago, fishing line trailing and dinghy in tow with the new outboard secured to its transom. Away from the shadow of the island the swells grew abruptly to four feet, and in moments the knot log readings plummeted from 4.5 to 1.5. The dinghy had flipped over, becoming a sea anchor, and the outboard was dragging below the water. Now the wind and sea were pushing *SC* down on a menacing reef. I pulled *T/T Southern Cross* alongside, turned her over, and untangled the fishing line. Lacking shelter and ample fresh water with which to flush the salt from the now-flooded outboard, I hurried on to Neiafu. There a Japanese cruiser taught me how to revive a submerged motor in trade for a miniature painting.

Dick and Theda, a former coast-to-coast truck-driving team on board *Gypsy Rover*, invited me for dinner—one of Theda's huge bowls of pasta with salad and garlic bread—to celebrate the resurrection of the motor. After dinner the subject turned to dinghies. They had noticed the multicolored patches spreading over my little red rubber boat. "You know, we bought that same dinghy for our trip, but the manufacturer replaced it before we even left Hawaii two years ago." The words went down like a dry, hard-boiled egg yolk. It was time to write another letter, only this time I had facts.

The next morning, sunlight filtered through jungle mist rising from the hills around the anchorage and bright yellow flowers floated by on the tide as parrots called greetings from frangipani trees. I sipped a hot, black mug of coffee and watched the daily stream of salesmen paddling their dugout canoes from shore to offer tours, boat care, and fresh fruit. When Aisea stopped at *Southern Cross* promoting his version of a Tongan feast at a beach on the opposite side of the island, near Tapana, I made a reservation for the next night.

On shore my errands began at the Moorings headquarters to show the staff twelve paintings of the town and outlying anchorages. They confirmed the rumor that they were opening a gift shop, but they were not interested in framed miniature prints. It was disappointing but not devastating news. There were funds in the kitty, and I knew the originals would sell.

The next night I joined several other cruisers and tourists at Aisea's feast of Tongan specialties served on banana leaves and in coconut shells. As we cruisers headed for our boats, Aisea invited us to church the following morning. "I'll be at the top of the hill above the beach at 9:00 with a ride to town."

When missionaries arrived in Tonga in the early 1800s they found a deeply respectful society formed into large extended families and following a single powerful leader, Taufa'ahau. He adopted the new religion brought by the Wesleyans and was baptized King George Tupou I. His people followed, and Christianity became the abiding cornerstone of Tongan life.

In the wake of the first circumnavigators came the recognition that the world needed an International Date Line in order to maintain a single calendar. The early explorers who had sailed west around the world arrived back home to discover that they were a day behind, and those going east were a day ahead. The line finally settled around 180 degrees longitude, between Fiji and Tonga. Eventually world progress brought the need for time zones. When the Tongan government decided which zone they would adopt, they jogged the International Date Line to fall east of their islands, so they could be the first people in the world to celebrate the Sabbath on Sunday. Strict rules dictated respectful behavior and dress for both visitors and locals on that day. Men were required to wear shirts at all times. Shops were closed. Fishing was prohibited.

Islanders took out their best clothes for church, immaculately clean and ironed. I chose a modest outfit from my limited dress-up wardrobe—something appropriate for a trip by small boat and a climb up the hillside—a pair of below-the-knees pants and a matching jacket in pale yellow linen.

I dragged the dinghy well above the high-tide line, tied it to a tree, and struck out to find our ride. The path rose into jungle overgrowth wet with overnight rains. Soon it became a muddy trough and then a gummy track that finally yielded to the thick red gumbo of the road. My sandals gathered the goo, and when I moved to the side of the road, straw from the fields mixed with the mud. My feet grew to ridiculous proportions as I waddled down the sticky, red rut.

The road stretched on with no sign of our waiting "ride." At last, I rounded a curve in the road and found a covered truck with a few people in the back and Aisea by the side. I scraped pounds of mud from my feet and sandals with a stick and climbed aboard. Spotless white dresses surrounded my red-streaked pale yellow outfit while we waited for other cruisers to arrive.

We pulled into a churchyard filled with Tongans. The women wore Mother Hubbards, some colorful and some white and lacy, and white straw hats covered with ribbons and flowers. Men appeared in *tupenu*, an ankle-length wraparound, and matching suit coats over white shirts and neckties. Everyone had the traditional *ta'ovala* wrapper around the waist. The men's were at least two feet wide and made from woven grasses; the women wore either a smaller, lighter version of grass or one crocheted with shells and beads along the bottom.

Legend held that shipwrecked travelers had been washed onto a Tongan beach long ago. When islanders invited them to meet the king they covered their naked bodies with a wrapper made from grasses. The wrapper itself had become a symbol of respect, and now no one would think of going to church without a *ta'ovala.*

We filed into the sanctuary, and I took a seat in the back, hoping no one would notice my disrespectful appearance. A heavenly sound burst from the congregation. Old, tired hymns that we sailors had left behind in our hometowns took on new life when sung by Tongan parishioners from their hearts. The minister followed. Caught up in his emotional message, he wiped away tears and blew his nose frequently while his stoic congregation listened dry-eyed.

Then he announced the collection. My neighbor Ty on *Azura* reached into his pocket and pulled out a $5 bill. From the front row, one by one, people walked to a table behind the pulpit to present their offerings. As they returned to their seats, the elder at the table called out the name of the person and the amount given while it was recorded in a large ledger. Ty reached back into his pocket to exchange the five for a ten. I was stuck with my $2; it was all I had. When Ty's turn came, he marched forward with his gift, and the elder switched to English to announce that this guest had just given $10 toward the building fund to finish their new church.

Back on board, I began my biweekly letter to my mother, passing along the morning's lesson on effective fund-raising. Her church in Illinois might use it for their next major project.

On a late afternoon breeze I sailed back to Tapana, thinking about another adult student my Santa Cruz flute teacher once taught. He had arrived knowing nothing and, after one year of dedicated practice, had gone on stage as a professional. It had been the only thing he did that year. I, too, would happily dedicate one year to such a goal. There was a small, half-finished studio on the point near Maria's. I could live there, paint, and make music everyday. But what would I live on? I'd still need food, gas, ice, and stamps. I anchored, and the days drifted by.

Cora worked out the flute arrangement for "St. Louis Blues," one of the group's new pieces, and I practiced it twenty-five times a day or more, preparing to unveil myself at an afternoon rehearsal. When the day came I walked through jungle-filtered sunlight, the butterflies in my stomach matching those that flitted through the warm, steamy air. With rehearsal underway when I arrived, no one paid attention as I unpacked and assembled my flute and stepped into the kitchen to warm up. The group was just starting to work on "St. Louis Blues" when I returned, and in a flash they were off and running. I picked up the beat with my toe, fingers poised to meet them the second time around.

They flew on by without a sound from me. Again they came to the beginning, my foot tapping with them. I played one note and they were gone. Over and over that afternoon they flew around and around the piece, while I sat in their dust. At last I went back to the kitchen to play it alone, just to know that I could.

Cora followed and put her arm around my shoulder. Later she brought her clarinet to *Southern Cross* to play a duet. I never expected to play with them, just dreamed I might.

The time came to leave Tonga, and I took photographs of them all. The one of Mejias and her saxophone joined the group on the head door as a reminder of what you can do when you really believe in yourself.

SHIP'S DIARY: 25 July 1991, 0944 Local, 19°22'S/178°35'W, motoring at 4.8 knots, steering 265M, no wind at all, glassy sea with a 1-foot swell from the NE, 10% cloud cover and 1013 on the bar, down 1mb from yesterday. Passed south of Fulanga early this morning, entering Fijian waters.

I arrived in Suva, Fiji's capital on the largest island, Viti Levu, late in the afternoon on Saturday the 27th—five easy sailing days from Tonga. Greetings over the VHF included news that the harbormaster's office would be closed until Monday, and all eighteen newly arrived crews were restricted to their boats for the weekend.

My carefully laid plans—to collect mail, shop, get permission from the Cultural Affairs office to visit outlying islands, sail northeast to Levuka on Ovalau to meet Dayle (as we'd planned back in New Zealand), and then go on to the other major island, Vanua Levu, to visit Barbara and Charles in Savusavu—began to fall apart. On Monday I discovered that *Fair Winds* was en route to New Caledonia via Suva to avoid a 50 percent import tax on their boat. "Sit tight," Barbara told me. "We'll be there in a few days. But keep your plans to sail to Savusavu for a little vacation. We have a maid and gardener to take care of you and a mooring for *Southern Cross*."

A bustling city of 75,000, Suva was overpowering after so much time in villages, quiet anchorages, and on the open sea. As the business week began, I buffeted through the crowded noisy streets checking in and running errands. On Tuesday evening I treated myself to a rare big-screen film—a fund-raiser showing of *Silence of the Lambs*—at the modern theater downtown near the post office. The spine-tingling movie was followed by an unsettling late-night hike back to the dinghy dock through the industrial district and past the jail—thankfully in the company of two other cruisers. Nighttime crowds surged along the main road, triggering all the survival instincts honed on visits to my cousin Claire's loft in New York City; every nerve twitched, and the hairs prickled on the back of my neck. At the dock I parted from my companions with their final warnings ringing in my ears: deadly sea snakes sometimes lurked in the dinghies, dinghies had disappeared from several boats, and ten days before a couple had been robbed at knifepoint aboard their boat in the anchorage. Thoroughly unnerved, I dreamed that night of locks and chains and knives, with the dinghy locked to the boat, me locked inside, and the air horn and flare gun by my pillow.

The next morning smiling, friendly Fijians on shore greeted me with their usual deep-throated *"Bula"*s. I put the flare gun and air horn back in the locker and left the companionway open to friendly breezes from the soggy, wet, jungle-covered hills behind the city.

My first errand Wednesday was a visit to the Cultural Affairs office. Coming to Fiji by private boat provided the rare opportunity to visit traditional villages and meet people one to one, without a tour guide. Far to the east lay the Lau group, where I longed to go. Known for their immense hand-carved war canoes that once carried hundreds of warriors on raids against enemy tribes, they were the most remote and traditional of the Fijian islands. But my allotted time was too short and the necessary permission too difficult to secure. Instead I chose the tiny island of Qamea and its hurricane-hole anchorage, just off Taveuni's east coast—an overnight sail from Savusavu, where I would visit Barbara and Charles's home.

Along with my port clearance, boat papers, and a detailed itinerary, I presented a formal request to the Cultural Affairs office for permission to visit Qamea. They consented, providing instructions on how to behave, what to wear, and how to ask the chief for permission to stay once I arrived at the island.

The next priority was getting a message to Dayle; the delay waiting for *Fair Wind*'s arrival in Suva would make our Saturday morning reunion in Levuka impossible to keep. Knowing only the name of the boat she had planned to take, I was crossing the street to the ferry company's office, wondering how to reach her, when I started at the sound of my name. Dayle had been in Suva just five minutes. We laughed at the mysterious workings of the universe and looked for a nearby restaurant reported to have a good Indian *thalli*, the popular lunch tray filled with assorted curries, chutneys, and condiments.

Fiji's Polynesian-Melanesian culture had been heavily influenced by British colonial settlers and their indentured Indian labor. The resultant blend gave Fiji its character, unique among the South Pacific islands. Huge, easygoing islanders, always ready with a smile, lived among industrious, business-minded Indians with their colorful fabrics and spicy foods, surrounded by the slightly tatty remnants of British colonial architecture and bureaucracy.

Politically the Indians and native Fijians coexisted in an uneasy peace, but by 1987 ethnic Indians outnumbered the Fijians, and their differences elevated to the edge of civil war. A coalition government was formed, but Indian domination broke the fragile accord, triggering the first coup in the South Pacific region. The uprising was quashed, but a new constitution favoring native Fijians continued to feed the tension.

After running down events in Russell, my visit to Tonga, and business news from the Blue Penguin, Dayle and I struck out for the huge central market to buy a mandatory gift, a half-pound of yangona root, for the chief on Qamea. I staggered at the press of humanity in the dusky, cramped interior. Small shafts of light fought their way through dusty air, giving a dull view of the products on display down the narrow, clogged aisles. The impression was a sharp contrast to Papeete's bright, colorful soaring arches and sun-drenched displays and Tonga's cheerful street market with foods spread on bright fabrics or in handmade baskets. We found the *yangona* in a corner of the second floor, both the dried roots preferred by the villagers and in powdered form. They would turn it into the mildly narcotic, peppery *kava kava*, a ritual drink used traditionally throughout the South Pacific.

We strolled palm-lined shady streets to the museum to shudder at displays of containers and utensils used for cannibalism. In 1874, after centuries of tribal warfare, a desperate King Cakobau, on the small island of Bau east of Viti Levu, had offered his kingdom to Queen Victoria for the peace her protectorate could provide. An agreement was signed on October 10th that year, and on the same day in 1970 Britain returned independence to the islands.

At an old waterfront hotel, one of the grande dames left in the dust of a retreating British Empire, we enjoyed a cool drink amid palms, latticework, and white-uniformed waiters—expecting to see Somerset Maugham in a nearby wickered chair. Back in the center of town we stopped at the visitor's bureau to pick up maps and brochures for Dayle's trip around the island. The offices were housed in a small, pale yellow colonial building, a vestige surrounded by tall modern construction, with a sea of locals relaxing in the shade of its verandah. We ended the day on board *Southern Cross* for dinner.

Dayle's visit came to an end and Barbara and Charles arrived with instructions for my holiday in Savusavu. I left August 7th with a mail stop at Levuka, Fiji's first capitol under British rule. Like Russell, it had once been a Wild West sort of place, filled with bawdy sailors and whalers; the wooden sidewalks and colorful, wood-fronted buildings, looking like a Hollywood movie set, still remained. I drew and shot photos.

Savusavu offered more scenes for painting in the towering, traditional thatched *bures* near Barbara and Charles's bungalow. Finally I reached Qamea. This outlying island stood well off the cruisers' well-worn "milk run" through the Pacific, receiving only seven or eight boats a year in its small anchorage. Here I hoped to be a special visitor in a little-known place.

The next morning a slim young Fijian squatted patiently in the shade on the shore, not far from *SC*. I noticed him as I cleaned the deck after the rough sail around the top of Taveuni and a night of debris-laden sixty-knot squalls at anchor. He was still there while I hemmed a piece of brightly patterned cotton fabric. A *sulu* and T-shirt were required for the visit to the chief of the village; all my sarongs were too thin or worn. The young man waited.

I landed, and we struck out for the village on the right. He took me directly to the house of the *tauraga ni koro* for the *sevu sevu* ceremony prescribed by custom. My escort presented the gift-wrapped roots to the chief, and we sat down on handwoven floor mats. The chief spoke reverently to the dried, gray-brown pieces of plant material while I waited for his acceptance. Once done, the village would assume responsibility for my safety and well-being and that of *SC*. To my relief, he wound up quickly, and I prepared to accept the anticipated invitation to return later and join in the next ceremony, when they would drink the *kava kava* made from my roots. But my escort walked me quickly through the cinder block village and back to the dinghy without a word about the evening. Perhaps there were no provisions for solo women travelers.

Relieved to end official duties, on board I turned to lunch, letters, and *Bonfire of the Vanities*. Shortly the tapping of a dugout canoe against the hull roused me. A handsome, smiling Fijian man in his late twenties held onto the side of *SC* waiting for a greeting. He asked a few questions, and requested to come aboard and see the boat. I said "no." Much as I wanted to meet the local villagers, being alone on *SC* with a man I knew nothing about was not what I had in mind. He smiled and invited me for tea, then paddled back to his village in a small, nearby cove. We met on shore and walked to his home through a poor but pretty little compound at the water's edge. He poured cups of aromatic tea made from a grass growing by the beach, and we sat on mats on the floor. Next to us his sister ironed clothes for a trip to Suva with a butane iron, using the floor for her ironing board. Carefully she folded her things, while her brother scolded me for visiting in a wrinkled *sulu*.

We hiked a nearby hill to a village of thatched huts planted in clipped grass lawns and surrounded by immaculately tended flower gardens. The chief, Moses, greeted us from the center of a cluster of men while other villagers waved from their communal work sites above, fulfilling their weekly obligation to donate one day for maintaining the shared spaces.

Billy, a slight, delicate man in a red-flowered *sulu*, emerged from the group carrying a small, fluffy white dog and exclaimed with delight to learn I had lived near San Francisco. He grinned, confiding he wanted to visit there someday. I would learn later that Billy's way of life may have been dictated by his position in the family: if an island family didn't have a daughter, the third son was usually raised as a girl. There were responsibilities and duties in every family that required a daughter to perform. Billy had a special place in his community.

Together we three climbed to the *fare* where Billy lived in the center of the most vibrant, beautiful garden of them all. He cut a huge bouquet of orchids, plumeria, and hibiscus for me. I returned to *SC* considering the valuable lessons in life the villagers in this remote cove had shared with me: how to treat visitors, how to care for communal spaces, how to show respect, and how to accept diversity in the community.

My few days at Qamea over, I prepared to return to Suva. A morning start would allow arrival before dark the following day if I took the channel between Mbatiki and Nairai. Going east around Nairai would mean a night waiting by the reef-lined entrance to Suva—a problem if the weather turned bad.

The chart showed a seven-mile-wide channel running between the reefs that surrounded each island. A full moon would light my way, the SatNav was working well, and the weather looked good. I confidently plotted the course and turned in for an early start.

The next day's sailing was a fast and rambunctious broad reach. I steered for the thrill of it, plotting fixes as the SatNav delivered them. *SC* held the course perfectly. The full moon lay behind a solid mass of clouds. I plotted a last fix four miles from the northern tip of the upper reef, turned from southwest to west-southwest down the middle of the channel, and changed sails to go wing-and-wing downwind.

As I studied the sails from the cockpit, the moon finally emerged from the clouds. It lit a boiling surf less than a mile ahead that stretched out on either side as far as I could see. I threw the tiller over to turn northwest and started the engine. The poled-out genny backwinded, draining my speed, but I couldn't leave the helm to take it down. Heart racing, I pushed the engine, struggling to pull away from the bubbling white mass of foam.

Long minutes dragged by as *SC* crept parallel to the surf line. At last the moon struck a path over smooth water to port, and the coils in my shoulders unwound. My held breath escaped in a "thank-you" to the silver-edged clouds above. I had come within minutes of joining those whose boats had been pounded and destroyed on coral reefs due to one brief moment of inattention, one miscalculation, an equipment malfunction, or an uncharted danger—their panicked voices on the radio calling, "Mayday, Mayday, we've hit a reef."

I put *Southern Cross* back on course and went below to pinpoint the failure. The trail of fixes followed a steady line along the course I had steered. But either the final fix was wrong or the chart was off—by at least five miles.

Changes in the government-supported satellite navigation system on board *SC* pointed suspicion at that final fix. Driven by U.S. military needs, a new global positioning system for navigation was replacing SatNav. The new satellites—which would provide continuous and more precise coverage—were already aloft. As the old circling SatNav satellites died, they were not being replaced, nor was the maintenance schedule that corrected the baseline data in each satellite being followed. GPS was the wave of the future, but the price of a receiver was still too high for many small boats. I relied on a faulty system.

Back in Suva, on August 20th, I heard on VOA that the Soviet Union was falling apart and Mikhail Gorbachev was under house arrest. Over the next few days the crew on a small Russian cruising boat anchored nearby spent hours in the U.S. Embassy watching the developments on television. I wondered what it felt like to them. The world was shifting. It seemed at once a time of tremendous promise and frightening uncertainty.

After a week of reprovisioning, replacing the starting battery, buying and processing film, and covering the usual unexpected expenses, the kitty looked very thin. On Malolo Lailai in the Mamanutha Islands, on the western edge of Fiji, the Musket Cove Yacht Club held an annual regatta to Port Vila, Vanuatu. One hundred boats were expected for the festivities, including the forty participants in the first Europa around-the-world-in-fifteen-months regatta. They were all possible customers for my miniatures. I also looked forward to finding many old friends among the arriving fleet.

On my last evening in Suva the heavy wooden Royal Suva Yacht Club door swung open to a busy, boisterous Friday night crowd. On his stool by the door, Charley, the elderly front-door security guard, made a towering island in the midst of the turmoil. Covered in pink lace and ribbons, Charley's four-month-old granddaughter lay cradled in his oversized hands. Their eyes locked as he whispered a Fijian lullaby and swung her through a gentle arc. Out and back, out and back, in their private world. His is the parting image of Fiji I carried as I sailed through the reef at the entry to Suva.

Two days later I entered the brilliant aquamarine waters of the lagoon at Dick's Place in Musket Cove to join the early arrivals for the four-day race. On shore, bulletin boards carried announcements of festivities for the participants—warm-up races, contests, pig roasts, a talent night, and parties. A $95 entry fee—beyond my means unless the next few days were highly successful—paid for everything, including gifts for each boat, a Vanuatu flag, and the $65 port charges due on arrival in Port Vila.

I checked in and joined the Musket Cove Yacht Club, as required of boats staying in the lagoon, then browsed through the gift shop looking for an attractive postcard to send my brother for his birthday. Finding nothing sparked an idea, and I made an appointment with the shop owners for the next morning.

They were enthusiastic about my proposal to do a series of paintings for oversized custom postcards showing Musket Cove and asked me to do a sample. On Viti Levu, six gift shops had expressed interest in a framed series of Fijian miniatures. With Dayle following up by mail for their orders I was optimistic again that ongoing business could follow my wake.

I shot photographs of the dry, golden, grass-covered hillsides and a white bubbling surf rolling over the lavender reefs circling the lagoon, processed the film, and painted the first piece—a flower-covered thatched *bure*. They loved it, but didn't want to pay royalties or a fee for using the art.

Dick's Place gave me space for a small exhibit in the lobby. I listened to the passing comments as I painted: "They're darling; we'll be back later." "I have lots of art in my home. You're very good." "These are really nice. I buy art all the time." Day after day I waited for customers to buy something, not just talk about it. I smiled politely, said "thank you" to each of them, then dinghied away from the parties to sit alone, wondering how to change things and dreading each day more.

The contents of my wallet diminished to $7. I checked the mail daily, waiting for a packet forwarded from Suva. Finally it arrived; the IRS threatened to place a lien on my bank accounts and property in California. But there were no accounts and no property. I wondered what more they would or could do.

At last a commission came for a full-size painting of a boat. I worked out the details with the owner and shot photos of his boat, but I had no money to process the film and couldn't begin until he sent pictures of the Mooréa backdrop he wanted. It would have to wait until I had a mailing address in Australia.

Cleared by officials from the main island, the racing boats left for Port Vila one daybreak amid laughter, good-natured taunts, and friendly competition. In the end, I had sold just enough miniatures to make the sail to Lautoka, on the west coast of Viti Levu, and check out of Fiji in a mixture of disappointment and optimism, sick from the antimalaria pills taken in preparation for Vanuatu.

EN ROUTE TO THE NORTHERN VANUATU ISLAND OF Santo and far from the regatta party makers, I awoke to absolute stillness. *Southern Cross* hung in the center of a dusky pink bubble with no horizon, no motion, no edge. Time and direction, up and down disappeared. Suddenly an explosion of water erupted to starboard, then two, three, six, eight porpoises jumped in a ballet, racing across the bow to meet another group of ten who made their leaps from port to starboard. I whirled to find more behind. The whole corps de ballet danced along the surface, leaping and pirouetting just for me, then vanished.

A light breeze appeared, and a small wiggly wake trailed behind. The undulating surface of pink picked up ripples of blue and lavender. As the top of the sun met the edge of the Earth, I went down to fix breakfast.

My emotions hung between wonder at the world outside and apprehension at what lay ahead. I compared the money in my purse to the expenses awaiting my arrival—$65 in port fees—and wondered again how long I could continue walking this financial tightrope. The only relief came at sea, where the disappointments and temptations of land disappeared.

October 1st, at noon, I passed through Selwyn Strait, entering Vanuatu between Pentecost Island and Ambryn. The air hung heavy and mysterious over the primitive archipelago. The moonscape volcanoes of Ambryn spread a supernatural aura over the islanders that a century of efforts by Presbyterian and Catholic missionaries had done little to dispel. On Pentecost the original bungee jumpers still leapt headfirst from high, rickety platforms, performing their act of faith with vines instead of rubber.

In 1906 the New Hebrides, as Captain Cook had named the islands in 1774, were claimed by both England and France. Together they established the world's only "condominium" government, ruling jointly until 1978. Two infrastructures, one English and one French, lived side by side. There were two school systems, two police systems, two religious systems—two of every government department and social service.

When independence arrived in 1980, the islanders chose Bislama, commonly called pidgin English, as the official language. But on each island some villages spoke English while others spoke French, and some inhabitants still used any of the hundred indigenous languages. The upper levels of government were a mixture of both systems, but each village maintained its traditional language, religion, and customs, regarding neighboring villages from "the other camp" with suspicion.

Central portions of some islands still had not been fully explored and mapped. Even though, during World War II, 250,000 GIs had been stationed on Santo, tribes of bushmen still lived untouched in the high mountainous interior, as they had for centuries.

I sailed with my own images of life fifty years ago in these waters and neighboring archipelagos, thinking of family members who had come here to save the world. In the distant mist lay the original Bali Hai, Aoba, the island that had inspired Michener, as a young serviceman, to write *Tales of the South Pacific*. Not far away, in New Guinea, my father and my sister's mother had lived out Michener's story in real life. He was a successful young officer separated from his wife and daughter. She was an attractive American nurse, his superior in rank.

The letter my father sent home had been addressed to "Mrs. Aileen Henry" instead of "Mrs. D. H. Henry." My mother had known without opening it that something had changed between them. It was brief and terse, not apologetic. She sent her answer back to the South Pacific pouring out her heart, burying her pride, and begging him to reconsider. He did not answer her plea. Ghosts from the past hovered over *Southern Cross*.

At 1600, with 45 miles to Luganville, on Santo, I reduced sail to dawdle through the night and delay my arrival until daylight. The pass between Aore and Toutouba Islands at the entrance to the port was broken in the middle by a smaller island, leaving less than one mile clear between the fringing reefs. The night passed, and *Southern Cross* wandered generally in the right direction. At 0300, in light winds, I checked my progress on the SatNav, then started the motor, estimating arrival at sunrise. I dozed in the cockpit with the autopilot steering alarms set at half-hour increments.

Lulled by the narcotic hum of the droning engine I slept through every alarm. Streams of sunlight poured into the cockpit, startling me awake. *Southern Cross* cruised a mile off the beach aiming at the center of the pass between the islet and Aore.

What-ifs tumbled incoherently through my head. Ten more minutes? My course more to port? Possible disasters lurked on all sides. *SC*'s angel had returned. I sent up another thank-you prayer and promised not to make this a habit.

At Luganville, the second largest city in Vanuatu, little evidence remained of those quarter million GIs who waited there fifty years ago for deployment on the Asian front. The jungle had reclaimed the forty movie theaters, bars, shops, and Quonset huts where they had lived and worked. The U.S. government took care of their remaining vehicles and equipment when they pulled out at the end of the war, shoving it all into the sea off Million Dollar Point after the Vanuatu government declined their bargain price offer.

The town trailed along, in the hot morning sun, on either side of a wide, paved road. Between jungle-covered gaps were tour agencies advertising trips to the interior to see "custom" villages (grass shacks with natives living a subsistence life), to the Blue Lagoon of Jean Simmons fame, and to Champagne Beach, where one could swim engulfed in sparkling bubbles. There were also grocery stores, handicrafts shops, and finally my target—the ice cream shop.

A blast of icy air hit me with a reviving smack as the door closed behind me. The small, refrigerated white cabinet held only four choices, but after a week at sea, flavor wasn't important. While I waited for a strawberry cone the door opened again, ringing a small brass bell.

A bushman no more than four and a half feet tall stood in the shop entrance. The chill air raised goose bumps over bare, dark mahogany skin protected only by a small square of cloth hanging from a cord around his waist and two decorative leaves dangling behind. He padded silently across the cold gray linoleum floor on wide jungle feet. Under a mound of grizzly gray hair, dark eyes studied the flavors. A piece of bone pierced his nose.

We exited together. Our eyes met in recognition for a moment over matching mounds of smooth, cold, sweet pink ice cream. In the noontime heat of the street, he joined his friends waiting for their ride back to an ancient, hidden village. I continued on to seek official permission to visit Vanuatu.

A week later *Southern Cross* sat besieged by dugout canoes, four deep on all sides, off Uri Island at Port Stanley on Malekula. Each canoe carried one or two young islanders, all male except for the canoe with Miriam and Elvina. Finally the boys left, and the two young cousins came aboard. We traded fresh bananas and papaya for jewelry, then they invited me ashore for "potatoes and pudding" and paddled home to prepare for my visit.

Following their directions down a narrow channel through the reef at the southeast end of the island, I landed on a narrow, pebbly beach. They were waiting, in fresh cotton skirts and blouses, to lead me past orchids, hibiscus, ginger, croton, and vine-covered trees, and over small creeks and winding muddy paths. Their small grass shack village nestled in a clearing by the sea. Neighbors were repairing nets and boats, tending the central garden, and visiting under the trees. Fishing nets draped over long poles, drying in the shade along the water's edge. Small garden patches backed against the jungle, and in the center of the compound stood a tiny Presbyterian church, the walls woven in patterns of green and white palm fronds.

Miriam led the way into the thatched home they shared. Everything there had come from their own hands . . . each piece of furniture, the mats we sat upon, their clothing, the house itself, the banjo they played, the garden outside, and the dugout canoe and fishing equipment they used. I was humbled.

Elvina served the "potatoes and pudding" and fresh lemonade, then waited for my reaction; in their culture it would have been impolite to join me. Similar to a baked sweet potato covered with thickened coconut cream, it was sweet and rich. Handing back an empty bowl, I invited them to *SC* the following morning for fresh banana bread; they smiled, pleased.

Later the teenaged boys in the dugout canoes, all from the island of Uripiv, just east of Uri, returned by one's or two's to visit, then ask for matches or other gifts. I gave them what they wanted, if possible. One young man, around seventeen, requested matches and then the box to strike them. I told him he could use a rock. He agreed but didn't leave, begging instead to "take a look inside," to "see the boat."

At last I broke down and allowed him to come on board "for one minute," as if he had any concept of a minute. He climbed into the cockpit. I stood in the companionway, half in and half out of the cabin. He peered around, then pushed by me to go below and see my strange home. I thought how amazing all of this—electronics, padded seats, gas stove, sinks, toilet—must appear in the eyes of one accustomed to grass walls and thatched roofs. In that small space, something shifted. He was staying too long. Alarm flashed across my eyes. Like a predator smelling the fear of its prey he saw that moment of vulnerability and grabbed me in the crotch.

My fear turned to anger. He saw that, too. I shoved his chest and shouted, "Get out; leave." He backed up the steps and disappeared, returning later while I was away to take new bungee cords from the self-steering system and short lengths of line used to hold deck gear secure at sea.

In the morning, when Miriam and Elvina came with their uncle, the chief on Uri, I told them of my encounter. He promised to talk with the chief on Uripiv. It reminded me of the obligations Fijian villages assumed to care for their guests. The following week in Port Vila, a cruising boat would arrive bearing all my small pieces of line and the bungee cords.

On October 12th I daysailed to Craig's Cove on the northwest tip of Ambryn and anchored for the night near a reef that promised good snorkeling. But the early Sunday sun flashed off large, unidentified silver bodies against the black sand bottom below *Southern Cross.* Not knowing what lurked below, I opted for church instead of chancing a swim with sharks.

Under a huge mango tree in the charming, colorful village on shore, children ate freshly fallen fruit, juice dripping from their smiles. I asked for directions to a church, and they pointed to a Catholic one in the center of their town, then up a path toward the next village where the residents were Presbyterians. The path took me past people gathered in a field, who motioned toward a creek and into the village on the other side.

I joined six hundred visiting worshipers that morning at the first service in a newly built Presbyterian church. Powerful *a cappella* voices rose in sure, sweet melodies and harmony. There were no hymnals, only a list of numbers on a board—106, 73, and 28. A visiting choir brought a keyboard, but their vocal confidence wavered with the unaccustomed electronic accompaniment. Gifts from neighboring Presbyterian churches decorated the altar with carvings and cut-glass vases.

As I walked back along the path, the mood of the crowd in the field turned cool, the children's smiles not as friendly. The seventy-four-year rivalry fostered between neighboring villages under Vanuatu's strange condominium system had not vanished with the colonizers.

October 15th I sailed a rough, windward passage to Epi, and on the 18th made a last island hop to Havannah Harbour on the west side of Efate, the governmental seat. It was an overnight windward passage into the strong trades. The lee rail sank and seawater raced over the deck as *Southern Cross* charged, plowed, and pushed into the waves. Chunks of salt water flew at me, and I ducked, grinning and laughing. She heeled farther; I stood one foot on the cockpit sole and one on the seat, braced, racing through thick black air.

My eyes squinched closed against the stinging spray, a nonstop wall of warm water hurtling over the dodger. And I welcomed the thrill. I was not the same sailor who had ventured timidly down the coast of Mexico and across the South Pacific to New Zealand. As a sailor, I had come far.

Dawn came. The sea was still in the lee of Efate Island. I found the pass, anchored near a spit of beach, watched men working on shore, and slept.

Two days later I sailed around the bottom of Efate into Port Vila harbor and picked up a mooring in the midst of a few remaining cruising boats, happy to find *Champagne* among them. I was thankful to see the regatta crowd gone. With shops, supermarkets, and cafés a constant reminder of empty pockets, my spirits bounced up and down. I fought a growing sense of doom over finances and potential future problems from the closing of my business. There had been no further word from the TWT attorney since I answered the judge's request for current financial statements the year before. Was no news good news? How far would the IRS reach when I had nothing to give them? Could anything in my going sailing be construed as illegal? My imagination worked busily in a vacuum.

I took breakfast up to the cockpit—a cup of rich espresso, French pastries, and fresh pineapple. Behind *Southern Cross* rose Iririki Island, once the British Commissioner's residency, now an elegant resort with cascading gardens dropping to the water's edge and spreading perfume over the anchorage.

Across the channel, Port Vila climbed the hillside in terraces of whitewash and bougainvillea topped by palms rustling in the morning breeze. Colorful umbrellas dotted the shoreline, pinpointing sidewalk cafés. To the left, more umbrellas clustered under the trees marking the open-air market where island women, in gaily patterned Mother Hubbards with ribbons and lace, sold fresh vegetables, fruit, and buckets full of flowers.

The clear, deep channel showed gardens of a different variety . . . coral with blooms of colorful fish swaying back and forth. In thousands of miles, Port Vila was the prettiest harbor city I'd seen.

Despite all the beauty, a large black cloud of worry shadowed my days. It seemed as if TWT was going to follow me for the rest of my life. Demons lurked, waiting to jump me from behind, feeding my fear and building fantasy catastrophes every minute I wasn't busy with something physical and demanding. Sitting in a harbor left too much empty time.

Unable to stand the pressure, I called *Champagne*. "Could I come over for a chat?"

"Come on; the coffee's ready."

Kathy, Joe, and I had often chatted long hours about many things, but pride had kept the mess I'd left behind out of our conversations. Now they listened patiently to the long story of TWT and all my fears. When it was finished, to my great relief, they didn't look at me with shock or contempt. Instead, they said to bring over the papers; they would see how bad it really was.

Joe, a competent and compassionate attorney, and Kathy, a successful CFO, dove into my piles of messy documents, and each provided recommendations and insights to consider. For the first time in a long time, I saw a little sunlight around the edges of the black cloud my imagination had created. No one was going to handcuff and haul me away. They helped me separate reality from manufactured nightmares and gave me direction for addressing the real issues.

Much as I valued their professional advice, their acceptance meant even more. They were my closest friends, and even knowing everything they still cared.

Champagne made ready for a passage southeast to New Zealand while *Southern Cross* prepared to sail southwest to Nouméa, New Caledonia. The final week in Port Vila cleared the gloom.

Dear Kit,

I arrived with next to zero, and less than two weeks later I'm sailing away with fuel, ice, propane, food, water, and enough money in my pocket to enjoy Nouméa. The French Embassy here at Port Vila offered me an exhibition. They wanted it for a week, but I only had time for one day. It was in a big space that opened onto the main street. After getting permission from a group of tribal elders at the Department of Cultural Affairs, I posted notices around town. All kinds of people came— French and English expats, tourists, cruisers, and best of all the locals. They were curious to know about the trip—especially the women.

I sold almost every miniature on display. But more important than the money was the encouragement. Now I'm anxious to start on the big pieces from my sketches and photos of the last few months in the islands.

On to Nouméa . . .

XXXOOOXXX . . .

Pat

─────────── NOVEMBER 1991

Southern Cross sailed out of Port Vila, and one day later *Champagne* followed. We'd made a schedule for radio contact on the newly opened marine band frequency, 6516 kilohertz, which fell within the range of frequencies my radio could access and opened communication with non-ham sailing friends. *Champagne*, like an increasing number of cruisers, had opted for a single-sideband radio, which, though more expensive than ham, offered ease of use and the absence of an exam. A single-sideband license required only money and an application. On SSB arrangements could be made ahead for parts, travel, haulouts, and other business affairs—including prices and payment—all activities forbidden on ham.

During the night I had spoken with Mom, Tam, and Shawn by phone patch. Everyone was waiting for today's big event—Terri and Glenn's wedding.

Each detail would be perfect and nothing left to chance. Everything Terri had done since the age of two had demonstrated that quality. With the exception of one college beau, she had never gone out with anyone more than once. Her list of requirements in a man lived indelibly imprinted in her mind: if a guy didn't measure up on the first date, he never got another. I could only imagine what qualities my daughter might desire: stability, a commitment to family values, reliability, the desire and capacity to provide for a family, neatness, fitness, and intelligence. Even though I had not met Glenn, I knew he must possess the traits Terri valued most. She had picked her husband with great care, just as she had made every other decision in her thirty-one years.

When Glenn had proposed to Terri after a friendship of several years, she had accepted on the condition that they would complete their master's degrees and build a new home before beginning their life together. This day would celebrate the attainment of all three goals. The rest of the family would be there, but she had not invited me. I had no money for the flight but still needed to know she wished I were there. Perhaps my mother had felt a similar disappointment when I presented her with the accomplished fact of my marriage. Her feelings had not been on my mind when Robert and I drove away in the old maroon Buick—only my own desire to be married. It had never occurred to me then that sharing this milestone would mean so much to a mother.

Mom forwarded her invitation. The memento marked a precious step in Terri's life. I prayed that whatever her vision might be of a happy home and family, she would find it with Glenn.

Champagne turned back to Port Vila after encountering 21 knots on the nose en route to New Zealand. We might have been in different oceans instead of 150 miles apart. I settled in the cockpit with a bowl of homemade trail mix and Mary Gordon's *The Company of Women*.

At midnight, I passed between Ouvea and Lifou in the Loyalties, east of New Caledonia, and turned to parallel the coastline. A light morning breeze increased to 12 knots, and blue skies reflected off almost flat seas. I picked out a Dick Francis mystery and went back to reading. Life couldn't get much better than this.

After tuna fish sandwiches and papaya for lunch, I checked the horizon on my twenty-minute schedule and climbed back into Francis's world of horses and foul play.

"BLAHHHH!" The blast lifted me two feet off the seat, and I looked straight up at the bridge of a large freighter. My heart raced. How could I have screwed up that badly in broad daylight, and where had she come from? I had sailed close across her bow. A shiver crawled down my spine.

The crew waved a friendly greeting and I responded, chagrined. As she steamed north, the name of a Russian home port on her stern triggered, for a fleeting moment, irrational alarm rooted in a Midwestern Republican childhood during the years of bomb shelters and the McCarthy hearings. The prevailing attitudes of that era had been etched on my DNA, but those anonymous, threatening Russians we had been brought up to fear didn't match the smiling men waving hello from the freighter. They must have heard by now that the Soviet Union was falling apart. What would it mean for them, and for the world?

I sailed on, thanking the Russians and my angel both for watching over me, but my hopes of an early morning arrival at the pass dimmed as the night threw 16- to 20-knot winds on the nose. SC made poor headway through thick salt spray, plowing southeast another long day. By midnight she hovered outside the pass, waiting for dawn and a favorable tide.

The sailing directions with their written instructions and charts showing the route ahead lay on the table as I made notes for sailing through the pass, around the bottom of New Caledonia, and into Nouméa. The two charts had been a gift from another boat. Studying them for the first time, I discovered that neither had a compass rose. There was no way to plot bearings to lights, beacons, or other points of reference. I looked through charts from places where I had already been and cut out a rose to tape onto each one.

The highlights from the sailing directions jumped off the page: ". . . entrance is about 1¼ miles wide . . . sea will break at times in the entrance . . . giving the impression it is breaking on reefs . . . a string of shoals and dangers . . . parallel to the south of the route . . . a local magnetic anomaly . . . flood current sets SW, and the ebb NE . . . 3 to 5 knots . . . great care should be taken . . . where several wrecks have occurred."

I made detailed notes: Line up beacons and lights on Cap Ndoua at 259M and sail approximately 7.5 miles from the entry until the light on the northeast end of Reef Ioro bears 124M. Change course to 224M for 2.3 miles, and then sail 282M . . . and so on for forty miles of turns and passes to the marina in Nouméa. I gathered everything within reach: charts, glasses, pencils, binoculars, parallel rule, dividers, handheld compass, directions, food, and drinks. The depth sounder and knot log were on, and so was the SatNav, though its infrequent fixes would do nothing to help on a minute-by-minute basis.

Dawn crept up slowly. I finished breakfast and the dishes, and *Southern Cross* made her way toward the narrow pass. A freighter drew close from the southeast. I took bearings deciding if I could make it in before she arrived, or needed to wait and follow her.

Anxious to get through and begin the long trek I called, "To the ship approaching Havannah Pass on the southeast side of New Caledonia, this is the small sailing vessel, *Southern Cross*, just ahead of you. Please come in."

"This is Professor Rozhdestvenski, *Southern Cross*, go ahead."

"I just wanted to be sure you knew I was here in front of you and to find out if you'll pass me before I reach the entry," I said, with deference to the professor.

"There's no problem; we'll take care to pass you safely."

"Thank you very much. I'll go back to monitor 16. Have a safe arrival."

I returned to the cockpit to recheck my preparations, thinking how amazing it was that the Russians were sending out professors as ship's captains.

Southern Cross slipped easily through the entrance, and I began taking bearings and watching the instruments as the large freighter slowly approached. She passed a half-mile to port, and as her stern came into view the large block letters read, *Professor Rozhdestvenski*.

Wet green hills slowly turned to dry, grassy terrain as *SC* sailed west around Grande Terre, the largest of the islands in the most remote of the French Overseas Territories. Napoleon III had annexed the area in 1853 and filled it with convicts. Then, in the late 1800s, the discovery of rich mineral deposits brought a wave of Asian immigrants to work the mines. Now less than half the population of 200,000 were indigenous Melanesians. Pressure for independence had brought violence to New Caledonia in the 1980s, making life uncertain for the large European population. France responded with increased autonomy and kept their heavy subsidies flowing.

At sunset Ty and Helen from *Azura* welcomed me to Nouméa with a fresh loaf of French bread, flowers, wine, cheese, and a letter from Kitty they had found in Santo after I had left. We exchanged it for one addressed to them that I had picked up in Fiji—the cruisers' postal service picking up where others left off. A few days later *Champagne* pulled in, Kat and Joe having decided that a downwind sail to Australia made a better choice for the cyclone season than the rough beat to New Zealand.

Nouméa, the Paris of the South Pacific, coaxed me ashore with sidewalk cafes, clean colorful open markets, supermarkets with delectable little packages of European foods I'd never seen before, stores full of books in French, chic shops, and people from around the world, including the French who, unlike those I'd met when I lived in France in 1969, were surprisingly friendly. I strolled the streets looking for galleries that might be interested in a local series of miniatures. One day with my portfolio under my arm I wandered into Galerie Tangram. The owners asked if I were an artist. I hesitated, then answered "yes."

Dear Kit,

Thanks for your very welcome letter.

There's such exciting news to share— a solo show. Galerie Tangram has invited me to come back in late spring with twenty watercolors, prints, and miniatures. Kat's fluent French helped us work out the details. Sylvie and Jean Luis, the owners, have only a smattering of English.

They'll provide a reception, invitations, PR, posters, and take care of the framing. I'll repay them for the framing at the end of the show. This should comfortably see me to the Mediterranean.

They're so excited that Jean Luis spent a day driving us around to gather photos of the colonial architecture and colorful foliage. There are several bungalows already tugging at me to start painting. I have scenes from the main plaza with fountains and the band shell under flamboyants and palms, the old library compound of verandaed buildings in a garden, men playing boules, and flower sellers in the quayside market— all full of vibrant color and light. With the success in New Zealand I now have the confidence to know these will become paintings.

Congratulations on your grant and your new gallery associations— especially Santa Fe. Those lucky children will have the best art teacher in San Francisco. Thanks for your comments on my work. You're right—I need more contrast. I'm so afraid to try anything new, and therefore only make progress in baby steps.

Reading of your visit to Russell and the Blue Penguin made me teary-eyed. Will we ever be in the same part of the world at the same time again?

Peter, I'm anxious to see you in one of Whoopi's films. Are you still doing the hand-painted shirts and jewelry? The one you made for me always gets compliments.

In the morning I'm leaving for Australia—checking in at Bundaberg and moving south to Mooloolaba. As soon as I have an address I'll write.

All my love, dears,

Pat

SHIP'S DIARY: 19 November 1991, 0400 Zulu, 23°26'S/162°48'E, sailing 250M at 6 knots with a 15- to 20-knot SE wind and 3- to 4-foot seas from the SE, 5% cloud cover, and the bar is 1010, unchanged. Cyclone Tia is still heading south and expected to veer southeast.

During the night I had spoken with Mom, for details from Terri's wedding, and with *Gypsy Rover*, in the Solomon Islands, for news on Tia. The cyclone had destroyed a thousand homes in the Solomons, but the dozen foreign cruising boats had survived safely. I curled up to rest and finish *Mama Day*, wondering if the supernatural powers of Gloria Naylor's character could bring me closer to my daughter. With ships lurking below the horizon—I'd seen two the day before—I couldn't allow myself to sleep soundly again until port.

On the 24th a gentle, 6-knot breeze from the southeast pushed *Southern Cross* over bay water held flat by the shadow of Fraser Island off Australia's east coast. The final fifteen miles to Bundaberg made quite a contrast to the previous day's 145-mile sprint in six-foot following seas.

The port operators required advance notification from incoming boats, and I was finally close enough to reach the harbor office operator on emergency channel 16. We hunted for a channel we could both talk on—my old VHF lacked the frequency range of their modern duplex equipment. At last we connected, and she passed instructions: "Anchor north of the red sailboat and wait for the officials to come clear you in." In the distance the smokestacks and gray clouds of Bundaberg's distillery turned the late afternoon sun an intense melon pink.

At the end of a day, when arrival after dark in an unfamiliar harbor following days without sleep was unthinkable and staying out at sea was equally unthinkable, landfalls always seemed to edge out of reach. In fading dusk, I slipped between red and green entry lights into a tiny anchorage that was half mudflats at low tide. The gentle breeze had turned to late afternoon gusts near land, and strong currents eddying in from the river mouth outside the entry worked against the rudder. The assigned spot north of the red sailboat held an earlier arrival. As dusk turned to dark, I searched in the small, congested space for enough water to keep *Southern Cross* floating.

I spotted a familiar boat, *Paragon*, acquaintances from harbors across half a world—Mexico, the South Pacific, and now the eastern coast of Queensland; they waved a greeting as I anchored just north of and slightly behind them, anxious for dinner and bed. Dave called over, "Are you happy with that spot? It looks a bit close to the rocks." A tall, riprap shoreline hovered not far away. He was right. If my anchor failed, *SC* would be on the rocks in a minute or two. He volunteered to help me move.

For the second time in three years, I accepted help anchoring. Dave came aboard and brought up the hook, while I drove out of the tight little corner to search for a safer spot. No space felt quite right.

Near the entry, where the chain could stretch across the bottom to the opposite side and there was ample room all around, Dave deployed the anchor. I pulled back, setting it well into the muddy bottom. But then, from below, a voice called over the VHF, "You can't stay there. You're blocking the entrance."

There was no arguing with Australian authority. As the darkness thickened Dave brought up the anchor, and the search began again.

Far too close to the shallows, but in the only spot left, I called out, "OK, you can drop it now." Silence. I called again. Still nothing. On the foredeck, Dave struggled, mistakenly pushing the windlass handle forward with all his might instead of pulling back on it. Muscles bulged as he continued to tighten the brake that held the windlass closed. Now it no longer worked in either direction. Complete despair and the fatigue of a weeklong passage through busy waters descended on me as I circled in and out of the harbor, back and forth, and up and down the river. Dave couldn't release the windlass.

I called to the mysterious authorities who were watching from some hidden office. "Please, may I come to the dock? The windlass has broken, and I have no way to anchor."

"We'll have to call Customs for permission; stand by."

Hovering in total darkness, we worked on the windlass unsuccessfully and waited for the answer. Then clearance came to approach the dock at the small marina inside. With no one on duty to take lines or give directions, I chose an opening in front of a large powerboat on an outside pontoon. The marina owner ran down the dock, yelling at me to move immediately to his fuel dock. He pointed to a tight downwind corner just off the riprap, and I asked permission to walk over for a closer look before trying to land there. I needed to be prepared with lines and fenders in the right places. But as I moved to step off the boat, he screamed, "NO! Get outta here. You're gonna break my dock."

He pushed on *SC*'s stanchions, trying to force her away from the pontoon against a strong beam wind. The sound of breaking fiberglass crackled through my imagination as I begged him to stop. Dave advanced on him, fists raised. Words flew instead. I gave up and returned to the river, assessing the situation yet again. The simplest solution was suddenly obvious—pick up the chain from the windlass and let it out hand over hand. Once again we entered the elusive protection of Bundaberg Harbour, anchoring in the last spot we had tried before. Dave promised to return in the morning to fix the windlass brake, then made a fast retreat to *Paragon* with portions of forbidden fresh cake. Nothing was supposed to leave the boat before the quarantine officer's visit in the morning.

Friends who had stayed in Mooloolaba during cyclone season the year before had recommended the marina there for my five-month stop. All through the summer and fall my correspondence had included the Mooloolaba address, leaving me two choices for checking in—Brisbane and Bundaberg. Mooloolaba sat in the middle. Grapevine reports indicated that Brisbane was home to a training center for Customs and Immigration officers and that they were excessively thorough and rigid in their procedures. With Australia already rumored across the South Pacific to be the most stringent of all countries for arriving yachts, I had opted for Bundaberg.

While I was still in Nouméa my preparations for the quarantine officer had begun with a list of prohibited items from the Australian embassy. I had emptied lockers of grains, dairy foods, dried soups with bits of ham, popcorn, rice, couscous, canned meats from various countries, and on and on, giving much of it away. While crossing the Coral Sea I had eaten everything fresh and transferred the forbidden French powdered milk into New Zealand containers. I had made wild rice cake to finish the eggs and wild rice both. I had planned my meals by the embassy list instead of listening to my appetite.

Champagne, following two days behind *Southern Cross*, kept our early morning radio schedule the following day. Disliking tight, difficult anchorages, Joe changed course for Brisbane.

At 8:30 A.M., Officer Dunwell from Quarantine arrived—a large, cheery man, bland but friendly. He was also the regional agricultural officer and was arriving fresh from a farm visit in his Wellingtons. Despite my efforts to rid *SC* of restricted foods, Mr. Dunwell filled a large black bag with 25 kilos of it, including eight varieties of beans, one of the mainstays of my mostly vegetarian diet, which had not been on the magic list. He remarked, chuckling, "Anything that could sprout, ya know." And on the way out he grabbed the feather from Shane, my reminder of the beach in Santa Cruz where she and I strolled and shared secrets. Perhaps he thought some bugs had survived for three years on that feather.

While he filled his bag with forbidden groceries, he carried on with questions about my travels: Where had I been? How long was I at sea? Did anyone die or get sick? Did I visit any farms? In a country with agriculture as a major component of its GNP, I understood his concern and cooperated. Mr. Dunwell finished, and I took him back to shore.

A slim, blond, clipped officer in starched uniform, from Customs and Immigration, waited on the dock for a ride to *Southern Cross*. As we pulled up to the boat he saw Dave on the bow with WD-40 and a sledgehammer. The officer fumed, "You're both in trouble, ya know." To Dave he said, "There's a $1,000 fine for boarding a boat before it's been cleared."

Dave fired back, "Were you gonna come out last night and give her a hand? She needed some help with that wind and current and no place to anchor." I was dismayed to have such a bad start in a new country, and upset that a designated port of arrival would provide no place to put a boat while waiting for clearance at the end of a long passage.

Dave continued pounding on the windlass while we went below to complete the paperwork. The officer demanded a record of my passage showing the exact route between Nouméa and Bundaberg. I gave him my radio reports of daily positions and weather. Pages of questions later we arrived at the meat of the matter—the information I had hoped to breeze over. "How much money do ya have?" The answer was none. I had less than $100 to live on for six months, but I couldn't tell that to an Immigration Officer.

Expenses in Nouméa had been high—it was a French territory after all. Each letter arriving at the post office through *poste restante* (general delivery) had cost 58 cents to pick up—more than the cost of the stamp. Fuel, ice, water, food, three days on the dock, and film for paintings had all eaten into what I had brought from Vanuatu. Tamara had written that she was sending a $900 check to Mooloolaba. The gallery in Carmel, California, had finally sold the primitive carving of a Naga fertility goddess from India that had filled one corner of my bedroom in Santa Cruz. That money would have to stretch while I waited for checks from Dayle.

To get an Australian visa I had had to satisfy the Australian Embassy in Fiji that I was solvent and wouldn't become a burden or take a job. Having no credit cards or bank statements, I had taken instead a record of business with the Blue Penguin, showing regular monthly income. That had been enough in Fiji, and I hoped their decision would satisfy this obnoxious officer's concerns.

Trying to reassure him that I wouldn't be looking for a job in Australia, I mentioned the Nouméa exhibition in June, wondering even as I said it whether I was volunteering too much. Concluding his inquisition for the moment, he directed me to take *SC* up the river to Bundaberg Town in the next day or two and report to him with my cruising plans fully mapped out. Back at the dock one parting look said it all: "Don't do anything more that you're not allowed to do. You're not off my list yet."

Returning to *SC* I found a gift from the friendly quarantine-agriculture officer—a fresh cow turd on the clean cabin sole where he had stretched his legs under the table. I hadn't been to a farm; it had come to me.

Thanking Dave for fixing the windlass, I left to motor eight miles up the Burnett River. It meandered through the sugarcane fields that fed the distillery and past ferry crossings. Wide, flat, fertile plains opened out on either side of *Southern Cross* as she skirted shallows at every turn, until the town of Bundaberg came into view, stretched along the high left bank.

It was a small, pretty, walking town with the same nostalgic air as Russell, taking me back to the American Midwest of the 1950s. In a community art exhibit, ladies displaying their work recognized me as a "boatie" by my small backpack and extended a welcome. There were stores where I could fill my shopping list and replace some of the items removed by Quarantine. I passed the post office and other charming, well-kept old buildings in the center of town and a leafy, green park with an Olympic-size pool, bowling green, and croquet court overlooking the river. The streets had an air of grace despite the town's nondescript new additions.

Other cruisers from boats moored down the center of the river appeared in the shady park. The family of four from *Souza* were the latest to run afoul of the arrogant immigration officer. Hearing news of an elderly parent's illness at home in New Zealand, the husband had hurried to buy a plane ticket for an immediate return. Anticipating a trip back sometime during their stay, he had already initiated the appropriate steps to name his wife as captain in his absence. Our officer had just accosted him on the street, yelling, "You didn't have my permission to buy that ticket. You gotta come see me first."

The *Souza* folks were dumbfounded. Borders between the Southern Ocean neighbors were open for travel, work, and even "the dole." He had never considered needing permission to fly out of Australia for a visit home. "Further-more, yur wife can't be the captain of that vessel."

"But she owns half the boat and is fully qualified."

"No, I won't permit it. She couldn't take the boat out alone, so she can't be captain."

I shuddered, wondering what he might have in store for me after I allowed someone on board before being cleared. The following morning I approached the Immigration Office with trepidation. He browsed through the detailed itinerary: "Bundaberg to Mooloolaba via Sandy Strait with overnight stops as required for rest and sightseeing. Mooloolaba to Brisbane via Morton Bay with stops as required for rest. Departure from Brisbane for Nouméa, May 1992." When he handed the papers back he included a package of postcards, with instructions to mail one at each stop, so he could track my every move.

Then he delivered the blow: "By the way, don't think ya can sit in Australia on yur boat and make paintings for yur show in New Caledonia. That'll be a violation of yur immigration status."

I imagined spies looking in my portholes and laughed inside. This small, clipped man waving his threats at sailors who had weathered storms, fatigue, reefs, and large ships could never shake their core of confidence. He had touched the raw nerve of my financial insecurity and triggered a fear that he would seize *SC*, but I turned my back and walked away, more indignant than cowed.

Cutting short my plans for a leisurely visit in this otherwise pleasant harbor, I sailed south toward Mooloolaba, looking for a more welcoming atmosphere.

_____ DECEMBER 1991

A WEEK LATER, EIGHT ENGINES HUMMED IN THE COOL, early morning air behind Inskip Point at the bottom of the Great Sandy Strait, the narrow, shallow, 30-mile waterway running between the shifting sandy banks of Fraser Island and those of the Queensland coast. Mostly strangers, we were making the day's passage to Mooloolaba as a fleet.

Between us and the open sea lay Wide Bay Bar, an often treacherous piece of water—shallow, with strong currents and frequently huge, turbulent surf. Each boat had followed instructions to call the Air-Sea Station at Boonooroo for the current sea state over the bar. They had responded, "Cross at 0600, slack tide."

One by one our anchors hit the chocks and were secured. Gears were engaged, and we pulled out of the anchorage, turned right, and headed east-northeast. Bundled in a sweatshirt, I sipped my coffee and watched the leading marks behind to keep *SC* tracking on a path away from the rough shallows.

It took five miles to clear the shifting shoals and sandbars on the south side of the course. Then our mile-long line turned south in damp, still, pale watermelon air for the run to our next harbor. I carried the big radial-head drifter to the foredeck and ran the lines, preparing for the anticipated light-air downwind run.

Sails slowly climbed masts along the line. On *Southern Cross* the dousing sock slid to the top, and the drifter filled gently in the first rays of sun over the horizon. Others began adding headsails and spinnakers. Gradually the air came alive with colorful ballooning Dacron. One by one engines were turned off, and race spirit invaded the fleet.

I shed the sweatshirt and sailed in my public uniform—an old T-shirt and underwear—unconcerned with impressions. Three of us were clustered together, and the fever became intoxicating as I tweaked and adjusted, constantly measuring progress against my neighbors. I couldn't believe my behavior. I was not a racer—I had said that at least a hundred times—yet I was doing everything I could to win. Maybe I had done that so no one would expect anything of me. All my life I'd measured myself against others, but most of the time they had no idea. I wondered what that had done to my relationships. Gradually the wind increased, adding to the excitement.

By midafternoon we were closing on our destination, where ominous black clouds loomed over the low coastline. With the wind coming from behind, I failed to realize that the mass ahead was advancing toward the fleet.

Suddenly, the wind began to build. I raced to the bow, but the dousing sock refused to come down over the huge sail that was snapping back and forth, stitches straining. I tried one thing after another, finally turning *SC* into the wind to depower the sail. But instead she heeled far over and surged ahead. Yanking up my baggy old underwear from below decency one more time, I ran forward again. *SC* was in serious trouble, roaring back to New Caledonia following the runaway drifter.

I gave up and dumped the sail. The blue, white, and green cloud floated over the surface of the sea, and I began hauling it on board by hand. Bit by bit the fabric rose, then stopped. Filled with water, it was too heavy to lift. The sail had become a huge sea anchor tangled in the trailing fishing line. In the vanishing afternoon the storm continued to grow. I winched in the sail an inch at a time, adrenaline pumping. The fleet had passed out of sight. I hauled and lifted until sail and fishing line lay in a heap in the cockpit, started the engine, and set a course for the harbor entrance, steering by hand. The autopilot had stopped working again.

As the wind screamed I replayed the last hour, searching for mistakes I hoped not to repeat. I looked at the piles of bright green rope at my feet—the drifter sheets. It was suddenly obvious; I could have released the sheets to ease the power in that sail.

Outside Mooloolaba, rollers crashed against the breakwater below the ugly, black sky. A fishing boat stuck its bow out, crashing and bashing past the heavy surf, and a cold chill stirred as I anticipated the ride through the turbulent entrance and the things that could go wrong that close to shore. Shivering from the cold air as well as my fears, I ducked below to call the club for a slip assignment.

In minutes SC had passed unscathed into the protected water of the channel. I drove up and down the narrow harbor, adjusting the course and running from stern to bow to prepare docklines and fenders. All had to be ready before turning down the side channel to the slip where friends waited. Approaching the dock slowly against a strong, outgoing current, I tossed the starboard bow line, and a minute later Southern Cross rested alongside the dock. I stepped off, and the storm hit.

In a boatyard nearby, two boats blew off their hardstands in winds over 60 knots. I imagined the sea outside and felt a flood of relief to be safely tied to a dock.

Inside the clubhouse I joined the lively southbound fleet—the only woman singlehander of the day. Everyone wanted to know what had happened—when last seen I had been flying at full speed northeast across the Coral Sea. I recounted the details, including what I should have done. Then Peter Willowby—the only male singlehander of the day—told his story. He had suffered a bad jibe and had to cut his preventer, the line restraining the sail from flying across to the other side of the boat. We toasted our safe arrivals with a fresh round of beers.

Peter moved next to me, and sparks jumped back and forth. He was a commercial artist my age, had rebuilt his boat, and had sailed solo along the Australian coast for the last six months. A long-distance cruise was next. Over the following week a budding romance kindled. We moved up the river where we could anchor for free, and it became our little haven. Seldom apart, we cooked on his boat or mine, ran errands together, sketched, talked into the night, then shared tender lovemaking and drifted to sleep on *Southern Cross*.

Our time together had the qualities of a vacation romance: no one expected us to show up for work or meet a deadline, so our days were filled with each other; we were surrounded by strangers who encouraged the happy glow of blossoming affection; and there was an end in sight. One day soon he would sail home to Sydney.

After eighteen months happily alone, I needed time and space to consider if I wanted it to be more than that. I liked Peter, but I wasn't in love with him . . . at least not yet. I enjoyed our conversations, the things we did together, and the physical closeness, but I wasn't ready to make any commitment, nor was I ready to give up my independence and time spent alone.

We promised to keep in touch and to explore the idea of cruising together with both boats. Perhaps with two boats, I thought, it might work. Finally I watched *Fruition* sail out of the harbor. The anchorage seemed too large and *Southern Cross* too empty without him. I had enjoyed the contentment of sharing my days with someone I liked, and I looked forward to his promised letters.

My arriving mail at the Mooloolaba post office included the $900 cashier's check, but the bank wouldn't cash it. Even if I opened an account it would take six weeks to clear. I fought tears of frustration, walking back through the sandy holiday town. T-shirt shops, pubs, and fish-and-chips signs greeted me along the streets. There were lots of ways to spend money but no way to earn it—no shops to market my miniatures and nothing interesting to paint.

Behind a long beachfront, the bland new West Palm Beach–style architecture and a canal community of expensive homes offered nothing beyond the flitting, colorful wild parrots to capture my imagination. Mooloolaba must have looked very different through my friends' eyes the year before.

Elke, my neighbor in the marina the week before, offered to deposit the check in her account and make me a loan while it cleared. We had exchanged only a few dozen words—I was touched and grateful for her generosity.

Champagne called from Brisbane to report the attractions of the city and its setting. "Come down for Christmas. We have holiday plans with *Fram* and *Northmoor*. There are wonderful scenes here for your miniatures."

"I'll do it! There's nothing but incoming mail holding me here. I'll see you in a week or so."

I sailed 14 miles up the winding river from Morton Bay to Brisbane at sunset. Story Bridge twinkled with tiny fairy lights as I passed under it, and around the bend a recently resurrected city center lined the waterfront. A graceful esplanade fronted handsome new high-rises that stood side by side with revitalized turn-of-the-century buildings; where these gave way to the Botanical Gardens, foreign boats moored on pilings bow-to-stern. More bridges twinkled around the next bend, and across the river dancers swayed, weaving their long, uplit shadows on the red sandstone cliffs.

Invitations flew for the lighted boat parade down the river, Christmas Eve caroling, Christmas morning gifts and breakfast on board *Fram*, and dinner at *Northmoor*. I looked up and down the river at familiar shapes and names: *Azura*, *Real Time*, *Kanaka*, *Souza*, and *Rose Rambler of Devon* with Rosie and Peter on board. Coming here had been a good decision; while spending the five-month cyclone season preparing for the show in Nouméa I would be surrounded by friends and a beautiful setting.

Peter wrote, inviting me to Sydney, but I had no money for travel and needed every minute to paint for the show. Slowly, distance overtook the sparks, and I put away the photos of the man with friendly blue eyes, a nice smile, and a sailing heart. If he had lived nearby, perhaps it would have turned out differently.

Each week Elke sold T-shirts at the Sunday open-air market that stretched for blocks along the waterfront. She brought my mail from the Mooloolaba post office, and I met her with cappuccinos to sip while we exchanged news and the mail. One day a letter with Dan's familiar writing sizzled on top of the latest stack as I threaded my way between booths of fresh herbs, home-made breads and pastries, pottery, dolls, clothing, crafts, and fresh produce. Back on board I eagerly sliced open the envelope: "Call collect as soon as possible. I have something to tell you."

I called. "Things are not very good here. Not in the office and not at home. I want to see you. I want to come soon—maybe Brisbane, or maybe later. Where will you go next? I've sent a package with a long letter explaining everything." Day after day and week after week I hounded the post office employees, searching for his package and letter. It never arrived. We talked every few weeks and settled on Bali for a rendezvous. My heart smiled all summer, through the long, hot, wet Brisbane days, in anticipation.

Libby came to Brisbane for a holiday, starting with a week on board *SC*. Her recovery had gone well, and she looked great. She went for beauty treatments while I painted, then we met for coffee each afternoon at 5:00 and visited and laughed through the evenings, going to movies or listening to street musicians. She had invited her on-again/off-again romantic interest for a week at a nearby hotel, then three nights at an exclusive resort on the coast. She rented a car, and I hoped she would ask me to join them for a day to see the surrounding countryside, or go to the store, or run an errand. But she did not.

I painted, printed, and sold miniatures to the museum and gift shops along the central mall, and the mail brought gifts of money from family members and checks from the Blue Penguin. Dayle had made my last payment for the new sail, and it also had arrived.

Through it all, paint sang across the paper while arias played from the radio. I dreamed watercolor scenes by night and painted them by day. Jean Luis and Sylvie, owners of Galerie Tangram, wrote to say they would be in New Zealand when the prints were finished. The printer agreed to hold the package for them to hand-carry to New Caledonia. They could start framing before I arrived. It appeared that every detail was under control as I prepared to sail east.

Over the months since Terri's wedding I had waited for a letter from her—something that would tell me she was happy. I was interested in their plans for the future, how she felt about the wedding and about being married—I wanted to know anything at all. She hadn't sent me a letter since August, or a photograph of her wedding dress. At last, in April, three beautiful, small wedding pictures arrived. Everything had been perfect.

The dinghy now limped to shore, gasping for revival and looking a lot like the dinghy with the strange black bubble that had given me a lift to shore in Nuku Hiva. Jim on *Nepenthe*, who had followed the saga from the beginning, insisted I write the manufacturer again. I shot photos from bow to stern showing the yellow patches and the gooey, black repair sealant Jim had found at a local chandlery. The manufacturer offered a $300 settlement, and I accepted.

Mornings I found myself unconsciously warming my wrist and thumb against my coffee mug, letting the heat soothe the joint. The long hours of painting and boat work were causing arthritis. Picking up a sheet of paper, sewing sails, and writing were no longer possible without sharp, needle-like pains. I tried not to think about it.

The cruisers organized a chart exchange, photocopying the best charts from each boat for all the other boats going the same way. For eighteen boats we copied 900 charts. At $1.80 per chart instead of $15 for the originals, we saved $11,900. Groups gathered, headed for the Red Sea or the Cape of Good Hope, to Indonesia or the South Pacific islands. Those who had already been somewhere gave advice and shared experiences with the ones who were on their way.

Somewhere in those interchanges I heard my first warnings of **THE TÉHUANTEPEC**—a name always spoken in boldface and all caps. It is a gulf on the Mexican west coast below Acapulco, near the Guatemalan border, and the culmination of my trip. The advice started with: "You either go 500 feet from shore or 500 miles; anything in between is impossible."

"Hurricane-force winds come right out of a clear blue sky. There's no way to see it coming. It can whip the seas to 20-foot breaking waves just two miles offshore."

The Téhuantepec went on the back-burner perpetual-worry list while I prepared for departure on the last bit of money left after paying for prints and living expenses. Fuel, filters, gas, oil, charts, and a string of small repairs and spares had wiped out every reserve, even after a loan from *Azura*.

Carolyn Moloney, a Brisbane friend I had met shortly after arrival, invited me out to dinner and offered to stop at a supermarket on the way home so I could shop for provisions. I fidgeted through our soups and salads, knowing when we got to the store she would see I only had $20. As we downed chocolate cake and coffee she announced that she and her husband, Des, wanted a painting of their home. With her deposit of $150 we flew down the aisles of cans, bottles, and packages, filling the cart with ingredients for culinary delights.

Two days later Ty and Helen from *Azura* joined me on *Southern Cross* to help with line handling at the fuel dock. We waved good-bye, promising to meet in Bali in September. *Southern Cross* and I were leaving a city that had made a perfect cyclone-season stop with museums, art theaters, galleries, coffee houses, Mrs. Field's Cookies, friendly locals, and an anchorage full of cruising friends. In the last days of my stay some had offered help in unexpected ways—like Peter from *Rose Rambler*, who had searched the city by bicycle looking for engine spares, and the crew of *Pou Sto*, who had brought a basketful of provisions. I had looked at that basket for two days, unable to accept that I was so poor people wanted to give me food. Finally pride won out over concern for their feelings, and I took it back, saying, "Something came up; I won't be needing this. But thank you very much." As I sailed across Morton Bay heading north to the entry I wondered where Peter was; if he would go cruising someday; and if he would remember the day we raced down the Australian coast.

SHIP'S DIARY: 10 May 1992, 0325 Zulu, 26°10'S/156°01'E, sailing 110M at 3 knots with wind ENE at 6 knots, seas ENE 3 foot, cloud cover 100%, bar 1012 mb, down 5.

By the morning of the 12th I had sailed only 350 miles in five days. The solid mass overhead and steel-gray sea below didn't look promising after a night with no wind. A small breeze blew across the back of my neck, ruffling my hair. It was welcome even if it came from where I wanted to go—northeast—and was not strong enough to push *SC* through the three-foot sloppy seas. At least I was going somewhere.

I checked the set of the mainsail and stepped down from the cabintop. My eyes riveted on a snaking wire backstay sagging first to starboard and then to port, as one of its two lower legs flew through the air. The U-bolt anchoring it to the hull had sheared off inside the caprail; there was no spare, and without the backstay's support I risked losing the mast. I dropped the sails, and *SC* wallowed in the sloppy seas with no direction and no driving force.

After scouring the boat for hardware, I stole a U-bolt from the life raft tie-downs and perched on the two-inch edge of the cockpit coaming with my tether around the boom. *SC* rolled first one way, throwing me forward across the open cockpit, then the other, suspending me over the sea. Between rolls, I worked two large screwdrivers against each other a quarter-inch at a time, loosening the turnbuckle nearly seven feet above the deck where the two lower legs joined the single section that ran from there to the top of the mast, then installed the bolt through the caprail and retensioned the stay while perched once more on the precarious coaming. By the next afternoon *SC* was under sail again, and I willed her to hurry forward.

SHIP'S DIARY: 14 May 1992, 0700 Local, 25°25'S/158°00'E, sailing 50M at 2.5 knots in 5-knot westerlies with NW seas at 2 feet, topped by westerly seas at 2 feet and northerlies at another 2 feet—the remains of yesterday's near gale. Cloud cover is 80% and the bar is 1016, up 6 mb from last night.

This same journey in November in the opposite direction had taken eight days. Now, in seven, I had not even covered half that distance. By turns I worried about what waited in Nouméa and looked forward to it. Jean Luis, Sylvie, and I had not set a specific date for the show, but mid-May was the time frame we discussed. I dreamed of a welcoming committee at the dock and someone from a local salon inviting me for a massage, a much-needed haircut, and a facial. In the next fantasy the critics were panning the show in their reviews.

Every penny I had was invested in prints and getting to Nouméa. The miles went by with unbearable slowness while I worried that they might open the show without me. I wandered north, unable to overcome the strong current in the light winds. On the twelfth day, I reached *Souza* in Nouméa and asked them to tell the gallery I was on my way and to find out when the opening was scheduled.

Souza called back the next morning. "No arrangements have been made and no date set. They couldn't pick up the prints from your printer; he hasn't made them. The originals were never released by Customs in Auckland."

My fantasies drifted off, and in their place worry settled down beside me as *Southern Cross* plowed on under overcast skies in short, choppy seas and light headwinds on her thirteenth day at sea with three more to go.

———————— JULY 1992

NEARLY TWO MONTHS LATER, ON MY WAY TO CHECK out of Nouméa, I gathered papers for the port officials and a letter to Kitty reporting on my first solo exhibition. No one had been waiting on the dock. I had walked to the gallery and begun seven weeks in a maelstrom of preparations for the show and for another passage.

Dear Kitty,

The show is behind me. What an experience!

Given the detailed arrangements made last November, I had expected that everything would be ready when I arrived on May 23rd. I thought I would only have to find something to wear from one of the lockers and get a haircut.

But instead I found Gallerie Tangram's enthusiasm had melted, their commitment had vanished, and our agreements had dissolved. It took more than two weeks to get the art released from Customs once it arrived from New Zealand. The show was open for a week before the prints were finally available. Framing diminished to gallery clips. The promised invitations, posters, and reception all became my responsibility.

Francine from *Baron Rouge* served as my interpreter but wound up holding me together. I fought tears as one by one the responsibilities and expenses landed on my shoulders. It looked impossible. As we walked out the door, Francine put her arms around me and promised that the show would happen; my cruising friends would see to it.

And they did. Francine, Nancy on *Windborne*, and Ginny on *Eagle* stepped in with loans and help. They said to leave the reception to them. "This is your night; relax and have fun." The day I sailed into Nouméa, Nancy, Ginny, and I had never met before.

I did get a much-needed haircut on the morning of the opening, but not free as I had fantasized. The price list in the window showed $3 for a shampoo and $15 for a cut.

When my chubby little stylist finished, her calculator indicated I owed $35. In disbelief, I pointed to the list in the window. Then the tall, skinny blonde owner, dressed in a flashy black outfit with shiny tights and elaborate jewelry, joined the high-speed French discussion. A heavy-set woman entered at that moment and said she would translate. At last, she explained that they were charging $17 for combing my 2-inch-long hair! It was in the small print on the bottom of the price list. We compromised at $30, the last of my money.

As I left, the translator remarked that the blonde owner's husband died "next" week. She wasn't slowly poisoning him as I imagined; he had been shot in the head, gang-style the week before, and the assassin had jumped on a plane for Tahiti.

There was no media for the opening—both newspapers and TV were on strike until the day of the show. But the turnout was the gallery's largest ever and included dignitaries who had never been to Tangram before. I smiled, greeted, and prayed that enough pieces would sell to keep me going.

I have learned a few things—like "get it in writing." But the best lessons were about friendship. It would have been impossible without Francine, Ginny, and Nancy. I realize now that I gave them something too—the fun of being involved in making the evening a success.

People admired the light, the color, and the intricate details in my paintings. Some pieces please me very much, some are okay, and others I don't like at all. Overall they're pretty mementos of beautiful places but lack content.

While sales were only $1,800, they covered expenses, the gallery's share, and the loans. I'll leave with $100 after getting *SC* ready to go—far from my visions of money for the next year and stacks of new boat gear. A GPS navigation system (like they used in Desert Storm) had been at the top of my list. My folks gave it to me for the treacherous passage through the Torres Strait above Australia.

The parting comment from Jean Louis and Sylvie was: "This was the most organized show we've ever had." It may have been a mistake, but I let them keep 6 originals and 65 prints, hoping they would have additional sales. If the pieces don't sell, they have to return them or pay the duty.

Much love and many hugs to you and Peter, too,

Pat

SHIP'S DIARY: 14 July 1992, 1400 Local, 16°10'S/154°48'E, sailing at 6 knots on a 295M course, wind SE 18–25 knots, seas SE 9–12 feet, cloud cover 100%, the bar is 1013—unchanged. Noon to noon—144 miles.

Eight days out of Nouméa, *SC* and I rode the edge between fear and fun, shooting down hissing ten-foot wave fronts. More frequently now I relied on the autopilot to do my steering in heavy offwind conditions, but using the ham radio at the same time frequently caused electrical interference with the pilot's internal compass, which resulted in a change of course. I switched from autopilot to wind vane for the ham net check-in. As my foot touched the cabin sole, *Southern Cross* lurched to starboard in a jibe, and a crash like a howitzer sounded above. The voice on the radio called again, "KM6DR, Kilo Mike 6 Delta Romeo, come in, please," but I was racing to the deck. I froze as *SC* skidded down a twelve-foot sea. The jibe had snapped the boom in the middle. I knew I should already have reefed.

I went below to answer the radio call with a report. Net control responded asking, "What are your plans?"

Darwin was sixteen days away, and Dayle was scheduled to meet me there August 4th with new prints to sign and money from recent sales at the Blue Penguin. Even if I diverted to a closer port, $100 couldn't pay port fees, buy fuel, and make any substantial repair. "I'll continue as planned and attempt a repair at sea."

I cleared debris from the deck and waited for the weather to improve. The wind increased to over 35 knots, and the seas went up to 16 feet, then increased again. I reduced sail until only the storm staysail remained, leaving me little control over my course. When the bow of a large ship bore down on me, I called, waited, and heard no reply; gradually she turned to starboard. The next morning looked the same, but by afternoon the wind was back to 25 and seas were only 12 feet.

As the wind eased, without the mainsail, *SC*'s daily mileage fell to 82 and then to 65. I made aluminum splints from scraps I found in the bilge, reinforced the concave grooves on the sides of the boom with a broom handle, and fiberglassed a bandage over the break.

With the yankee up and poled out to port, I raised the staysail, sheeted it to the end of the boom to starboard, and by the following noon, sailing wing-and-wing, had made 120 miles.

The halfway point came on July 20th, two hundred miles south of the coast of Papua New Guinea and two days before the Torres Strait. This narrow link from the Indian Ocean handled most of the traffic between the South Pacific and Africa, Europe via the Suez, the Middle East, and Southeast Asia, mandating a 24-hour watch on channel 16 for all vessels. The channels and few open areas were edged with reefs and small islands and scoured by six-knot currents and 20-foot tides. It would take two days to transit, with no opportunity to sleep.

I hit Bligh Entrance at midnight on July 22nd and Bramble Cay, the powerful lighthouse that points the way to the eastern end of the passage, at 0500. When ten-minute catnaps no longer sufficed, in one of the few clear areas away from the shipping lanes, I stretched out below. Soon the drone of a small, low-flying plane and a squawk from the radio stirred me: "White sloop, white sloop, calling the white sloop." *SC* was a cream-colored cutter. Relieved, I shut my eyes again.

The plane buzzed lower and called again. An Australian voice answered my response on the VHF, demanding to know where I was coming from, when I had departed, where I was going, how many people were on board, our nationalities, my home port, and on and on. The flight was part of a daily coastal surveillance that began at the bottom of the Great Barrier Reef, carried around the northern Australian coast, and extended partway down the western side. It included a radio interview and photos of each vessel encountered. Australian officials were worried about Indonesian infringement of fishing areas and illegal entry to Australia as well as smuggling. The plane flew away, and I gave up the nap.

I brushed by reefs off Dove Islet and Twin Island, holding my breath and willing inches to come between *SC* and disaster. Imaginary radio talk shows played through my exhaustion, and I repeatedly turned the watch over to an invisible partner. At the end of the second day a freighter passed a half-mile away, her stern lights vanishing as dusk turned to night. She would have required five to ten miles to stop and almost as far to execute a turn to avoid a collision.

My eyelids hung, each lash a lead weight. Brain waves tangled in the masses of cotton balls filling my head. With ships coming and going, I fought to stay awake just a little longer. At 2125—two miles past Booby Island, three miles out of all the traffic lanes, and past my physical limit—I gave up.

The sun rose, piercing the cloud cover, as *SC* drifted across the Gulf of Carpentaria heading west, five miles south of shipping traffic. I would never know how close those nearly silent steel beasts might have come in the night.

SHIP'S DIARY: 24 July 1992, 1300 Local, 10°46'S/140°51'E, sailing 4.5 knots at 262M in SE winds at 10 knots and 2-foot SE seas, cloud cover 90% and the bar at 1010, down 1 mb. I've entered "The East."

I took my pasta dinner and a glass of red wine to the cockpit. Gone were the deep cobalt blues, seas washed with a tinge of purple, the sky vivid and rich with cherry-red sunsets edged in gold and orange. The panorama here came from an ancient Oriental book with delicate brush paintings between verses of poetry. Creamy turquoise water lapped at a pale melon setting sun with warm blushes glowing in the sky above, hazy and wispy. Soft and mysterious.

In Brisbane I had made arrangements with an Indonesian agent for a group rate on eleven cruising permits at $160 each instead of the usual $200 fee. Our permits granted two months in Indonesia, beginning on the date we predicted we would arrive instead of the date we pulled into port. Mine said August 1—already impossible—and I still had to take the boat out of the water, paint the bottom, and prepare for the passage to Bali and on to Singapore.

The project list grew: Repair every sail but the new main. Reweld the broken bow rail mountings. Repair the autopilot mounting bracket. Replace the autopilot—the motor in the old one was sounding a death rattle. Before the show in Nouméa, Jan on *Eldevik* had insisted I try their backup for this passage. If it worked I could buy it. With no money at the end of the show, I had put it away.

By noon on July 30th I was passing Elliot Point, heading toward the quarantine anchorage on the west side of Darwin. I had made it from New Caledonia, as predicted, in exactly twenty-four days, despite the broken boom. The harbormaster instructed me to anchor just past the cattle carrier and wait for the officer to board.

Mr. P. J. Blackadder arrived and packed his black plastic bag with 18 kilos of forbidden food. On the way out he spied poppy seeds in the spice rack and said, "I'll have those, too," for a bit of *déjà vu.*

Word spread quickly through the Fannie Bay anchorage on the east side of Darwin—a singlehanding woman . . . broken boom . . . an artist. David Fiddler, a local news anchor, arranged an interview for the evening news. The news team spent an hour filming *Southern Cross* and visiting with me. I watched the show at the Darwin Sailing Club. As the "hard" news ended, the announcer introduced the segment, saying something about a woman sailing "in abject poverty." I was too stunned to hear the rest of the 30-second clip. The woman who had done the interview sat at the next table. "Why did you say that?" I asked her. It had been her response to my story about arriving in Tahiti with $3.

For all the financial difficulties along the way, I had felt impoverished only once—in New Zealand, when I was poor in spirit as well as money. In Tahiti and at other "tight" junctures, I had believed the circumstances were uncomfortable but temporary. If I had asked Miriam, in Vanuatu, "Do you live in 'abject poverty' in your handmade hut on Uri Island?," I think she would have said "no" for the same reasons I would. She had food to eat, a shelter of her own, and people who cared for her nearby. And for me each day there were things I enjoyed waiting to be done. Abject poverty is a black, hopeless hole.

Dayle arrived, pale and exhausted. The Blue Penguin was becoming too difficult for her as myalgic encephalomyelitis (ME) manifested in extreme fatigue and numerous allergies. At times her elderly father had to carry her to the apartment above their home. We parted at the end of the week with plans to meet again in the Mediterranean.

There was nothing in the mail from Tangram, but with money Dayle brought from sales at the Blue Penguin, the final payment from Des and Carolyn for the painting they'd commissioned, the $300 manufacturer's refund on the dinghy, and proceeds from a one-day show in Darwin, there was enough to refit *Southern Cross.* A builder of aluminum boats offered to weld the boom and the broken bow rail in exchange for a set of Bay of Island miniatures that showed his brother's store. Jan, on *Eldevik,* traded the autopilot for a painting of the cathedral in Neiafu. One by one, jobs disappeared.

Taking advantage of Darwin's 21-foot tides, I ran *SC* ashore on a grid at the beach to check, clean, and paint the bottom. The cost was far less than a haulout, though it meant racing to complete the work between tides. When the first tide receded it exposed hundreds of tiny blisters swelling under the old bottom paint. I panicked. It could mean months of stripping, drying out, and resealing the hull—time and money I didn't have.

Before leaving Santa Cruz four years earlier, I had applied a preventive multilayered epoxy barrier coat to *SC*'s bottom, hoping to avoid the problem of fiberglass blisters that boats built after 1973 often encountered, especially in the warm waters of the tropics. Dismayed but resigned, I slapped on the last of the fresh bottom paint as the second day's final low tide turned; the blisters would have to wait until the next haulout. The following day another cruiser said his boat had also developed tiny blisters after using the same barrier coat product I had used, but they were all between the gelcoat and the barrier coat—not in the hull itself. I comforted myself with that possibility.

From a circle of all-women boats—*Tethys, Cacique,* and *Southern Cross*—I joined Nancy, Patti, Sue, Rona, and Jacque for an evening with the Women's Embassy of Darwin. The organization invited me to speak. As I told them about my voyage and its genesis, the words flowed on their own. At the end a line of young girls waited for autographs with new dreams kindled. I hoped that sometime in the future, when life was especially challenging, they would remember my words: that a crisis had provided the impetus for my trip, that I had found a way to solve the problems along my path by believing I could, that they must never give up their dreams.

Tethys was heading around the bottom of Sumatra for Sri Lanka and the Red Sea. Rona and I were singlehanding to Bali, and Jacque was flying down the Queensland coast, returning to her naturopathy practice. Before leaving, she came to examine my hands—the pain of arthritis had become so acute that I bound each arm to a rolled-up magazine at night in order to sleep.

Jacque prescribed changes in diet—teas and juices—and a new way to look at the source of the pain. "Your own ideas and attitudes are killing you. You're trying to 'hang on.' It's time to let go." Her words brought an image to mind: As I had struggled with financial insecurity I grasped hold of everything in desperation—money, bits and pieces of boat gear, precious minutes, and even scraps of useless paper. I resolved to try her advice. I had what I needed each day; the trick was to accept and enjoy that. A change in viewpoint had healed my back; perhaps it could do the same for my hands.

THERE WERE DESTINATIONS AROUND THE WORLD THAT hung like ripe plums, pulling me forward even when things were grayest. Bali was one of those places. A friend in Nouméa, who had lived in Bali for several years, described the best way to see the island: walk across the rice fields to a village, arrive as a simple foot traveler without fanfare, and ask if there is a home where you can stay. Experience the island at that level, and you will know it.

The natural allure of Bali was heightened by nine months waiting in anticipation for Dan's planned visit. As I sailed out of Darwin on August 26th, thirty-five days remained on my Indonesian cruising permit from the original two months allowed.

SHIP'S DIARY: 28 August 1992, 1200 Local, 12°07′S/128°17′E, Timor Sea, sailing at 1.5–2 knots, steering 265M, wind N 2–4 knots, seas NE 1.5 feet, 30% cloud cover, bar 1008. In 4 hours made 6.5 miles. Noon to noon—58.

Every cruising boat up to 600 miles west of Darwin reported "no wind." Surrounded by pale, creamy aquamarine water and a sunset of muted pink, peach, and lavender, I fantasized how 10 knots of wind would feel against bare skin. These nights came from an Illinois childhood summer—before air-conditioning—when my bed felt like a puddle of warm water. By 1000 the deck was hot enough to cook breakfast.

Under the shelter of the green-and-white striped sunshade, I watched yellow-and-black banded deadly sea snakes, lavender, peach, and pale blue jellyfish, and small orange crabs drift by. Only the small, wiggly line following *SC* gave the impression of forward motion.

SHIP'S DIARY: 31 August 1992, 0830 Local. Only made 6 miles all night—the wrong way—south. Motoring now.

I thought about Dan's impending visit and wondered if he would like to hike across rice paddies, seeking a place to stay in a village, or would he prefer the Hyatt? To me his life seemed so narrow—only concerned with home and office. Could I still sit in rapt awe at his every word, having seen the world for myself? Would he still find that quality in me that drew us together in the beginning?

September 1st, in the evening, the wind arrived, and the new weld on the boom opened. Only the pop rivets between the lower track and the sleeve held it together now.

SHIP'S DIARY: 2 September 1992, 1200 Local, 11°48'S/124°02'E, sailing at 5–5.5 knots, steering 265M, wind south 8 knots, sea SW 1.5–3 feet, 90% cloud cover and the bar is 1010. Noon to noon, 80 miles. I should be less than a day from Bali, but instead I'm only halfway.

On the 5th the island of Sumba rose to starboard, pale magenta in a clear rose sunrise sky. Three hundred miles to Bali.

Fellow cruisers, friends, and family had all asked about piracy. "Aren't you worried? You do have a gun, don't you?"

"I'll just invite them on for coffee," I had answered. "There're no weapons on *SC*, and I don't know how to use one anyway. I'm not sure I could pull the trigger on another human being."

Australian authorities had issued reports and warnings. They were seizing Indonesian fishing vessels for infringing on territorial waters, and retaliatory attacks on sailboats sometimes followed—not true piracy, but still frightening. Later my route would take me through one of the world's most pirate-infested passages—up the Strait of Malacca north of Singapore. From here to the Mediterranean, I would view any approaching vessel with suspicion.

That evening a fishing boat crossed a few miles ahead and turned to parallel my course. As she drew near I hid the binoculars and GPS, started the engine, and took off at 6 knots. She slowly changed course toward me. My heart raced. She fell off, came back again, then trailed one mile away. After two hours she left. Perhaps they were only curious, but finding a woman alone might have provided an irresistible opportunity.

SHIP'S DIARY: 8 September 1992, anchor down 0900. The harbor is crowded and shallow.

Careened Taiwanese fishing boats, looking like old shoes with the soles curled up at the toe, covered a large mud bank in the middle of Benoa Harbour, on the southeast end of Bali. I imagined the Old Lady and all her Children emerging from the rakishly canted tall, skinny cabin on the stern, just like the nursery rhyme, and shooing the fishermen off the deck.

Three weeks remained on the permit when I checked in with the harbormaster, quarantine officials, customs, the navy, and finally immigration, filling in mountains of forms while swearing that no one had died en route and I didn't have any monkeys on board.

I boarded a small, seat-stuffed *bemo*, an overloaded van that served as a bus, to look for the post office in the city of Denpasar. We rocketed down congested roads past fields, construction sites, motorbikes carrying entire families, and a bicycle piled six feet high with thatch—all but the legs of the rider hidden. Traffic squeezed and tangled over six-lane roads and into two-lane streets as uniformed police controlled its flow and pedestrians dashed through cracks in the wall of cars, trucks, buses, and motorcycles. No check and no letter from Nouméa awaited me.

The phone office produced equally disappointing results. Dan would not be coming to Bali. There were problems at the office. He could come, but it wouldn't look good in the midst of cutbacks and layoffs to leave for a vacation. He sounded relieved as I muttered compassionate platitudes, when what I longed to say was, "What about us? I've been looking forward to this visit since January."

"Maybe Singapore," we said, and hung up. Letting nine months of anticipation go, I wondered again what propelled him to the office every morning and kept him there late every night. His voice no longer carried enthusiasm for what he was doing. The passionate young man who had captured my heart had vanished under a pile of irritations and conflict that had little to do with the music of architecture. He never talked with excitement about new projects, about a breakthrough, about how it felt to know he had solved a problem or produced something of beauty. His reports were only of lawsuits, difficult employees, unreliable workers, and clients who wanted to take advantage of him. What would it take to let the Dan I thought I knew emerge once more? I still wanted to believe in the old dream that someday we would work together. But I knew I couldn't endure the environment he described in his office, and I wasn't sure I could replace it with something better.

The weld in the boom had failed because the loose-fitting round sleeve installed in Darwin allowed play between the two parts. In Bali, the land of teak carvers, I hoped to find someone to shape a teak plug matching the complex curves of the boom. Bali Yacht Services found just such an artisan, but his estimate for the job was over $240. Exquisite, intricate statues the same size sold for less than $100. I reassembled the old parts with two new 6-inch bolts from *Baron Rouge*, and replaced the broom handle with aluminum tubing for a few dollars.

In the Denpasar market I searched the narrow, dark aisles, shopping for provisions and fresh produce in suffocating, dense air. Beggars pulled on my arms and reached for my change from the stallkeepers. Jim on *Nepenthe* arrived, anxious for an update on the dinghy, and invited me for a private tour to Lake Batur. After visiting temples and artists' villages we stopped for lunch at the lake. Forty hands shoved through the open windows of our minivan with merchandise or open palms.

In the early 1970s, Bali's rural villages leapt from the seventeenth century into the jet age with the construction of an international airport. Western dollars and investment brought income to a neglected Hindu island buried in a jealous Muslim country, but also changed a spiritually centered, giving society forever.

Dear Kitty,

No money from Nouméa yet, but I'm still hopeful it will be waiting in Singapore. The cutoff date for the gallery comes October 1st—return the work or pay the duty.

I had a three-day show at the Nusa Dua Hyatt in an exclusive resort area at the south tip of Bali. With 700 rooms fully booked, I had high hopes, but only a handful came to the little shopping area in the gardens.

It took nine days to organize, prepare, stage, and dismantle the show, and I wound up with $65 after expenses and the gallery's percentage. For that I gave up my dream to walk through rice paddies, visit a small village, and touch the Balinese people.

The arts are the core of Bali's culture. They make theater, art, dance, and music as offerings to their Hindu gods. Everyone is an artist and expresses a joy and celebration of life by creating. I want that feeling in what I do.

In three days I'm leaving for Singapore—as soon as I finish shopping and getting *Southern Cross* ready.

Hugs to you both, love,

Pat

In *SC*'s visitors' book there were photos and messages from the young staff at the gallery. Beautiful Nana Nindiya, with sweet pink lips like a lotus blossom, invited me to her Hindi wedding in a small village near Singaradja on the northern coast. I pleaded with the Muslim authorities, going higher and higher in the navy, for the two extra days I needed on my permit. Their final answer was "no."

I RODE THE BALI COUNTERCURRENT NORTH ALONG the coast, watching the surf build and smash against the rocks ahead at Bias Putih. Gone was the thrill of departure I had come to expect, gone the anticipation of the next port. I had left Darwin with high hopes, but they had melted in the steamy air of Bali. No journeys by foot to Balinese villages, no money from Nouméa—and no Dan. It wasn't good to arrive anywhere with too many expectations, including expectations of myself.

I sailed into each new port with impossible lists of repairs, errands, housekeeping, sightseeing, painting, and selling, then left disappointed if I could not accomplish it all. I made the challenges and set the schedules but no longer felt in control. This voyage had acquired its own life.

Southern Cross and I both showed the wear. Her boom was back together, but she needed a new one. The dinghy was more patches and goo than original material; $300 couldn't replace it. Sails had disintegrated on every passage. The life raft had not been serviced in four years; it was supposed to be done every year. I sported calluses, scrapes, bumps, and bruises. We made quite a pair, *SC* and I.

Quick, one-day shows and individual sales kept food on the table and diesel in the tank, but they would never buy a radar or replace another sail. I wondered how long I could continue this way, but never considered whether or not I should.

Because I was a traveler at heart, the allure of foreign place names on my charts still drew me forward. But telling people I was "going around the world" had turned it into a project, with a beginning and an end, instead of a way of life. The forces that had pushed me out in the first place were all but forgotten. My focus was ahead as I looked for the means and stamina to finish what I had begun.

The fantasy of "sailing around the world" typically cast a dreamy haze over a person's eyes when we met for the first time. "I've always wanted to do just what you're doing." I'd heard it a hundred times.

"I know," was always my response. "My job is living everyone's dream. Someone has to do it." They'd look perplexed, and then we'd laugh.

I tacked away from Bias Putih.

Morning brought rough seas, a thin haze, and no wind. Without the engine *Southern Cross* slipped backward at 1.3 knots. Multicolored boats and the fish traps they tended produced the only traffic. At the surface of the sea 8-foot anchored bamboo poles floated vertically, marking the traps. Until I cleared the area my fifteen-minute sleeping pattern would have to continue.

At midnight, as I entered the pass between Madura and Sapudi Islands, off the northeast coast of Java, in the inky black air ahead an even darker shape loomed directly in front of *SC*'s bow. I grabbed the spotlight from below. Its beam bounced off the sail of a small fishing boat without lights and revealed a lone man—asleep. In a few seconds more, if we had collided, he might have been dead.

The next day dawned with a light breeze from the southeast. The fields of bamboo poles grew in all directions, like an endless drive-in theater, as I entered the Java Sea, nine hundred miles from Singapore. *SC* ghosted ahead while my mind floated back to Illinois and family.

Mom had waited almost a year for an invitation from Terri for dinner, a tour of her new house, and a chance to see the video or the photograph album of the wedding. Try as I might, I couldn't relate to Terri's actions. Was she afraid to show love or did she not feel it? Or was she doing this to punish me?

SHIP'S DIARY: 5 October 1992, 1200 Local, 06"36'S/114°01'E, sailing 4 knots wing-and-wing under 130 and the main with one reef on a course of 308M, 10% cloud cover, and the bar is 1005 and steady.

Today Tamara turned thirty-five, but who would butter her little nose? It was a family tradition that someone crept up from behind and slapped a gob of butter on the end of the birthday celebrant's nose, claiming it would make the next year slip by smoothly. No one remembered how the tradition had started. I missed the butter more than birthday cakes or presents.

The message on her dog-eared Mother's Day card helped soothe my guilt at not being there through her marriage and painful separation. She would find her own path, but a part of me insisted I could have helped. "Mom, there are so many times I have wished you were here," she wrote. "But, instead of your presence you have given me the courage to take risks and a sense of adventure about life. Thank you."

I said a thank-you prayer for being entrusted with the life of this beautiful person and tried to forgive myself for all the mistakes I had made in my decisions—letting her leave to live with her father, not giving her the home I had envisioned when she returned, not stepping in when I might have as she navigated her difficult teen years and—in my example—marrying too quickly, being a perfectionist, trying to squeeze the last second out of every day, and not evaluating consequences carefully before choosing a course of action. She seemed to look past it all to what was in my heart.

The quick dusk of an equatorial sunset dropped into the sea as the unending poles and their attendant fishing boats continued to rise above the edge of the earth. I had been awake for sixty hours. My thoughts were getting fuzzy. Another fifteen minutes. . . .

The alarm rang; I slept on while a guiding hand steered *SC* through hours of poles and boats.

SHIP'S DIARY: 6 October 1992, 1200 Local, 05°30′S/112°33′E, sailing at 4.8 knots on a 300M course, wing-and-wing under 130 and a reefed main, bar 1005—unchanged.

I passed Bawean Island at sunrise. The sailing directions described a less-than-favorable anchorage, and I kept going.

The autopilot stopped working. *Southern Cross* jibed, and the poled-out 130 shook violently. A freighter loomed directly ahead. She didn't answer on channel 16. I scrambled over the deck, releasing and adjusting lines to alter course and move out of her way. An electrical connection had corroded inside the autopilot. Exhaustion built, and big-ship traffic grew on all sides. How could I do this for eight more days?

On October 7th, 80 miles off the south coast of Kalimantan on Borneo, a solid, dense black squall raced down on *Southern Cross*. As the angry mass flew across the water, I dropped sails. Forty-five knot winds drove into *SC*, pounding her with large, pelting drops of horizontal rain. My eyes, squinched tight against the blinding squall, strained forward, waiting for the slicing bow of a huge ship to emerge from the black air. No one would see me. Even if a ship had had her radar on, *SC* would be lost in the rain clutter on the display screen. For three hours, the cords in my neck taut and my fingers stiffly gripping the edge of the dodger in fear, I hunted for traffic I knew was out there. Ten ships had passed in the two hours before the storm.

Finally the air cleared. Less than eight miles away ships traveling in every direction surrounded *SC*.

I had managed one brief nap in 120 hours. Fifteen-minute catnaps between rings of the kitchen timer did little to help. At dawn, a ship I hadn't even seen approaching passed just one and a half miles away. If only I knew what waypoints they were using, I could lay a course clear of them.

I called the tanker *Arctic Trader*, outbound from Singapore, to ask for their waypoints and course. The captain asked if I had charts on board and a radar, then told me to steer 320. "You'll find Singapore and lots of ships."

He didn't understand my problem, but if 320 degrees and its reciprocal were what the inbound and outbound ships were steering, I would do anything but steer 320. Fifteen miles north of my previously planned course, the traffic dropped off to one ship in eight hours.

The Java Sea fell behind, and the South China Sea took over. Traffic began to increase again as we all headed for the western end of Serutu Island, until the view to starboard looked like an L.A. freeway. I called the tanker *Western Bulk* to ask what waypoints they were using, but the radio operator responded with my position and directions for reaching Singapore. He didn't understand that I just wanted to go where they weren't.

A large, dark squall gathered south of Serutu, and another ship approached. This time the English-speaking officer understood what I wanted——and why. They were steering 300M from the tip of the island. Ten miles north of that line I would be clear of traffic. But could I stay awake that long? My arms and legs were filled with sand and my head stuffed with steel wool. By morning, I would have gone 168 hours without real sleep.

For an hour visibility disappeared, then the air cleared, but squalls continued moving out from the islands and over the traffic. Serutu passed. Ten more miles. Nausea, exhaustion, and tears weighted me to the cockpit seat.

Another ship appeared ahead; her lights indicated she would pass very close starboard-to-starboard. I spent my last energy jibing the pole and switching sails and lines to get out of her way. She changed direction to a collision course. There was nothing left inside me to do the deck work again. I called repeatedly on channel 16, gave up, and played the searchlight on my sails to catch her attention. Again on the radio, I called, "Is anybody on the ship just approaching Serutu Island bound southeast? Please, please respond."

"Oh, good morning," came a friendly response.

"What are your intentions please, to pass starboard-to-starboard or port-to-port?"

She adjusted her course.

Eight miles northwest of Serutu, I turned off the engine, set the kitchen timer, and went below to sleep for thirty minutes. *Southern Cross* sailed 330M at 2 knots, while four miles behind me ships traveling eight or ten times as fast passed steering 300M. Four hours later, I jolted awake in a boiling squall. The sails were backwinded, and the deck was in bedlam. I couldn't think. There was wind, but how much? And there was a ship ahead. I pushed myself to move— to get the sails under control and start the engine.

Her navigation lights should have told me her course, but the combination she displayed made no sense. I had to decide immediately which way to go. I tried the radio. No response. Then I trained the spotlight on her desperately, trying for a response. Still she held her course—a small, local fishing craft with nonregulation lights.

Heavy squalls built wind and seas on the nose, driving *SC* north toward a charted reef. I could do nothing. For two days, I existed in a blur of nausea and severe headache, barely going through the motions of living. The second evening I emerged—took a hot shower, fixed a stir-fry, cleaned the cabin, and went back to bed. Only two ships had passed since the encounter with the fishing boat.

On Columbus Day, the Voice of America broadcast a presidential debate between George Bush and Bill Clinton. The event was more than just half a world away. In my corner of the South China Sea, conditions eased, and I altered course to port 15 degrees, toward Singapore.

SHIP'S DIARY: 13 October 1992, 2000 Local, 00°00′/106°44′E, just returned to the Northern Hemisphere. I'm on the way home!

Crossing the equator again after more than three years, I toasted Father Neptune with a little $2 wine from New Caledonia, wrote a note telling who I was and when I was here and launched the bottle, said a prayer of thanks, baked a loaf of pumpernickel bread, and indulged my returning appetite.

A harvest-sized full moon laid a diamond-studded path across the water. I felt like the richest person in the world, to be alive and there to see it. That afternoon I had calculated a budget to fix all the problems on board, add new equipment, and take me to the Mediterranean. Then I turned the matter over to the Universe with a note tacked on the bottom: "If $12,200 isn't possible, my real bottom line is $3,000."

On October 14th, I motorsailed through light traffic in a contrary current. At 1700, at the Strait of Singapore by Horsburgh Lighthouse, I waited like a turtle preparing to cross a six-lane interstate. Twenty-eight ships approached from east and west. When they had all passed by, I began the five-mile trip with only one approaching ship to port. Inching toward the middle of the channel, I took bearings on her bow every few seconds. The numbers held steady, which meant we were on a collision course. I retreated to the edge while she slid by—the largest ship I had ever seen, a ULCC—ultralarge crude carrier—500,000 tons and more than a quarter mile long.

Again I put my toe in the stream, dodged and darted around barges and tugs, freighters and tankers going both ways, and emerged two hours later on the opposite side. Ships were anchored three-deep along the edge of Singapore Island in the distance, their lights melting into the city lights beyond.

The south coast of Johore, Malaysia, passed. *SC* turned up the channel leading to Serangoon Harbor on the top of the island with all the required supplies at hand in the cockpit: GPS, pencil, binoculars, chart, paper, hand-bearing compass, parallel rules, and my glasses. This one time, I would violate my personal rule prohibiting landfalls after dark in strange harbors. Something moved along the coast far off to port. Now and then tiny red lights darted in the distance ahead—fishing boats, probably.

The waypoint for each turn down the channel and into the anchorage was logged and numbered in the GPS and marked on the chart but not numbered. *SC* slipped into the shallows along the Malaysian side of the channel, and the depth sounder bleated a warning. I counted the flashes on the navigation aids ahead and took bearings, but they didn't tally with the chart. Without matching numbers I couldn't tell which one came next. The current and engine together swept me ahead at more than six knots as I scouted periodically for traffic but worried most about my location. In the dim light on the cockpit seat it was impossible to plot it, and the Singapore shoreline offered few clues. The only other vessels moved far in the distance.

At Fairy Point, I could just make out a forest of masts to port. I was home safe. My shoulders unwound as I put the engine in neutral to set up the anchor. In the quiet of Serangoon Harbor, away from the press of big ships, I walked out to the bow, untied the cord restraining the anchor on the roller, lifted a few feet of chain through the hawsepipe, and lowered it to dangle just above the surface of the water—ready to drop when I found a good spot.

Turning to go back, I froze. Ice water surged through my knees. High above the stern of *SC*, stacks of red and white lights glowed menacingly, the vessel below them invisible in the dense black air. Something very large and very close was under tow and being carried by the same current pushing *SC*.

I jumped into the cockpit, pulled off the autopilot arm, threw the engine into gear, and opened the throttle, turning to port—away from the looming monster. When the danger receded, my heart thudded still as the questions raced through my head. Why didn't her captain see *SC*'s navigation lights? Why didn't he call? Maybe he did, and I couldn't hear him above the engine. Where did she come from? Was she the vessel I saw earlier by the shore? How could she be that close and not hit me? I found a spot near the other cruising boats, dropped the hook, and sank down on the settee, still shaken.

Over breakfast I watched a steady stream of shipping traffic passing in the channel that had seemed only a backwater the night before. Two oceangoing tugs left for offshore oil fields towing towering cranes that extended over the bows of the tugs and rose twice the height of passing tankers. Perhaps one of them had made the light pattern that crept up on me the night before. If so, even if the tug captain had seen *SC*, he could never have changed course in time.

Once again I had been delivered by Divine Protection, this time from fishing traps, ships, reefs, and finally, in the moment of arrival, from a brush with death.

Mr. Tan greeted me with a sour-plum smile and an arm's-length welcome at the entry to the Changi Sailing Club. For $25 per week the club offered landing docks for cruisers' dinghies; hot showers; fresh water; fax, phone, and mail services; use of the bar and restaurant; and access through the front gate to Singapore—once past the watchful eye of Mr. Tan, the front-door "public relations" officer.

The village of Changi, a suburb at the northeast corner of the 24-mile-long island nation of three million, was a long bus and mass rapid transit (MRT) ride from the heart of the action in the city of Singapore, but the small village center a half-mile from the club provided some basic needs. Tampines, where the bus ride ended and the spotless, streamlined MRT began, offered a Prime Supermarket and a small shopping center on the ground floor of a high-rise housing complex, and the center of the city supplied everything else.

I checked in with the port captain, Customs, and Immigration, receiving the standard two-week landing pass. A stack of letters waited at the post office, but there was nothing from the gallery in Nouméa. The die was cast. I would be here for a year, not just two weeks, in order to replenish my cruising funds and refit *Southern Cross*. With that decision made, the pressure of uncertainty eased. I might be letting Mom down by extending the trip another year, but there was no way to go on.

My cousin Claire wrote, "I'll be in Singapore for the second week of November. Find some good restaurants." Claire had inherited her father's fondness for gourmet food and would want the best from Singapore's palette of Chinese, Malay, Indonesian, Arab, Indian, Filipino, Thai, and continental cuisines.

Mom and Stubby sent photos from their visit to Terri and Glenn's home and a full description of each room, the dinner they shared, and everything that was said. It had meant more to Mom and to me than Terri could imagine. Tam sent a letter filled with happy news, photos from her garden, and a tone of promise and enthusiasm.

Immigration extended my permit for two more weeks.

The sailing club agreed to a small exhibition one Sunday afternoon, and then to my proposal to do a painting of their facilities in exchange for a six-month membership. Gradually a nest of friends and activities grew around me, turning Singapore into a "home." The lady who sold the $2.50 tickets for the twice-weekly symphony concerts at the Victoria Theater began to greet me with a smile. Inexpensive movies, cheap dinners at the popular hawkers' centers offering ethnic specialties, and art openings filled my evenings. Days disappeared in the old sections of town as I searched for images to paint and investigated galleries.

The ethnic neighborhoods looked like a confectioner's display, with multicolored, pastel buildings—homes and shops—lining narrow streets. Plaster curlicues, rosettes, and ornate trim surrounded doors, windows, and eaves. Multipatterned tiles filled panels and covered walls and floors, while delicately carved wooden privacy screens fronted open doors and filled arched openings above windows. The colorful display marched down Joo Chiat Road, River Valley Road, Boat Quay along the riverfront, in Katong, and up Emerald Hill. The old city thrived in pockets behind concrete, steel, and glass high-rises. Indian music, sweet incense, spices from Indonesia, clanging music from Chinese street opera, curries, and sweet tropical flowers blended in the air while faces and costumes mixed in the streets.

On Sunday mornings, Chinese men gathered in a small corner plaza, their bamboo-caged exotic birds hung from an overhead rack. With glass cups of sweet coffee they visited, listened to the suspended orchestra, and plucked their sparse beards one whisker at a time. Foreign maids collected in the

Botanical Gardens to sit in the shade of a small pavilion and talk wistfully of their families in the Philippines.

The Sunday Claire arrived, as planned, Mr. Tan sent a message to let me know she was waiting in the clubhouse bar. For a week we ate our way through Singapore's gourmet offerings—Claire's treat—pausing only for a dinner on *Southern Cross* in the middle of a torrential downpour. Family history and news of our numerous cousins filled the hours. My father had been her father's favorite brother and her father my favorite uncle—irascible, sometimes obnoxious, but straightforward and funny. He had once described me as a "war casualty." I had no desire to be considered a casualty of anything. Understanding, compassion, and acceptance left self-esteem intact; pity did not. He and the rest of my father's family had never approved of my father's second marriage, but had made no effort to stay in touch with me until I was an adult.

One evening after Claire's departure, Wilma Falconer, a recent arrival from New Zealand, sat next to me at a classical guitar concert. It was her first trip to Singapore and my fifth. She had come on a two-year contract with an expatriate public relations firm. Together we explored more corners of the city.

Rona, one of our circle of women sailors in Darwin, pulled into Changi with a smashed bow—en route from Bali she had T-boned a small freighter. At the limit of exhaustion, thinking the freighter would pass well off her course, she had gone below to rest. Some instinct pulled her on deck seconds before *Cacique* rammed the ship's side. The helmsman stared down incredulously at this six-foot skin-and-bones naked woman with a wild head of scraggly blonde curls who was shouting epithets and frantically waving at him to get away. She reported that after she had gone below he had changed course for a closer look at her 27-foot boat and had misjudged her speed or course, causing the collision. *Cacique*'s rail and bow roller were broken, the deck-to-hull joint sprung, and Rona had three broken ribs. Every pull of the oars for the mile-and-one-quarter row to the sailing club brought Rona wincing pain as she went back and forth making arrangements for repairs.

Immigration reluctantly extended my permit for another two weeks.

Kiwi Star joined us in the anchorage with an ailing new Spanish diesel and searched for a mechanic. Lynn, my old acquaintance from Bay of Island days, had arrived singlehanded again after carrying crew from New Zealand to Bali.

Immigration said I absolutely had to leave in two weeks, whether or not the dentist had finished with my root canal. And added, "Did you come to Singapore just to get dental work done?"

With Wilma's permission I gave Immigration a letter stating I was leaving my boat in her care to travel through neighboring countries. They gave me three days to go, and I caught a bus to Malaysia. There I changed to the next bus back to Singapore—as a tourist, not as a "boat person." That maneuver put me in a new category and a different Immigration Office.

I painted a series of miniatures and began working on larger pieces. The arthritis increased. Jacque's recommendations—wedges under my hips for an hour a day, black currant juice, and barley water—made little difference, and my ongoing attempt to change my attitudes about scarcity had been unsuccessful as I hunted for sources of income. A notice for a traditional Chinese medical facility offering herbs and acupuncture in exchange for a small donation caught my attention.

Forty pairs of curious brown eyes swiveled toward the door when my blue ones peered into the waiting room of the Buddhist Free Clinic . From behind the reception desk strange, pungent odors wafted out of hundreds of small bottles. The staff looked for someone who spoke English and returned with tiny, shoulder-high Soh Kok Moey. Her index finger scooted her glasses higher on her nose as we filled out the forms. I paid the voluntary, recommended donation of $1.25. Kok Moey handed me a number and pointed to the flashing sign at each examining room. I joined a young woman in her late twenties on one of the hard, brown leatherette benches. She smiled, and we began to chat, her English a little shy and my Chinese nonexistent after the greeting "zao an." Then Jenny Lim's number flashed over one of the rooms, and she left for her almost daily treatment.

Arthritis ran in my family, but this early onset was unusual. Life on the boat had not been kind to my hands: washing sheets and towels by hand, engine work, and heavy maintenance projects continuously irritated the joints. Equally at fault were the long hours spent painting intricate details with tiny brushes.

As I waited, memories returned from my first visit to an acupuncturist. On board *Windy* in Singapore in 1980, a skin fungus with white spots and itching had developed on my neck and jaw. A Western-trained doctor prescribed Selsun shampoo. "Put it on each night and wash it off in the morning for one week." When nothing had changed in six days, I visited a Chinese doctor.

In his traditional Chinatown shophouse office I found a room full of human pincushions connected to small electrical machines. I had assured myself I would not need needles for a skin condition.

In the examining room the doctor had popped three needles inside each ear and returned twenty minutes later with his assistant. She had handed me a vial of pale yellow powder, saying, "Dip gingerroot in and scrub this on your neck and jaw." The next morning the fungus had vanished, leaving no sign it had ever existed. It was not difficult to imagine that the doctor at this Buddhist clinic could cure arthritis. I only hoped it would be fast.

My number flashed on the sign above room number 3, and Kok Moey waited at the door. Four patients already sat on the three tables with needles at work. I sat next to Jenny while Dr. Lee Poh Kheng took my pulses and looked at my tongue, nodding her head as Kok Moey explained the problem. She popped in the required number of needles, fresh from their sterile bubble packs, while Jenny and I continued our conversation.

Shortly Dr. Lee removed the needles and handed me a prescription for a vile black liquid—worse than pure vanilla—and hundreds of tiny, round, black pills. "Take sixteen of these four times a day." I slipped down from the table and for the first time saw Jenny Lim's distorted hands. Her smile and lively conversation distracted anyone from noticing the progressive damage arthritis was doing to her hands and knees.

I handed the receptionist my prescription. She collected the medication from the tiny, smelly bottles behind her desk and gave me a bill for 65 cents.

The pain slowly receded through four months of visits several times each week to the clinic in the Kallang district. Sometimes I went as much to see Jenny, Kok Moey, and Dr. Lee as for the treatment. They tried to teach me Chinese, took me out for lunch, and guided me through the supermarket, explaining all the strange items I habitually bypassed on my shopping trips. We chatted about our families and lives, but they never mentioned the Buddhist temple that funded their clinic.

Jenny invited me to her mother's home for Ancestor's Day, a strictly family affair during Chinese New Year's celebrations. There were two tables set—a large one for all of us, and under a small shrine a small one with one place setting for those who had already left this world. When Jenny's family decided I had not eaten enough, they fed me morsels of vegetables, seafood, and meat cooked in the rich, steaming broth of the "steamboat" at the center of the table.

I invited the group from the clinic to visit a freshly scrubbed and polished *Southern Cross* with their husbands and children one Sunday. Clouds opened, the rain poured down, and we squeezed into the tiny, steamy cabin. Kok Moey and Jenny turned pale green in the gentle rocking motion. Clutching plastic bags they climbed into my bunk and struggled with the snacks I had just served, while I watched nervously over the pale peach cotton blanket that I'd just ransomed from the laundry for $6.

As my visits to the clinic diminished, the days filled with painting, boat maintenance, and becoming acquainted with the varied cultures of Singapore. The predominant Chinese population carried a patina of the flavors, designs, and colors of Malaysia from their migrations over the centuries down the Malay peninsula. Malaysians comprised the next largest group, followed by Indonesians, Indians—both Sikhs and Tamils—and remnants of the British colonialists. Middle Eastern families were scattered throughout the city, as were expatriates who lived in luxury apartments while on assignment from home offices in New York, Tokyo, Brussels, Djakarta, and all the major economic centers of the world. The texture of Singapore was shaped by this blend of customs, costumes, food, and beliefs.

On a Saturday afternoon in March, steamy, tropical heat rolled over me as I descended from the bus, arms full of shopping bags, anxious for a cold shower at the club. An arcade of mango and frangipani trees arched over the long driveway, and bougainvillea, hibiscus, and spidery palms followed the sides of the road to the clubhouse and a small public beach next door.

A young family played in the warm, shallow water, finding some relief from the sauna-like air. The father, a handsome dark man with a neat clipped mustache, in navy blue shorts and light blue T-shirt, tossed a ball lazily with his young son. The boy romped through the water, occasionally splashing his little sister as she sat nearby, making sand pies.

At one end of the beach stood the mother, with her back turned to her family. Through the crocheted bars of her *chador* she looked toward the boats bobbing on their moorings in front of the club. In black from head to toe, with veil, cape, robes, gloves, and socks, she stood in the sun looking. I wondered how old she had been the last time she felt sand between her toes or knew the joy of tossing a ball, the kiss of a cool breeze, sun on her arms, or fresh rain falling on her face. Some of the sights and customs around me were beyond my understanding.

Dear Kitty,

The prints and paintings finally arrived from Nouméa (short the ones they sold), but with no money! A French friend of mine called to ask for the payment, and they refused to send it. He said later, "Never do business with the French." Now the gallery has gone bankrupt.

I explored teaching at the university and at the American School, proposed a project to the Singapore post office for mailgrams, outlined a cultural development idea to the government, and wound up painting again.

In the back corners of the city are glorious old buildings in the most fantastic colors—pale lavender with deep purple trim, yellow with blue, orange and blue trim on a peach-colored background. It's a feast for an architect turned painter.

A new series of minis and prints are selling in several gift shops. But Dawn Poh at Art Focus Gallery has turned out to be my salvation. She took both minis and prints from my first two pieces, paying for everything. She doesn't work on consignment. Then she ordered ten prints from the piece I had started of the old, classic Raffles Hotel.

When it was finished I began another painting, praying for funds to do the printing. Day by day, money trickled out. Finally, I was down to $3, a little gasoline for the dinghy, enough on my transit card to go to town twice, and a small balance on the phone card. I packed a peanut butter sandwich for lunch, the two paintings, money, and cards, and left for town. On my way through the club, I called to make an appointment with Dawn.

Gathering my courage I showed her both new pieces, then explained that I didn't have any money to make the prints. If she would pay me for ten that day, I would give her twelve when they returned from New Zealand in three weeks. She thought for just seconds, reconfirmed my proposal, and said "yes." She paid for ten from each of the new pieces, and bought other prints and some originals too.

I walked—no, soared—out the door with a check for $1,200 and went straight to the bank to cash it. Then I called Wilma to invite her for a glass of wine after work. She had thought she would be bringing me a care package that night. I feel like a real person again with money in my pocket.

I am now painting almost every day in the Alcove, a lovely shop in historical Cuppage Terrace just off Orchard Road, the main shopping street in the city center. I had noticed the store on my visits to Della Butcher's gallery (the first in Singapore) just down the hall, but every time I passed, it was closed. Finally I asked the proprietor, Mary Ann Middleton, if she would like me to keep it open in exchange for letting me paint there. She didn't jump at the offer, but just weeks later, when Della died, her assistant Fawziah came to work at the Alcove, and Mary Ann offered me a corner in which to paint and display my work. The forty-five-minute commute isn't too bad—I write letters on the MRT.

The exposure has been excellent. A freelance writer, Ellen Ettensperger, stopped one day, then came back the next to do an interview for a newspaper. She threw a lunch to introduce me to her friends, and one of them, Molly Robertson, invited me to live in her apartment complete with maid for five weeks in July and August while she and her family travel.

I've joined a figure-drawing group with Claudia Russell, an architect from the States, and Max Millen, an artist from Berlin. It's pushing me artistically; I'm used to the straight edges of architecture and the anything-goes freedom of foliage. Max is incredible to watch. He's a perfectionist in every stroke from his life as a commercial artist, but totally loose after twelve years of travel in search of a personal vision. His imagination hands him amazing images and his talent makes them believable. Every brushstroke shows his confidence. I'm jealous.

I must do a show in the fall to raise the funds to continue my voyage, but I have no idea where or how. Dawn's place will be undergoing a major remodeling. For such a large city with so many cultured, well-to-do people, there are few galleries. Government support and interest has all gone to the performing arts—music and dance.

I saved my biggest news for last. I'm flying home! Tamara wants me to come. Kira and Shawn need me in their lives. Mom didn't think I would be willing, but only the money held me back. Mom, Stubby, Tamara, and Terri all contributed to the $1,200 ticket. It's embarrassing not to be able to do this for myself, but I'm overjoyed all the same.

When I started this trip I don't think I gave much thought to the impact on my family. It took Tam's concern for her children to bring it home.

I'll spend ten days in Illinois with Mom, Stubby, Terri and Glenn, and Stu and his family, then ten in Santa Cruz with Tam, Kira, and Shawn. I'll be meeting a new son-in-law and a new granddaughter for the first time. Finally I go to Portland for a visit with Libby. Dan will fly there to meet me for a few days, too. He was supposed to come here, but that didn't work out. Can you come to Santa Cruz between June 15th and 25th to visit for a day? Drop a note when you have time. I miss you so much, my dear.

Love and kisses,

Pat

The Immigration Office (the one for tourists now, not cruisers) gave me two extensions, then I caught a ferry to a nearby Indonesian island. On my return the officer—who no doubt had encountered tactics like mine before—insisted that this extension would be my last. With the help of Dennis Donahue, director of the U.S. Information Service and the Cultural Affairs Officer at the U.S. Embassy, I presented a request for a three-month extension that would allow me to stay as a visiting artist with a plane ticket out in June. With my three-month extension and the new one-month visitor's pass I'd have on my return from the United States, I was finally free from the Immigration Office until August.

One day in April Fawziah arrived at the Alcove with a tiny, elegant Chinese lady in tow. "Pat, this is Rose Quek, a dear friend of mine I want you to meet."

After studying art and fashion design in London, Rose had returned to Singapore in the early 1950s and opened the first original-fashion boutique in the city, on Beach Road near Raffles Hotel. But tropical life lacked the verve of London. Eventually she and her husband, Donald, moved to England.

Then Donald's business affairs brought them back to Singapore. Rose ever after longed for the life she had known in London, including the open and easygoing art scene with life drawing groups available any time. In prudish Singapore, nudity for almost any purpose had been banned.

Our Wednesday-evening life-drawing group had somehow slipped through the censor's net. The meetings at the neighborhood center in the central district lacked the London atmosphere, but Rose was pleased at my invitation to join us the following week. We agreed to meet at Ali's Lebanese Restaurant, downstairs from the Alcove, at 5:30 for a quick bite before the gathering.

As we polished off *shwarama* dinners of pita wrapped around barbecued meat and vegetables, I suggested we hurry to catch the subway. Rose froze. In all her Singapore years she had never ridden the superefficient and 100 percent safe MRT. I cajoled, reasoned, and encouraged until we were on board for the ten-minute ride across the central district, bypassing the traffic-clogged avenues overhead. Minutes later we joined the all-Chinese-male group with Max and Claudia, Rose still amazed that she had ridden the subway. Later she found a group that better suited her schedule, delighted to be drawing again.

Departure day drew close as I managed last-minute details, preparing to leave *Southern Cross* on her own for a month and get to the airport by 5:00 A.M. with everything I needed—gifts, phone numbers and addresses, prints to sell, a portfolio of the articles accumulating about my trip, tickets, and a range of clothes to accommodate hot Illinois, cool Portland, and anything in between.

SC moved to a "mooring"—a 75-pound anchor with 200 feet of half-inch chain that would hold her in the pudding-like bottom of the bay even through the occasional heavy winds and thunderstorms known as Sumatras for their source.

―――――――――JUNE 4, 1993

IN MY BUSINESS-SUIT LIFE BEFORE "THE TRIP," AT least once every month I had climbed on board an airplane for destinations from Miami to Bangkok, and loved it. I knew by heart the maps of cities all over the globe. In truth, the desire to make traveling part of my work had partially inspired the launching of TWT. In the end, though, my business had cost much more than many years' worth of airline tickets and hotels.

My simple, scaled-down existence on *Southern Cross* included no flights, no bustling airports, no dashes by cab for the next meeting or the next plane. I measured travel in weeks now, not hours.

This morning, once again, an airport scene surrounded me—Singapore's shiny new Changi International. Then I hung suspended miles above the Earth, waiting for my destination to arrive. The Pacific flowed below, its cresting waves and small boats invisible at 30,000 feet. My body felt the rise and fall of those thousands of hard-won miles, now almost instantly lost as I flew back over my sea path.

Quickly Singapore became Chicago. My mother's arms wrapped around me, and Terri held me close, our tears mixing. We touched to reassure ourselves it wasn't a dream. While we traded news, our eyes sought the telltale changes of four years. We covered the highlights as Terri drove south to Bloomington: her promotion at State Farm, Glenn's just-diagnosed diabetes, Stubby's retirement at eighty-four, and Mom and Stubby's planned move to a new home. Mom had plans for family dinners and an outing on Stu's pontoon boat, as well as a list of old friends who wanted to see me.

Terri had contacted a local framing shop to arrange for a one-day show of my paintings. A small ad in the paper brought out faces from my past, some long forgotten, and new ones I had never met—Roxie, our ham angel, came with a red rose. Childhood friends challenged me to "Guess who I am? Don't you recognize me?" I searched old memories for a link, trying to look past the hundreds of new faces and names that had entered my life in the past four years.

Glenn's 6-foot 4-inch body stretched even thinner than the wedding pictures had shown, but his doctor said the diabetes could be controlled for a while with a careful diet and oral medication. The changes Glenn had wrought in Terri showed in her relaxed hairdo and casual look. He had even convinced her she could leave home in unironed shorts. We toured their new home, its empty rooms waiting for the right furniture—one step at a time, and not on credit. What about children? I wanted to ask, but wouldn't. Glenn remarked as we drove through town, "Oh, look at that cute baby stroller!," and I knew grandchildren were in the future.

Terri and I celebrated her coming birthday over brunch. I longed to reach inside and talk about something meaningful. Instead we visited on the surface—about clothes and favorite perfumes, about her job aspirations, and recipes. I wanted to say, "Invite your grandmother over now and then; call her to say hello," but I held back. Terri's family relationships teetered on a knife edge, and I wouldn't be the one to tip the balance.

We drove through town to see new neighborhoods—shorn, modern, and sterile—then toured the old streets of my childhood, where handsome elderly trees still arched overhead to make green tunnels for bike rides on shady sidewalks. I looked for the good memories.

Mom was frantic about the antiques and treasures she and Grandma had gathered over two lifetimes. Stubby's job as the director of the Immanuel Bible Foundation had given them a fully furnished mansion for a home, and for the past thirteen years their possessions had accumulated next to Grandma's in the unused attic. Retirement meant someone else would move into the house. "Please, come help me sort through all of this and make some decisions. Isn't there something you would like to keep?" "Where?" I wondered.

Small notes in Grandma's green-ink handwriting told when each small treasure from my childhood had arrived. "Note from Patsy, Jerseyville, August 10, 1948." She had saved them all.

We visited the retirement center where Mom and Stubby had made a reservation many years before. As we walked into the tiny apartment on the corner of the third floor, it felt like the last door in Mom's life was closing behind her. I wanted to rush away from the place. We drove home in silence, and I tried to sort out what terrified me more—losing her or facing my own old age. Stubby's children joined Stu and me in quiet conversations, exploring possibilities. I pictured Mom and Stubby surrounded by sunshine and a patio filled with flowers, not snow and the windswept barren fields outside the window in that apartment. I pleaded with them to take their time making a decision, to explore alternatives. When I left for California the question still hung in the air.

The peace of Tam's place soothed me. I slept in the loft over her stained-glass studio and woke up to silence and brisk West Coast air. She shared eleven acres in the Santa Cruz Mountains with her boyfriend, Bob. The trailer where they lived, while they built a new home to replace the one he'd lost in the 1989 earthquake, looked over blue-green treetops. We ate fresh strawberries from the garden and visited in the sun.

Shawn had begun studying piano a year before, and by Christmas had accompanied the school holiday concert. He played for me with an exceptional talent that could offer endless possibilities if he chose to follow them. I hoped he would find the confidence and encouragement he needed, from his father as well as from Tam, to answer a calling from the heart and not the wallet. He beat me at countless games of cribbage until my last day there, when I finally won.

Day in and day out Kira chose a book, and we curled up for story hour. A high-energy bundle topped by lively green eyes and long, blonde hair, she clung to every minute. We played house on the deck, holding imaginary tea parties as I had with my grandmother, my mother, Tamara, and Terri. These links wove back and forth unbroken over generations.

Shane and I scouted the beach for a new feather for *Southern Cross*. "I wish our paths had crossed in Bali," I told her. "I wanted to see the house where you lived and meet the family of wood-carvers who taught you, but there was no time. Your Bali was much different from mine."

Kitty arrived for an afternoon, and we tied up threads of conversation begun in our letters. Peter had hepatitis C and had been in a near-death race to the emergency room only a few months before. Their lives circled around the virus in his body, putting everything else on hold. Now they waited anxiously for word of a liver donor. Kit brought slides of bold new pieces—paintings on black velvet. She pushed me for still more contrast in my paintings, while she worked in total dark and light in her own.

I talked to a bankruptcy lawyer, gathering information, but took no steps. To do more would require money I didn't have. The lawyer handling TWT affairs said there was nothing to do. The cases were following their own course; she would be in touch. The CPA had nothing to add beyond what she had written. Records of TWT's affairs were not available; she had lost contact with the bookkeeper who had them.

Tam, Shawn, Kira, and I packed the van for a three-day camping trip north to meet Libby in Eugene, Oregon. The colors of northern California flew by along I-5, dusty moss-green, gold, and peach, and then the wet green of southern Oregon rose around us.

On Sunday Libby gave me the keys to her car and apartment. I left for Portland, and Tam drove south. My heart rate accelerated as the miles to go dropped. I found the apartment ready for a romantic reunion with Dan. Libby had stocked the refrigerator with wine, fresh strawberries, orange juice, fruit, fine cheeses, and freshly roasted coffee, imagining that we would not be able to tear ourselves apart long enough to go out for food.

I thought back to the beginning of our affair in 1968, a quarter century before. I was a twenty-seven-year-old University of Illinois junior whose daughters had just gone to live with their father. Dan was trapped in a marriage he hadn't wanted. He cried when we made love for the first time—whether for joy, for loss, or because he was being unfaithful, I couldn't ask. Degree in hand, I moved to California and met Lars in 1971, leaving Dan on the pedestal where I'd placed him seven years before.

We saw each other from time to time over the years after my divorce from Lars, but those brief encounters provided only a taste of what I imagined might happen if we could spend days together—time to develop a more intimate language than that expressed in letters or in a single night. A shared vocabulary of inflection, glance, and touch could only be discovered slowly. In this time together, our first in six years, we were going to have that gift of days.

The doorbell rang, and all my nerves ignited. There he stood, his face careworn and bearing new creases but every inch familiar—the one enduring constant in a history of ephemeral relationships. He gathered me in a strong, quiet embrace, then stepped back smiling. A little shyly we reconnected the threads of our lives, talking for hours about the problems in his business, his children, mine, and my experiences on *Southern Cross*. Then slowly we approached the subject we both felt had to be discussed, but with which neither of us was comfortable.

In the years since we had last seen each other, the AIDS epidemic had moved the topic of safe sex into the public dialogue, but for many children of the 1950s like us it remained an alien and uncomfortable concept. He thought of my roving life and envisioned a "man in every port"—though in fact I hadn't looked at another man in two and a half years, since receiving his phone call in Australia. I did not know if he and his longtime significant other had been faithful. We stumbled around the subject, then fumbled with preventive measures like awkward teenagers. But in the end it was the death of spontaneity.

We lay wrapped in our private thoughts, a pair of sad and disappointed fifty-somethings, then rolled apart to sleep. In the morning I looked at that solid, secure back and wanted to draw my arms around him, to hold him close, but something held me back. Maybe, after all those years, I still had him on that pedestal. I waited for the overtures to come from him.

By day we explored the city, browsed through Powell's, the largest book-store in the world, drove and hiked along the Columbia Gorge, and by night ate intimate dinners at quaint restaurants. One evening as we contemplated the menu, Dan said something about his "wife." I thought it was just a convenient means of referring to his significant other, but when it happened again I stopped him: "Why do you keep talking about your wife? You're not married, are you?"

"Of course I am, you knew that."

"I had no idea. You never told me."

"I wrote that we were getting married when you were on the coast of Mexico in 1989."

"I guess a lot of mail went missing there."

I was stunned. Perhaps I did not know him at all. The long-term relation-ship had been an open subject between us, but he had never suggested the pos-sibility of marriage. By degrees I reassured myself that, in effect, nothing had changed. We were still the same two people, with a shared history of love, or at the least affection. I knew enough to believe that his marriage wasn't one of passion. When I was married he had always continued to live in a special com-partment of my heart; perhaps that was where he now kept me. In any event, after waiting eighteen months for this short time together, I didn't want this news to spoil it.

Soon I was driving him to the airport, both of us frustrated by our unful-filling tryst. Neither of us willing to release the thread that still held us together, we chose Greece to meet again.

Libby and I filled my last few days in Portland with shopping. There were boat parts, art supplies, and new underwear to buy—items even mod-ern Singapore didn't offer, or sold only as expensive luxuries, or carried in the wrong sizes. We shared news: her romance in Eugene that never moved forward, the job she wanted to change but didn't, and her plans for trans-forming the apartment she had purchased in a 1930s-era historical building in the center of the city. Another anniversary saw her free of cancer for three years—and still doing well. I told her of my plans for the year ahead—new places and new directions—and of Dan. She was almost as disappointed as I was that the carefully orchestrated interlude had fallen short.

Thirty days had slipped through my fingers under the pampering and nurturing love of my family. I had floated through the experience—seeing people and visiting, but never feeling completely there. One day in July I found myself emerging from a plane in Singapore as if from a dream. Immigration granted a one-month visitor's pass at the Changi Airport, and Mr. Tan actually smiled as he welcomed me back to the sailing club. I picked up my waiting mail and boarded the club launch for a ride to *Southern Cross* and a return to boat life. The next morning I awoke on board as if the trip home had never happened. Only the photos and letters we exchanged confirmed that it had.

I wondered whether we had really seen each other as we were now, or only as the shadows we remembered from long before. Could love bridge every span of time and distance to understand the new person in front of us wearing a familiar face, or were the gaps left by unshared experiences too wide to cross? How could I imagine their lives, so removed from my existence on the sea and in foreign places, and how could they imagine mine, far from the comfort of daily routine and dependable expectations? Could I ever fit into that life again? Did I want to?

The wind and waves, sun and stars had worked their magic on me. I would be a sea person . . . perhaps forever.

——————— JULY 1993

BY NOW THERE WAS LITTLE THAT WAS DEPENDABLE about my only link to shore—*T/T Southern Cross*. I unfolded the rubber dinghy, installed the delaminating floorboards, and worked the foot pump. As she filled I felt a certain respect for her tenacity. Returning to the dock to find she had been stolen was never a worry, but finding that she had deflated and sunk was becoming a definite possibility.

A few days later Jim on *Nepenthe*, still worried about my transportation, left a large, white, spare dinghy as a gift. The walls were as thin as a shower curtain. Thinking of the occasional sea snakes on the long route to the clubhouse, I declined the offer.

The next day, I returned to the dock and found a note from a Brazilian boatie: "Hi Pat! I leave the dingui at your boat. I will explain later the deal 'good!!' The boton of the dingui it's full of [here she drew a dinghy with lots of barnacles hanging from the bottom], I will talk with you later. Have a nice sleap. Nivea."

A huge, old 16-foot Avon with a slow leak in the port pontoon waited at SC. It was better than my old one, but within a few hours, unless I removed the mounting bracket and the outboard hanging on the stern, it began to deflate. Each morning I pumped up the mushy left side and dreamed of owning a new dinghy.

There had been a French singlehander in Darwin the August before, his boat and sails a floating billboard. They were covered with the names of sponsors who had donated equipment for his trip around the world. He had planted a seed that finally sprouted as I looked at T/T *Southern Cross* and the equipment list for the rest of the trip.

The old wind vane was no longer dependable, and singlehanding with only an autopilot was risky. A furling system would let me change the size of the headsail or douse it with ease from the safety of the cockpit. Radar with a rest mode and alarm would allow me a little sleep in traffic zones. The old sails could not last for the rest of the trip, and a furling system would require a new headsail. Finally, my correspondence list had grown at every stop. Letters poured in at a volume I could no longer maintain on the little portable typewriter. I needed a laptop.

My mind filled with reasons why a potential sponsor would turn me down, and my conscience nudged, saying that asking for help was not right. Everywhere people had offered their support, and in return, I hoped, felt that they were part of the voyage. But asking for something was a different matter entirely. The inner voices prodded, asking "Where is your sense of pride? Why do you think the world owes you anything? Who do you think you are?"

Ignoring the negative messages, I found the name and address of the top manufacturer for each piece of equipment, then wrote letters offering a painting in exchange for the needed item. I told them I would probably be the oldest woman to sail alone around the world, as if that were something special. The promotional packages included photos of artwork and articles about the trip. I mailed them with prayers that someone might answer.

A few weeks later a fax arrived at the Changi Sailing Club from Profurl, in Fort Lauderdale, Florida. My letter had gone to the main office of Proengin in France, and they had forwarded it to Mike McLaughlin, vice president of the Florida subsidiary. He wrote that they got requests like mine every day and routinely turned them down. However, he continued, "my almost-fifty-year-old, avid sailor wife has threatened unmentionables if I don't give you the furling unit." I let out a squeal that stopped every typewriter in the clubhouse office.

Molly Robertson and her husband and children left for their five-week vacation in the States, and I moved into the luxury of their two-story, three-bedroom apartment with Olympic-size pool and maid. It felt like I was living someone else's life.

As I stretched into that first heavy, languorous Singapore morning, sweet, damp scents of wet tropical foliage stroked my skin. The air carried land sounds—birds, hedge clippers, children, and Filipino maids chattering just outside. The morning smells and sounds told me where I was in the world. At dawn on *Southern Cross* there was little to remind me I was half a world away from home.

With a flood of guilt I left the bed unmade and my clothes heaped for laundry, ironing, and repair. Lenore's soft tones drifted through the window as I showered and planned the day.

Downstairs the table was set, coffee ready, and Lenore waited for my breakfast order. Nothing was too much to ask; she was used to four. I was almost a holiday. While she cleared the dishes, I set up to paint at the table by the patio, surrounded by palms—a dozen types—and bougainvillea in five different colors. Explosions of tropical plants and the sweet, liquid air pulled me into the scene on the watercolor pad, a garden on Sentosa Island, south of the city. Lenore scrubbed and dusted and polished, washed clothes, and cooked while I painted.

We chatted some, but she was reserved. Maybe she was thinking of the husband, four daughters, and mother she had left behind in the Philippines, or perhaps wondering if her husband was faithful and if he was taking care of the money she sent each month. When her family called to say the box of clothes and gifts she sent had arrived, she smiled all day. She had worked for a week carefully packing each item—paid for by the second job she worked on Sundays—her day off.

Lenore did my shopping at the produce market down the road; she was a better bargainer than I. From time to time she prepared a special Filipino treat, but the bitter vegetables and the strange texture of okra were not for me. I feigned pleasure, not wanting to hurt her feelings, but turned down seconds.

I invited friends for breakfast and chose Sunday, Lenore's day off. When the guests left I made the kitchen sparkle before she returned. But one sign still remained from my busy morning.

Lenore walked in, and her nose wrinkled at the bitter scent of a burned breakfast roll. She found the source and looked perplexed. "How can this seemingly smart Western woman not know how to use a microwave?," must have run through her mind. She couldn't imagine it was my first experience. She fought to rid the smell from the kitchen, then reported the episode in full to the maids' evening forum just outside the door. Perhaps Lenore enjoyed her moment of superiority.

The immigration office for visiting tourists granted a one-month extension.

Lenore picked up her pace of polishing, dusting, and scrubbing; curtains, spreads, and rugs came down for washing. Richard, Molly, and the kids returned, and I moved on—but only a few doors down, in the next building in the same complex.

In February I had looked for a professional photographer to shoot photos of my paintings, and the search had led me to this apartment and Helen MacKinlay. She and her husband, Rod, both from New Zealand, had become part of my life from that moment on. The walls and shelves of their home were covered with awards for the marathons they ran, art and artifacts collected during their travels and sojourns in Europe and the United States, and Helen's photography. Singapore had become home when Rod's Silicon Valley firm offered a Far East assignment.

Rod and Helen left to climb Kilimanjaro, and I resumed painting. There was no maid this time. I would miss the ease and pampering, but maybe not the guilt.

New paintings accumulated day by day, some as large as 18 by 28 inches, and thoughts about a show grew. I explored the possibilities. Spaces to rent were expensive. Dawn's place was not available, and after Nouméa, working with any other gallery held little appeal. The project appeared overwhelming, but nothing else would prepare *Southern Cross* for the long trip to the Med.

In August I called Ellen Ettensperger for a brainstorming session on the subject of "an exhibition." Tall, willowy, and dark haired, with a sort of Diane Keaton look, Ellen could calmly pull together any organizational challenge she accepted, like a puppet master with her marionettes. Her business and academic credentials were as long as my arm, but her warmth and enthusiasm were what ensured her success.

That day we discussed a small, one-day show in October using a room at the American Club. With coffee service for a hundred guests, it would cost $100.

Dear Kitty,

I enjoyed our day together more than you can imagine, my dear. We can't let it go so long again.

It's time for another exhibition. This time there won't be a gallery involved.

Using my fund-raising experience on the Cabrillo Music Festival Board, I hope to pay for invitations, framing, the reception, and prints from new pieces with grants from the expat corporations here. I know it won't be as easy promoting myself as it was describing the work of a new composer or a visiting artist.

Two of my paintings were selected by Riding for the Disabled, a local charity, for their annual fund-raiser—Christmas cards featuring local artists' work. I was pleased, as they only do eight cards each year. Their printer will use one of those images for my invitations. Ellen is inviting her friends for lunch, and with their secret mailing lists we'll have an invitation-addressing bee. The details are falling together.

What is the news on Peter's health? I'm praying the phone rings soon with a donor. How difficult it must be, living in limbo every minute.

Love to you both,

Pat

I caught a ferry from Changi to Pengili, Malaysia, had a cup of coffee in a beachside restaurant, then picked up a two-week visa on my return to Singapore.

Rose came for tea one day with a box of pastries. Having spent all those years in England, she had certain expectations of an invitation for tea. To me it meant a bag in a cup of hot water and good conversation. She tactfully suggested I warm the milk and bring the tea water to a full boil. We shared the good conversation, the pastries, and our portfolios, then ended the afternoon with a photo of us in front of Rose's favorite bigger-than-life photo of a nude male.

Later that week a call from Fawziah sent me hurrying through the noon-time crowd at the MRT station. The doors closed and the train accelerated away from the platform. In the back of the car, a flutter of butterflies in exotic colors and patterns chatted avidly. Wearing the typical Muslim *baju kurong*—tunic and long skirt—and a complementary *selendang* over their hair, they appeared elegant and comfortable. Each one expressed her own style in some way: color, jewelry, a different sleeve design, or some small detail.

Across the aisle sat two of their Muslim sisters, *dakwas*. Each was shrouded from head to toe in a heavy dark *chador*, her hands and feet covered in long gloves and socks. I wondered what went through the minds of the women behind those crocheted masks, watching their brightly dressed sisters who worshiped at the same mosque and read the same Koran, but lived such different lives. I couldn't begin to understand their acceptance, nor the men who created the rules that put them there. The sight tore at something deep inside— my sense of justice and the right to freedom and personal dignity. I wanted to ask them how they felt, but I did not.

I crossed from the Centrepoint station to find out what was worrying Fawziah. Usually so full of bubbles and lightness, she had sounded despondent on the phone. In the cool courtyard below the Alcove, the silk man whispered, "Cheap silk, cheap silk," to each passing lady. I hurried by and mounted the creaky, old wooden stairs of Cuppage Terrace.

A shaft of light caught Fawziah from the skylight above. The pattern played gaily across her purple silk blouse, then picked up the sadness in her dark Saudi eyes. Beautiful Fawziah had been Miss Singapore before she was given away in an early arranged marriage. Her life had been unhappy ever since. Now she was seeking a divorce.

"Things aren't going well. The mullahs turned me down."

"But your husband said many times 'I divorce thee.' Can he just do that?"

"It's true, and he can. But not frivolously. Muslim law states that if he has done it more than three times during our marriage, I can request my freedom. But I must have a witness, and they won't accept mine. It has to be a man; my witness is my husband's mother.

"Oh, Pat, I don't know where this will end, and I just want out of it all." I struggled for words to show I understood what I could not fathom.

During evenings with Rose and Fawziah, stories unwound of Rose's life— one of easy luxury neither Fawziah nor I had known. With servants for the chores and household marketing, Rose and her friends had filled idle hours visiting, shopping, and playing mah-jongg, until they discovered the Singapore Stock Exchange.

Periodically the group had checked into a nearby luxury hotel and spent a day or two trading on the exchange, with room service breaks in their suite. Each one had made an initial investment and agreed not to increase that with personal funds. Their getaway expenses came from trading profits.

Fashion magazines had stacked up unread as Rose pored over the financial section of the newspaper and studied public offerings and annual reports. Her stake had multiplied steadily, and the men at the bourse had begun to notice the attractive group of well-dressed women in their midst.

Then the bubble burst. A crash swept them up and spit them out with just what they had when they started. With the glow gone, the rest of the group had looked for new games to play. But for Rose it had been more than a game. She didn't miss the clandestine days of hotel living, nor the curious glances from the men at the exchange. For her it had meant the end of a secret dream.

Her earnings had been pegged to her freedom—her own English cottage. Donald, a generous and caring husband, had no desire to return to England, but Rose dreamed about it every night. The dream was finished, but not the longing.

Kit, dear,

Show preparations are progressing perfectly. Four sponsors are committed for the invitations, framing and printing expenses. I offered them prints equal in value to the money they are donating. That may not have convinced anyone, but I feel better giving something in return.

With 1,100 invitations, it's become a two-day show for 400 with wine and canapés at $600. Ellen assured me, "Don't worry about a thing. If you find a sponsor to pay for the reception, great. If not, I'll pay for it." I haven't found one yet, but I will.

Friends have offered transportation, help with sales during the show, setting up, and taking everything down.

I've raised $1,800 from the sponsors, but expenses are running up to $2,700. Friends came up with plans to cover the difference plus money to live on. Wilma threw a private party/art show at her home that brought in $500. Monique, a friend from France who I met at the Alcove last spring, arranged for me to join a two-day private show. That Saturday, I made $1,300 and breathed easier.

I'm in the home stretch. The last paintings just left for printing in New Zealand.

How is Peter doing? Any news?

Hugs my dears,

Pat

Rod and Helen returned, and I moved into Richard and Pauline Kean's large three-bedroom detached house near Changi. With 80 percent of Singapore's population living in high-rises it was rare to be surrounded by a yard and gardens, with windows on all four sides.

Pauline left to look at land for a tree farm in her native New Zealand, planning for the day when Richard would retire. As the troubleshooter for Lear jet owners from Hawaii to India, he spent most of his time away from home. "You could help us for the next month by forwarding the faxes that come in for Richard. We'd love to have you stay, and it would make things much easier getting ready for your show," Pauline had reasoned, and I had agreed.

The fax machine hummed not only with Richard's faxes, but messages from my mother, Dan, the boom manufacturer on the U.S. East Coast, Profurl (for shipping arrangements), and a local supplier for new engine mounts. Endless details for the show rolled in daily.

Mom wrote to say she had contacted the *Guinness Book of World Records* for details on how to record a singlehanded sail; the editors had responded that I would need to go through antipodal points. I looked in the dictionary. Somewhere my path had to cross through a point in the northern hemisphere exactly opposite a point on the route through the southern hemisphere.

I had expected them to say that the Suez and Panama Canals, with their requirements for pilots and line handlers, would pose a problem, assuming the presence of others on board for those few miles would interfere with my singlehanded status. But the canals were not mentioned, and using them hadn't disqualified Krystyna Chojnowska-Liskiewwicz or Tania Aebi. My route was almost identical to the one Tania had followed. I wasn't seeking recognition, but if gaining it would encourage others, especially women, to pursue their dreams, I would at least consider fulfilling the requirements.

Mom's fax went on, "We are not moving to the retirement center now. Someday, but not yet. Dick and Kay Hoffland [Dick had been my choir director in junior high school] have offered their new home on the Lake of the Ozarks. We'll move this month." I could feel the lift in her words.

And every two weeks I took the ferry from Changi to Malaysia for a cup of coffee and another two-week pass.

None of the other letters seeking sponsorships were answered. Then one drifted in from the wind vane company saying they thought I should sell my art to tourists so I could buy one of their units at $2,600 plus freight, less a $200 discount.

That was the end of the sponsorship search.

I invited my friends at the Buddhist Free Clinic to my exhibit, to show them my view of their city. The morning of the show a florist delivered a huge bouquet of red and white roses, carnations, and baby's breath trimmed with cascading ribbons and a message of "congratulations." It was from Jenny, Kok Moey, and Dr. Lee—the traditional Singapore way to pay tribute. They skipped the crowd on opening night and came the second day, when we could visit and make promises to stay in touch.

Dearest Kitty,

It was a smashing success!

I located a sponsor to replace Ellen, but that couldn't make up for the hours she spent on phone calls, the two luncheons, nor the hundred behind-the-scenes things she did to make the show possible. I gave her a painting of the courtyard under the Alcove where we met as a thank-you.

Days flew by, with many moments of success and a few of horror. My last shipment of prints arrived from New Zealand two weeks before the show, wet along one end and smelling of Chinese medicine. I opened the package in front of the postal officer, and together we examined the ruined prints. I filed an insurance claim and had them reprinted in Singapore. I rode a roller coaster of hope and anxiety through September and the beginning of October.

The ten press packs and hours on the phone produced no publicity, but I didn't need it. At least 400 people came between opening night and the next day.

Ellen served as Mistress of Ceremonies and Dennis Donahue from the Embassy gave the official opening speech. I told a few sea stories, and the party began. Every original sold, plus almost 80 prints and 50 miniatures. Friends handled the selling and accounting so I could visit with the guests. At the end of the evening I handed out thank-yous of minis and prints. After all expenses I made just over $10,000.

It felt wonderful to be enveloped by success. But a creative life produces an insatiable appetite. Finish something, leave it behind, and start again. It takes challenges to produce growth. The show has given me the confidence to know I could stay here and make a good life as an artist, and the idea is attractive, but I would be letting too many people down if I quit now—my family, sponsors, and most of all myself. The things in life I've left unfinished remain to haunt me. This voyage cannot be one of them.

Enough of things from this side of the world. I am anxious to hear your news and, especially, to get an update on Peter. How can you endure the waiting?

Much love to you both,

Pat

At the end of the show Molly, a former bank manager, handed over the proceeds and asked how I would keep in touch with all my friends in Singapore. She immediately began lobbying Kirk Moul, a fellow board member at the American School and regional head of Compaq Computers. Kirk agreed to provide a laptop computer and a two-hour crash course in how to use it.

Two donations of major equipment from my sponsor wish list of six was good. I wanted to show my appreciation. Profurl had only asked me to keep in touch, though I had offered them a painting and sent a print. I insisted Kirk select a collection of Singapore prints for his office.

I had returned to *Southern Cross* the week before the show, putting the big gray dinghy back in service and continuing to remove the engine and its mount at night. For a few days during the exhibition, the dinghy sat at the dock unattended while I stayed with Rod and Helen ashore. In the rush to leave I had forgotten to remove the outboard. Sloppy harbor chop had bounced the dinghy against the dock, forcing out air faster than usual. The precious two-year-old outboard had spent two days submerged and was beyond resuscitation.

I could not leave without solving my ship-to-shore transportation problem. The dinghy that would answer all my needs cost $2,300—almost enough to live on for a whole year. But it was the answer, and nothing less would do.

Helen picked me up to go shopping one day with the news that she and Rod had just bought property at Lake Tahoe. Their plans bubbled out: "We need to start the permit process right away. It can take forever. We'll just use a stock log cabin design to get it rolling, and change it later." I cautioned her that once their application for a permit was accepted, they could have a great deal of trouble changing anything. The design in their application should be the one they ultimately wanted to build, and that would require some soul-searching about how they wanted to use their house and why they were building it.

From that brief discussion, they decided I should design their new home. When they told me their decision, my confidence hit the floor. Ten years had passed since I had held a drafting pencil. I was out of touch, out of practice, had no equipment—no T square, no paper, no reference books—and I was sailing to the Med. I told them I simply couldn't do it, but they were determined. "You can do it from the Med and send us the design. We'll give you an advance now."

In the end I agreed, but only if they would try my approach. I didn't want to talk about bedrooms and bathrooms. Instead, we would look at the activities in their lives and what was required to enjoy them. They answered my pages of questions about the intimate details of their daily existence and how they celebrated special occasions, about their possessions and how and when they used them. This house would have tailor-made spaces for everything. Soon they had pages of notes and taped answers to the probing interrogation.

With their advance and part of the exhibition proceeds, I ordered the Avon Roll-up of my dreams. Dinghy problems would be a thing of the past. Once again, I thanked the Universe for another lesson in Manifestation. When the beautiful new rubber boat arrived, I sat a little taller every time I used or even looked at her.

Fawziah, Rose, and I met for our last dinner together, swearing solemnly to one day reconvene at Rose's English country cottage. We were certain that I would finish my trip and find my way to England, that Fawziah would get her divorce and be free to travel at will, and that Rose would once again live in England enjoying proper tea, lively art groups, and life in her cottage. The three of us agreed that anything one believed in enough would come to pass.

_____ NOVEMBER 1993

THOUGHTS OF STAYING ANOTHER YEAR HAD COME and gone. I recognized that life happened best on the days when I didn't know what to expect—a state guaranteed if I kept moving. The mystery of every port ahead and my drive to experience it pulled me out of the bunk each morning. My boundaries drew in, turning from town to boat, from art to sailing. The edges of *SC* curled up around me, and my focus narrowed back to the journey.

Preparations for the more than 5,000-mile-long trek through the Strait of Malacca, across the Indian Ocean, and up the Red Sea to the Mediterranean filled my days, and the familiar pressure of impending departure grew. Sometimes it felt like I was in "fast forward" with the sound left on. With the club-house pay phone glued to my ear, I made arrangements for galvanizing the anchor chain; ordered batteries, a sail, and a new boom; arranged to have the boom installed; and found someone to check and repack the life raft, fix the mounting bracket for the autopilot, and shim the tiller. My wallet, so unusually full in October, needed a tourniquet from the daily hemorrhage.

I bought six months' worth of groceries at Prime Supermarket. Five people wheeled the five carts of food to the elevator and out to the taxi. The driver angrily pointed out that he was not a delivery truck, but drove me to the club anyway. My purchases filled the new dinghy a foot above its sides, leaving just enough room for me to sit in one corner and run the borrowed outboard. It took five hours to move everything from the dock to the boat, onto the deck, and into the cabin for later sorting, repacking, and stowing. A six-inch-wide path between stacks of cans, bottles, and boxes led to the bunk.

Piles of stuff grew around me. *Southern Cross* and all the paraphernalia of voyaging seemed to own me. My days revolved around shopping for stuff, installing stuff, maintaining stuff, cleaning stuff, repairing stuff, stowing stuff, or getting rid of stuff. I went for a haircut and dissolved into tears when the attendant washed my hair. Her touch reminded me that it had been months since I had taken time for myself.

Every departure by sailboat was crazy, but this time there was additional pressure to hurry. My sister was coming to visit me in Phuket, Thailand.

When we had set the date, months before, as always, it looked fine. I had seen no reason why I would not be there by mid-December, ready for some fun. She would come for two weeks, and we would sail among the islands off Phuket before I left for Sri Lanka. The two weeks changed to three and a half for a cheaper ticket. I adjusted my itinerary, dropping a stop in the Maldives and shortening my stay in Sri Lanka.

I had planned to haul the boat out of the water in Singapore in early November, right after the show, and finish every project needed for the sail to the Mediterranean before leaving for Phuket. The sailing club office accepted my reservation to use their railway, the only place in Singapore where I could do my own work, and the only facility I could afford. The following day they dropped a boat, ramming its keel through the hull. All future reservations were canceled. My plans began to disintegrate.

After more than a year, *SC* could not move if the bottom were not cleaned first. Singapore Harbour had been measured as the fourth dirtiest in the world. No one was available or willing to dive below to do the job at a reasonable price, and I would not submerge myself in that water. With a wooden oar I scraped as much of the bottom as I could reach from the dinghy.

An inspection of the newly galvanized chain showed that one foot had been eaten away by the surface water in the harbor. The links had lost half their size at the point where the chain entered the toxic floating mix of petro-chemicals and organic pollution. There were 120 good feet on one side of the ruined section and 79 on the other, but neither side was long enough to use. I pulled out the 160 feet of rusty chain that had come with SC, but I lacked the time and money to galvanize it. It would have to do.

Every muscle ached. My body had forgotten the agony of boat work in the cushy months of apartment living and painting, of dressing up to go out with friends. I was back in scruffy shorts and old, holey T-shirts with grease under my nails.

The Profurl unit arrived, and I installed it with help from friends while *Southern Cross* sat at anchor—not recommended by the manufacturer. I had carried an auxiliary external antenna and power connection for the handheld GPS from Nouméa. The new setup would improve reception of satellite signals and eliminate the need for the internal, short-lived batteries. Since everyone I knew had experienced problems after completing this installation, I had waited until Singapore, where a representative would be nearby. I followed the manufacturer's instructions, wiring the GPS to the antenna and to the boat's batteries, and predictably it failed. The local representative said he could fix it, but while sitting in Singapore I had missed the warranty deadline by four months. It cost $200 to replace the defective parts.

Thursday—Thanksgiving Day—was my deadline at Immigration. Two weeks had passed since my last ferry trip to Pengili to renew my tourist pass. Either I took the ferry again, or I checked out and got on with my voyage. The officers in Customs, Immigration, and the Port Office looked perplexed when they studied the documents showing I had stayed more than thirteen months, slipping through their careful program to move yachts quickly out of town and up the coast to Malaysia. The last one commanded, "You be out of here by midnight tonight."

On Friday morning I threw a party for the sailing club staff with pastries and coffee—my thank-you for the countless ways they had helped me through the year. Mr. Tan shook my hand and turned away quickly.

On Friday evening twenty friends came to wish me bon voyage at the clubhouse docks. We toasted a year filled with good times. Photos recorded faces I would miss. I would stay in touch with some, while others would slip away into fond memories from one of the "homes" along my route.

I left the dock to moor out for the night. My world drew in to 31 feet by 9 feet 6 inches. Scenes of the city, with faces from streets and markets, buses and shops, friends and strangers who had touched me in some way, filled my dreams. A one-inch mooring line was all that held *SC* now. In the morning the only tie would be in my heart.

There was a deadline pulling me north up the Strait of Malacca to Phuket. It was time to move on.

40°N

TURKEY
Marmaris

GREECE
Lindos
CYPRUS

MEDITERRANEAN
SEA

Suez Canal

30°N

Suez
Sharm el-Sheihk

EGYPT
Safaga
SAUDI ARABIA

Sharm Luli
RED SEA

Gwilaib
20°N
UNCHARTED REEF
Suakin
YEMEN

SUDAN
Aden

Mitsiwa
(Masawa)

ERITREA
Gates of Hell
Socotra

10°N

ARABIA
SEA

GIANT
UNDERWA
SPOTLIG

INDIAN
OCEAN

0°
(EQUATOR)

30°E   40°E   50°E   60°E

PART THREE
To the Mediterranean

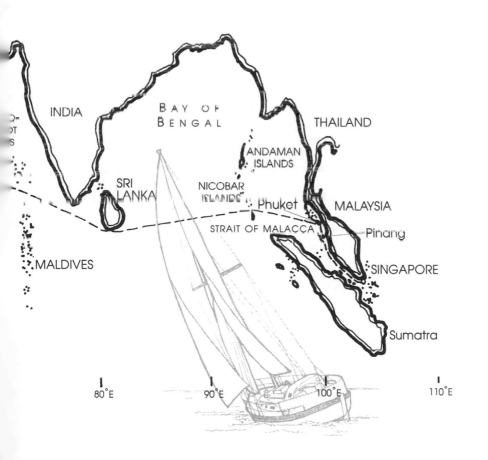

INDIA

BAY OF BENGAL

THAILAND

ANDAMAN ISLANDS

SRI LANKA

NICOBAR ISLANDS

Phuket

MALAYSIA

STRAIT OF MALACCA

Pinang

MALDIVES

SINGAPORE

Sumatra

80°E

90°E

100°E

110°E

TWO HUNDRED SHIPS PER DAY PASSED THROUGH THE Strait of Malacca between Sumatra and the Malay Peninsula, making it the second busiest shipping lane in the world. Since the mid-1800s the narrow waterway—some five hundred miles long and just thirty miles wide at its narrowest point—had also been one of the world's most notorious pirate lairs. The previous five years had been marked by increasingly frequent and sophisticated acts of piracy. While most assaults had been made against commercial ships carrying large sums of cash or valuable cargo, attacks on small vessels had also been reported.

My 700-mile passage through the strait to Phuket began at noon on November 27th in the midst of a violent Sumatra storm—with gusts over 30 knots, a torrential downpour, and lightning daggering down on all sides. *SC* was halfway between the mooring and a floating diesel barge on the northeast side of Singapore when it hit. I pulled alongside, and the scowling fuel attendant emerged from his dry, cozy office to switch on the diesel pump. Other cruisers heading north had left Singapore weeks before in a loose convoy, seeking safety in numbers. After numerous delays I followed them . . . alone.

Shipping traffic ran up and down the middle of the strait in a continuous chain, confined by regulated traffic lanes and the shallow waters and shifting banks on either side. *SC* traveled outside the shipping channels along the Malaysian coast, where I shared the water with fields of fishing traps and fishermen. With mild weather and no protected anchorages near land, I simply dropped the hook each night in shallow water a few miles from shore and hoped the neighborhood pirates wouldn't notice.

At sunrise on November 29th, the sound of rattling chain launched me out of a deep sleep on the settee. Outside was an open boat loaded with slight, dark, wiry fishermen who were struggling to raise my anchor. Tired, hungry, and frustrated, I looked around at miles of empty sea, wishing I had not chosen to spend the night in their favorite fishing hole.

Without a common language I couldn't explain that I had problems to resolve before I could move *SC*—a bilge full of water, an oil leak, a diesel leak, and a stomachache from not having eaten the night before. Skipping meals had turned into a bad habit. Finally they seemed to understand that I would leave as soon as possible, and moved away to wait for my departure.

The fuel leak had started long before and had destroyed an engine mount. In Singapore I had hired a fellow cruiser who had been a professional ship's mechanic to replace all the mounts, fix the leak, and adjust the valves. Now diesel oozed down the side of the engine with every lift of the fuel pump; seawater dribbled through the stuffing box; and the gasket under the valve cover draped around the top of the engine like an old lady's slip.

I ate breakfast, climbed behind the engine to tighten the stuffing box, adjusted the gasket, added oil, tapped a new hole and replaced the bleed screw to stop the diesel leak, and prepared to leave.

The first thirty-five feet of *SC*'s old chain rode up easily over the manual windlass, then it began slipping. Enough material had corroded away during its years at the bottom of a locker to let it slide through the toothed gypsy that should have gripped it. I had to haul 90 feet of bad chain hand over hand before reaching another section that fit snuggly in the gypsy. Only $550 worth of new chain would solve that problem.

On December 3rd the low-lying, jungled land of Malaysia was barely visible to starboard behind a shoreline of mangrove and shifting beaches as I skirted shallows fifteen miles offshore. Behind *SC* a white powerboat—most likely not a fishing boat—had paced my speed for an hour. I hid money and valuables, preparing for the worst. Another hour went by, and she gained only a little distance. My nerves stood on edge. She could outrun me easily. I had no idea why she was holding back.

When the suspense became too much, I grabbed the VHF microphone and with all the authority I could muster called, "Will the white powerboat following the small sailboat heading north off Kuala Selangor please state your intentions."

A slightly abashed New Zealand voice came back, "This is *Astron* responding. Are you *Saracen*?" *Astron*'s crew—Brian, Louise, and Hedley—were a family attempting the first circumnavigation of the world in a small powerboat by New Zealanders. After introductions, they apologized for scaring me half to death. At that distance *SC* had looked like their friends' green-and-white boat, *Saracen*. Gradually *Astron* picked up speed and disappeared ahead.

That night off the Outer Kra Bank, a high-powered fishing boat pulled near, forcing me from my course and herding me toward shore. At first I assumed he was trying to protect fishing nets and traps that I might not see in the dark, but the closer to shore we went, the more nervous I became. I turned back toward my course, refusing to follow him farther. He turned and raced at me head on. Ten-foot daggers of water flew up from the dark sea on either side of his plunging bow. I felt the black eyes of the captain burning across the water as he stood in the glare of his deck lights. A cold void inside froze me to the deck as his vessel loomed closer. At the last minute, I powered the engine, turned out of his path, and reluctantly followed his lead again. There was no other choice.

As he forced me toward shore, my doubts surfaced again. Off to port the nets and traps being tended by other fishing boats were marked with small lights, but there had been no such lights visible in my path. I feared he was pushing me toward a waiting gang and wondered if this was what a pirate looked like. But a half-hour closer to shore, he let me go—only an angry fisherman.

On December 6th I pulled into the channel between the island of Pulau Pinang and the mainland of Malaysia to service the engine, sleep in my bunk (instead of on the settee), and buy fresh provisions. Rumors of a new, unfinished marina and boatyard on the upper east side of the island had carried to Singapore and indicated it might be a place for the haulout *SC* desperately needed. With 6-knot currents in the channel, I pulled cautiously toward the new concrete fuel dock, prepared to jump off and secure the lines, but an invisible back eddy near the landing pushed *SC* from behind, forcing her into the unprotected raw concrete dock. After five years and 16,000 miles, *Southern Cross* sported her first scars. In dismay I surveyed four dark gashes in her cream-colored topsides.

The marina would haul *SC* out, but the price was more than $1,200, and slips were $50 per night. Instead I anchored close behind *Rose Rambler*, waving a greeting to Rosie and Peter. Our paths had crossed briefly after Brisbane, in Darwin and Singapore. With limited swinging room in the shallow, crowded harbor, I laid out only 80 feet of chain in the custard-pudding mud bottom, then pulled out tools and supplies to change the engine oil and automatic transmission fluid.

The hours slipped by in one mishap after another. When the oil pump quit, I pulled the plug at the bottom of the pan and caught the old oil in plastic bags. I was covered in oil and so were the bilge, the floor, and the cockpit.

No sooner had I cleaned up the mess, replaced the parts, and put away the tools than a great black cloud swept down from the Malaysian mainland. The leading edge hit with sudden ferocity, and *Southern Cross* danced backward down the channel. The gale's intensity grew, and even with the engine running *SC* sailed quickly past one boat after another, dragging her anchor as she went. She came to rest at last behind *Astron*. Brian, Louise, and Hedley waved a greeting from their back deck, seemingly unperturbed by my arrival. The storm passed, and I reanchored by Rosie and Peter, this time with my usual 120 feet of chain on the bottom. I could never again say that *Southern Cross* hadn't dragged at anchor since the Baja coast.

In the morning, with bags of oily garbage, documents, and a shopping list, I left to explore Pinang. A water taxi dropped me off at the end of a block-long rickety dock edged by the wooden stilt homes of local fishermen. Friendly greetings followed me through the watery neighborhood.

Peter had suggested skipping the check-in procedure for a stay of only one day, but I decided to follow the rules, checking in and out simultaneously. I found the port captain and Customs offices easily, but after failing to locate Immigration at three different addresses, I wished I had listened to Peter. The last office directed me across an 8-mile bridge to the mainland city of Butterworth. I had anticipated time in my one day in Pinang to stroll through the interesting old part of the city, to explore the remnants of British, Chinese, and Malay culture along back streets, to sit in a nice restaurant and slowly savor a good meal, and to shop. A 16 mile round trip to Butterworth wouldn't leave time for any of that.

As I turned to leave, the guard glanced toward the gate to the harbor officials' compound and exclaimed, "There he is now. Hurry. The man by that car; he's the Immigration Officer."

"Excuse me, you're in charge of Immigration?," I asked. "I need to check in. I just arrived, and I'll be leaving early tomorrow for Langkawi."

"You'll have to come over to my office in Butterworth; I don't have my stamp with me."

"Couldn't you just sign my passport and write a note in it?" He smiled, but shook his head, knowing what an inconvenience the trip to the mainland was for everyone. His office had been moved from the island the year before.

"Perhaps I could ride over with you? It's a long way, and I don't know the city."

This time he laughed, "Oh, wait a minute. I see some of my men over there. They were checking in a ship. I'll get a stamp from them."

In the heart of the old district I found the Eastern and Oriental Hotel restaurant, a throwback to colonial days with its tuxedoed waiters and a too-British menu of roast beef and limp vegetables served on starched white linen. In the hushed atmosphere I felt as alien as ET, as I sat back massaging one painful foot with the other under the cover of the long tablecloth.

After lunch I hunted for the supermarket and a few boat parts, wincing as I stepped through the bright sunny afternoon. A sign announcing "Reflexology Studio" caught my eye, and my feet took me across the street and through the front door without asking. I eased into the half-reclining seat and the practitioner began working over my tender soles. When he reached the middle of the pad just behind my big toe I couldn't breathe for the pain. "You need to take care of your stomach," he cautioned. "Don't skip meals." He was right of course, though I couldn't imagine how he knew about my irregular eating habits.

On December 8th I followed *Rose Rambler* northwest toward the Malaysian island group of Langkawi, 65 miles away. With two seasoned racers on board, *Rose Rambler* quickly outpaced me, surging off through the steep, short seas. I pounded miserably into them. Looking at lists of work needing to be done in Thailand, when *Southern Cross* came out of the water, I broke down in tears of exhaustion. I had not relaxed for a single day since long before the exhibition, and questioned why a sane person would choose to live like this.

In less than two weeks Libby would arrive for her holiday. I knew she would not enjoy spending it in a boatyard, and it was unlikely that I could finish and be back in the water before she arrived. I had looked forward to this visit—sailing around the islands, snorkeling, sampling Thai cuisine, and sailing together back to Langkawai. This time I would have a little money and time to take a vacation with Libby, and I needed one as much as she did.

By 2100 I realized that entering through the reefs after dark at Langkawi's main port of Kuah in rough conditions using the charts on board would be foolish. I changed course and three hours later arrived at a small bay on the south side of Dayang Bunting Island, where I could easily stop to wait for daylight. At last, in calm water under a brilliant night sky, I went forward to lower the anchor. The pounding seas had jumbled the chain into a solid mass that would not move an inch. *SC* drifted back out to sea while I crawled over the gear stored in the V-berth, reached into the chain locker, lifted pounds of chain to free six inches, climbed back to the deck, pulled that little bit through, and went back down to start on the next six inches. At 0245, I set the anchor and collapsed . . . without dinner again.

In the morning I sailed between hilly, jungle-covered islands down a protected channel into Kuah. Three days later, I was on the last leg to the Thai island of Phuket, gritting my teeth for the haulout and the rush to catch the February–March Indian Ocean weather window, when the northeast monsoons would push me to Aden safely before typhoon season. In mid-March the harsh northerly winds and adverse currents of the Red Sea would be at their most favorable for a northbound voyage. *SC* needed to be in top condition for the more than four thousand miles of hard traveling between Phuket and Suez.

The newly repaired GPS stopped working just as a cluster of islands rose over the horizon. I took bearings and plotted them while the old SatNav warmed up and began gathering signals to reactivate itself. The simple process of picking out edges of land with the hand-bearing compass and drawing a line from that point on the chart toward *SC* reconnected me to the sails, wind, boat speed, and sea. I hadn't noticed how much awareness the fancy electronic GPS had stolen from me. My instincts had lost their edge with the ease of reading numbers from its screen, just as wearing a watch slowly erodes the natural sense of time.

Almost reluctantly I repaired the unit that afternoon to guide me into the anchorage at Ao Chalong, the main port on Phuket, on December 12th.

_____ __ DECEMBER 1993

"HAULOUTS" CAME IN ALL SHAPES AND SIZES, BUT seldom in pretty wrappings. The moment would arrive when the dripping, wet bottom rose from the water, revealing the smelly accumulation of marine growth and possible damage from the previous year or two. Uncertainty would turn into hard-edged work lists; the budget would take on its own life; and the fear that I might never again leave the boatyard would become real.

By my count, I had participated in twenty-six bottom jobs: eight on my own boats and the rest on big trimarans belonging to friends. (I counted each of the tri's as three, since there were three hulls.) The routine was etched in my memory: the preparation, the materials and tools required, the sore muscles, the toxic fumes, and the boatyard camaraderie. I knew all about crawling out of bed each morning and into the stinky work clothes from the day before, lowering the supplies and tools down by bucket, and climbing down the ladder with a stabilizing cup of coffee to start again—grinding, sanding, fiberglassing, and painting—until the sun sank out of view and the smelly clothes came off for a maybe-hot shower. My sister was going to love this vacation if I could not get the job done before she arrived.

Jim from *Nepenthe* and I went together to make arrangements at the only haulout facility in Phuket—Boat Lagoon. The earliest they could haul our boats was December 16th. Lib would arrive on the 18th. The second piece of bad news was the price. They handed us the 1994 price list, but we argued that neither of us would be in the yard when New Year's Day dawned. Finally they dropped my charges to $700—five times the cost of my New Zealand haulout.

Early on the 14th we waited in the shallow bay by the first post marking the long, winding channel into Boat Lagoon. With pilots on board we paced past the markers down the serpentine path and into the marina complex. I waited on the bow to pick up the mooring as my pilot guided us across the basin. He backed off on the throttle and killed the engine, turned quickly to restart it, and burned out the starter motor. That unplanned repair and extra expense moved to the top of my list.

The following morning I was, surprisingly, not altogether depressed. Some perverse side of me enjoyed occasional opportunities to forage the dark sides of towns where grimy men in greasy clothes made things work again—machine shops, welders, places selling hoses and pipes, and electrical repair shops. I followed leads from one part of town to another and located a small shop with no workbenches. A young guy ran a few tests on the starter while squatting in an open spot on the floor, and confirmed my suspicion that the solenoid was bad. Within an hour the motor worked perfectly again. I paid the $40 bill and let out a sigh of relief, remembering the two previous repairs at more than $200 each.

Boat Lagoon was the most beautiful haulout facility I had ever seen. Flowers blossomed everywhere. Lawns were clipped to fairway perfection. The owner had expansive plans to add condominiums, marina docks, and a yacht club and restaurant, but at this point there were no facilities—no telephones, fax, or even an office. There were no workers to hire, no woodshop, no lockers, no laundry, no restaurant, no food of any kind, no high-pressure wash to clean the bottom when it first emerged from the water, and only one outdoor toilet and shower. At night we waded through knee-high tidal water wondering what might be floating or swimming next to us.

The visionary who had created Boat Lagoon owned a huge power yacht and now had a nice place to keep it, but he knew nothing about boatyards. He left day-to-day operations to his manager, but one day he arrived as a vessel emerged from the water. When the owner of the boat began scraping off marine growth before it dried and cemented itself to the hull, Mr. Boat Lagoon rushed over shouting, "Stop! You're making a terrible mess in my boatyard."

I pulled into the channel below the up-to-the-minute 80-ton travel lift early the following morning, thinking that a machine like that would only take minutes to lift *Southern Cross* and move her to her assigned spot in the yard. I should be scraping within half an hour. Hours later she still hung in the slings while men on each side of the lift pulled tiny chains over one pulley after another, raising *SC* one slow inch at a time. Incredibly, they only used the travel lift motor to drive boats around the yard, not for lifting them. At the end of the day *SC* had finally been scraped and blocked, ready for her face lift. I noticed corrosion on the rudder gudgeon and added an investigation of that to the projects for the days ahead.

I opened and drained some of the hundreds of tiny bubbles all over the bottom, checking the odor. Real blisters smelled distinctively nasty. These did not. They were between the hull and the barrier coat, just as I had hoped. If everything went without a hitch, I might be back in the water by December 23rd—in time for Christmas.

Lib arrived on the 18th and found my message with detailed directions to the boatyard on the big board at the airport. By midafternoon we were in a happy hug, swapping stories and making plans. She thought the haulout looked like a great adventure and offered to help. I apologized again and again for the inopportune timing, but she decided it would be a different kind of vacation. We left in a buoyant mood for dinner in town and a look at things to do when the boat work was finished.

SC once again rang with Libby's humorous dynamic. She found a StarMart at the turnoff to Boat Lagoon and howled with pleasure. "It's just like Oregon," she said. When she could not sleep at home, she went down to the Star-Mart in the middle of the night for a cup of coffee and to watch the people go by. Lib announced that she would be right at home here. She was looking and feeling good, approaching four cancer-free years since her surgery with constant encouragement from her doctors.

I found a German named Walter who declared himself an expert on fiberglass work after years doing car repairs in Germany. Libby stood to the side observing our negotiations. She had a good eye for male anatomy and later endorsed my choice of assistant with the comment that Walter had a great ass. "Someday if you write a book about your trip, he could head up the Good Ass chapter." I made a note, and we laughed like boatyard cronies everywhere—only most of them were men.

The visit unfolded with new developments each day. Hauling buckets of dirty dishes (since the sink could no longer be used), tools, laundry, huge bags of ice, and all the shopping and supplies became old and wearing for both of us, but especially for Libby. Her muscles, so used to resting on a comfortable chair behind a desk, complained about new tasks. Her nails and skin took a beating. For a change of pace I suggested she make a trip to town for errands. She set out cheerfully with maps, lists, and samples of bulbs, batteries, and O-rings, and returned dejected with a sprained ankle and empty hands. Even her fax wouldn't go out.

Libby repaired the cabin floor. The supports always broke about the time she came to visit, and by her third trip, she knew what to do. We worked together under the boat, filling the little holes I had opened and dried. Walter pursued his various epoxy projects, but the stuff he mixed failed to harden. He left for the evening wondering what had gone wrong. Libby and I dressed up after cold, outdoor showers and joined the rest of the boatyard group for a Christmas party.

On the morning of the 23rd, I looked at the still-gooey epoxy and knew I would be lucky to be in the water before New Year's. The power went off and on all day. My electric dual-action sander broke, leaving hundreds of little humps marking all the new patches on the hull. The replacement set of bronze gudgeons and pintles supplied by the boatyard where SC was built didn't fit the rudder. There were no workers to hire for the woodwork I needed to do. I gave up. Libby and I went to town for dinner at our favorite lemon chicken restaurant again.

I silently resolved to hang my miniature Christmas ornaments on Christmas Eve, thinking they might bring a little cheer to soften the growing gloom. The 24th followed the pattern begun the day before. At the end of the day I had managed to sand two-thirds of one side of the bottom with the small orbital sander. Libby left to pick up the dual-action sander from the repair shop, and was handed a box with a hundred pieces of the sander inside. Friends brought cookies and eggnog to cheer me.

Lib returned and entertained me with stories of her unfruitful day. She had looked for tongue depressors to mix the new epoxy by going from store to store with her tongue hanging out. Her one success was finding two fly swatters so we could be twice as effective.

I worked late on Christmas Day sanding, cleaning up Walter's mess, and fuming. Libby spent the day coaxing me to take the day off, which made me fume even more, since I was only trying to get done so we could have a nice vacation. She fixed a baked chicken, and at the end of the day we joined Jim and another singlehander for Christmas dinner. We never got to the decorations, which were nestled in their little boxes behind the settee.

The next day Libby announced that she was leaving to travel around on her own and look at temples. I wallowed in self-pity, wondering how she could leave when I needed her so much. I conjured up every old issue from every other visit and reminded myself how thoughtless she had been before. I swore that next time I would say, "No, you cannot come," and, "No, you cannot stay for three weeks just because the ticket is cheaper." I fumed and boiled and growled at everyone.

Walter and I screamed at each other and nearly came to blows. How could I know anything about it; I was only a woman—I heard it under the surface of every retort. No one had pointed out to him the monumental difference between boats and cars—they don't go underwater for a year or two in the dynamic forces of the ocean—until I came along and his workmanship failed.

I finally got through to him that epoxy wouldn't stick to the old bottom paint he had not bothered to sand off. Reluctantly he began to clean up the mess, grinding away on the hull as well as his teeth. The teeth fared better; he went all the way through the factory gelcoat in several places, breaching the integrity of the barrier. I reglassed and swore at Walter again.

I muttered away in anger at everything, jealous of Libby's perceived ease in life. When had she ever had to worry about money? I asked myself. Dad had been there providing what she needed. Everything had come easy for her—jobs, friends, recognition, and material things. She'd always done just what she wanted even if it didn't work for anyone else.

"Phuket! More like Fuck It!" I sneered, and began to think what I would do if Lib did not show up when the boat was ready to go back into the water on Friday, New Year's Eve. "I'll leave. That'll serve her right for abandoning me when I need her help . . . Going off to have a good time while I slave away . . . I want a vacation too . . . I deserve it as much as she does. . . .

"She always complains that so and so is never there for her. When has she ever been there for me? She wants me to stop work and go play; well, when did she ever take a day off when I went to visit her? She never writes to say 'thank you' after she comes. I'm the one who writes to thank her for visiting me." The internal monologue went on and on. I fanned the flames as high as I could and stoked my boiler for a full head of steam. The morning of the 29th, Jim stopped to tell me I was awful. "How can you even think of leaving her stranded in the boatyard?"

I found a young guy to fix the duckboard in the bottom of the cockpit and did the rest of the woodworking jobs myself—shimming the tiller and making backing blocks to mount new navigation lights. Turning to my last problem, the new rudder hardware, I had one hole in the gudgeon elongated into a slot to fit the holes in the hull, bought new bolts when the bronze ones broke, and mounted the old stainless steel pintle back on the rudder.

By the 29th *Southern Cross* looked beautiful again, with more than two coats of deep red paint on her clean bottom. Her cream-colored hull and dark green trim belonged in an old-fashioned Christmas card.

The next morning, I decided to wait for Libby, but by that evening, sitting in the nightclub-level lighting of the cabin, I was again wallowing luxuriously in self-pity. The replacement halogen bulb for the fixture above my table didn't exist in Phuket—Libby had looked everywhere. I blamed her for everything that didn't work and for making me feel so miserable. It was easier than looking inside. Moodily, *Southern Cross* and I swung in the sling, ready to drop into the water early the next day and catch the tide for the one-hour trip back to deep water.

New Year's Eve dawned. Mr. Sim, the yard manager, reported a problem with the wheel bearing on the travel lift. *SC* was suspended 20 feet away from the water in a piece of equipment that couldn't move. The workers removed the wheel and disappeared for repairs.

Libby arrived, and we chipped through the icy air. She had sat in a hotel room for days, never venturing to the beach, let alone seeing any temples. Good, I thought, she was just as miserable as I was. We didn't ask each other, "What went wrong?" or, "How are you feeling?"

I set up the docklines and opened lockers to check that nothing leaked as we entered the water—before they cut *SC* loose. We waited in silence. At 1:00 the tide would turn, and we would be leaving as the water dropped—always a bad idea.

We hit the water at 1:00. Everything checked out, and I opened the throttle to make time down the channel while I still could. Things looked totally different from the trip coming in. No pilot this time. The little rods that served as channel markers confused me. I wandered back and forth just outside the entry to the marina, asked a passing boat which way to go, and finally took off as someone called a warning, "Several posts have shallow water next to them. Don't get too close to posts 68 to 73."

As we approached the shallow stretch, I eased away to port. From the companionway Lib called out the readings on the depth sounder, "10, 12, 68, 3, 151, 0."

My first thought—oh no, it's broken—vanished with the realization that *SC* was sitting bilge-deep in mud and I was driving her farther into it. She wouldn't back out. We were in tight, stuck, not going anywhere until the tide turned again in six hours. *SC*'s first grounding.

Libby went below looking for books with advice, while I rowed out the main anchor and tried to pull us back to the channel. *Southern Cross* leaned slightly to starboard, toward the stream. One book said to prevent her from falling over toward deeper water. I lashed oars to the starboard rigging as supports, and they sank into the soft mud. I rowed another anchor out to port and buried it with a line tied around the mast to help hold her upright. *SC*'s beautiful new paint disappeared under brown, slimy mud.

We sat in the cockpit and Lib thumbed through *Smart Seamanship* looking for more ideas while the water vanished all around us, leaving a sea of wet mud. Finally the absurdity of it overtook us, and we began to laugh. Far off to starboard a narrow little stream meandered by, and occasionally a skiff passed on its way back to the harbor. We waved and acted as if we really wanted to be right where we were, ready for the fireworks.

We downed a New Year's Eve dinner of tuna fish sandwiches, potato chips, Bailey's and coffee, sultana biscuits, and a *pomelo* (similar to grapefruit), and waited. The water began to return. I retrieved one anchor and pulled up the oars. We slowly rose. As we broke free, Lib hauled the other anchor in quickly, and I drove toward the channel. With the spotlight she led us from stake to stake, back to deep water.

Midnight. Anchored off a nearby little island we watched the fireworks on the other side of Phuket, wished each other "Happy New Year," and had another Bailey's.

After two days of sailing and snorkeling, Libby left a week early to fly home. There were no harsh words between us, just, "I found an earlier flight." We never talked about what really happened in our hearts. We never opened the door to heal the feelings that surfaced. We just went on as if it had never touched us at all. Watching her go, I wished that she wasn't flying home disappointed and that I didn't feel guilty about it. I knew it was my own defenses and old, unresolved jealousies that made me want to point out her mistakes instead of looking inward. Her true feelings were still a mystery to me. I loved her, but did I really know her?

I sailed alone back to Langkawi.

AFTER TWO WEEKS OF PROVISIONING, SMALL REPAIRS, last-minute maintenance, shopping for spare parts and gear, and picking up the new sail and installing it, I had just four jobs remaining my last Thursday in Langkawi. I needed to buy fresh vegetables and ice, check out with the authorities, and fill the diesel and water tanks. As usual I dressed up to see the port officials, donning beige silk shorts, a red silk blouse, and my favorite silver earrings, a gift from my mother long ago. They were large hoops, not quite closed at the top. Things were always catching in that small gap.

As I put them on, an image of one earring flying through the air flashed through my mind. I hesitated, thinking it might happen in the dinghy, then shrugged it off and left for town with a large bag and a luggage cart to haul my purchases.

I hiked through sunny, dusty streets to a small produce market on the other side of the village, and made my selections from a minimal assortment of pineapples, carrots, potatoes, green beans, and things I didn't recognize. The bill was tallied, and we settled; I pulled open the cart to strap on the heavy bag of purchases. Something caught my right earring. It flew through the air and disappeared.

Busy shoppers stopped and jumped in to help me search the dirt floor— first for the small silver back that held it in my ear. We plowed through baskets of pineapples and potatoes, over and under all the racks and crates strewn about the shop. Nothing—no back and no earring. Then I spotted the earring hooked around one of the uprights of my luggage cart, just like a ringer in a game of horseshoes.

I turned the earring over in my hand. Everyone gasped. The silver back was still firmly mounted over the post on the back. Wide-eyed, superstitious villagers drew back from me, wanting no part of this white woman and her spells. There was no blood, and no enlarged hole where it might have pulled through my ear, but I could find no other explanation. While Islam ruled their lives from loudspeakers on the minarets, ancient beliefs were still passed on in hushed voices.

Superstitions and sailors have always gone hand in hand, intertwined in the mysteries of that great blue expanse with its power over life and death. The long, solitary hours and the link to the cosmos, which rule courses and currents, play deeply in the hearts and minds of seagoing people everywhere. Over the centuries, sailors around the world have grown to accept such admonitions as: "Never leave on a Friday. When you step a mast, put a gold coin under it. Always coil your ropes clockwise. Never change the name of a boat." And of course, there are many dire warnings against allowing women on board ships. Of these, only the Friday rule was sacred on *Southern Cross*.

On Friday morning I left for an anchorage by the waterfalls behind Tanjong Sawa, ready to sail the next morning across the Andaman Sea toward the Bay of Bengal. I hoped the sea gods would acknowledge that this was not a real Friday departure.

Sri Lanka, on the opposite side of the Bay, had been my home for one year in 1979–80, on board the trimaran *Windy*. Old friends were waiting to see me in Colombo, the capital. My last visit had been in 1983, after the sadness of racial wars began between the majority Sinhalese and the Tamils of the north. I wondered how much my friends had changed in eleven years, and how much I had.

I knew that I had arrived at a new understanding of the meaning of "failure." One day, somewhere along the way, I had passed a newsstand with the current issue of *Forbes* on display. In the upper right-hand corner a quote had jumped off the page: "I would never hire anyone who hadn't failed," said Malcolm Forbes. It was as if a lifeline had been tossed to pull me out of the morass of TWT's failure.

It made perfect sense in that clear tropical light, far from telephones and pressures. The only way to fail was to take a chance. No one achieved success without taking risks. I could have done many things better, but retreating to the realm of "safety" would never have made me happy. I thanked Mr. Forbes for that insight. At last I could ask myself whether, if someone should want to hire me, I *wanted* to be hired.

The freedom of the cruising life, the peace at sea, the pride I gained from tackling physical problems and solving them, and my budding success as an artist were bringing about some of the changes I had sought in the beginning of this journey. Going back into "the system" no longer appealed, but it was nice to see myself again as someone who had something to offer.

Days slid over the horizon as I sailed west at 5 knots, without traffic, and with nothing pressing to do but watch the sails, the GPS, and my musings. Occasional moments of exhilaration brought me out of my reverie as *Southern Cross* flew down a wave front at 7 knots, but when she settled back to 5, my journey turned inward again.

Just before I left Singapore, Dan had written recommending *The 7 Habits of Highly Effective People*. It had changed his day-to-day interactions and his approach to conflict resolution. I had found the book in Pinang and now added Stephen Covey's input to my contemplations.

Covey's effective people did three major things I didn't. They guided decisions according to a mission statement; they allocated their time to fulfill the mission statement; and they involved everyone concerned in the process.

I had picked up *What Color Is Your Parachute?* by John Bolles when TWT failed and I was trying to figure out who would hire me and what kind of job I could do. In the back of the book was a section on determining your mission in life, but at the time, the word "mission" had carried a Mother Teresa–like overtone, and I had decided I wasn't the type to sacrifice everything to selfless service.

I pulled Bolles out again, and this time understood that he wasn't asking us to wear a hair shirt, but instead to find the thing that would bring the most joy. He said to consider what activities would make time evaporate and you would find the source of that joy. In the 1970s I had taken a photography class. I would enter the darkroom at noon and emerge at 9:00 P.M., wondering where the sun had gone. On *SC* I was already doing the thing that brought me the most joy at this time in my life—sailing around the world, stopping in beautiful places to paint, and meeting people from many cultures. I wondered whether this could be my mission in life.

It seemed too selfish, but I finally concluded that the world needed people who reached for their dreams, so that others could know it was possible.

Being an inveterate list maker, I took immediately to Covey's plan for organizing time in accordance with one's mission statement. He said to list all my roles in life and map out each month, week, and day to include some activity for each role. When I included the aspects of my mission that involved my family, friends, and personal interests, the list of roles and activities mushroomed. As a mother I might write my daughters a letter. As a sailor, I had hundreds of jobs to do. As a role model I could write an article or give a talk. As a budding flute player, I wanted time to practice. Then came assigning a priority to each task. The stack of pages grew. My week began to look like Kilimanjaro, and old issues of "time" arose. I panicked.

One morning, before *Southern Cross* came into my life, I had been consumed by the idea that when TWT was finished I would become a bag lady without a home or job. Walking on the beach, I had begun a mental list of things to be grateful for: a home, food to eat, clothes to wear, good friends, a caring family, a challenging job, and enough *time* to do it all . . .WHAM! With the sudden realization, my body had gone into shock. The wave had run from the top of my head to my toes and stopped me dead.

"Time" had never been a gift I used to nurture myself, but only an instrument with which to accomplish the impossible everyday. Hours and minutes had come between me, friends, and family. If I could squeeze in one more thing before an appointment, I did. The same held true with dinner engagements, meeting friends, or visiting Tamara. Each night I had looked at the list of projects to be done that day and chastised myself for not finishing them all.

When I taught at San José State people had said, "There're no flies on Pat." I hadn't stopped running long enough for flies to alight. Whenever friends called, they immediately apologized for taking my time. If they invited me to do something they prefaced it with, "You probably don't have time, but. . . ." I had never questioned whether this was good for me or if there was another way to be.

Sitting in SC's cockpit, I tore up the lists and weekly plans I'd just made and considered the third major strength of effective people—group decisions.

Covey's plan was not just for individuals, but for any entity from a couple to a large corporation. Their mission statement was to be written by the group as a whole, with each person's input considered equally valuable and used to reach a point that satisfied as many people as possible. Joint decisions were then tested against the statement.

When I was six and had moved back with my grandparents in Draper after an absence of six months, an amazing thing had happened to all the other children in town. They had learned to play softball. I hadn't. School had started, and the activity at every recess was a softball game. I hadn't known where to go on the field or what was expected of me, and kids had jeered and made fun of me as kids do. It left an indelible mark, and I had hated team sports ever since. I chose swimming, tennis, skiing, running, and golf—solitary endeavors, with no one to make me feel like I had let them down.

Group process was not my strength. I either took over when I had good ideas, or I backed out of a discussion altogether. Covey was asking the impossible, or at least the very difficult, from me—to be a member of a team. It took a special kind of confidence to join a discussion, a confidence that your ideas would be respected.

Memories of childhood dinners still made me cringe. Typically they had begun with a challenging question from my stepfather. I never found the answers he wanted, and he'd spend the rest of dinner pontificating on what I should have said. As adults we had once argued about the pronunciation of "hydrogenated." Even when I brought out the dictionary, he had declared I was wrong.

At school I had never raised my hand to ask a question and show what I didn't know, assuming everyone else already possessed the answer. When the teacher asked a question I seldom volunteered, and then only if I was absolutely positive my answer was correct. I was totally amazed when I graduated seventeenth in a class of 260. Since one B on a report card made me a failure in my stepfather's eyes, I had only known I wasn't good enough.

That was old history, but the patterns didn't die easily.

SHIP'S DIARY: 24 January 1994, 1100 Zulu, 07°34'N/93°28'E, sailing 265M at 4.5 knots with 10 knots from ENE in 2- to 3-foot seas from the ENE. I love the furler and my new sail!

SC passed through Sombrero Channel in the Nicobar Islands, marking the end of the Andaman Sea, and entered the Bay of Bengal. The name conjured up images of maharajas and mystical jungles in which handsome tigers waited beyond the edge of the campground.

The next morning I awoke floating inside a huge gray ball without edges; the day after brought an electric-hot-pink sunset ahead, with pale-blue clouds above and the moon rising behind.

Other boats reported heavy traffic and a total lack of wind on the morning ham net. Perhaps they'd left port on a Friday. My route was blessed with no traffic and 8 to 15 knots of following wind.

The Indian Ocean and Red Sea passages ahead created a spicy mix of time pressure and worry, and my stomach responded each night with rolls of pain. The next two months offered the only time to cross the Indian Ocean with favorable winds and an absence of storms. In the Red Sea at the end of March the area of strong adverse winds and currents would begin expanding. I had to get there as quickly as possible or battle every inch of the way north. And on both shores lining the sea, politics created uncertainty and reduced the possibilities for stopping to rest and reprovision.

I changed my diet. Of the three medical books on board, one said, "Don't drink milk." The next said, "Use milk to soothe and coat the stomach." I charted a path down the middle that helped at times.

In *You Can Heal Your Life*, Louise Hay said about the cause of ulcers: "Fear. A strong belief that you are not good enough." I dreamed my stomach was full of gooey green tar.

Two areas emerged that might have changed the course of my life, if Mr. Covey had only lived a couple of decades earlier—my relationship to my daughters and the failure of my business.

When my daughters had said they wanted to live with their father, if I could have reached beyond my own pain and discussed the options with them, if we could have all talked about our fears, dreams, and perceptions, the result would surely have been different. Instead I had shut them out and erected a barrier against further hurt.

Before the voyage, whenever I had been happy, I had always felt that everything that had occurred before was necessary to get me to that point. Now other paths I might have chosen were emerging bit by bit. Had I considered, after graduation, returning to Bloomington or moving to another city in central Illinois to work as an architect? Eventually I might have opened my own office. Did I think about taking longer to finish school so I could spend summers with my daughters? I could have insisted that Terri come to California at least to visit . . . I could have quit school. . . .

At TWT Kelly and I had often wondered when the world would discover we didn't know what we were doing, but we both feared giving up control. Perhaps everything would have changed if I had brought all the staff into the process, trusting we would make the right decisions together. My ego would have fought it, but it might have saved us the agonizing death TWT endured.

Sometimes something could be right in front of me, but I could not see it. Now it was Sri Lanka. I was only 17 miles from the coast and 25 miles from a 6,000-foot mountain, and I saw nothing. I was approaching Dondra Head on the south tip of the island for the seventh time in my life, and at night again.

It had been a very black night the first time the three of us on the trimaran *Windy* had sailed around the south coast of Serendipity, as Sri Lanka was called centuries ago. We had strained our eyes for the fishing traffic lit by glowing braziers for miles in every direction. There were hundreds visible and many more without lights.

A terrified fisherman in a small boat to starboard had spun in circles as we hooked his net, lying across our path to an unlit boat on our port. We had cut the engine and carefully passed it under our small keel. There had been no common language in which to apologize.

Now I worked my way through the middle of a sea of fishing boats again, searching for the fleet's edge. The audio book *A Time to Die*—a gift from the farewell party in Singapore for some night when I didn't dare to fall asleep—played on my Walkman. I hung on each word and peered into the dark.

At dawn I waited off Galle, my home for four months in 1980, anxious to see how the little town had fared in fourteen years. The entry was tricky, and the GPS proved useless. No doubt the positions it was giving me were accurate, but my charts were off, or everything had been moved.

I dropped anchor near the middle of the harbor and waited for instructions. The comfortable glow of "coming home" descended. Other boaties came by dinghy to help me move into the new star-shaped mooring arrangement unique to this place. As I hauled in chain to move, a powerboat roared alongside SC, and an officer in dress whites bellowed at me, "MOVE THAT BOAT! We're bringing in a ship."

He didn't know that this town had once been my home, that I felt an attachment to this island and its people, that I had known another side of the Sinhalese. I dropped the bow anchor and backed into the star, and my fellow cruisers carried the stern line to a huge buoy in the center.

——————————— FEBRUARY 1994

ON FRIDAY MORNING BEFORE DAWN I SETTLED ONTO a hard, leatherette seat on the train to Colombo. Cool, damp salty air lifted my hair as the rhythm of the wheels picked up. Wood smoke from small wattle and daub huts along the tracks drifted on the breeze. Misty, pale-rose sunlight spread between the trunks of palms, and the surf beyond danced over a teal-blue sea. Small towns, where children played in dirt yards surrounded by flowers, broke the texture of the wooded terrain. More than two hours passed, and the outskirts of Colombo, the capital, crowded the rails with boisterous life: small, wiry people—men in sarongs and T-shirts or long, white shirts, women in colorful saris, children with big, shy smiles calling, "school pen, school pen, lady"; stark white Buddhist *dagobas*, Hindu temples in flamboyant colors and stacked high with gods and goddesses, and the rare mosque for the two percent Muslim population; open markets with carefully arranged pyramids of fruits and vegetables; small, dark shops selling fluorescent, ultrasweet soda pop that made teeth cry to look at it; busy, streaming crowds vying for space with blaring cars, buses bursting with passengers (bodies plastered on the outside around the door), three-wheel taxis, and bicycles; and mounds of young men lounging carelessly in heaps and watching it all go by. The late-nineteenth-century station we pulled into was covered in the arches and embellishments typical of British colonies around the world. In moments I was in a taxi to Shanti's home in Wellawatte, a suburb south of town, for the weekend. It had been more than ten years since my last visit, but her busy home hadn't changed.

Late that night the din of the three "outside dogs" set off the three "inside dogs." I looked at my watch and rolled over in Shanti's bed. The three-year-old in the tiny, closet-sized room opposite cried. Soft, comforting sounds from her mother crept past the door. Light filtered in from outside. I tossed a few more times and faded back to sleep until the dogs found something new to announce, wondering how Shanti ever managed a night's sleep.

We had met in Trincomalee, on the northeast coast, in 1979. I had been living on *Windy* in front of the old British fishing club at China Bay and had made friends with a group of New Zealanders hired to manage the new Sri Lankan–owned yacht-building operation nearby. Shanti had come for a weekend to visit her New Zealand boyfriend, chief of the finish carpentry crew.

At the time, Shanti had worked for an export company. A few years later she had opened her own operation and supplied wooden masks to TWT and other products to the Middle East. Eventually she had joined a United Nations program with offices in hot spots around the globe. Her assignment was to assist victims of violence in Sri Lanka. The civil war with the rebels in the north took her into homes where there was suffering on both sides of the conflict. Day in and day out she witnessed firsthand the results of the ethnic strife that had struck a line across Sri Lanka in 1982. The problem had begun far back in history, but that was the year it had erupted onto the front pages of papers around the world. That was the year when travel had become difficult, or maybe impossible, in the northern part of the island.

Beyond remnants of the aboriginal Veddas, settlers from southern India formed the original Sinhalese population when they crossed Adam's Bridge, the narrow intervening waters, 2,500 years ago. Each subsequent invasion from southern India was repelled until the thirteenth century, when the northern tip of the tear-shaped island became a Tamil kingdom. In the sixteenth century the Portuguese arrived, then the Dutch, and finally the British in 1796. With the last invader came international commerce and plantations—tea, rubber, and coconut—and the need for cheap labor. The British brought Tamil workers from India. The modern Hindu population descended from both groups comprised 20 percent of Sri Lanka's population of 16 million in

1982. The Buddhist and Sinhalese represented 70 percent, and the balance were Burghers—of European ancestry—and Muslims. The roots of discord between the Tamils and Sinhalese lay in ethnicity, not religion.

Since the granting of independence in the late 1950s, when the colony of Ceylon became the country of Sri Lanka, the Tamils struggled against an eroding voice as Sinhala replaced English and Buddhism became the religion of the government. Disenfranchisement of the plantation Tamils further fanned the discord, and violence erupted off and on. But the Tamil demand for a separate nation in the northern third of the country finally escalated to general violence in 1982. Jungle skirmishes gave way to urban guerilla warfare, and a line had grown across the country. The population of Trincomalee, once half Sinhalese, had become all Tamil as everyone else fled south. Travel had ceased, and the peaceful place I had known was no more.

In 1980 Shanti's household on Chapel Lane had been a beehive of visitors and those needing a helping hand. On a normal day some relatives would have dropped by, a few friends, someone from her office, a poor soul from the neighborhood, the relative of her maid or someone else's maid. As the day had progressed the airy living room with deep-red polished floors, tropical plants, and simple local furniture had gradually filled, and Shanti had extended hospitality and help in whatever way she could. For me it had been a bed for the night, a wonderful local meal, and friendship whenever I traveled down from Trincomalee.

In her roomy one-story bungalow surrounded by a small garden in a quiet neighborhood on the outskirts of town, we had sipped strong, black local tea, sharing our dreams and experiences. At the time Shanti had decided her nine-year marriage was untenable, divorce had not been common in Sri Lanka. She had walked out with the clothes on her back and her two young sons. The laws had not smiled on a woman leaving her husband—regardless of the reason. He kept all her jewelry, clothes, and household effects, and she began again. I had never probed for details, but in those days the mixed marriage of a Sinhalese granddaughter of a Kandian chieftain to a Tamil businessman must have added its element of stress.

Shanti's family came from the hillside capital of Kandy, the last royal seat of the country to fall to foreign invaders. When she was growing up independence had been new, and English had still been the language of the educated. As an adult, Shanti spoke English more naturally than she did Sinhalese and had long forgotten how to write the latter. Her parents, both educators, had chosen high-quality schools for her, and she too had become a teacher.

Her first assignment as a new, young graduate had taken her to the Maldives and given her a first taste of independence.

Before my last visit in 1982, Shanti had barely escaped with her life from a Sinhalese antiguerilla attack in Colombo. Searching for Tamil Tigers and their supporters, young Sinhalese warriors indiscriminately stopped cars and demanded proof of ethnic origin. Shanti still carried the Tamil name of her former husband (for the sake of her children). She spoke Sinhalese sufficiently and by some intervening miracle had been saved from the rest of the test—writing the intricate, curlicued script. Those less fortunate had been burned alive in their cars.

Petite, with olive skin and short, wavy black hair, in her sari Shanti conveyed a quiet Oriental demeanor. Underneath, though, burned a fierce sense of right and wrong and a brilliant mind. When an international organization had announced her nomination for a high level "woman of the year" award, she had thought I made the recommendation; I wished I had.

For twelve years we had kept in touch by mail. And now I was back in that happy, chaotic house, spending another night as one of Shanti's guests.

In the morning, I took a quick, cold shower in the small bathroom off the kitchen and prepared for the van and driver loaned to us for the day by our mutual friend Dushi, who had been a school chum of Shanti's from childhood and a friend of mine since the early days of TWT. Shanti's and my mission for the day was to deliver gifts to a girls' orphanage on behalf of "Mrs. Z." Daris Zinsmeyer had been a widow in her seventies when we met cruising the coast of Mexico in 1989. After a lifetime sailing around the world with her husband, she had ordered a 65-foot power yacht to continue her annual travels. There had been many evenings on *Sirad* spent visiting and playing dominoes, while she smoked her signature cigarillos and talked about her life. When I sailed on, we kept in touch.

Mrs. Z had sponsored a young girl at the orphanage for the last twelve years. I handed out forty small bags with butterfly stickers, sweets, and earrings, a hair ribbon, or a headband to the excited children. We took photos for Mrs. Z of Indika, her "adopted" child, and left to visit more old friends.

The main event of the day pushed us home to shower and change for dinner with Dushi. Memories flooded back of visits to her sumptuous three-story home when her husband had still been alive and their twelve-year-old daughter's battle with scoliosis had just begun. My stepniece had also suffered with this spinal curvature, and my mother had begun a correspondence with Dushi sharing advice and information. Now Dushi's daughter had just graduated *magna cum laude* from the University of Pittsburgh, and Dushi beamed with pride as she greeted us and shared the news.

The rest of the guests arrived. Laughter and stories flowed down the stairs and into the van, which was overpacked with all of us and all of the dishes, crystal, food, and necessities to put on a feast at Dushi's new garment factory far outside the city. We bounced over the rough country roads: Dushi, Shanti, the cook, the maids, two German visitors, their Sri Lankan butler, the driver, and I. Her sparkling new building finally emerged from the surrounding jungle, and we were swept away on a tour.

One of the few woman factory owners in a male-dominated industry, Dushi had thought of everything her 375 employees might need, including colorful, well-lit workrooms, attractive uniforms, living quarters, and medical care. She had put her heart into this facility as she had her first one, which still ran with 100 staff. We found our way to the boardroom-cum-dining room, transformed through the efforts of the cook and maids. Food, wine, and conversation filled the hours until long after midnight, when we bounced back over the well-worn roads to Shanti's home and our waiting beds.

The dogs greeted us with the usual din, but quickly settled down. More strangers had arrived in the intervening hours and found places here and there on the floor. It was odd having a whole bed to myself while people doubled up everywhere else.

Quiet had descended around us for at least an hour when Thikshan, Shanti's eldest son at twenty-nine, arrived home from a trip to Hong Kong. The dogs gave him their formal greeting, then we came out to welcome him while he unpacked gifts for all the family—including a colorful skirt for me. Silence again engulfed the little house on Chapel Lane.

The outside dogs announced the next visitor, and the inside dogs picked up the tempo. A knock sounded, and one of Shanti's younger son's friends called for him to come quickly. There had been a drowning. They needed Sujeeyan's help. People scurried around, hurrying him out the door to help with the father of the young victim. Shanti sent us back to bed, but sat alone praying for the family.

Several more outbreaks came from the outside dogs, then finally one that also engaged the inside dogs as another knock came at the door. Staff members from Shanti's office needed her urgently. One of their employees, a young man, had just been arrested. Could she please come to the police station to help get him released? She was all too familiar with these unexpected arrests; both of her sons (one a banker and the other a businessman) had been rounded up at random by Sinhalese militia in the past year. Shanti raced into the night to do what she could. I went back to bed.

Just before dawn the dogs were at it again. This time it was a phone call from Shanti's brother in Australia with more disruptive news.

Daybreak came, and we all struggled out for breakfast: the three-year-old and her mother, various unidentified people from far corners of the house who had needed help during the night, Thikshan and Sujeeyan, Shanti, and I. No one seemed nonplussed by the night's activities, but everyone was anxious for more details. Shanti calmly poured strong Ceylonese tea and served up toast with marmalade while filling everyone in on the events as if every morning began in just this way.

I packed my bag, made plans with Shanti for her visit to *Southern Cross* the following weekend, and caught a ride from Grand Central Colombo on Chapel Lane to the main train station downtown, thinking I would need to make a tape of dogs barking and a little noisy chaos so that the silence of *Southern Cross* would not keep her awake.

Colombo crawled by. City gave way to country, with beaches and surf on the right and waving palms on the left. Small bungalows surrounded with hibiscus, bougainvillea, and fresh laundry dotted the side of the road where people strolled and old men sat on the edge of the pavement, oblivious, their backs turned to the passing traffic. Evening descended and oil lamps flickered in cottages where women prepared painfully hot curries, grinding their spices and chilies by hand. Some might serve fish for dinner, if the tourists didn't buy it for more money than the fisherman could afford to give up.

Shanti was called to the troubled area in the north and could not keep our date.

As I tackled shopping and errands, preparing for departure, I explored old haunts around Galle, the oldest European town on the island, with a living, walled city at its center. I bought a Sri Lankan sapphire at the jewelry store in the rambling, old Oriental Hotel inside the fort, succumbing to the notion that it could be resold for a fortune in Europe, and put it away for a rainy day.

I had fabric and supplies on board from Singapore for a new cockpit awning to replace the green and white stripes SC had worn since Mexico. A young woman near the anchorage accepted the job and also agreed to mend a torn sail and sew the courtesy flags I would need to fly in host countries from Sri Lanka to Greece. In town I found an inexpensive long mirror; years of not seeing anything below the shoulders was telling in my expanding shape. It fit perfectly behind the family gallery on the inside of the door to the head.

Friends joined me for dinner at the Closenburg Guest House high on a bluff above the harbor. With high ceilings, gleaming wooden shutters and furnishings, wide verandas, and romantic suites draped in mosquito netting, it had been the plush home of a former Pacific & Orient ship's captain. A little worn around the edges but still clothed in an air of aristocracy, it was the high spot for a night out.

The Galle post office had mail waiting for me: letters from family, Dan, Helen, and a late package of holiday greetings from Tam, who forwarded the mail from my post office box in Santa Cruz. Helen had enclosed an article on new discoveries about ulcers. Recent research had shown that certain bacteria played a major role, and with antibiotics eliminating the bacteria, most ulcers could be quickly cured. Stress was not the only culprit.

Dan's letter asked me to call collect. "I want to meet you in Greece," he said when I reached him. "When will you be there?"

"I should be in Lindos on the island of Rhodes by August 1st. That would be terrific."

I splurged and hired Simon, a local boat worker. At $5 per day, even I could afford a little help with cleaning and polishing.

Simon had worked on the trimaran for a few months in 1980. He knew about boat work—what to do and what not to do. I reminded him to not touch the expensive new red, ablative paint I had just put on the bottom in Thailand. He acknowledged with the local side-to-side head wobble that began from the joint at the base of the skull (and looked like "no" but meant "yes"), hopped down into the dinghy, and started to work enthusiastically—first to clean the topsides, then to put on a coat of wax, and finally to buff them. I returned to my project inside the cabin.

Several hours later, at lunchtime, I climbed down to the dinghy and looked in horror. He had just scrubbed off all three layers of the new paint where I needed it most—at the waterline in the midsection for ten feet on each side of the hull—where the dinghies came to land. This special soft paint was designed to slowly slough off as the boat moved through the water, leaving a fresh surface to discourage barnacles. It was vulnerable to abrasion, and Simon had gone at it with a scrub brush. For the next two years *Southern Cross* would look like a boat needing some TLC instead of the well-cared-for vessel that had sailed into Galle. I wanted to cry. I wanted to kill Simon. I tried to forget how much my Thai haulout had cost. Instead, I took him to shore for his lunch break and accepted what could not be undone. It was my fault for not staying with him to see that he understood the instructions. Simon worked for several days until every inch of the top-sides and stainless gleamed, then hand-carried jugs of diesel and water to fill the tanks.

Departure day drew close with only two jobs left: stocking fresh provisions and shipping the painting requested by one of my exhibition sponsors in Singapore. Around the world, I'd found express mail service to be the best system for sending almost anything anywhere. Every country had some version of international EMS through its own postal system, providing receipts and tracking numbers to ensure that one could trace a package if it disappeared. I always bought insurance, too—just in case.

As usual, I wrapped the package securely between layers of foamcore with heavy brown wrapping paper and strapping tape. The postal clerks shuttled me from person to person and finally to the postmaster. "We don't handle EMS here. You'll have to go to Colombo to mail that."

"A three-hour train ride just to mail a package?"

"That's right."

The only person versed in any aspect of EMS was on tea break, but it didn't matter. It couldn't be done from Galle. In Colombo, the post office first demanded that the package be unwrapped. When I pointed out that they didn't sell the materials needed to rewrap it, they relented, then gave me a choice: send it by EMS without insurance or send it airmail with an insurance value of $40 maximum. The painting was worth $500.

They won, of course. I sent it via EMS without insurance and caught the return train to Galle, chuckling over old encounters with the Sri Lankan post office. In the summer of 1980, my neighbor Jim had had an urgent gift to send to Italy (for his girlfriend's forgotten birthday). Racing into the post office, he had asked for the fastest means possible to send his package. The clerk had taken charge; Jim had paid the money, accepted his receipt, and left, relieved that everything was under control. The following week he had been sitting on the veranda of the Closenberg, sipping his morning coffee from a dainty china cup, when a note regarding a package arrived from the post office with instructions to come to the office.

Jim had presented the note to the same clerk from the week before. In no time the fellow had returned from the back room and handed Jim's birthday package back to him. Incredulous, Jim asked what had happened. The clerk responded with the familiar side-to-side wobble, "Oh, you paid too much."

Many things in Sri Lanka had come a long way, but the post office was not one of them.

Lightning crackled on all sides, and rain pounded down in torrents. Ships loomed in the distance as Sri Lanka disappeared over the horizon. The winds shifted from 12 knots out of the northeast with 4-foot chaotic seas to 12 knots from the north-northwest with lumpy seas. I tucked myself into a dry corner under the new sunshade with roll-down sides—a design improvement offering protection in almost any weather.

Sailing toward the southern tip of India on my second day at sea, I considered the story I had heard of Lynn's experience on *Kiwi Star* not far from this area. The previous year Lynn had made the trip north from Singapore and turned west to cross the Indian Ocean. Off the southwest coast of India, four open boats full of fishermen had approached her boat asking for food, then realized she was alone. Forty Indians had boarded her boat, jeering and taunting her. One had slit the straps of her jumpsuit with his knife, then spit betel juice at her while the others had stolen jugs of fuel and water, food, money, electronics, lines, and even the windlass handle. They would have left her helpless 200 miles from Cochin, India, but for a final taunt she threw at one of the men. "You call yourself a Muslim, and you'd leave me here with no fuel." He had turned back, looked in her eyes, and put down the jug he was carrying.

Days unwound in pleasant beam-reach to close-reach sailing with 6- to 12-knot winds from the north to northwest while I worked on concept studies for Rod and Helen's house. Listening to their voices on tape, I made bubble diagrams with notes about views, sun, sound, privacy, how they celebrated Christmas, and what they did first when they awoke in the morning.

A gauzy, pale-yellow sunset with soft tinges of pink grapefruit and peaches and cream was followed by a cold, hard white sunrise and a sea covered with mysterious tiny, brilliant electric blue and turquoise objects—not quite animal in appearance, but no other explanation fit.

Five hundred miles out from Galle, I passed through Nine Degree Channel in the Maldive Islands below India. Ahead and to starboard rode a fishing boat with a small cabin and men working on deck. I started the engine, dressed in loose clothing, and put on a man's hat. With my flare gun for a weapon I opened the throttle to maximum, leaning over now and then to talk with an imaginary partner below.

My heart pounded as we drew closer together. Then I saw the net strung far off to their side. They were working and paid no attention to *SC*. I imagined the disaster that might have followed if I had changed course to pass them on the side with the net and realized that my fear could have been more dangerous than the potential pirates.

For eighteen months the new Navico autopilot had been a reliable partner, but that afternoon it failed. The motor ran but the arm didn't respond. I switched to the wind vane and dismantled the pilot. Aluminum shavings sparkled over the inside surface, and the housing on the worm gear slid freely back and forth with its threads stripped by the stainless steel gear.

Winds dropped to 5 knots from the north to northeast, and the vane steered halfheartedly. In Darwin, tired of fighting its erratic behavior, I had switched to the Navico full-time. Twenty months had passed since I had used it last. *Southern Cross* slowly wandered 60 degrees on either side of the course while I worked, catnapped, and now and then took the tiller.

SHIP'S DIARY: 28 February 1994, 1100 Zulu, 10°31′N/068°19′E, steering 286 at 3.3 knots, wind 4–5 knots northeast, and sea at 1 foot northeast. It's a long way to Aden steering by hand.

On the tenth day nothing would keep *SC* on course. As night fell I gave up, unlashed the tiller, and stretched out in the cockpit. The same reliable tenth-day peace of the Pacific crossings and the Coral Sea passage to Darwin descended; despite the steering problems I was, to some degree, enjoying myself. I laughed, wondering if I were just a little crazy.

At 0405 I awoke to inky black air, but the water underneath *Southern Cross* was lit by a sixty-foot circle of light, as if a giant, underwater spotlight were suspended below. It floated away, and another circle appeared in my wake.

The morning ham net carried stories of various strange phenomena from other boats. Lloyd and Judy on *Batwing* had caught a fish for dinner. They stored the excess in a plastic bag in the refrigerator. Later, in the dark, they noticed the contents of the bag were glowing.

Small, shining turquoise creatures, glowing fish, and huge circles of light—they all brought to mind ancient mariners' fantasies of strange sea creatures, mermaids, and ghost ships. The rational possibilities—a whale or a large school of fish disturbing a body of phosphorescent plankton or a substance dumped or spilled overboard—couldn't explain the perfect circular shapes I had seen. I preferred joining the ancients and feeling the sea's mystery around me.

On day twelve I reached the halfway point to Aden (Yemen's arrival port at the bottom of the Red Sea). It looked like the passage I'd hoped to complete in twenty-one days might take twenty-four. A celebratory glass of Pernod with water, no ice, slid down smoothly. The cloudless sky defied my depth perception and made the setting sun seem only one mile away. In the thin light, I reviewed my budget to reach the Med. There was only $250 for Aden, and I needed $600. Of that, $100 was for fuel and then came the autopilot repair, provisions, an Egyptian visa, a dozen jerricans, port fees, and living expenses. The money from Singapore had melted away.

From the tape deck Pete Seeger sang a song about sailing the next morning, and my mood lifted. I wondered how I could have spent two weeks at sea and not thought once about how lucky I was to be out here doing this.

In my drawing pad, the stack of bubble diagrams for Rod and Helen had been steadily growing. I looked through them with satisfaction, remembering how much I enjoyed solving design problems. Someone had once told me of a man who was searching for the common link among singlehanders. Eventually he found himself in a discussion with a group of long-distance solo sailors. One of them was contemplating an ocean crossing by kayak. The others immediately jumped on the project with suggestions: You should try this for food storage. . . . I'd handle the drinking water this way. . . . Now how about communications. . . . He realized at that moment that the common bond was a love of problem solving.

The broken autopilot taunted me. I examined the unit again, checking off various supplies on board and waiting for an inspiration. A friend had once mentioned repairing an engine with Marine Tex epoxy filler. The repair had lasted for years. I packed the acetone-clean housing with epoxy filler and slid it over the silicone-coated gear. It worked for half an hour, then the tiny motor sounded a death rattle.

One small, pathetic fish sacrificed himself to my handline, but when I filleted him, one of the small white balls inside that looked like gobs of fat stretched out and began to move—a parasite of some kind. I tossed it back to the sea and opened a can of tuna.

SHIP'S DIARY: 11 March 1994, 1100 Zulu, 14°02′N/054°57′E, steering 264M at 1.6–2 knots, wind 4 knots south-southeast. Lloyd and Judy on *Batwing* just called to congratulate me on passing the halfway point around the world.

SC was moving again. The day's tally hit 68 miles made good, with 520 to go. The fickle wind raised my hopes, then dashed them again, as boat speed wavered between 1 and 2 knots. I tried to force myself to do nothing but steer, but I couldn't. I had to move, eat, read, walk, anything but sit hour after hour at the tiller.

Sunday afternoon brought wind. The knot log hit 2.8 and I broke out in a smile, but it didn't last long. That night I fell asleep going backward, listening to slapping sails. *Southern Cross* lurched in the wake of a ship a half-mile away and tossed me across the cabin.

At dawn hundreds of leaping four- and five-foot fish roared down on *SC* like an approaching detachment of jets. The entire horizon undulated with their bodies.

By evening *SC* was almost steering by the sails and almost on course. With the genny sheeted to the end of the boom, the main out over the rail, and the staysail up, I was on a port broad reach. While I searched for the magic sweet spot where she could balance without effort and I could sleep, I enjoyed a glass of wine and the sunset—electric red-orange, not round but elliptical, with a band of mauve at the bottom sitting on orange water with textures in pink and blue. One little silver jet trail shimmered above.

The wind began to fill in the morning. *SC* sailed well, but only with me glued to the tiller. I checked inside the autopilot one more time. The motor was only loose, not dying. I tightened the screws holding it in place, and that afternoon while the pilot steered, I finished listening to Rod and Helen's tapes. It felt like they had been along for the passage.

By Wednesday at 0600 the wind was up to 10 knots, and five-foot seas with a knot and a half of favorable current pushed *SC* toward Aden. The autopilot began slipping again. My handmade threads had worked for 18 hours—now I knew how to do it again.

After 87 miles made good that day, *SC* made 63 the next, then 78, and finally the last 31 miles into Aden Harbor. The passage had taken 28 days.

Chuck, from *Viki*, pulled alongside before the anchor hit bottom. "Here's a little care package from Dot with some local oranges, bread, and dates. Hurry, get your papers together, and I'll take you in to clear. They're ready for you." He couldn't wait to see the expressions on their faces when a woman singlehander arrived to check in. They examined my paperwork in polite amazement.

THE *MUEZZIN'S* CALL TO PRAYER BEGAN LONG BEFORE sunrise and blared above the quiet harbor. Below, *SC* sat in a thick, black sea of gooey tar. A storage tank on shore had been shelled in the last skirmishes between North and South Yemen, and the oil had pooled behind a concrete wall. Now it was slowly seeping through the ground and into the harbor. Each boat wore a wide black band at the waterline. Dinghies, fenders, and lines were all coated, and by the time we arrived at the jetty in the guarded Custom's yard so were Judy, from *Batwing*, and I.

Dressed in conservative slacks and long-sleeved tops, we picked our way past the rubble of shelled and abandoned buildings and through the dirty streets and refuse of Aden. It sat only a day's sail from the narrow opening into the Red Sea at the Gates of Hell—Bāb al-Mandab. The surrounding terrain looked like a small piece of hell itself—no flowers, no plants, no playgrounds, no cafes, no sign of joy. Children climbed over the rubble looking for ways to entertain themselves. Women peered down from inside the shadows of dingy apartment buildings. The civil war between North and South Yemen had ended four years before, but it could have been only hours for all we could tell. The city lay in a pall of gray air and dirt.

The conservative republic of the north and the radical Marxist south had attempted a confederation in 1970, each keeping its own president, capitol, and political leanings. Russia had come to the South, bringing military support and economic aid, and the wealthy had fled north to Saudi Arabia. Then in 1986 a coup in the South had ended the fragile association with the North, and war had followed. Russian aid evaporated with the fall of the Eastern Bloc at the end of the 1980s, and the South had gone back to the table in 1990. A new accord had been reached, North and South Yemen had merged to become the Republic of Yemen, and peace had returned. But after four years of calm, Aden appeared to be part of a country unable or unmotivated to rebuild and move ahead despite its offshore oil wealth.

We made our way toward the small street market, passing the post office, narrow gift shops carrying a smattering of small electronics and knick-knacks—a front for discreet black market money changers hidden in the back—the bakery, and clusters of young girls on their way home from school. They wore long white robes from head to foot with small black cloths like aprons covering their eyes. A shiver ran down my back as I thought of all the vibrant young women in countries along my path who were running, swimming, playing tennis, and reaching out for all that life could offer.

During the Russian years veils had nearly disappeared from the streets of Aden. Perhaps, in part, the custom returned from Saudi Arabia with the wealthy. With 70 percent of Yemeni women illiterate, the girls on their way from school may have come from those well-to-do families.

Something in their manner felt so familiar as they chattered and giggled. Everything but the full fabric covering spoke of youth. Like a first bra, lipstick, or high heels, it was their symbol of maturing. Looking at them, I could only see the price they were paying.

The streets were filled with women covered in black robes, veils, and long gloves. Occasionally a foot peeped from under a hem, painted with henna in intricate patterns reminding me of a South Seas tattoo. A flash of red high heels and Levi's suggested stories of another life at home or traveling abroad, out from under the head-to-toe *balto*.

An all-black figure waited ahead of me in line at the bank. Twenty minutes later at an intersection she drove by alone, unveiled and waving to me with a large smile. I wanted to sit with her over coffee and hear her thoughts, to know if she chose this or was forced into it by her Sha'fi Sunni branch of Islam.

It was not the first time, nor would it be the last, that I would grapple with confusion and anger at local customs regarding the rights of women. Arriving in strict Muslim countries concerned me enough to take care in my own dress and behavior and hope that Mohammed's instructions on how to treat women would apply. There was nothing in the Koran, I had been told by several Muslims, dictating that women should wear veils or be repressed and treated abusively. Just the opposite. Women were to be cared for and respected. As in most religions, contemporary leaders interpreted ancient writings to suit their aims.

Yemen was one of a few countries in the world where women's life expectancies were shorter than men's. I had my own ideas about the relationship between their well-being and their religion, but I wanted to hear the truth from them.

Our Immigration passes clearly restricted us to the area around the port and Aden city proper. But hearing that others had managed to visit the ancient city of Ta'izz in North Yemen by taxi, Judy, Lloyd, and I arranged an excursion to see the marketplace inside the two-thousand-year-old city walls. We found a willing driver in Husein and met the following morning at 6 A.M. in the parking lot west of Customs.

As we drove north through periodic checkpoints in the pale-yellow light, a stark landscape of sand and rock unfolded, overpowering in its austerity, with long sweeping vistas of barren land, jagged rock outcroppings, and distant mountains. Built from the pink, black, green, and white stone of the surrounding countryside, villages melted into the rocky terrain. Few signs or embellishments broke up the harmony of buildings and environment, except the steel doors on every building. They were painted outlandish, bright colors in geometric patterns, and provided relief from the sameness.

A cold, wet gray mist cloaked the mountain city 4,593 feet above sea level when we arrived five hours later. We huddled together in an open-air cafe sipping strong coffee and gazing over a neutral blanket of low buildings laid across the hills in all directions. Husein drove us through a denser version of the villages we had passed in the morning to the gates of the ancient market. We explored on foot through rough, cobbled streets with large rocks and muddy ruts. Displays of wares—fabrics, antiques, household goods—crowded around the doors of the small shops, spilling over the crumbling walks to the edge of the street. Pushcarts and street vendors filled the corners between, selling sweets, qat leaves (the mild stimulant chewed by Yemeni men), brooms, baskets, spices, pulses, and produce. Men and women thronged the streets, some in colorful costumes from the surrounding countryside and others in the somber black and white of the city. The bustle and strangeness of the place pulled us this way and that through the colorful bedlam.

Forty youngsters soon surrounded Judy as she passed out red, white, yellow, and green balloons, until her pockets were empty and the children disappeared. Men paraded past in white sarong-like *futahs* trimmed in bright colors or long white robes with curved daggers at their sash-wrapped waists without splashing a drop of mud on their spotless hems. Each one modeled a black-and-white checked *kaffiyeh* (the headdress Westerners associate with Yasser Arafat) wrapped in a personal style.

We sampled local sesame and clove sweets, bought gifts from the antique *jambiya*, or dagger, dealer, and found a shop with fabrics. I picked out my own black-and-white head scarf for a shawl and began to wrap it around my head. Husein jumped up to help arrange it in his favorite fashion, and the shopkeepers joined until they were satisfied it was right.

More fabrics found their way to the counter, and Judy and I looked through the men's *futahs* made locally on backstrap looms and stitched by hand down the center. I selected a soft white one with bright pink and green in the black design along the edge. Again the two shop owners rushed in to correct my South Pacific–style women's wrap. I assumed a stern, menacing scowl, ready for battle, then did a little dance around the open-air shop, and looked up just as a tiny lady walked by covered completely in her black *balto*. She tossed me a thumbs-up sign, her eyes snapping behind the veil. I knew I saw her smile.

After a lunch of ten mezes-style Middle Eastern delicacies, an entire meal of appetizers served in small dishes, we climbed back into Husein's battered taxi and snoozed our way down through the mountains to the sea, seeing again the young girls in white on their way home from school. That night my thoughts drifted through the past year to other women living under the strictures of Islam—Fawziah seeking her divorce, the women on the Singapore MRT existing in *purdah*, denied their freedom of speech, dress, and choice, and the young mother staring out from behind the crocheted bars of her *chador* at the sailboats bobbing freely at anchor.

I wondered whether all these women had accepted this path willingly. Did they have any regrets or wish to live another way? I had often heard that many preferred the *chador*, that it gave them a sense of privacy and security. Could there be a kind of freedom behind those bars? Was it possible to set your mind free when you were not concerned about impressions? In my pinstriped suit had I really been so free, or had my stripes been the bars of a different fabric jail?

Nick Hawkins, a British sailor who had been working in the oil industry in Aden for several years, had just discovered the cruising community the week before I arrived and had offered to help anyone find the supplies and services they needed. He ordered clutch plates for *Batwing* and parts for my autopilot. They arrived hand-carried from England in a few days. In payment for my parts he accepted a bank draft from Dayle that had been waiting at the Aden post office. The bank exchange rate was a small percentage of that on the black market, but the money changers wanted half of my check for their service, while Nick could deposit it in England for full value.

All nine boats sharing the harbor shopped, stowed, did maintenance, and worried about the Red Sea. Westbound sailors leaving Southeast Asia faced two choices: to go around the Cape of Good Hope on the south tip of Africa or to head up the Red Sea. I had no desire to sail into the large rolling seas off South Africa, but more than that, the Mediterranean had been calling to me ever since Mexico.

Back in Brisbane the New Zealanders on *Sunglo* had shared their advice for the grueling Red Sea passage: Go slow; plan on two months; if the weather looks good, leave at 5:00 A.M.; be ready to stop at 2:00 P.M. if the wind picks up; if the weather isn't favorable, stay put and wait. Shipping traffic used the middle; I would travel the sheltered edges, between the barrier reef along the coast and the fringing mainland reef. Anchorages in *marsas* (mini fjordlike lagoons entered through a break in the fringing reef along the coast) and behind the outer reefs and islands would provide rest and escape from the harsh northerly winds.

Water, fresh food, diesel, and propane for two months were my biggest concern. The east side was off-limits from Aden to the Sinai. Stopping in North Yemen was discouraged, and all of Saudi Arabia's coastline was prohibited except in an emergency. The Saudis would provide fuel and water and send you out immediately. No female would be allowed on shore.

On the west side, Eritrea had welcomed the first visiting yachts in thirty years the previous spring. Their war of independence with Ethiopia had finally ended; they were celebrating and open to visitors again. Americans were discouraged from stopping in Sudan, though many pulled in, disregarding the warnings. There had been recent attacks on tourists in the historical areas of Egypt I wanted to visit, and gunboats near all the border areas were a threat. Many uncertainties lay ahead as I sailed out of Aden just ahead of *Batwing*.

Every boat leaving Aden with its necklace of tar smears around the waterline stopped at Jabal Aziz, renamed "Clean-up Island." Gasoline and fiberglass cleaner took off the top layers, and time might remove the rest. Old cooking oil and dish detergent softened the goo coating my almost-new dinghy. I blocked out thoughts of the money spent in Thailand and Sri Lanka to make *SC* look her best and those of the fish swimming in the cleaning-operation residue.

In the morning, one by one, we left for Bāb al-Mandab, the narrow entrance to the Red Sea known as the Gates of Hell. What possible images could come to mind from such a name other than smoldering boulders, roiling black clouds, a murky sky, chaotic seas shoved by racing currents, screaming winds whining through the rigging, sails torn asunder, and me prostrate in the cockpit as freighters drove down upon me? Reverend Jonathan Edwards, the archetypal fire-and-brimstone 1700s preacher, could not have painted a more forbidding picture than my fears dreamed up on April Fools' Day 1994.

Yet the evening's passage was perfect, with following seas and 20 knots of fresh wind. I laughed at my apprehensions, wondering where huge winds and seas would have come from under that clear night sky. Traffic passed in a steady stream to port; a break came, and I crossed to the west side of their lanes with no sign of a ship for more than an hour. The sun rose over flat water on the first day of the 900-mile voyage up the Red Sea.

SHIP'S DIARY: 3 April 1994. 13°57.6′N/42°43.3′E, anchored at Zuqar Island. Celebrated Easter with a hike over the island with *Batwing* and *Jack Fish*.

For two days *Batwing* and *Southern Cross* convoyed from anchorage to anchorage to the south side of Umm Es Sharig, a three-mile long, 30-foot high, dun-colored pancake of an island covered in brush. The anchorage I chose offered protection in every direction but east. At 0300 the wind swung east. *Southern Cross* pitched violently. Plunging into seawater up to my knees as the bowsprit dropped below the wave crests, reared back, then fell again, I worked for an hour to release the snubber, ease out more chain, and reattach it. In that time the line had jumped out of its roller and worn a groove an inch deep in the wooden bowsprit.

I left at 0630 for Adjux Island with wind on the nose. Behind lay the barrier between the lower portion of the Red Sea, where wind came out of the south from the Gulf of Aden, and the rest of the passage to Suez, which would deliver nonstop headwinds. The March window, when the barrier was at its northernmost limit, had come and gone before I arrived. From this point on, I would face an unrelenting plunge north.

Charts for the Red Sea provided poor information for small boats cruising through the coastal reefs, and most were offset one to two miles from real-world GPS positions. I plotted the GPS coordinates of each day's anchorage on the chart. The chart error began a mile and a half southwest; later it shifted into the northeast.

On April 9th, relying on the chart of Port Smyth on Isola Shumma, information in the sailing directions, and a view from the mast of the grass-covered low-lying shoreline, hills, rock outcroppings, and reefs, I held my breath as I approached the hoped-for entry and slid between the reefs into a placid lagoon.

Two young boys swam toward *SC* from shore a half-mile away as I anchored. After Southeast Asia, where few young people enjoyed water sports, it was a surprise to see them so at home in the sea. Thirteen boys from thirteen to eighteen years old lived alone on the barren island, tending herds of 400 goats, 350 sheep, 25 camels, 50 oxen, and some cows. The food and water delivered by boat once a week from the mainland was overdue. I took them to shore by dinghy and gave them cookies and a jug of water. In their home, a dirt overhang with a few cots, a couple of chairs, and some dishes and pans, I accepted the chipped cup of tea they offered. A bony young boy swung a goatskin filled with milk idly back and forth, making butter while we visited.

One of my escorts reported that he went to school in Asmara, the mountain capital of Eritrea, and studied geometry, chemistry, geography, English, and mathematics among other courses in an ambitious program. He said he would return to school after six months of herding, but didn't explain why he had been chosen in the first place.

On SC I started the borscht I had promised Judy and Lloyd would be waiting when they arrived, along with fresh pumpernickel bread. While they limped north with another broken clutch plate, Judy baked a blueberry cobbler for our dinner.

When Batwing pulled in at the end of the day we delivered more food— rice, sugar, tea, onions, beans, and cookies—matches, and another jug of water to the young shepherds on shore. The boys herded their flocks into the camp and the air filled with hundreds of lambs squealing after being held for the day in nearby pens. Mothers answered in their distinctive ways, and silence fell as each baby latched onto the right teat. Having run among the scrambling animals milking the mothers for their own dinner, the boys offered sweet sheep's milk from a large, not-so-clean pan. We sampled, too touched by the gesture to worry about hygiene.

As the African sun set beyond the edge of the now-purple lagoon, we sat down on SC for our feast, wondering how the folks at home were spending this beautiful April evening. None of our books, magazines, or friends had painted this interesting picture in their images of sailing the Red Sea. I had not thought about the people I would meet, only the struggle against the elements and the politics.

The next day, sailing west down the South Mitsiwa Channel between the red and green harbor entry markers, past freighters, a U.S. Navy search-and-rescue ship, and on to the small anchorage for visiting yachts, I found Jack Fish and Rose Rambler. Batwing followed with another engine problem.

On shore we were greeted by the friendly, redheaded chief officer from the navy ship, in Mitsiwa on a mercy mission to clear the harbor of a sunken freighter that was blocking the commercial dock. "If there's anything we can do for you, please let me know."

"Oh yes," I replied. "I need help from your machine shop, a haircut, and a doctor."

The ship's machine shop made a new part for my secondary fuel filter that stopped the old air leak for good, and their barber gave me the best cut I had had in years. But the medical crew was not available to tell me what to do about my chronic stomachache. I thanked them with a signed print to hang in the mess.

Word had passed down the Red Sea from earlier boats that a visit to Asmara, the capital, would be worth the seven-hour bus ride. Judy, Lloyd, and I picked up our visas and planned a two-day trip to the mountains.

Our fair hair stood out in the backseat of a bus full of locals as it pulled out of Mitsiwa. We were still half-asleep in the predawn light, surrounded by a mélange of local costumes and dark skin. Surreptitious glances from behind veils and under turbans turned our way, as our fellow passengers indulged their curiosity. Thirty years of war had kept visitors at bay, but now we came, one or two at a time, to see the new Eritrea, formerly Ethiopia's seaside property.

Control of Eritrea's seacoast had passed through many hands over the centuries. It was settled around 1000 B.C. by Semitic nomads from across the Red Sea and enjoyed twenty-two centuries of self-rule. Then the region passed first to Ethiopia, then to Turkey, and in the 1860s to Egypt. The Egyptians also won control of the northern and western regions of the country, which had never before fallen under foreign rule. Ethiopia claimed it once again for fifteen years, then Italy took it as a colony in 1890. When Britain ousted Italy in 1941, Eritrea became a protectorate of the Allied powers, who gave it to Ethiopia in 1952, when a friendly government ruled from Addis Ababa. The Ethiopian Federation, established then, granted Eritrea autonomy with its own government, constitution, and choice of language. But Ethiopia reneged on the agreement, and Eritrea's independence vanished in 1962. No one had asked the Eritreans what they wanted, and not one country in the world had protested when Ethiopia assumed full control.

The parched coastal lowland rolled by, covered in scrubby plants and an occasional abandoned armored vehicle. Shell craters in the road bore mute reminders of both pain and triumph to most on board. Blank eyes and the stumps of limbs on several freedom fighters on the bus testified to their sacrifices. We three wondered where they had found the courage to fight for their country against the ten-to-one odds of the Ethiopian armed forces backed by the Russians.

Slowly, as the bus neared the mountains, they took us into their midst, sharing stories of heroism and hardship through one English-speaking man in the backseat by us. He told how they had asked for help around the world, and none had come. Today they need not thank anyone but each other. They had wanted their freedom enough to build the best guerrilla army in the world to fight for it, without an air force, without antiair defenses, and without guns or munitions except those they captured from the enemy.

From the row ahead, flashing dark eyes peered over silver veils, and mustached men peeped backward, lacking words for questions they held poised in a strange language. Our smiles conveyed our willingness to converse, and slowly a dialogue of photos, hands, and universal understanding began. The Rashaida women's tribal costumes—rich in red, black, yellow, and green patchwork and heavy with silver trim—tempted cameras from our bags. We stopped for tea and a prayer break for the Muslims on board; the Rashaida women brought out their best jewelry, dancing on fingers and arms, to pose for us as camels sauntered by.

At another stop, the mother, sons, and wives from the seats ahead encircled us as we sipped tea away from the glaring midday heat in a cool, shady room by the side of the road. Everyone laughed when Lloyd pantomimed Judy's need for a rest room. The horn called us back to the bus. Higher and higher into the mountains we rose through terraced fields to Asmara, a city untouched by the war. Perhaps both sides had loved her beauty too much.

Mountain coolness crept through our airy seaside clothes as we scouted for the White Hotel with rooms at $3 per night. Sidewalk cafés, shops with hanging cheeses and sausages, and the sound of escaping steam from espresso makers told of the days when Italy had created a Mediterranean town in the African mountains. Elegant, statuesque Eritrean women strolled through shops in stylish clothing and cornrow hairdos fit for *Vogue*.

Over small cones of gelato, our freedom-fighting friends from the bus called out greetings from a café. Blond and black heads mixing again, we embraced one another like long-lost companions, laughing and parting once more. Judy, Lloyd, and I sipped chianti over garlic bread and pasta and strolled spotless, friendly streets. Our fellow busriders called from their hotel balcony. The men dashed down for formal greetings, while their wives and mother waved and smiled behind their veils from the second floor.

In the cool, mountain morning, we found steamy hot cappuccinos and fresh bread for breakfast, then poked and prodded the wares behind shop doors, found a late-nineteenth-century post office with gleaming brass letter-box doors and fresh plants, and passed a Coptic cathedral undergoing restoration. Everywhere we felt the pride of people caring for their homes and shops.

In the mad scramble for return seats on the bus, our Rashaida family's faces fell to find us in the front while they wound up in back. Photos from the day before—extralarge enlargements—were passed to the back of the bus. They giggled, showed everyone, and the poses began again.

A regal beauty just across the aisle flashed a smile, displaying two teeth of pure gold surrounding two others that were filed to perfect points. When I smiled back, my teeth cringed.

More stories followed of hardship and heroism from the man next to me, his cousin, and the bus driver. "I've come back for the first time in thirty years. We fled to Italy when it became too difficult to live here anymore. I wish I could have helped win the independence, but I was too young then. This is my cousin; he stayed and fought.

"He wants me to tell you this was his command post, right here. They had a restaurant behind the pile of rocks over there, and his office was under that bridge. In the middle of the war they still held classes—English, math, whatever they could manage." He wanted me to know what had happened—battles won and lost and daily life.

The driver stopped for Lloyd to video an abandoned tank. I followed the men to hear more of their stories, but they were looking for relief, not just a view of the tank. I hurried back to the bus where the other women waited.

Hot, sticky coastal air seeped in through open windows, and Mitsiwa's lights came into view. We passed freshly planted flower gardens and trees, happy, laughing people, clean streets, and restoration projects in process. The contrast with Aden, both in the physical surroundings and in the spirit of the Eritreans, struck us sharply.

On the way back to *Southern Cross*, I passed a young sailor standing by the navy ship. He asked me, "Look, we're here because we have to be, but why would you come?" My answer had to do with dreams and having the faith and strength to see them through, as the Eritreans had.

Jack Fish left one morning, I left the next, and *Batwing* waited for more clutch plates. Five days and four anchorages later I pulled into Suakin, Sudan. A portly, uniformed officer waited on the high commercial wharf to board *SC* and check my paperwork. He lowered his face away from me, saying, "We would be ashamed to let a woman go alone like this"—as if they would have let her down in granting her that freedom.

I cried inwardly for any Sudanese woman who longed to go into the world and do something alone. Certain that deep inside we were all the same, I knew we must share common wishes, hopes, and dreams. This man would never understand that women have passions for testing their limits and experiencing life just as men do. I hoped my arrival in his port placed at least a seed of doubt in his view of the world.

The "new" town of Suakin wrapped around and protected the lagoon where *SC* anchored, and the lagoon in turn surrounded an island. At 9:00 the next morning a tap, tapping on my hull came from two young Sudanese boys in a dugout canoe. They brought an invitation for coffee on shore, as they did for each boat stopping there. The children pointed to the island and a tiny beach surrounded by an illusion of ancient Egyptian ruins. Three thousand years ago, Ramses III used Suakin as a port for trade across the Red Sea, but these remains only appeared to be that old. They actually had been part of a thriving Ottoman slave-trading post in the nineteenth century.

Peaches-and-cream spires and fluted white columns floated over still, turquoise water. Crumbling coral building blocks, slowly returning to their former underwater home, made a Daliesque image against a background of small huts, palms, and camels on shore across the narrow isthmus that connected the island to the ramshackle town.

On the way to shore my mind played with images of Ginn, the ancient legendary demon of Suakin who impregnated the seven virgins marooned here by a storm on their way to King Solomon as a gift from Sheba. My two escorts, Kuri and Taj, waited on the beach—happy I had come as promised.

On the edge of the sand a small shack leaned against the crumbling ruins. Entering its dark interior I found three young men lounging on narrow beds that lined the bare, unpainted walls, and in the center one tiny, ancient man in a long, white traditional galabia squatted by a glowing brazier. I sat on the edge of one of the beds, wondering at my nerve in being there. This was a man's world, and I was outnumbered. Awad, with his three long ceremonial scars on each cheek, watched through curious, piercing eyes as his cousin Hashim greeted me. They were both self-appointed yachts' agents, helping cruisers with fuel, shopping, and changing money. Their friend sat by silently, his dark face a mask for his thoughts.

I gradually relaxed to the rhythm and music of old Hussien's mortar and pestle grinding fresh coffee. He told of his latest wife, a twenty-five-year-old Nubian, mother of the two boys. She had left to visit her family in the high mountains to the south. I wondered how many other wives had shared his eighty-some years, and how many children had preceded those two. Had he inherited his powers from Ginn?

Stories, fantasies, and dreams wove through the perfume of strong, fresh coffee and smoke-thick air. Tiny cups were filled with heavy, sweet, foamy *jeb-bana* coffee, and conversation ebbed. Less than 400 miles away, hundreds of thousands of Sudanese clung to life in refugee camps slowly dying from starvation, disease, and war.

Climbing into the dinghy as the sun slid behind the ghostly ruins and toward the distant desert, I had to turn down the old one's offer to join my expedition, do my laundry, and make Sudanese coffee every day.

By midafternoon the following day I had reentered the reef-lined coastal channel en route to Egypt. *Southern Cross* shuddered as her bow plunged into six-foot walls of blue-gray water while wind laden with stinging sand pounded her—almost on the nose. My target was a small break in the reef leading into Marsa Gwilaib, a protected anchorage surrounded by sand dunes.

It took engine and sails together to push forward while the distant landscape slowly changed, and one hill slid past another an inch at a time. Just before the point of no return—when it would be too dark to enter on arrival and too late to turn back—I gave up searching for the pass and turned south for Abu Imamah, ten miles downwind.

After eight hours the next day I had traveled seventeen miles into the calm waters of Gwilaib. It was like stepping into a secure, warm mountain cabin in the middle of a blizzard. To seaward, creamy white mounds of sand stood out against the intense turquoise of the lagoon water and the blue of the sky behind. In the other direction were hills washed in lavender and deep blue shadows—a waiting painting, if only I had the time. The night sky slid down over the scene and a full moon turned it back into daytime. This was the nature of sailing the Red Sea.

The wind blew all the next day, and I waited. The following morning I motored out past the fringing reef, the channel, and the outer reef into water that the chart showed open. I went below for fifteen minutes to plot a new course, not knowing that a huge, uncharted reef stretched from horizon to horizon less than two miles ahead.

In the past two weeks two other singlehanders had lost their boats on Red Sea reefs. One had been on his third circumnavigation of the world, and the other was a very experienced blue-water sailor. I said a thank-you prayer for the guiding hand that pulled me up on deck just in time to skirt the unmarked reef.

If I dwelled on the possibilities, setting out each morning would have been impossible. Another singlehander waited out the strong winds in a *marsa* nearby, frozen in fear. It would take him two more months to complete the journey north. The self-forged shackles of fear were more destructive than any danger met underway.

SHIP'S DIARY: 27 April 1994, 1430 Local. 22°00′N/037°05′E, motorsailing in light winds past Elba Reef to port . . . not visible.

The border between Egypt and Sudan lay ahead. At times all of the land in both countries had belonged to Egypt, and at other points in history Sudan had ruled both nations. Between those extremes the dividing line had floated back and forth. Near the border political tension still ran high. I swung out to sea to avoid the patrolling gunboats.

Eighteen miles short of Marsa Alam, one of the few *marsas* with life on shore, I gave up again and this time sailed back to Sharm Luli. I had had visions of dinner in a restaurant to celebrate reaching the three-quarter mark in the first month of the passage, and of buying ice and fresh food. Inside the *marsa* at Sharm Luli I found *Viki* and *Cygnus*. Chuck insisted on taking me to shore to check in with the Egyptian authorities, just as he had in Aden. The officials had watched my arrival and would be waiting.

Chuck escorted me to meet the military detachment garrisoned on the north shore. Three men lounged in the small office, drinking tea. They straightened up and tugged at wrinkled uniforms as we entered. The man at the desk made notes in his ledger from my passport and boat papers, handed everything back, shook his head, and stared at me, a woman sailing alone. It was becoming a common reaction from the Arab world.

We stopped outside to visit the soldiers' camel in his "corral." The huge, handsome animal stood docilely in the center of a large square of sand. Two of his legs were loosely tied together, but still allowed him to walk. The boundary of his keep was marked by a small mound of sand less than ten inches high, and at the center of each side was a three-foot break in the mound. He could easily have walked through those openings or stepped over the little mound. His only fetters were in his mind.

For three nights we waited for a break in the wind, but by 0700 every morning it blew 20 to 30 knots. We read, visited, or scouted the shoreline for shells—Dot's passion—then gathered on a different boat each evening for dinner and a visit. I welcomed the break in routine but was anxious to continue. The prevailing winds would intensify day by day over the approaching summer season. When each break came I needed to gain miles before the next northerly picked up momentum. The uncertainties of weather, supplies, politics, and attitudes hurried me on, and each day spent in the Red Sea claimed a share of my dwindling funds without offering an opportunity to replace them.

With the winds calming late every afternoon, I convinced the others to make a break for it on the third day. At 1545 we left in a convoy en route to Safaga. Familar voices joined our radio chitchat as five other shelter-bound boats also departed from surrounding *marsas* and island anchorages. At midnight we converged outside the port and made plans for a trip overland to Luxor and the Valley of the Kings.

Only 220 Red Sea miles remained. The voyage had gone much better than expected. I had waited for calm weather only three and a half days over the past month. Some boats had spent three and half days in each of ten different places.

I anchored behind an island off the channel into Safaga to wait for daylight, and the other seven pulled in around me. Quiet descended. In the morning, after checking in, I moved north of town. The sign on shore said "Safaga Paradise"—a desert oasis with cold beer, a restaurant, laundry service, fresh water, fax machines, and phones. We let out a collective sigh, anticipating all the luxuries that awaited us.

─────────── MAY 1994

THE VHF BUZZED WITH PLANS FOR OUR TRIP TO Luxor, home of both the eleventh- and twelfth-dynasty pharaohs and the New Kingdom dynasties, on the banks of the Nile River. Some of us were going by taxi and the rest by bus with the locals. I teamed up with Rosie and Peter for a side trip to the lesser-known ruins at Dendera along the way. By mid-afternoon everyone had arrived in Luxor. The others checked into a nice but reasonable hotel at $25 per night. My budget sent me to the Nour Home on Sharia Mohammed Farid for $4. I climbed into bed with visions from a long-ago semester of ancient architectural history.

A soft knock on the wooden door announced breakfast—tea, bread, and jam delivered by a small boy in the cool, predawn darkness. I sat on the edge of my small, lumpy bed to eat and finish selecting three tombs to visit in the ancient necropolis at the Valley of the Kings. The others were going by taxi, but I had answered a call from the heart and arranged to ride by donkey.

My Bedouin guide arrived in his flowing white robe. "You're my only customer today," he announced, with a look of disappointment. But he had agreed to the price the night before and did not argue. We set off on foot for the ferry to cross the Nile. Crowds milled about on deck with their bags of produce, boxes of pastries, luggage, and small children not yet ready to be up. On the east bank the blush of dawn rose over Luxor behind a skyline of piercing obelisks, temple remains, and columns.

The ferry docked, and the scrambling crowd hurried away. At the donkey corral nearby we mounted and left for the distant hills to the west. The air turned pale pink and yellow and began to warm as we bounced down the side of the narrow road. My breath caught. An old lecture slide came to life. Out of the dewy fields ahead rose the Colossi of Memnon. We paused. It was too much for a photo.

Our donkeys climbed steadily up the hills. The temperature rose with the sun. They were sweating, and so were we. Up and up the hillside we rode, until my guide stopped by a rock. He would wait while I made my pilgrimage below. There was no shade, no tree, only the very hot sun. "Please don't take too long, but see what you wish," he asked.

I hiked down into the valley, loving the feel of earth beneath my shoes, the motion of my strides, even the sun on my back. I bought the three-tomb ticket and one extra for Tutankhamen, but my three choices were all closed for work. Instead, I descended into the cool, damp air of the last resting places of Ramses IX, Ramses III, and Sethnakht/Tawsert. The magic and mystery stole my breath away as cool spirits brushed past, drawing me deeper into the silence. The walls, columns, pilasters, and tombs covered with rich detail in brilliant colors and molded surfaces defining muscle and structure—lost in photos— mocked the gray stones I remembered from college textbooks and lecture slides. I filled my pockets with this moment stolen from history, mine to experience alone in the still-early hours. I wondered how it would feel to be the first modern person to see such a place. I wished I could share this experience with Shawn.

Back in the now beating sun, I thought about my poor guide and the donkeys above and hurried up the hillside. As we crossed the dusty terrain, vendors offering "antiquities" popped out of the shade from behind rocks one by one. They claimed to have gathered their small treasures while working at one of the excavation sites. Other salesmen approached with alabaster or cool drinks.

I succumbed to the lure of a "very old," tiny, pale turquoise scarab. This small beetle had special significance. In college, "Scarab" had been the honorary scholastic fraternity for architecture students. History pulsed in my palm. I saw visions—ancient rites and rituals—in which it had played a role, and tucked it away with a trace of guilt for encouraging tomb robbery.

Queen Hatshepsut's tomb stretched out, wide and stately, across the head of the valley below us as if carved from the cliff behind it—a powerful statement from the first woman to rule as Pharaoh. The scale deceived me from high above, giving the impression of an architectural model or a stage set in pale sienna until I saw the tiny people walking about. As we rode away my guide instructed me, "Just remember hot chicken soup." I rolled it around on my tongue, realizing that most of his customers wouldn't already know how to pronounce Hatshepsut.

We descended the trail and stopped at an alabaster factory. The owner embraced my guide in a huge bear hug, welcoming him as if they were great friends. Perhaps they were, but I also knew this was how my guide made his money. They smoked a *hookah* on the terrace and left me to wander through shelves of delicate, almost transparent stone bowls, plates, and artifacts.

My host produced cool drinks and poured on the charm. He couldn't live without me. He was in love. I quickly chose one small bowl and remounted my donkey; he counted his money and returned to his *hookah*.

We bounced down small paths through lush fields fed by irrigation ditches from the Nile and passed others jouncing on their donkeys to market, to work, to the fields, or to visit families—but no tourists. Everywhere I heard the soft "hoosh, hoosh, hoosh" of riders telling their donkeys to keep moving.

At my guide's small home I met his parents, siblings, children, and wife. They offered me mint tea, buffalo cheese, pita bread, and a seat in the cool interior. His young son took me to catch the ferry and return the donkeys to their corral.

I landed in hot, sweltering noontime Luxor wearing my visor and dark sunglasses against the glaring sun. A shopkeeper standing by his door called out, "You have beautiful eyes." How could he tell? Similar comments had followed me down every street in Luxor and Safaga, far more than in other countries. Egyptian attitudes toward their own women were more open than in many Muslim countries—I had seen no veils—but still men would not attempt such familiarities with an Egyptian woman. I had grown tired of the unwelcome aggressive attention.

On the return bus to Safaga and *Southern Cross* the next morning, the soft "hoosh, hoosh, hoosh" of the conductor urged the passengers to move along to the back of the bus. They squeezed closer, and the Egyptian men eyed me, searching for the right line to begin a conversation. Something like, "You have beautiful eyes," or "I can't live without you."

With fuel, water, ice, fresh provisions, and a new packet of mail on board, at 1730 on May 11th, I left Paradise for the Gulf of Suez—the 180-mile-long, 15-mile-wide body of water stretching from the Strait of Gubal, with its famous scuba diving destinations, to the Suez Canal.

SHIP'S DIARY: 12 May 1994, 0430 Local. 27°29'N/034°15'E, in a gale with 6- to 8-foot short, steep seas. Miserable with a fever of 101.

By noon I was anchored in an open, clear area—no buoys, no nets, and no markers—in the northeast corner of the bay by Sharm el-Sheikh, near the tip of the Sinai Peninsula, protected from the northeast wind by surrounding hills. I stowed gear, covered the mainsail, and cleaned the decks, then ducked below for a bite of lunch and a snooze.

The afternoon winds began to gust from the southwest, and boats swung to face it with their sterns straining toward a nearby reef. *Raconteur III* slid backward toward danger, and her crew scrambled for the anchor. I watched smugly, confident in my anchoring, but not for long. *SC* dragged next.

I started the engine, turned on the autopilot, and drove forward, bringing up chain hand-over-hand with an eye on the reef lurking behind. By the time I saw the small orange floats trailing along the side of the hull and raced back to disengage the gear, it was too late. The heavy monofilament line connecting the floats had already wrapped around the propeller and disabled the engine. Fishing net and more line from the bottom of the bay encased the anchor. I could neither stay put nor go. *SC* slid closer to danger.

With my heart racing I unfurled the gennie and sailed away from the reef, around the boats on nearby moorings, and back to sea, then cleared the anchor. It was too rough to go overboard to cut free the propeller. Returning to the bay under sail, I dropped the hook in the protective curve of the southwest side.

In the morning *Raconteur III* reported that the police wanted to see me about "600 feet of damaged fishing net." I knew the net was only 30 feet long and 3 feet wide, and it had been abandoned on the bottom of the bay.

I left for shore, not to talk about fishing nets but to inquire about a permit for the famous nearby Ras Muhammed dive site—hoping there was a place to snorkel, a place to moor, and they would allow me to stop.

The port captain scowled at my request then relented, giving me permission with restrictions: "You have until noon to get there; you can't anchor, fish, or throw things in the water. And be gone before dark, or I'll take your license." I headed for the door, nodding all the way. "What do you know about a damaged fishing net?"

I shrugged my shoulders. The money in my pocket would barely get me through the canal. There was nothing for *baksheesh*. I knew I had not damaged a fisherman's means of livelihood . . . only the port captain's source of pocket money.

At Ras Muhammed the mooring buoys were all underwater, out of sight; I passed by and sailed into the protection of the nearby, five-mile-long Mahmud reef as the wind rose and the chop increased.

For three days I waited behind a low spit of land, surrounded by reefs in every direction, while the Abenaki weather stick from my brother held firm in the strong winds. Until it moved things were not going to improve. The dun-colored coastal plains of the Sinai swept away to the north and east, then turned south five miles away.

SHIP'S DIARY: 18 May 1994, 28°14′N/033°37′E. Tor Harbor. Arrived at 0730 this morning. Last night the wind ran 25 to 30 knots with 6- to 9-foot seas—short and steep.

Tor was a small, industrial-looking place partway up the Sinai shore. On my budget of $15 per week there was little point in going ashore to explore. Two other boats waited not far away, but putting the dinghy together was too daunting. For weeks at sea I had been contented alone; now, knowing there were people nearby brought a wave of loneliness.

That evening the net reported that fellow cruisers on board *High C's* had rescued more than 21 people from a burning ferry somewhere near the Strait of Gubal at the bottom of the gulf. *High C's* had been first on the scene, going in close to the flames to pick up survivors. U.S. Navy ships and commercial vessels had responded soon after. Their combined efforts had saved all but seven of the 500 passengers.

On May 20th at 0330 I gave up waiting for conditions to get better and left Tor, expecting to arrive in Port Suez the following morning. All of the remaining fuel on board had been budgeted for the passage to Cyprus, but without the engine to help the mainsail, *SC* didn't stand a chance against the strong winds and blunt, 5-foot seas.

By midnight I was tacking back and forth across the busy shipping lanes, approaching Suez but making little headway. Shortly after sunrise, only two miles off the cliffs of the western coastline, an airborne desert hid all sign of land as it blew down on *SC*, leaving a sticky, gritty brown dust in its wake.

There were seven boats hoping to reach Suez that morning; but only three made it, and *SC* was not one of them. With all power on and sails set my best speed made good was 2 knots. At noon I gave up and sought refuge at Ras el-Sudr, on the east side of the gulf.

Behind the protection of a small hook of land I spent the 22nd watching tour buses arrive at the windswept resort beach in the middle of nowhere. The sand gradually disappeared under a blanket of colorful people and umbrellas, and above them the wind howled. Women in their fanciest holiday clothes and head coverings sat in beach chairs visiting while children and men in shorts ran, played soccer, and swam. It was the annual four-day weekend Egyptians chose for weddings and celebrations.

The next morning at 0345 the Abenaki stick turned downward, indicating good weather was coming. I left with one spare gallon of fuel beyond what I needed to get to the Suez Yacht Club. At noon I reached the "Prince of the Red Sea," my agent for the canal transit, by radio. "*Southern Cross, Southern Cross. I've been waiting for you for a long time.*" Not as long as I've been waiting for you! By 1400 *SC* was secured to a mooring in the Suez Yacht Club basin. It felt like I had been plucked from the far north and dropped in the middle of Miami beach—palm trees, blue skies, balmy breezes—and a million flies.

The Prince arrived in his flowing robes with a welcoming cake—shredded wheat soaked in honey and covered in chopped almonds. He invited me to join him at *High C's* that evening for a video of the ferryboat rescue. Later, while someone taped the occasion, the Prince gathered us in *High C's'* saloon and surprised me with another cake in honor of my voyage. It was embarrassing under the circumstances. *High C's* had risked their lives to save those passengers. I was only making a trip to save myself.

With the Red Sea behind me, that night an air of nostalgia filled my dreams for the people and places my path had crossed. The shepherd boys of Smyth Island, Rashaida nomads on a bus to Asmara, tiny cups of coffee in a small shack in Suakin, riding a donkey at sunrise to visit ancient tombs had all disproved the expectations accompanying me through the Gates of Hell.

The Prince offered laundry, ice, and fuel services, but my budget couldn't meet his prices. I washed clothes and bedding by hand, found a taxi to deliver ice, and landed my dinghy in the tugboat basin to walk through the harbor gates and buy fuel from a filling station on the street for $0.40 per gallon instead of $1.08 from the Prince.

On a shopping trip into the shabby town center I hunted for a reasonable place to make the thirty-nine photocopies required for my transit documentation. There were two men in the small stationery store when I arrived—the proprietor and an elderly, white-haired fellow visiting with him over the counter. When my copies were ready and I turned to pay, the old man waved me away with a smile. He had paid my bill. My feeling toward Egypt changed in that single gesture.

The night before my transit an Egyptian engineer from the Canal Authority and a representative of the Prince came to determine if SC would be fit for the trip. As the engineer finished his inspection—a series of questions on SC's preparedness—the man from the Prince of the Red Sea's office stepped in to ask if I would have a gift for the pilot the following day.

"Of course. I have the usual $5," I responded.

"Good. We've picked a very special pilot for you. A very devout, religious man. Be ready before 0900 in the morning. Good night." He said nothing about his arrangements for the second day's pilot.

Six hundred years before Christ, the first attempt to link the Mediterranean to the Red Sea was made via the Nile and Great Bitter Lake. A hundred thousand laborers died before the project was abandoned, but a century later Darius of Persia completed the effort. Then, over the centuries, it was dredged, filled in, used, and abandoned. In the nineteenth century interest in a direct passage arose once again, and under a ninety-nine-year lease the Suez Canal Company began construction in 1859.

The lavish four-day opening festivities and subsequent weeks of celebrations in 1869 had driven the *khedive* of Egypt, Pasha Isma'il, into severe debt. The British government's purchase of nearly half his shares in the Canal Company rescued him, and control of the canal passed to Britain. It was nationalized by Gamal Abdel Nasser in his first year as Egypt's president in 1956, closed for eight years by the Six-Day War in 1967, and reopened by Anwar al-Sādāt in 1975. Since that time the canal had produced Egypt's primary source of hard currency, carrying 50 ships per day in a steady flow from Europe to Asia and back. Large ships passed through the canal in convoys going one direction at a time—it was too narrow for two-way commercial traffic. The transit took them fifteen hours; *SC* would need two full days to do it in a one-way convoy of small boats, hugging the opposite side of the lock-less canal from the ships.

Sondra, one of two doctors on board *Reva*, arrived early the next morning and quickly confirmed my suspicions. "Yes, it looks like an ulcer, even though right now the pain is only at night. You're doing exactly what you should, but increase the Tagamet or Zantac and take antacids night and morning. The antibiotic treatment might work for you, but you need to have brushings from the stomach lining to be sure before you start that."

At 0900 Murbarak, my pilot—a shy, quiet man of forty—arrived carrying two loaves of bread. He surveyed *Southern Cross,* quickly preparing to guide me through the first half of my final passage to the Mediterranean. We waited for the go-ahead with the engine running. At 1030 our convey began; the fastest boat left, followed by *SC,* then *Philmar.*

The northbound current pushed us at more than seven knots up the long, straight, narrow waterway toward Al-Buhayrah al-Murrah al-Kubrā (Great Bitter Lake). Large ships passed so close to starboard, heading south to Suez, that our margin for error was measured in feet, not fractions of miles. The pilot's job was to keep the boat close to the left side of the canal, maintain communications with the signal stations, report our progress and any problems en route, and tell us where to go in the open areas and at the beginning and end of each day's passage.

At noon Murbarak asked for fresh water in a bucket. On the foredeck he washed his head, face, arms, hands, feet, nose, and ears, and then the deck. Finished, he turned to face Mecca, knelt, and said his prayers.

Following an impromptu race under sail with *Philmar* across the huge lake, a second long, straight section, and two more prayer sessions, *SC* anchored in Ismailia, a new town built for canal operations and supply on Lake Timsah. I dropped Murbarak on shore with three packs of cigarettes and an envelope with his $5 "gift" sealed inside. I had worried for nothing about spending the day alone with a Middle Eastern man. He had been a gentleman and treated me with respect. The unpleasant experiences in Luxor and Safaga added to warnings for women travelers in the region had produced a feeling of dread for a day that ended well.

The dishes were dried and put away, preparations started for lunch, and the day's charts ready when a launch pulled alongside the following morning. I struggled to hold the heavy work vessel and the large black tires swinging down her sides away from *SC* as a small, wiry man in a white uniform jumped down to the deck. A burly, greasy crew member above demanded cigarettes, but I told him I didn't have any. I did, but they were all allocated—two for the launch who would pick up our paperwork, two for the launch that picked up the pilot, and two for the pilot. There were no extras. He demanded to see the captain. "I am the captain." They backed away as my new pilot, Mohammed, beat a quick path below to the main cabin.

I arrived as he reached for the radio controls and hailed another pilot. Signing off, he spun and grabbed me in an embrace, trying to kiss me. "Stop that!" I said. "This is a business arrangement, and you aren't going to touch me. You're here to take my boat through the canal. Nothing more."

"Oh," he whined, "don't be so touchy. If you were a man, I'd do the same. I hugged your friend Dave on *Paragon* the other day."

"Well, you're not hugging *me*. Just do your job and keep your hands to yourself."

We drove back into the narrow corridor of water. The day was punctuated by occasional pungent odors from the small oases along the side of the canal and by the hundreds of flies that had hitched a ride from Suez. We swatted flies, and the stack of their dead bodies grew between us along with the heavy air. Mohammed rolled his eyes over my clothed body. I hugged myself and felt violated, then turned away with my knees gripped together and counted the miles and the hours until I could be rid of him.

All morning he whined, "No coffee, no tea, no soft drinks, no alcohol, no kiss. No, no, no." I fixed lunch, offered coffee or tea, and emerged from the galley to see the concrete sidewall of the canal five feet from the bow as Mohammed daydreamed at the tiller. I yelled, and he jerked back on course.

We passed hours with nothing to look at but each other, the ships, the waterway ahead, or the stone and concrete walls. Even the flat, featureless desert beyond was out of view.

Mohammed demanded his "gift," then ripped open the envelope scowling and complained bitterly at the $5 inside. He begged for T-shirts or hats with the boat name, luxuries found on larger, well-funded boats but not on *SC*.

At last we arrived at the Said station. Mohammed handed the crew list and one pack of cigarettes to the police launch. Their second pack had disappeared. They pulled away, glaring unhappily at *SC*. Then the pilots' launch arrived and stayed to help me secure *Southern Cross* in the unfamiliar mooring style used throughout the Mediterranean (stern- or bow-to the jetty) at the Port Said Yacht Club dock—a truly helpful and unexpected gesture.

Mohammed jumped on board the launch, while the crew looked expectantly at me for their cigarettes. There were none. Mohammed had taken all five packs.

While heating leftover bean soup for dinner, I reminded myself of all the good encounters in the past month. The children who laughed and giggled when I answered their "What's your name?" with the same question back. The face of the old man in the photocopy shop. The men in Suez who loaded my jerricans of fuel into their truck and drove me back to my dinghy in the tug-boat basin, refusing any money. All of them had expected nothing and had given me a reason to return someday.

I turned my face into the fresh, clean Mediterranean air, drinking it into every pore, washing away the grit of North Africa and the stickiness of the Red Sea. The light changed to clear, deep blue above and below. I left behind the weight of *chadors* and leering men, of feeling undressed when I was covered from neck to knee to elbow, and self-conscious of every move. The Med called with music and dancing, trees and flowers, wine and good food, beautiful anchorages where I would find friends, and charming villages with ancient winding streets and old architecture where life still happened.

With the challenge of the Red Sea behind and *Southern Cross* and I still intact, thoughts surfaced of the other women who had passed alone up that stretch. Both Tania Aebi and Lynn Service had crossed almost the entire distance under sail alone. Their courage and perseverance had kept me moving forward, and I hoped I would do the same for others behind me. We each said of those who had gone before, "If she can do that, so can I." I thought again of *Guinness*'s; I would write to see if they would consider "the oldest woman to circumnavigate solo" for a title.

————————JUNE 1994

AS SOON AS THE OFFICIALS FINISHED CLEARING ME IN on June 1st, the day after I arrived at Larnaca, Cyprus, I looked for the post office. Other than four letters in Port Said, three in Safaga, and a small bundle in Aden, I had not had mail since Sri Lanka in February. The clerk handed me a big stack and took the letters I had written over the past month—to my family, *Guinness*'s, and friends scattered across half a world.

Outside were clean streets filled with happy, chatting people—men and women. Small shops lined the sidewalks with beautiful, colorful displays. And there were no flies. Across the main road and down a narrow walkway I found a small café, Aunty Lulu's, with Kelly green umbrellas and green-and-white checkered tablecloths, a perfect place for letter reading with anise tea and a pastry.

Dan had sent a birthday card and $100. "Sorry I couldn't take you out for dinner. Have a nice one on me. See you in Greece." A letter from Dayle carried a welcome check. Life in Cyprus was beginning to look much better. The anchorage area at the marina entry was wide open to the sea, and her check would help pay for a stay at a dock inside. I savored all the letters one by one, while I sipped tea with the writers' faces in my mind to keep me company.

Dayle's illness had advanced, and no buyer had materialized for the Blue Penguin. Her father came several times each week to help at the store. Mom and Stubby had moved into the retirement center. They sounded like newly-weds as they wrote about decorating their new apartment at Westminster Village. They were surrounded by old friends and family, and Mom had her patio filled with pots of flowers on the ground floor. Peter, Kitty's husband, had his new liver and each day brought him a breath closer to health—but ever so slowly and often painfully.

In the marina, old and new sailing friends began handing out advice about my ulcer. The trail led to Ed on *Fiddler's Green*, who had taken the new antibiotic treatment in Israel the summer before. Ed gave me the magic formula, with the names of the medications and the dosages, assuring me I would have no problem finding them in Turkey.

The open central market became a mecca in my daily rounds. Fresh cherries and apricots were $0.75 a pound, and I bought them by the kilo, wondering if I could ever tire of the familiar fruits. Much as I had loved mangoes in the tropics, these fruits meant "home." I found a small bakery that sold loaves of fresh, whole wheat bread filled with seeds and oats. Slowly, new impressions and memories began to replace those from the slot through the desert with its pounding winds and seas, empty shops, and annoying men.

One afternoon as I crossed the street to the harbor gate a voice called out behind me, "Where are you from?"

Without looking, I knew the accent and the question. I asked back without turning, "Where are you from?"

"Egypt."

"Yes, I knew that." My guard was back in place.

"You did?" he asked, catching up with me.

It had been more than a week since I had been bothered by anyone on the street. How nice it had been to walk about unconcerned. The beauty around me, the cleanliness, the well-cared-for old stone buildings, and the deep blue sky and sea didn't compare with the joy of not being noticed.

The next day my usual morning rounds of post office, market, bakery, and tea at Aunty Lulu's included an introduction to the owner, Troulla. I asked if she knew a place to dance *bouzouki*, the music produced by the mandolin-like instrument of the same name that is the heart of Greek music. "Tonight my son is playing for the first time at a hotel. I'll pick you up at 8:30."

On *SC* I climbed aloft to scrub Africa from the rigging—forty trips up and down the mast with buckets, scrub brushes, and the hose. As the last bit of daylight oozed from the sky, I showered and looked for something to wear. Too late to iron something nice, I dressed in clean jeans and a pretty—but baggy—patchwork shirt.

Troulla's small red Volkswagen pulled up at the marina entry, and she hopped out to let me squeeze into the backseat. My heart sank. I faced four gorgeous Greek Cypriot women dressed for a night on the town. The morning's invitation had not included a dress code. It was too late to turn back now.

Troulla made quick introductions, and we sped off. Her daughter Cia sat in the middle, sixteen and six feet tall, elegant and teenage gawky at the same time. There was Mary, Troulla's sister, trim but with round curves, curly dark hair, and a face that lit up when she smiled. Then Theolaura, petite, with short cropped reddish hair, in tight black pants, a black silk shell, and high heels. The others wore long, slim dresses with bare arms. Makeup and perfume said this was a carload of WOMEN—all but me, huddled in the midst of the tigresses.

We pulled into the hotel parking lot and made our way toward the distinct sound of the *bouzouki*. A big table waited for us, reserved by friends of Troulla from England who were living in Cyprus as part of a military detachment. More introductions followed, and in minutes they were all on the floor moving in the intricate patterns of the traditional dances.

They coaxed me to join them. I longed to move as they did, to feel the rhythms and lose my body in the motions. But I hesitated, embarrassed by my outfit and by the fact that I knew none of the steps. In the middle of the floor Theolaura spun slowly and sank down low, then sprang up, slapping her heel behind. That perfect execution of almost making the step, pausing, then coming down in a syncopated beat that is the essence of Greek dancing—she had it. I wanted it, too.

Slowly the pace, the motions, and the attitude penetrated my skin. I stepped onto the floor and danced all night, forgetting that I was wearing jeans and a baggy shirt. I asked at the end, "When can we go again?"

Lying across ancient Mycenaean and Phoenician trade routes between Europe and the East gave Cyprus its place in history. Coveted by every neighboring power, the island passed back and forth from Eastern to Western rule—Assyria, Egypt, Persia, Macedonia, Egypt again, Rome, and Constantinople. Then the Byzantine Empire and Islamic powers fought for control, each side using the island as a base of attacks against the other, and Cyprus changed hands eleven times between the seventh and tenth centuries. Conquered in 1191 by King Richard I the Lionhearted and his crusaders, Cyprus passed in the fifteenth century to the Venetian empire, and in 1570 for the next three hundred years to the Ottoman Empire. In 1878 Turkey ceded Cyprus back to England. Always someone else had determined the island's destiny.

With independence in 1960, the turmoil shifted from outside sources to internal struggles between the minority Turkish Muslim population of the north and the Greek Orthodox of the south. Constitutional changes threatening the rights of the country's 160,000 Turks provoked threats from Ankara, and intercommunal violence broke out among Greek and Turkish enclaves. In 1964 the United Nations dispatched a peacekeeping mission. Then Greece sponsored a coup d'état in 1974, placing former guerilla leader Nicos Samson in charge and putting Cyprus under Greek control. Turkey exercised its right as a treaty guarantor to respond by invading and occupying the northern third of the island. The Greek population fled below the Green Line that divided the country into north and south. Turkish Cyprus declared itself an independent republic in 1983, but only Turkey acknowledged the new country. Now travelers could visit north of the line on a one-day pass, entering through the divided capital, Nicosia. Travel in the opposite direction, however, was restricted to a minute population holding property below the line.

Two weeks later I stood in line at the Larnaca post office with a letter for Kit, a large envelope of sketches and notes for Rod and Helen, and a little prayer that they liked my interpretation of their anticipated life at Lake Tahoe. The line stopped while the tea man, looking like the waiter at a fancy restaurant in black slacks and white shirt, delivered small cups of tea from a large round tray swinging from his hand by three chains. He made his appointed rounds every morning and afternoon, delivering to offices and shops around the neighborhood.

Dear Kitty,   Larnaca, Cyprus

At last I can breathe again—in more ways than one: the air, the men,
and I have a little money. After five years I'm finally here.

George Day, who writes for the sailing magazine *Cruising World* and is
here with his family by boat, offered me a ride to Nicosia one evening.
There was a special art exhibition, and I jumped at the chance.

The retrospective show displayed expansive canvases with amusing
characters from Greek mythology—all with the same huge nose and
dignified forehead. Given that the show covered some 20 years of work
though, I thought the artist might try something new. It was a strange
evening, to be in the middle of 500 people without one of them saying
a word to me. It's the most lonely I've felt in the past five years.

I spent a day in nearby Agia Anna shooting photos and sketching
400-year-old buildings. At noon I sat on a rock across the street from
the elementary school to eat some bread, cheese, and fruit. Soon I was
surrounded by youngsters, and eventually the teacher came too. She
invited me to tell them about my trip. The walls of the classroom were
covered in photos from North Cyprus, across the "Green Line." As she
told me about each photo, her subtle comments reminded the children
to carry on the hatred. How will the old pains ever die?

My palette has shifted with the warm Mediterranean light and the
brilliant cobalt of the sky—the same color they paint the trim around
doors and windows. The mellow old stone used for building glows in a
peach and gold like Mavro Daphne wine, while the hibiscus, bougainvillea, and geraniums sparkle like fresh fruit. I can taste the scenery.

Every time I stop painting to move to a new part of the world, I
think I will find a looser, freer style when I begin again. But I become
ever more controlled and precise. It is growth of one kind, but I am
hungry to be wild and paint with abandon.

I had a small, private show at the marina for one day, and that will
keep me going until I reach Turkey.

I talked to Dan last week; he is coming to Lindos, on Rhodes. I'm
not sure if he will be there by August 1st or not, but I should arrive by
then. Please write to the Lindos address. I am anxious to hear how
Peter's recovery is progressing.

Love and hugs,

Pat

◀ 1938: the way every little girl wants to remember her parents, Dave and Aileen Henry.
▼ 1945: four years old and already looking for the end of the rainbow.

◀ 1986: grandmother Mildred Tobiassen turns 100 with granddaughters Tamara Myers and Terri (Myers) Wilson. ▼ October 1988: a farewell dinner on board *Southern Cross* with grandson Shawn, daughter Tamara, and friend Shane Scott.

Neiafu Harbor, Tonga

The Gables, New Zealand

▼ December 1989: Libby, my sister, greets me in Opua, Bay of Islands, New Zealand.
◀ May 1991: scrubbing the hull on a grid in Russell, New Zealand, before departure.

eptember 1993: my Singapore Rose (Quek)
eautiful Fawziah (Almashoor).
eptember 1994: a visit from my daughter,
ra Myers, and my grandson, Shawn.

The Chinese Garden, Singapore

▼ July 1994: sailing the
Turquoise Coast of
Turkey.
◄ September 1994: my
granddaughter, Kira,
visits me in Turkey.

◄ Marmaris, Turkey.
▼ Caribbean Market.

July 1994: at anchor in Kastellorizon, Greece, safely three miles away from the Turkish immigration officer.

➤ December 1995: enjoying a stop at the Canary Islands before crossing the Atlantic. ▲ February 1997: a small exhibition at Bonaire, the Dutch Antilles, en route to the Panama Canal.

At $6 per day, the marina became too much for my budget as I stretched my funds to provision for the Turkish coast, buy fuel, repair parts, copy charts, fill gas bottles, repair the new Compaq laptop, buy shoes, and take a two-day trip to the four-hundred-year-old, famous lace-making village of Lefkara in the foothills of the Troodos Mountains. The small, once-a-day bus passed through golden, rocky terrain covered in small trees. The towering cedars of antiquity had never recovered from the building of Cleopatra's navy.

Worn cobbled streets ran between hushed stone walls and under graceful arches. Flowers peeked from vine-covered terraces and from inside courtyards, glimpsed through open doors. Moorish arches, an Orthodox cathedral on the hill above town, the English voices in my old hotel, and the varied aromas of sixteen little Greek-Turkish mezes plates at dinner reflected the history of the island.

Southern Cross moved outside the marina to the open anchorage for my last week in Cyprus. After several days of settled weather I decided to invite Troulla and the dancing group for a Sunday sail. But when I left to pick them up that morning the anchorage was growing choppy.

As I waited for them inside the marina, Mauricio from *Aphrodite* walked by. "What a beautiful dinghy you have," he remarked. I glowed with the compliment. My pleasure and pride in *T/T Southern Cross* had not diminished in the least.

Troulla and her son arrived, and we left for the boat. By the time we reached *SC*, she was pitching up and down in a two-foot swell. Lacking a boater's instinct for shifting his weight to stay balanced, Troulla's son moved awkwardly to the boarding ladder, the dinghy surged forward, and *SC* crashed down upon it. A sharp cotter pin at the base of the bobstay sliced through the port tube of the inflatable dinghy. With a loud hiss, the air escaped.

Panic ensued. Troulla and her son scrambled for the safety of the deck while I secured a lifting line, removed the outboard, and climbed out of the knee-deep water in the rapidly submerging dinghy. A call by VHF found a willing cruiser to ferry the other passengers out, and we left for the promised sail. The beautiful *T/T SC* lay in a shriveled heap on top of the cabin.

We sailed, ate fresh bing cherries, visited, and enjoyed the outing. On Monday I sewed and patched the four-inch gash and tried to forget how pretty she had looked before the accident.

The next day Troulla brought a charm with a deep-blue eye at the center, a God's eye to frighten away evil. Handing it to me, she explained: "When a baby's born we say to the parents, 'What an ugly baby' to ward off the danger of pride."

I looked at *T/T*'s fresh scar and replaced pride with affection.

—————————— JULY 1994

THE COAST OF TURKEY TUGGED AT ME. IT WAS SO close but a continent away—Asia Minor, the bridge between East and West. The line dividing Turkey and Greece had floated back and forth across these waters so many times over the centuries that both countries carried elements of the other in their food, music, dance, architecture, and customs. The Greeks bristled at the idea of similarities; the Turks didn't mind.

I sailed from Larnaca around the east end of Cyprus and northwest to Taşucu, Turkey, arriving July 4th. The port captain welcomed me, pulled out a comfortable chair, doused me with the traditional lemon water, poured a cup of apple tea, and settled down for a chat. If all Turks were like this it might be a perfect place to stay for the winter. I had until October to decide where I would spend the stormy season. My heart leaned toward Greece, but many friends who had stayed in Turkey the year before had reported wonderful people, prices, and facilities. The decision still floated between the two.

As I stood to leave, the port captain pulled out his binoculars and studied *Southern Cross*. "Get that flag down and buy a correct flag immediately. The star is not straight!" The young seamstress I had hired in Sri Lanka had not noticed the tiny, important detail showing one white star on the red field precisely placed between the ends of the white moon. The star was not in the correct location, and it was cockeyed. I went to change money to buy a new flag and a few groceries.

I didn't count the money or even look at my receipt in the bank; the exchange rate seemed close to what I remembered from the guidebook on board. At the small grocery store the owner told me how much I owed for a loaf of bread and a few onions; a quick calculation showed $4. The woman nearby heard me mutter that things were certainly expensive, and she agreed, adding they were much cheaper in Ankara.

At the dock I discovered the exchange rate had been 25,000 Turkish lira for $1, not the 2,500 shown in my book. Bread and onions had cost 40 cents. I hurried back to stock up on fresh cherries for 50 cents a pound and peaches and apricots for 35 cents!

Flying the new Turkish flag, *SC* sailed to a nearby cove and anchored in the shadow of a crusader castle. A crew of three dark men and an attractive blonde woman waved from a small fishing boat nearby as their nets drifted through the air and settled on the water in a gentle rhythm.

On shore I explored a tidy vacation park looking for people, a laundry, ice, and quiet trails where I could smell pine trees again, instead of palms. There were two small shops with groceries.

On the edge of the campsite a sixtyish man with a neatly trimmed mustache and gray hair relaxed by his trailer in the shade of a large tree. He smiled, greeted me, and introduced himself as Ihan. He chatted a bit in English, his words emerging from the back of his mind where they had been stored for forty years. He shook his head when I asked about a laundry, then mentioned his wife. She had a new half-size washing machine under the trees beside the trailer.

"How much does she charge?" I asked. He waved his hand and shook his head.

At that moment the blonde woman from the boat ran across the beach, waving and smiling broadly. She grabbed my hand enthusiastically, then disappeared inside the trailer and emerged with cherry juice and small cookies. Sonya was Ihan's wife. We continued an arm-waving, pantomimed visit while she showed me her washing machine. I agreed to come back in the morning at 9:00 and asked again about the price. Sonya only shook her head no, "*hayir.*"

I brought ten days' worth of laundry and soap to shore in the morning. Sonya offered me a chair at a small Formica-topped table under the big tree and brought out pita bread, eggs, rusks, fresh tomatoes, homemade cherry marmalade, and strong tea. Each summer for thirty years they had come from their home in Adana to spend a few months at this beach. With Ihan's retirement they were extending their stay.

At last I understood her reluctance to quote a price for my laundry. Sonya was not the local laundry lady making her "egg money" to help the family over hard times. Ihan had retired from a career as a bank manager. When we finished washing my piles of dirty clothes she handed me a small traditional, brightly colored head covering with beads stitched around the edge—a thank-you gift for coming to do my laundry and sharing my morning.

The next morning brought the same longing it did each year when Terri's birthday arrived. I surveyed the paths our lives had taken—linked at one end but year by year moving farther apart at the other.

Dearest Terri,   July 7, 1994

At times it is hard to imagine that the little bundle held up for me to see in the delivery room thirty-four years and ten hours ago is now a mature, married woman. I have missed twenty-six of those years.

If I could change one thing in my life, it would be the day your father came to ask you to live with him. You were only eight. I could have said "no." The court would have agreed. But I couldn't deny your wish. It was the saddest moment of my life. My father hadn't wanted me and my daughters didn't either. It was more than I could handle. I built a shield around myself so that a pain like that could never happen again.

School ended three months later. We packed your bags and met your father at the halfway point. As you climbed into his car and closed the door, a gulf opened between us that we have never closed.

I hoped that some day we could bridge the distance, but I didn't have the courage to put myself on the line. To share my feelings and go through the pain to build a true relationship. To say I'm sorry for the hurt I must have caused you and for the feelings of loss and abandonment you may have carried all these years.

Can we try now? I want to know what is in your heart. Your dreams and fears, your passions and worries, who and what you are. I love you without knowing you, but knowing you would fill an empty place inside. Can you forgive my mistakes? Can you trust me enough to let me in?

I send you wishes of joy, happiness, and inner contentment on this special day.

With love and kisses,

Mom

I sailed west past an evergreen-covered coast, with the ancient history of Turkey spread over its hillsides and mountains: Byzantine and crusader castles, abandoned cities—Hittite, Greek, Roman, and Byzantine—Lycian tombs carved into the walls of high white cliffs and sarcophagi that had stood in open fields for thirty centuries, Greek theaters, Roman baths and temples, aqueducts and amphitheaters, a graceful Seljuk tower and a nearby boatyard cut from the rock walls of the shore, medieval fortresses, minarets of Islam, and a romantic beach where Cleopatra and Marc Antony once played. There were traces of every invader since the Hittites ruled 4,000 years ago. The rich plains and valuable East–West trade routes had led to periods of war and conquest between centuries of peace and prosperity; culture and refinement followed abuse and despotic rule. The reign of the last powerful Ottoman sultan ended in 1909, and the modern Turkish Republic emerged in 1923 under the guidance of Kemal Atatürk.

With Atatürk's Western orientation he pulled Turkey into the twentieth century, democratizing the political system, secularizing the government, rewriting the laws, adopting a modified Latin alphabet, and outlawing the veil and fez along with polygamy. He reshaped an entire society and became revered as the father of modern Turkey.

I skimmed across Antalya Körfezi to Kemer in perfect conditions and anchored SC between two all night discos. Between their noise and my nightly stomachache I tossed and turned for hours, waking up more tired than when I had gone to bed.

Over breakfast I consulted Louise Hay's *You Can Heal Your Life*. She said, "We rip our guts apart trying to please others. . . . Love is the answer. . . . Be gentle and loving to the child within, and give it all the support and encouragement you wanted when you were little." It brought back memories from 1981. I had gone to a chiropractor with a stiff neck. He had worked on me over the following months and one day announced he would do a "bloodless surgery" on my abdomen for some kind of "blockage" he had detected. As he pushed deeply with the tips of his fingers on my right side, just below the ribs, my father's face had appeared suspended two feet above my own. "Okay, now let go. Release it." As the knot in my side eased, my father's face had floated away and disappeared.

I had known what it meant. For a year and a half after my sixteenth birthday, I had had gallbladder attacks every time I had seen my father. The last time, after only two days of a weeklong vacation with him, I had returned home and my gallbladder had been removed. One doctor had come to interview me for a study he was making of unlikely candidates for gallbladder surgery. I had been very unlikely—young and not overweight. His theory had centered on the influence of emotions. Hay said gallstones meant: "Bitterness. Hard thoughts. Condemning." She said to affirm each day, "There is joyous release of the past," and again admonished to love the child within.

I gathered my backpack and camera and caught the little stuffed bus called a *dolmuş* to Antalya, where a packet of mail including a check for $77 from Dayle waited. At the pharmacy I asked at least five times whether there was any penicillin in the three medications I was buying, but I did not speak Turkish and the pharmacist did not speak English. With a history of allergies and reactions to several antibiotics, I was nervous.

The next morning the question mark still hung in the air, as I reread the tiny print on the containers. The options pulled me back and forth. Should I go to shore and take the pills with someone watching; call someone from another boat to come watch; stand by the radio and hope, in the event of an attack, there was enough time to make an emergency call; or forget the whole thing? The last was not an option. I took a breath and downed the potent combination of high-powered antibiotics.

Nothing happened. I sat in the cockpit, thankful to be alive and praying that Ed's magic formula worked.

On the south side of the bay, Club Med rocked with music and tourists every night. I arranged to put up a small display with the local carpet, jewelry, and gift shops on their market night. The local tradespeople gathered me into their midst. They bought my dinner, set up lights, and invited me to their homes—but the tourists only looked at the paintings, paid compliments, and walked away.

I made banners—"the GALLERY"—to fly from *SC*'s spreaders and flyers to hand out as I worked my way slowly westward to the anchorages at Phaselis, Çavuş, and finally Kale. There by day I anchored in front of the small village below a Byzantine fortress, amid the countless tour boats, charters, and the occasional cruiser, to paint the scene on land. From split-timber and white stucco waterfront restaurants and homes the town climbed steeply to the fortress walls in shades of umber and ochre. Carpet shops, fishing boats, hanging laundry, and women in harem pants splashed spots of color under the dusty green of olive trees and warm sienna tile roofs, while over it all a pale turquoise sky warmed the painting.

At night I moved into the protection of the nearly landlocked bay by the village of Üçağiz. One day I stayed inside the bay to explore and along the main road found four Turkish women in colorful baggy harem trousers, blouses, and head scarves seated on a hip-high wooden platform. They chatted in the noontime shade of a small roof while waiting for customers for their hand-painted scarves and *borek*.

I paused, waiting for a lull in their conversation, then said, "*Börek, lütfen.*" They smiled in response and scooted around to make room for me. Who was

I? What was I doing in this tiny village at the southernmost end of Turkey? When they understood I had come alone on a small boat, they threw thumbs-up and pronounced that I was a "good *capitan*." Coming from a village of fish-ermen, they knew what it meant to go to sea.

One woman rolled the flaky pastry around two wooden dowels making it thinner and thinner, until it was a perfect two-foot circle of dough ready for the charcoal-fired griddle. When it was cooked she filled it with crumbled cheese, chopped onions, and parsley, then folded the *börek* in quarters and handed it to me. Another filled a glass with *ayran*—ice-cold water, yogurt, and salt blended to a refreshing drink. I ate and drank, and they watched.

As I finished the woman on my left pulled her pant leg up to show me large welts at the top of her thigh, asking my advice. Walking my fingers up my arm and making biting motions with two fingers, I suggested little creatures. She emphatically shook her head "no." "Perhaps it's an allergy," I offered.

Then the chubby little woman on my right pulled her pants down to show me the rash developing between her legs. I tried to explain that in the heat of summer, the pretty, flowered polyester fabric of her trousers might be causing a heat rash. They nodded. I paid my bill and departed from the Üçağiz Ladies Club while my medical mystique was still in place.

Each day while I painted, I hung the banners and wished someone would buy a print or a miniature. Friends from Australia pulled in on their boat *Timshel*—Geoff, Wendy, and their teenage daughters, Debbie and Kathy. The girls had been waiting two years, since my show in Darwin, for the miniatures they wanted, and now they dinghied over to buy them. That broke the ice and more sales followed.

Day by day the two-week medication regimen for my ulcer passed. Slowly the pain subsided, and the bacteria were conquered.

——————— AUGUST 1994

I SAILED AROUND THE POINT TO KAŞ TO CHECK OUT of Turkey for Lindos, on Rhodes, looking forward to Dan's arrival, but with a stop on the way at Kastellorizon. The stories surrounding Kaş harbor author-ities were an endless part of eastern Mediterranean sailing lore—like the one about a $1,000 fine for dishwater carelessly discharged into the sea. I anchored

SC in the bay across from the infamous harbor, avoiding the risks inside, but I still had to see the officials for permission to sail from Kaş to Greece.

Old retired desks, barren except for typewriters turned up on end, filled the port captain's office. He offered apple tea in a small glass cup while examining the stacks of documents I handed him. At last he signed and stamped the necessary exit papers and sent me to the next mustached officer—from the Customs Police—in a neat, crisp uniform. I passed his inspection too.

They then sent me back across the central plaza with its small kiosks selling Dove bars for most of a daily wage and handmade trinkets for far less; past the harbor where fat, beamy local *gulets* for the tourist trade were tied side by side with foreign yachts; then up the hill searching for a police station hidden in the midst of a residential street. I entered a roomful of chattering men, breaking their comfortable rhythm. The first officer finished with me quickly, eager to reclaim the arid masculine atmosphere.

Then an unkempt, sneering Immigration officer beckoned from his scratched and sorry wooden desk. Dismay rolled over me when he asked for my crew list and I realized it was two miles away on *Southern Cross*. Contempt spread across his face as he tore a precious sheet of paper neatly across the middle for me to write my list of one name.

I gave it to him, and he handed it back for my signature. That signature had grown slowly since I'd changed my name at forty-five back to my birth name. A lifetime of old swirls and curls had held on tenaciously, but now a sort of flower blossomed whenever a signature line appeared.

I signed and passed it back. "What's that?" exploded from his creaky, straight-backed chair.

"My signature, of course."

One and a half miles from Kaş, *SC* crossed the territorial boundary between Turkey and Greece. At last I was there, ready to live my dream. Layers of color radiated from the end of the narrow channel into the port of Meyisti on the three-mile-long island of Kastellorizon, made famous in the film *Mediterraneo*. Open fishing boats painted white, green, blue, red, and orange bobbed in the blue-green harbor water along the curved stone quay. Mounds of turquoise and green nets sat in front of white buildings trimmed in bright blue, green, and red. From the waterfront the village stepped up the hillside in progressively deteriorating rows of structures, untouched since World War II, toward the olive-green foliage and red-brown earth that spread behind.

People crowded the quayside tavernas, and yachts filled the small basin.

I found a spot close in, dropped the hook, and stowed the sailing gear. "Perhaps you're a bit close there," a neighbor said, pointing to a shallow area toward the quay.

"You might be right."

I moved, reanchored, and decided I didn't like the feel of the new spot either. I moved again and was told the water barge would be arriving and SC would block its way. I moved far out, away from everything, anchored, and began fixing breakfast. Someone called out, "You'll be in the way when the ferry arrives."

I pulled up the anchor by hand one more time and moved in closer. As I finished laying out the chain and setting the hook, a fat taverna-owner on shore shouted. "You can't anchor there." I was far out from the quay in front of his place and in no one's way. I refused to move. He told me he wanted to keep the spot open for a large charter yacht to tie up and possibly eat at his restaurant. I refused again.

"If the harbormaster asks me to move, I will."

"I'll come out and move you myself," he threatened.

I went below to cool down. Was this the Greece of my dreams?

Once ashore I tried calling Dan to see what his plans were, but the call did not go through. Fearing he might already be in Lindos, I planned an overnight passage. But the late afternoon winds failed to die down that night, and I pounded into head seas, tacking the 70 miles to the island of Rhodes. The autopilot broke again.

Reaching the check-in port at Mandraki Harbor seemed impossible. I pulled into Lindos instead. On the southwestern side of the bay, ancient fortress walls topped a massive stone promontory standing watch over the four-hundred-year-old town. The hillside houses gleamed brilliant white against the deepest blue sky I had ever seen. Red and magenta shot from flowers peeking over walls and cascading from grape-covered terraces above. In the far distance the soft mauve of a barren hillside rose above the scene.

A path crawled down from the town above to a collection of buildings on the beach and a few fishing boats waiting on their moorings. I was anxious to get to shore—to explore, pick up mail, and reach Dan, perhaps even to meet him. As I changed clothes and fixed breakfast, the harbor police arrived to check my papers. I explained the problem with the autopilot and asked permission to take a bus to Rhodes Town to check in to

Greece. "Of course, no problem. You will go today?"

"No, tomorrow, if that's okay. I'm pretty tired today."

"No problem."

I climbed to the village and explored a narrow labyrinth of stone paths between white walls. They were punctuated by wooden doors surrounded with carved peach and beige stonework and fronted by "doormats" of small, thin stones set on end in intricate patterns. Some were dated from the nineteenth century. Color sang overhead from hibiscus and bougainvillea. The entire village was a living museum, preserved and protected from development. Through the occasional opening in the walls I glimpsed the deep blue water below and *Southern Cross* at last happily anchored off a Greek village.

On the end of town near the coastal road, I found the tourist office, buses, and phones, and called Dan. Office problems were keeping him home; he would come sometime later in the fall. I tried to understand one more time and let Lindos fill the empty space inside, while I waited for the promised visit.

The man in the tourist office looked down his nose at me with eyebrows raised high, "We don't have time for that in the summer. I can tell you where to go for disco dancing, but not for *bouzouki*."

The post office produced a pack of letters. Guinness wrote saying it would not consider anything but speed records—no national records, and nothing gender-based. I let the idea go. There were more ways to encourage others than by competition. A letter from Tam said that she was coming for a visit in September, and my mind filled with plans for all that I wanted to show her and the children.

Rod and Helen wrote to say they liked the direction my sketches were going and were anxious to see the next stage of drawings. My attorney sent a packet of forms from the judge requiring my notarized signature. The papers constituted a mutual dismissal of all charges against all parties to TWT's default: Lars, the S&L officers, the Federal Savings and Loan Insurance Corporation, and Kelly and me. At long last this would end the nightmare of TWT, except for the IRS claims against me. For six years only the attorneys had benefited from the messy legal entanglement. Other than the expense (and much of that had been covered by liability insurance) none of us were either further ahead or behind. But who could measure the price in time and emotional pain? The entire affair had taken on a life of its own.

I built a routine in Lindos: painting in the mornings from photos of Cyprus, Turkey, Kastellorizon, and Lindos, then a swim across the bay and finally a climb to the village for errands, a chat with a friend, and a coffee. Far too often the day included a visit from the captain of the tour boat *Aphrodite*, which was anchored near *SC*. I didn't know his name but always thought of him as Mr. Aphrodite—and not fondly. He would swim over in his underwear, crawl on board, sprawl out in the cockpit with his legs spread wide, and leer at me with dreamy, half-closed eyes. Somehow I always managed to get rid of him until a few days later, when he would arrive again.

Looking for a place to do laundry, I met Sheila, an American who had married a Greek, bought a house, had a family, and now operated a laundry and small library in the center of town. She introduced me to Will and Mavis Manus (both writers and residents since the early 1960s) and other expats from around the world who were living in Lindos.

The village took on the feeling of home, but it would only be short term. There was no ice, water, showers, or fuel available in Lindos, and after early October the harbor would be exposed to winter storms. Conditions at the dock in Rhodes's Mandraki Harbor didn't sound much better—*Southern Cross* would be Med-moored either to a stone quay or a poorly supported floating dock. There was no place to buy ice nearby, showers were not available in the marina, water was impossible to buy in the small quantities I needed (it was only sold by the ton), and diesel cost $3 per gallon.

Greece had other strikes against it too. Prices for food were high—butter was $6 a pound and a head of cauliflower the same. In a slick, modern little coffee shop in Rhodes I asked for ice cream. The sign said that ice cream cones could not be eaten inside; I ordered two scoops in a dish so I could sit down and relax. One scoop cost 200 drachmas (just under $1), so two, I assumed, would be 400. The bill came to 750! The owner explained that he was charging me 350 drachmas for washing the dish, but I could have ordered a Greek coffee for 300 with the dishwashing included.

Half of my financial dilemma in choosing a place to winter was the cost, but the other half was earning money. There were a few galleries in Rhodes, but the quality of the work was soulless. They cranked out one painting after another . . . they even numbered originals.

Dear Kittikins,   Lindos, Greece

I was so glad to hear that Peter continues to improve. Tell him I hope he will soon be making his beautiful pins and painting shirts again.

Greece isn't turning out to be all that I had dreamed it would, but I love Lindos. I've visited many of the "captain's houses" dating from the 16th-century Ottomans. Each home is actually a number of structures arranged around a plant-filled court. An intricate paving of tiny stones flows from the courtyard on into the rooms. Stone carvings arch over the doors and windows. And the terraces above offer views over the rooftops and down to the harbor. Every one is a painting waiting for me.

There are no galleries here, but I had a three-day show at an Italian ice cream shop. However, my most delightful sale happened yesterday.

The Baroness Beatrice Mondi Della Corte invited me, along with five of the people from the 130-foot yacht anchored by *SC*, for an alfresco dinner on her rooftop terrace. An Italian friend of hers brought wine from his vineyard in Tuscany and fresh fish he caught in the bay, prepared in his own style. The moon and stars shone down as we savored every morsel plus an ice cream cake from the shop where I had the show. A call from one of the other guests the next morning led to a sale of two originals.

I'll let you know where I'll be spending the winter as soon as I figure it out. I need a drafting board and a big space. Doing architecture again feels wonderful.

Much love to you both,

Pat

The autopilot manufacturer sent a replacement plastic gear—the one piece they had omitted in the package of parts sent to Aden. I installed the gear and left for Rhodes Town looking forward to Tamara, Bob, Shawn, and Kira's arrival the next morning. They were staying for three weeks, and I had lists of things to see and do in Turkey and on Rhodes when we returned. I was looking forward to sharing my world with them.

While I checked out with the authorities for a visit to Turkey, they explored the fourteenth-century Knights of St. John walled city near the harbor. We celebrated a belated fourth birthday for Kira after dinner and left for a night sail over flat, black water under a million stars. Ten-year-old Shawn and I stood watch together. He shot compass bearings on approaching traffic and plotted GPS fixes on the chart with serious intent.

My old school friend Harry Stern had made plans to join a special Moorings–*SAIL* magazine charter flotilla for a cruise along the Turkish coast beginning two days before Tam's arrival. After making arrangements by radio, we met Harry, his wife Marlys, Judie Bey, and her friend Hugh under Atatürk's statue in the center of Fethiye. Harry kept shaking his head in wonder, "Just imagine us kids from Bloomington meeting here in Turkey. Amazing, isn't it?"

Marlys unloaded a care package from their dentist, a Bloomington sweatshirt, and a bag of art supplies from Mom. Everyone talked at once as we downed a mezes lunch, and Harry mapped out plans for the next day. "The flotilla is going to Stone Wall Bay for dinner, and you're all invited. They'd like you to give a talk about your trip. Amy Ullrich, the managing editor from *SAIL*, has asked to meet you."

We sailed across flat turquoise water between the islands and the mainland of Turkey for a festive night. In the morning Amy invited us to visit the spacious *gulet* carrying the group from *SAIL*. When she learned I was paying my way around by painting, Bob and Shawn were dispatched to bring back paintings and prints from *Southern Cross*. The Moorings flotilla packed off tubes of prints, and I tucked $900 into my wallet. Amy promised to stay in touch and invited me to send articles along the way. Harry and his group left while we slowed down and relaxed—swimming, snorkeling, fishing, and sailing the coastline north and west toward Marmaris.

We visited a carpet merchant where Tam and Bob shopped for the new house they were building, and Shawn soaked up the salesman's every word. Eventually he chose his own small silk carpet with a 10 by 10 grid—the highest quality—made, according to the salesman, in the area of the finest craftsmen in Turkey. "It's an investment," he announced to the amazed salesman and his own gaping family. Kira took up belly dancing and, after buying her own bangled costume, entertained us as she shimmied and wiggled her way around the deck by the hour.

At anchor off the islands we slept over every flat surface of *SC*. When we stopped by towns they moved ashore to a hotel. In Marmaris I tied up amid luxury at Netsel Marina: water, electricity, white marble shower rooms with Turkish carpets, and daily fresh flowers. The charming little town that stretched along the seafront captivated my artist's eye. An Ottoman castle built by Süleyman the Magnificent in 1522 topped the hill in the center, and down the sides and along the shore whitewashed buildings capped with red tile roofs sparkled above the blue-green harbor. There was even an ice shop at the end of the dock.

We left by car to visit Cappadocia, southeast of Ankara in central Turkey, with stops along the way for carpet shopping and sightseeing. The first night we stayed in the 4,000-year-old city of Konya, original home of the Whirling Dervishes (or Mawlawiyah), in the midst of the immense, sweeping Anatolian steppe. Its conservative, religious atmosphere was our first exposure to the countryside of Turkey, away from the tourist-oriented coastline.

We checked into the Şems Tebriz Otel opposite the tomb of Mevlana, the name given to the great mystic philosopher, Jalal ad-din ar-Rumi, whose religious and poetic writings in the twelfth century led to the Muslim brotherhood of the Dervishes.

In the morning, after a traditional breakfast of fresh warm bread, sliced tomatoes, sheep's cheese, black olives, and strong tea at the hotel coffee shop, we met eighteen-year-old Yildiz, on duty at the reception desk wearing the region's traditional *bez* head covering and long coat. She told us of her wish to fly to all the countries of the world, see the cities and the people, climb the mountains, and dive to the bottom of the seas. In her youthful passion, she was nearly airborne sharing her dreams. Her conservative clothing suggested limitations to me, but not to her. Our souls touched—two dreamers who saw the whole world as our neighborhood. I hoped my grandchildren would grow up with that vision, as Tamara had.

By noon we reached the moonscape of mushroom shapes, wind-carved from soft tufa stone, for which Cappadocia is famous. Eons ago the area had been a solid landscape of the highly erodible stone with hard stone boulders buried beneath. Over the centuries, as weather removed much of the tufa from under the boulders, each one was left sitting on top of a column or cone of the soft stone. The overall effect was a village of whimsical Disney fairy chimneys. Far back in history dwellings and churches had been carved inside the outcroppings, and when threatened with invasion, entire cities had retreated underground.

A tired and cranky crew tumbled out of the car back in Marmaris the next night. There had been too many long hours in a small vehicle, with Shawn and Kira testing their limits at every chance. We needed a break for a day. I found a gallery in the marina and signs announcing a large regatta at the beginning of November. "Would you be interested in doing an exhibition of my work during the regatta?" I asked them.

"We'll be closed, but you can use the space and put on your own show." With that offer I moved a step closer to resolving my winter address.

Back in Lindos I introduced my family to everyone I knew and showed them my favorite corners of the village. We swam, fished, and climbed to the acropolis inside the hilltop crusader castle, following Kira, who went by donkey. Then one day I took them all to shore. A taxi took them to the ferry back to Athens and the plane home. The visit had gone too fast. Back on *SC* I found a little trail of turquoise bangles and beads and imagined the little blonde belly dancer and her big brother back on board in other ports someday.

SC's small space and our busy schedule had left no opportunity to hear Tamara's concerns and joys. I wanted to know how she managed raising two children with two demanding and often unsupportive fathers. Was there a balance in her life? Was she happy? At times I had seen a shadow passing across her face and felt the tension in her shoulders. I feared her self-imposed demands to be the best mother, partner, and person and still keep a little piece for herself pulled her in too many directions at once.

The weather turned. I finished one more painting, took a few last rolls of photos, and made plans with Sheila for a show in April to coincide with the opening of her new, larger library and laundry facility and my return to Lindos. In Rhodes Town I finished shopping for things not available in Turkey and supplies for my exhibition and finished a painting of the Alanya market full of detailed clothing patterns, chickens, eggs, olives, and all the unique produce of the region.

A storm hit the day before my departure. It rolled in from the southeast and pushed at the stern of *Southern Cross*, Med-moored by the bow to the floating dock and held back by her stern anchor. By the second night the winds stretched the stern line taut and pounded her bobstay against the dock. At 3:00 A.M. I hauled the 35-pound C.Q.R. and 170 feet of chain to the dinghy and bashed through the chop to set a second hook in the center of the harbor, then collapsed in my bunk while the wind screamed overhead and *SC*'s lines groaned as she yanked from side to side.

The next morning crews worked to raise the smaller, open boats that had sunk all along the quay. Torrential rain had wiped out the highway and the utilities to Lindos. Two people had been killed when the road caved in below them. Rhodes had not seen such a storm in many years.

I left two days later for Marmaris, planning to stay for the winter—on the hook, at the city quay, or in the marina. There was one piece of unfinished business going with me—the TWT papers from my attorney. On Rhodes there had been no one qualified under U.S. federal law to notarize my signatures.

Colorful spinnakers flew across the entry to Marmaris Bay. I hurried into the harbor and dinghied to shore. The same lady I had spoken with before was just closing the marina gallery when I arrived. "Don't worry. The regatta isn't until next week. Sorry about your show, but we've decided to stay open and do our own."

November 1994
Marmaris, Turkey

Dear Kit,

I had a one-week exhibition during the annual fall regatta here. It took a week to find a space, but I wound up in the marina, just above their own gallery. Two hundred guests came from the racers, cruisers, and locals. The day after the show I tied up inside the Netsel Marina with hot showers and all the amenities.

That decision was a huge leap of faith—$1,262 for five months. On the last day of the exhibit, I was still $400 short, with no money left for food. Then George Sackett on *Sesame* offered to loan me the $400, and I accepted.

The marina has everything I could desire, except ice. The plant doesn't deliver in the winter. And mail is slow. However, on the positive side, the Turkish people are generous with warmth, friendship, and a helping hand. In Greece, if I asked a shop owner for something he didn't have, he rolled his head back, raised his eyebrows, shrugged his shoulders, and sneered. In Turkey, if they don't have it, they take me by the hand to their friend's shop who has it and insists I sit down for an apple tea and a visit.

The marina gallery was closing for the winter. I proposed to keep it open with my art and pay them 25 percent of the sales, and they agreed. It's a light, airy place to work and offers a view over the harbor. With the loan of a large table from the restaurant upstairs, photos and sketches from all over the eastern Med, and the peace of being settled for the next five months, I am ready to work.

My new pieces are fascinating and complex, but a few lessons from you would be so welcome. I keep vacillating between seeing myself as an artist who sails and as a sailor who makes art. For the most part it's the latter. When the trip is over I hope I can change that and get serious about my art (or do I mean unserious?).

Have a wonderful time in Hawaii. You are right; it is just what Peter needs for his recovery—warmth and the sunny light of the islands.

Love and hugs,

Pat

The phone at the gallery rang now and then—my mother and Dan. Dan had a big project with problems, but he might be coming in January. I wasn't surprised anymore at the constant change of plans that kept his visit moving continuously forward—just disappointed, but still hopeful.

The days took on a rhythm tied to the hours posted on the gallery door. People wandered in to watch me work, visit about my trip, and occasionally buy something. Late one afternoon my eyes swept up the length of a gray cape to the upswept blonde hair, enigmatic gray eyes, and Mona Lisa smile above. Jütta swayed gently and held out a tiny bouquet of purple wildflowers, expecting me to know already who she was. In Lindos, Will and Mavis had given me her name and address. "You must meet Jütta when you are in Marmaris. She's an artist and a very intriguing woman." I had written, and she had answered. Eventually we had spoken by phone, and now she was here.

"We must go for a wine when you're finished. I'll meet you," she said, then disappeared.

Jütta had come to Turkey in the early 1970s and married a fisherman. She had become a Turkish wife in every way for more than ten years—speaking the language, adopting the head covering, observing the customs. When her artist's soul had needed more she had left him and moved to Marmaris. There she had built a small apartment block, painted, and raised her children.

Jütta could do absolutely nothing, like a languid cat, stretching out and letting her body mold to the place where she sat, not moving. I found that impossible—and intriguing. I was more like an electric spark, jumping from one thing to the next.

She floated in and out of my days, and sometimes, it seemed, almost in and out of life—the cord tying her to this world so tenuous. She wondered why she should go on living. I urged her to think of her future grandchildren and her son and daughter, to not be selfish, but she only smiled that one-sided smile. I had never been this close to a suicide before, apart from my own brief brush with it in New Zealand. Her slow contemplation was frightening.

The TWT attorney wrote with an ultimatum from the judge. If the judge did not receive the original signed copies of the mutual dismissal offered by FSLIC's attorneys, he would withdraw it. The U.S. Embassy in Ankara was too far away. I found a U.S. Consular Agent in Izmir and called for the address and the cost to notarize my signatures. I had to be on the 6:45 bus the next day for the five-hour trip.

At 5:00 A.M., icy cold water bit into my skin, and my breath hung in clouds. I hurried to finish my shower, longing to climb back into bed under blankets and sleeping bag. My head ached, my throat hurt, and my chest rattled. I was in no condition for the long ride to Izmir.

My existing wardrobe on *Southern Cross* did not include winter clothes to match the weather. I put on a thin pair of dressy gray slacks; a long-john top; a quilted, dressy white sweatshirt; and my black-and-white checked Arafat shawl for a "coat." The bus was stiflingly hot, but I didn't have a layer to remove. Smoke filled the air, and I coughed my way north under overcast skies past the gray, barren winter landscape. By the time we got through two long tea stops and arrived in Izmir, I was burning with fever, and my nose ran incessantly.

Biting, cold wind stabbed through my clothes as I searched for the consular office, using one tissue after another. The agent watched me duly sign on five sets of dotted lines, signed and dated each document herself, and sealed the papers with her stamp.

I paid the $100 fee and left to hunt for a reasonably priced fax service to send the required pages as proof. The attendant in the small photocopy shop across the street directed me to the post office but warned, "They'll charge $16 per page and keep your originals!" A businessman, waiting for his photocopies, invited me to his office and sent them for free.

At the post office I dropped the registered envelope containing the original documents in the slot and walked away into the bitter cold wind outside. The door clicked closed behind me. Finished. TWT was dead. The rest was between the IRS and me. I waited for the euphoria or the grieving to start, thankful I had not stayed behind to see it through. My presence would not have changed one thing in the entire episode.

I soothed myself with hot tea in a warm shop and an omelet for lunch, then the bus ride home, a glimpse of the sun, and a feeling of peace as the lights of Marmaris greeted me.

One rainy Friday Jütta picked me up to go marketing. We brought home more food than we could carry—cheeses, tomatoes, olives, yogurt, lettuce, eggplants, fresh herbs, and garlic. All evening she cooked for cruising friends and me. It was like watching a dance as she chopped and peeled and simmered her pots, and the aromas wound around us. With music playing, we ate *meze*-style for hours with *cacik* (yogurt and cucumber salad), *patlican salatasi* (eggplant salad), *taramasalata* (caviar dip), *dolmuş* (stuffed grape leaves), *köfte* (grilled meat-balls), and more, drinking bottles of wine, then coffee, and finally Metaxa.

She came for me one cold, crisp, sunny Monday for a drive to English Harbour and lunch with Sadun Boro on board his boat *Kismet*. We parked in a grove of tall, spindly trees near the long, narrow dock where Sadun waited with his rowing dinghy. *Kismet* and Sadun had traveled around the world in the 1960s.

He spread out lunch for us in the cozy cabin and the hours slipped away over fresh octopus spaghetti, green salad, halvah, tangerines, wine, coffee, and Metaxa. He talked of his voyage and the days before when he spun the yarn, wove the cloth, and made his own sails. Every inch of his boat came from his hands. When he sailed home, Turkey welcomed him as the first Turkish man to sail a small boat around the world and honored him with a stamp com-memorating his accomplishment. We lifted our glasses to boats, sailing, and the world we had both explored. Jitta and I drove back through the woods and the last rays of a deep red sunset.

Batwing radioed an invitation for Christmas in Fethiye. After several months in the Red Sea waiting for clutch plates and battling headwinds, they had emerged at Port Said at last and worked their way along the Turkish coast for the winter.

Wrapped in my new, heavy, black winter jacket, I caught an early morning bus. The seat next to me swallowed the tiny bones of a little old lady who looked just like a dried-apple doll. Her feet dangled above the floor. She folded her hands in her lap, and I looked out the window. Miles passed—a stark Turkish winter landscape between Marmaris and Fethiye. Rocks, ever-greens, and barren deciduous trees marched up hillsides. Small, humble cot-tages with curling smoke from coal fires huddled against the terrain. Far in the distance, snow-covered mountains shimmered in a pale-blue sky.

The bus stopped, and my traveling companion hurried down the stairs. Soon she returned with a large basket covered by a red-and-white checked cloth. She left it by the driver and scooted back into her seat. The index finger on her left hand was bleeding, and she carefully protected it with an empty candy wrapper.

I found a Band-Aid and turned to offer it to her. She smiled and held up her finger like a child to have it wrapped—to make it feel better. I put the Band-Aid on and turned back to my book as she rummaged in her black purse.

She tapped my arm and held out her hand. I held out mine, and she placed a beautiful, tiny, hand-carved wooden spoon in my palm. I thanked her, "*Teşekkürler ederim*," with a smile and a tear.

Lloyd, Judy, and I feasted in the warmth of *Batwing* and traded news. Yanmar had offered Lloyd a brand-new three-cylinder engine. It would be waiting when they arrived in Holland. I had followed the clutch plate history of *Batwing*'s Yanmar with interest; the engine on *SC* was identical and the same age. His had plagued him since the Maldives, while I had had no problems. They mapped out their plans for the coming year: sailing west, then transiting the canals of France to collect their gift from Japan.

Astron and *Timshel* were anchored nearby. They frequently traveled in tandem to provide company for the teenaged crew on both boats. On board *Timshel*, Kathy pulled out a children's book for me to see. I browsed through, appreciating the quality but missing the all-important detail—the author was Kathy Davies. At sixteen she had published her first book and had another already under contract.

On my way back to Marmaris the next morning I thought about the incredible "boat kids" I had met along the way and wished I could have given that childhood to my girls. I had known nothing of this lifestyle until they were already grown. Poised and comfortable with adults, these children melded into cultures around the world, absorbing languages and making friends with confidence. Their home school or correspondence educations were put to use in the real world every day. Geography and history in their travels; math as they helped with navigation and dealt in foreign currencies; English as they kept journals; science in the natural world around them, observing the weather and the changing flora and fauna of other places. Their parents had given them a priceless gift, and the young people I had met seemed to appreciate it.

Back in the gallery I finished the last details of Rod and Helen's new home. The steep terrain of their building site, covered in boulders and trees, called for a model. When I finished, the miniature house sat nestled into the hillside in the middle of four large foamcore boulders and a grove of wooden skewer trees. I shot photos, made copies of the drawings, sent them to Singapore, and held my breath.

The daily visitors to the gallery slowly grew in number. One afternoon an attractive woman with short dark hair stopped by. She had moved to Marmaris for the winter from Istanbul for her health. Nazan studied my paintings and then bore into me with intensity, certain we had been destined to meet. We found common areas of interest in metaphysics, music, art, and philosophy, and began a friendship. Nazan called me her "sister" and bought us matching watermelon-pink sweaters to wear on our outings.

Evenings on board *Bonny Day* with Margaret and Neville playing Crazy 8's and Okey, a Turkish form of Rumicube, had become a weekly event. Bubbly, freckled, red-haired Margaret with her Scottish brogue and tall, bearlike Neville with his gray butch haircut and Yorkshire accent kept me rolling in laughter with one story after another from their travels and Neville's years as a mechanic. They found humor in everything—even when Margaret had to retrieve her camera from a public toilet.

One Saturday early in January, Neville and a few other fellows from the marina were all abuzz with their great adventure of the night before. Haki, the owner of one of the quayside restaurants, had taken them on the most delicious, risqué outing. Their telling of the events raised the temperature in the room.

He had taken them to a remote residential area in Marmaris where he promised they would find a very special private home. The taxi had made stop after stop, seeking directions to the house. At last the driver had pulled up in front of a large, white-stucco, two-story home. People were coming and going through the gate in the wall, and they had joined the mostly male crowd.

Inside, the room was full of people visiting, smoking, and drinking while the women who ran the establishment circulated. The fellows had sat down on cushions in an open space on the floor. To one side, two musicians were playing music Neville described as strange, wailing, and toneless. The woman who owned the house came to greet them and ask what they would like to drink.

Their story went on with innuendoes and hints at the true nature of this house—a nature they, of course, as faithful married men, had not pursued to its ultimate end. Nevertheless, they were clearly delighted with their prowl on Turkey's wild side.

A few weeks later, Nazan invited me for an evening of classical music. She had just found a wonderful private coffeehouse. We circled the far outskirts of Marmaris to reach the two-story, white-stucco house with people crowding around the gate.

The wonderful sounds of exotic half-Eastern, half-Western Turkish music slid out through the open door. We found a mix of young and old visiting quietly in small groups and enjoying the concert. Over thick Turkish coffees, we laughed as I told Nazan about the guys from the marina and their hot night out—at the coffeehouse with classical music.

Dan called. He'd be in Marmaris in March. His wife had filed for divorce.

At last a letter from Rod and Helen arrived. They loved the design. Helen said she could see the thoughts that had gone through my mind as I visualized them working, playing, entertaining, and relaxing in a house that fit like a glove. Their letter reminded me of the dreams that had driven me, with my two young daughters, to the University of Illinois in 1966 to become one of ten women among eight hundred men in the architecture department, and why I had worked to pass the licensing exams in Illinois and California despite an overwhelming bias in favor of men. It reaffirmed for me the satisfaction I felt in solving problems and creating something unique.

I had missed that process intensely and had often considered, in those long stretches at sea, why I had not stuck it out through the thin times. Women had not been welcomed to the profession—tolerated at times, but not encouraged. Those were the days before affirmative action opened some doors if not some minds.

When the firm I had worked for as a project architect ran into serious financial trouble in 1974, I decided to quit and go into business for myself. Within three months San José State offered me a faculty position. I snatched it—not for the security of a job, but from a desire to share what I had learned and experienced. My passion for designing had continued, but had found few outlets. Rod and Helen's project had given me back a piece of myself that I had missed more than I realized.

Dan called again; he would be arriving in April now, just one week before my five months at Netsel Marina ran out and my deadline to leave for the show in Lindos arrived. The divorce was proceeding. For the first time, the only thing standing in our way would be us.

The bus from Marmaris to the airport at Dalaman did not coordinate well with Dan's arrival. I waited in the drafty, cold, empty airport for two hours—fidgeting, reading, drinking coffee, and pacing the length of the waiting area while fantasies of our future together rewrote themselves across the airport walls.

I had always dreamed of our working together, but perhaps he was ready to move on from an occupation that no longer seemed to bring him satisfaction. While he put his affairs in order and joined me for frequent visits, I would finish the trip. Then we would have *SC* for travel by boat and his home in the States for the rest of the time. There would be days filled with sailing, painting, sculpting, exploring the world, listening to opera, and cooking fabulous meals together . . . things we both enjoyed or wanted to. In my mind the question was not, "Would we or would we not be together eventually?" but only "When?"

Dan broke into my reverie as he walked through the door—tall, rugged, blond, and blue-eyed. The years almost vanished. The old electricity almost came back. We hugged and held each other expectantly, but we both seemed shy and tentative in this new environment without established boundaries. The drive back to Marmaris by rental car was filled with busy conversation—most of it mine—personal news, and plans for the week, but not for the future.

I had stored as many of my excess possessions as possible to make room for Dan, but still *SC* was too small for him. "I could never live like this," he said. "What would I do with all my art and sculpture? No, it's too claustrophobic for me."

We visited a 65-foot boat so that he could see how spacious and comfortable boat life could be. But he didn't say, "Oh, now this is more like it; this I could enjoy."

Over the week we traveled by car to ancient sites—Ephesus, Priene, Miletus, Didyma, and Milas. I had waited decades for us to have this much time together, but something was missing. It felt like he had left half of himself at home. In the three years I had waited for this visit—since the phone call in Brisbane—I had not gone out with another man. Reading between the lines of the long letters he had sent—but that had never arrived—I had manufactured expectations of a shared future. If such a dream was not his too, why would he come thousands of miles to see me, why all the phone calls? Why was he keeping the connection between us alive if he didn't see a future? But I waited in vain to hear him say the words I thought were in the missing letters. Our moments of intimacy did not bridge the gap either; tired the first night and preoccupied the others with his dissolving marriage, his office problems, and his children, he pulled away from me. Then he caught a cold and drew further away. The last two days of his visit I was distracted by preparations for my departure from Turkey and upcoming exhibition in Rhodes. And then it was over.

He flew home, saying "maybe in the Canaries," and I put the idea away with less assurance than before that it would happen or that it would live up to my expectations.

Southern Cross and I were ready to let the lines go, to slide out of our safe haven at Netsel Marina just south of where the Mediterranean and Aegean

Seas mixed their distinctive waters and climates. I had chosen the perfect place to spend the winter. With its enticing blend of tastes, smells, rhythms, faces, and emotions—not of the West and not of the East either—Turkey was like the child of a mixed marriage—its features more beautiful than either of its parents.

The slow winter pace in Marmaris had not been quite a hibernation, but a time to recover from the Red Sea, the Indian Ocean, and the high pace of Singapore. A time to curl up under a warm blanket and read, bake coffee cakes for my women friends, and contemplate the summer ahead in southern Europe, on the way back to where I had begun.

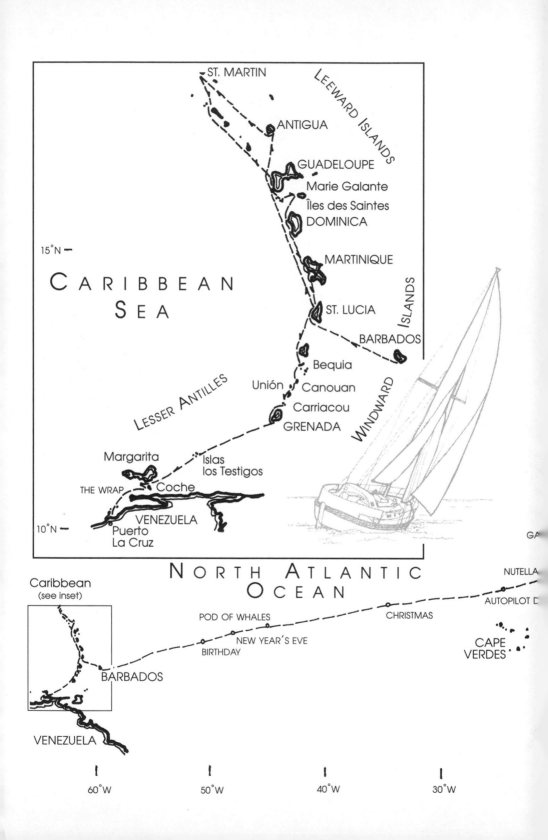

ST. MARTIN

LEEWARD ISLANDS

ANTIGUA

GUADELOUPE

Marie Galante

Îles des Saintes

DOMINICA

15°N —

CARIBBEAN
SEA

MARTINIQUE

ST. LUCIA

ISLANDS

BARBADOS

Bequia

Unión   Canouan

WINDWARD

LESSER ANTILLES

Carriacou

GRENADA

Margarita   Islas
los Testigos

THE WRAP   Coche

VENEZUELA

10°N —

Puerto
La Cruz

NORTH ATLANTIC
OCEAN

Caribbean
(see inset)

GA

NUTELLA

AUTOPILOT

POD OF WHALES

CHRISTMAS

NEW YEAR'S EVE

CAPE
VERDES

BIRTHDAY

BARBADOS

VENEZUELA

60°W   50°W   40°W   30°W

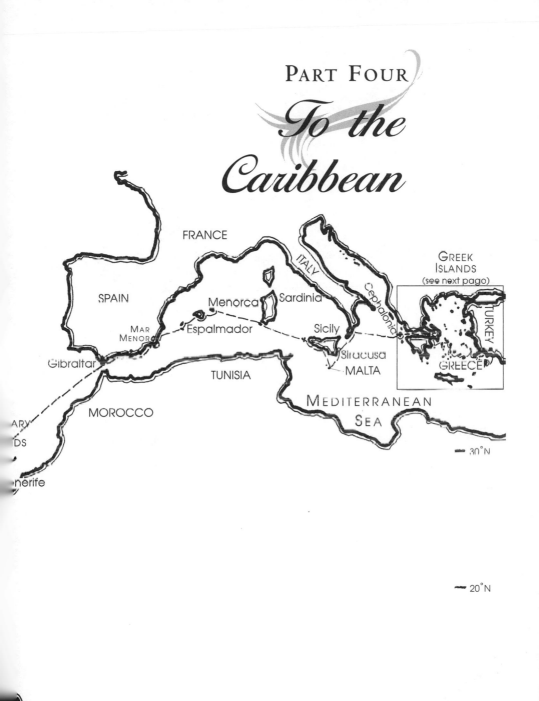

PART FOUR

To the Caribbean

GREEK
ISLANDS
(see next page)

FRANCE

ITALY

SPAIN

Menorca

Sardinia

Cephalonia

TURKEY

MAR
MENORCA

Espalmador

Sicily

GREECE

Gibraltar

Siracusa

MALTA

TUNISIA

MEDITERRANEAN
SEA

ARY

MOROCCO

DS

30°N

nerife

20°N

10°N

(PRIME MERIDIAN)

10°W

0°

10°E

20°E

Northern
Greece

Delphi
○

Galaxidhion

Ithaca

Petras

Athens
○

Cephalonia

Corinth
Canal

To Italy

38°N—

GREECE

The
Peloponnese

Póros · Kéa

IONIAN
SEA

37°N—

36°N—

35°N—

21°E   22°E   23°E   24°E

EGEAN
SEA

MEDITERRANEAN
SEA

Tinos

Mýkonos
Páros

Kallmnos

Amorgós

Astlpálaia

Kos

Simi

Tílos

TURKEY

Marmaris

Rhodes

Lindos

Crete

Cypress

26°E   27°E   28°E   29°E

THE SOFT COLORS OF TURKEY SLID AWAY IN THE WAKE of *Southern Cross*—silvery green olive trees, dusty peach-colored old brick and rounded stone, and pale turquoise water—a hint of the Orient, reminiscent of the Torres Strait. In the short twenty miles to Rhodes, the quality of light, color, and form changed to stark blue and white, splashes of cherry-red, hot pink, and magenta hibiscus and bougainvillea, and the rugged shapes of dark cliffs and rocks.

With considerable relief at finding *Aphrodite* no longer anchored in Lindos, I hiked the hill to town. Along the path, people who had never spoken to me the fall before welcomed me—not with *kalimera*, the usual "good morning," but with *yasou*, a greeting saved for friends. Coming back had moved me into a different category of visitor. Sheila said that in twenty years they would still remember me.

If I ever choose a place to call home, Lindos will be high on my list. The peace of its quiet pathways, the feeling of history in the old buildings, the clarity of the air, and the easy pace of life draw me back there. I imagine living in one of those captain's houses with their clean, unencumbered spaces reminiscent of Shaker simplicity and filling my days with painting the colors of Greece on a rooftop terrace, eating a fresh seafood lunch in the filtered sunlight of a grape arbor with sun-warmed tiny pebble paving under my bare feet, letting 400 years of history from the walls of my bedroom invade my dreams.

Sheila's new, expanded laundry and library operation was a scene of total chaos. No one knew how to install the dryers. There were problems with the ironing equipment bought to do guest-house sheets. Every available corner was piled waist-high with bags of dirty clothes, and boxes of books waited beside library shelves. Several friends hovered over mechanical equipment manuals, studying solutions. Sheila's red curls and freckles surfaced from behind a mound of laundry. She was frazzled but laughing, though too preoccupied to discuss arrangements for the grand opening and the art show—a combined event scheduled to take place in less than a week.

I posted flyers around town and by the beach village and shopped for wine and snacks. *Bonny Day* arrived from Marmaris, and Margaret and Neville joined me with brooms, rags, and buckets of water to clean the library and hang the show.

We covered the walls with my year's work in the Mediterranean: castles in Turkey, markets, a quiet corner inside the walled city of Rhodes, doors and courtyards from Lindos, the colorful harbor of Kastellorizon, and the town of Simi wrapped around a tiny harbor with pastel buildings in pink, pale blue, peach, and yellow layered one on top of the other high up a steep hillside.

Opening night the library looked gala with 150 guests sipping wine, visiting, and enjoying hors d'oeuvres. Among then were my old friend Kay Green and her friend Cheri Kennedy, recently arrived from Champaign, Illinois. Kay had rented Mavis and Will's two-hundred-year-old house for a week. Our friendship had begun when she was my golf instructor and we were both young, single moms at the University of Illinois. We had kept pace through the years—romances, careers, and grandchildren—following each other through letters and visits.

The month in Lindos sped by with Kay's visit, Greek Easter festivities including *bouzouki* dancing in the square, the show, time with the crew on *Sesame* who were on their way west, and making arrangements with Sheila for future business—miniatures and prints from Greece and the ink-drawing cards of the village she had commissioned. I hoped she would be a Mediterranean Dayle.

At the close of the show, I gave Sheila an original painting in appreciation for use of the space. She insisted I take her son's old folding bicycle. "He never uses it. Send him $100 sometime when you can spare it.

"You must stop to see my friend Dr. Kanopoulis in Kalimnos. He collects art. I know he'll want to buy one of your paintings. I'll call and tell him you're coming—be sure to stop."

Even with $2,000 in my pocket I would still have to fly "the GALLERY" sign over the summer to make it through the Med and across the Atlantic. A short detour to see the doctor made sense.

I left for Simi, the next island northwest, then sailed on to Tílos in light southwesterlies. I anchored, put sailing gear away, and prepared to receive officials with boat papers and my passport as a small, official-looking launch drew away from shore. When the boat approached, my heart sank; it was not the officials at all, but Mr. Aphrodite. Not wasting a second, he climbed on board *Southern Cross*, an expectant look in those dreamy, dark eyes.

Mr. Aphrodite waited for me to be overjoyed and reached over to pat my knee. "No," I said sharply. He was downcast for a moment, then beamed and asked me out for the evening.

"I have too much work to do."

"You're always busy," he whined.

"Oh, yes, I'm sorry, but I have a lot of work—always."

"There are so many things I want to do with you."

I could imagine what they were. He left dejected. I went below to fix lunch, wondering why, in the middle of our conversation, I had said I was sorry.

Two days later, after an overnight stop at Kos, I pulled into the town quay at Kalimnos, the heart of the ancient Greek sponge diving industry. Dr. Kanopoulis ushered me into his office. It was obvious when I introduced myself he had not heard from Sheila. He called out for the young man in the waiting room to come in too, and I turned to leave. "No, you can stay."

The doctor took care of the young man, then called out for the old lady in the waiting room. She entered, talking a mile a minute and hauling handfuls of medications from her purse. The doctor said to me over her voice, "She does this every day, morning and night, and there is nothing wrong with her." Finally he shoved her out the door and locked it. My alarms began going off, especially in light of the television show he had been watching when I arrived: swimsuit models wearing fabric postage stamps.

He wanted to entertain me, he said, and I was anxious to sell art. We walked out of the office harboring divergent goals. His home overlooked the ocean from high on a rocky hillside. There were walls and walls of art, but nothing similar to mine. Every time I tried to steer the conversation in that direction he did a quick end run to another topic. The doctor mentioned that his wife was in Athens, then invited me to lunch—after he had a very large scotch.

We drove north on a narrow, coastal road that gripped the steep hills, displaying a new, breathtaking view around each curve—the foamy white of pounding surf against the deep blue Aegean, rocky cliffs dropping into the sea, white pocket beaches, bougainvillea—and above, the blue of a Greek sky that defied description. When I used that exact same shade in a painting it seemed such a sky must be impossible.

He stopped on a side road by his small, fresh, and airy weekend house with bleached natural-wood furniture, white walls, and brightly colored cotton fabrics. Another large scotch was followed by a long lunch at a garden restaurant down the road. The coastal road, the weekend house, the garden restaurant—with the right partner it could have been the stuff of dreams. The doctor had two beers with lunch. Thinking of the road we had just traversed, I shuddered.

Back at his vacation house, he played music—very, very romantic music—and asked me to dance. I declined, but he persisted. Moving like a steel rod at arm's length, I danced with him for one, then two, and at last three songs. "I must go; I have to get back to work," I begged.

With gratitude to whichever Greek god or goddess had heard my prayers, I arrived safely back in Kalimnos town. The doctor deposited me in front of *Southern Cross*. I could not bring myself to play the doctor's game just to sell a painting; we never discussed my art. The price of his patronage was too steep for me.

Inside a minuscule church that was squeezed between neighboring buildings on a narrow side street, an old lady, dressed all in black and no taller than my shoulder, stood to greet me. Her dark eyes sparkled with excitement that someone had come to visit her church. She tried Greek, then Italian, disappointed that we could not find a common language. I left on the farewell notes of "*Adio, adio*," as we each wiped away a tear for the words we lacked and the recognition that as women we had much to share. There are moments when souls touch without words, without physical contact, without a mutual culture, times when we disregard the beliefs and customs that make us different and experience the emotions that make us all the same.

Around the corner an old man with a crumpled hat sat on the curb in the shade of a tree, selling salad greens from his garden and visiting with a friend. He smiled and held out samples for me to try. I bought some, and he made a gift of a small bundle of fresh herbs.

The sail to Astipálaia, the butterfly-shaped island to the west, began with shifty winds and gusts and ended nine hours later in a 35-knot *meltemi* and 2-meter seas. These were the conditions that made sailing the Mediterranean in the summer difficult and anchoring overnight risky. The strong summer winds that blew from the north to northwest grew between the pressure differentials of Pakistan's low pressure area and the Azores high. In addition to sudden weather changes, traffic or rocky shores were never far away.

Above the anchorage, homes and shops clambered up the steep island side from Skala, the town by the harbor, to the *chora*, a hilltop village above, with a cluster of windmills and a thirteenth-century castle. I hiked to the top and shot photos of red poppies against the dry golden hillside and deep blue sky and of geraniums backed by stark white walls and bright blue trim.

"The GALLERY" made $880 one day. A traveler from England and a young couple on a small boat from Sweden came to buy prints. Then a German couple from a boat anchored next to me came aboard, announcing that they only bought abstract art. They left with an original of the Nouméa library—more impressionistic than abstract. It was not the money they gave me that mattered, but the stamp of approval from "art collectors."

For sixteen hours I bashed through the sea between Astipálaia and Amorgós in conditions ranging from chaotic 6-foot seas and no wind to strong north-northeasterlies. On the windward side of the island the monastery of the Panayia of the Presentation hung on the side of the cliff—the building so thin it looked as if it had been painted on the rock, the white walls a slash against the dark crag. I planned a pilgrimage for the next morning.

Over a rabbit *stifado* in a restaurant on the quay, I asked the owner about the monastery. "Yes, you can catch a bus along this road. It'll take you to the gate. Be careful of the monks! If they invite you to see their rooms, don't go."

The bus ambled up the scrubby western side of the hill to the *chora* above the harbor and the end of the line. I hiked to the crest in the warming sun, then down the switchback path—back-and-forth across the steep east-facing side, past the monastery gate, up hill to the entry, and then up several flights of steep stairs. There I learned that my jeans were not modest enough, and I was sent back down for a long skirt from a rack by the entrance.

Back up stairs a young novitiate led me through the public spaces, brought me candy, and then schnapps. My antennae on alert, I declined, and he disappeared. On the way out I stopped to help a monk who was struggling with a large bag of dirt, then turned up the road.

As the sun rose higher, the steep switchback path looked less and less inviting. In my heavy jeans and skirt, I wished the bus did run all the way to the entry as promised by the restaurant owner. The monk I had helped offered me a ride in his van to Katapola, the harbor town on the other side of the island. He drove down the narrow highway, but passed the road to town and turned instead toward the beach. Stopping at a small chapel, he told me not to worry; he would take me to town when he finished the gardening.

He opened a tap, and water from a spring-fed cistern on the hillside above filled a channel along the upper edge of the garden. One by one, with his hoe, he opened the side channels running between the rows. When one was drenched he closed it and opened the next. On and on he went across the expanse of vegetables. I hiked to the beach below in clean blue air perfumed with herbs and salty sea smells.

When the monk finished he insisted on showing me a grove of trees by the spring. The nearby tiny chapel was his home, he explained, as he returned from inside with a jar of Vaseline. "I have a very bad back. Can you rub it?"

"That won't do any good. You need to see a doctor. They'll have to cut your back open to fix that," I answered, hurrying down the path to walk to town.

Southern Cross island-hopped through the Cyclades: Páros; ancient, mythical Dhílos; modern mythical Mýkonos with its famous, deep-blue domes above pure white stucco—only the domes were surrounded by wires and satellite

dishes. I dashed between hydrofoils in busy ferry lanes. Like giant water strid-
ers, they skimmed across the sea at lightning speed. I wondered if they could
see me and how fast they could turn or stop. On the southeastern end of
Tínos, five-hundred-year-old Venetian dovecots dotted the windswept yellow-
ing grasses of the 2,000-foot-high hills. I touched at Kéa and finally Póros, in
the Saronic Gulf, to pick up my mail. All across the islands I had been writing
and sending letters home. This was the first mail stop since Lindos.

Nineteen letters waited. When I gave the attendant my name she lit up,
happy to have so much to give me or perhaps just glad to clear the shelf. I
sent Dan a package with tapes of Turkish music, Mary Lee Settle's *Turkish
Reflections*, photos from our visit, and a letter. But there was nothing in the
mail from him. I had counted on a letter—something to tell me how he was
doing, thoughts on our time together, plans for another trip. Even though
the long-awaited visit in Turkey had fallen short, there was nothing to indi-
cate we would not go on as before, staying in touch and seeing each other
now and then. I wanted to know what it all meant to him, or if he thought
about it at all.

Dear Kitty,   13 June 1995

Thank you for your letter. I've been out of touch with everyone for a
month, but it feels like much longer. Gibraltar is my target by October—the most favorable time to sail from there to the Canaries.

The island scenes in the Aegean have been captivating. If I spent the
rest of my life right here, there would never be an end to the inspiration
for paintings. Instead I'm collecting photos for future pieces and moving too fast to do it right.

The process of watching my vision come out on paper has been so
satisfying, if only I could accept that as being enough. But I need the
approval and acceptance of others, and when they give it I don't believe
them. I think honest art only comes when you paint to answer the inner
voices, and I don't trust them yet.

Have you ever noticed how watercolor pulled across a fresh piece
paper makes it sparkle?

When you make the coming move to Hawaii it will surely take your
work in a new direction. I can't imagine you two in that languorous setting after the pace of San Francisco.

Thank you for the clipping on Alviso, California. What memories that evoked of the months we shared living on *Miss Petunia* on the side of the slough; doing architectural design in the little migrant worker's shack in town; going out for dinners at Maria's; sharing bottles of wine with the guys at the boatyard; and being young and happy. Those wonderful, carefree days.

Many, many hugs to you both.

Love,

Pat

The islands had passed by, each with its own character and its own encounters. Some were unforgettable for their charming architecture—like Astipálaia and Simi—or for their breathtaking vistas, like Kalimnos. But others were clouded by encounters with the likes of Mr. Aphrodite and the doctor. More time might have changed this. I had never gone beyond a first impression before it was time to move on. The experiences I sought could only happen when one stayed a long time and slowly became part of a village, as I had in Lindos.

On June 16th *SC* sailed across the gulf and arrived at the southern end of the Corinth Canal, ready to transit the next morning. The canal was expensive and could be difficult to negotiate against strong opposing wind and current, but the alternative—sailing through the chronically heavy weather around the bottom of the Peloponnese—was more discouraging.

I hunted through the small town on the eastern side of the cut for ice and fresh provisions, then stopped at an outdoor café for a cold drink, asking, "Do you know where I can buy ice?" A group of young men at the next table promised to get it—in a little while, after their beers. Then they preened and paraded, clowned and danced for their audience of one. I could not believe it! It was the first time anyone had danced spontaneously in the five months I had been in Greece. They continued drinking, and things turned ugly, hovering on the edge of a fight. Menacing moves fanned the skirmish; someone shoved over a table, and broken glass flew. The manager stepped in and took control.

New arrivals brought a shift in mood. One man crawled from table to table on his hands and knees barking, then mewed like a cat. Others sat alone staring into space. I expected a film crew to arrive for a Greek version of *One Flew Over the Cuckoo's Nest.* When I stood to leave they all jumped up, saying, "Wait, we'll get your ice now."

I waited. The young men returned with ice, insisting I needed their help transporting it to *SC*. Two of them climbed into the dinghy, and I gave up arguing. Letting them see the boat would be a way to say "thank you." On board SC the situation plummeted. They chided and probed. "Why can't I smoke on your boat? Why do I have to take off my shoes? Maybe I should take my pants off too. You don't have a boyfriend. When was the last time you had sex? You need to have sex again." It took two hours, but at last I was rid of them—tired, hungry, and upset. I was angry with myself for getting into the situation and with them for creating it. A lifetime of practiced manners got in the way; setting boundaries and drawing firm lines were not skills we had been taught in the benign 1950s.

In the morning SC moved inside the canal basin. I arranged for transit and paid the exorbitant fee—just $14 less than the two-day transit of the Suez. This canal was just 3½ miles long and would be over in less than an hour with no pilot on board. It was the most expensive stretch of water in the world.

SC's engine hummed, and I waited for the canal to open. Ahead a constant stream of cars and trucks between Athens and the Peloponnese filled the bridge at the surface of the water. Traffic halted, and the now-empty bridge sank below the sea. When it reached the bottom there were 20 feet of water above the guardrails, and the light turned green. I held back, waiting to follow a large oceangoing tug docked ahead of me, but its crew waved at me to pass.

I approached a narrow slit cut into the red stone cliff ahead, the walls on either side rising sheer for 270 feet. SC entered the 70-foot wide canyon—only twice as wide as she was long—and I held my breath, pushing the engine to the maximum and gripping the tiller. There was no room for error, and using the autopilot was impossible.

In ancient days ships were dragged across the narrow isthmus. Then Greek and Roman rulers sought a way to create a canal; Nero began digging in the first century A.D., and in 1893 the French finished cutting the slot in use today.

A blast sounded from behind—the large tug was rapidly bearing down on SC. She sounded again, and a voice called on the radio below. It was prohibited to pass; there was no room; and I could not leave the helm to respond. She blasted again, looming closer. I pulled over and let her by. Someone shouted angrily from the deck. Her wake hit, tossing SC close to the rocks along the side. Then the water calmed, and the taste of adrenaline vanished bit by bit. I was lost again in the beauty of the red stone topped by a bold cobalt strip of sky until the next bridge dropped below the water and SC exited the canal.

The oracle at Delphi hovered in the mountains above the Gulf of Corinth as I sailed past. "Can you tell me something about my life?" I wondered. "Where am I headed and why? Is this the right direction?" Grinding sounds answered from the autopilot. On shore in Galaxidhion, I sent a fax asking Navico to send two new plastic gears to Malta.

Southern Cross waited at anchor in Galaxidhion while I made a day trip to Delphi. Picturesque photos of most seaside villages in Greece showed sailboats circling around a town quay, and in years past tying to the wall had been free. But in January 1995 every little village had begun charging. They offered no water, electricity, showers, or facilities, and the fees ran midnight to midnight, so that an overnight stay counted as two days. The port captains reasoned, "We're not running a hotel." Fees for *Southern Cross* would have been more than $15 per day—out of my budget. I sent a little prayer to the weather gods while my bus toiled into the mountains.

The town of Delphi climbed up Mount Parnassós like a Swiss village. I walked out the far side to the ancient site and felt my way among remains from which the mysticism of the oracle's inscrutable proclamations still emanated. Greeks of the sixth century B.C., when Delphi was the center of the world, celebrated architecture, sculpture, music, poetry, and theater as inseparable components of sacred life. Contributions from city-states and foreign rulers to the temples of Apollo and Athena had included works from the finest artists rendered in precious materials: gold, bronze, ivory, and marble.

Inside the museum the bronze Charioteer drew me. The wind lifted his flying reins, and I could feel the weight in the drape of his clothing. The Three Dancers in marble pulled me over and stole away my breath with their delicate faces and graceful bodies. They had stood 40 feet high atop an acanthus column in 335 B.C.

I had been here once before, in 1969, but I saw things as if for the first time. There were no old memories. How could I have looked at all this before, I wondered, and not been so moved? The young woman I was then had come to gather history lessons, and now I was seeking to understand the lessons of life—learning to know myself as instructed by the inscription above the entry to Apollo's temple where the oracle made her proclamations. Back on the bus, looking over the treetops to the Gulf beyond and the setting sun, I realized that the oracle lived inside me, if I would listen for the answers.

The next morning *SC* left for a partially finished marina on the island of Trizónia. The small village on shore was living on high hopes of future prosperity from visiting cruisers. For the time being, tying to the unfinished docks was free.

After the camaraderie of the South Pacific, Southeast Asia, and the Red Sea, the Mediterranean had been a desert. My fellow cruisers had spread out to far-flung destinations and kept in contact only by radio. In most anchorages or on town quays I had been surrounded by charter boat guests who arrived and immediately set out for restaurants and shopping. There were people all around, but I felt more lonely than I'd ever felt at sea. Alone and lonely were not the same. Loneliness happened when people were present but looked straight through me.

The waiting cluster of boats at Trizónia had formed a temporary community sharing potlucks, visits, books, and help. We were all starved for conversation and friendship.

Southern Cross sailed on to her last Greek island—Cephalonia, in the Ionian Sea.

Legendary Ithaca, the home Ulysses craved in his travels, lay across from the anchorage at Áyios Eufemia. For me home was not a place on land or sea anywhere. Instead, the home I was searching for dwelled inside, and I would arrive the moment I was at perfect peace with who I was.

In my last days in Greece I still longed to dance *bouzouki*. One was advertised for July 1st; I would stay for one last chance. Dinner was an endless affair, and I waited impatiently as the evening wore on. At last the music began and the dancers emerged—not us but a hired troupe. They danced well, but I wanted to be moving with them on the floor, not watching from a chair.

July 3rd I tied to the long empty town wall in Argostoli, on the south end of Cephalonia, to shim the tiller and change the oil before crossing to Italy. As I finished dismantling the steering and draining the oil, the harbormaster dropped by, asking me to stop in his office to check in sometime that afternoon. I promised to do so as soon as I had the boat operational again. He smiled and said good-bye.

Midafternoon I made my way to the harbor office. "You're in the wrong area," the office attendant said. "You should be inside the basin behind the gates. That's a commercial zone where you put your boat, and the fees are $50 a day—midnight to midnight."

SC was tied to the open section of wall my sailing guidebook indicated was saved for boats that had already checked into Greece. There were no signs indicating otherwise. When I told him this, he backed down to $15. I moved across the channel to spend the night and left for Italy in the morning.

I had invested five years in a dream. Expecting to discover the Greece of Zorba with music, dance, and an unending passion for life, I had found lust and arrogance instead. How could the Greeks I'd met have descended from the godlike men who created all that beauty long ago? Their modern counterparts seemed another breed.

The moments of pleasure I had found in the physical beauty of the land, the ancient sites, and a few precious people were offset by anger and disappointment in the men I had encountered. Egyptian men had been silly and irritating, but the Greek male's behavior from my first encounter at Kastellorizon the summer before to the last at Cephalonia was obnoxious and meanspirited.

—————————JULY 1995

DEPRESSION SETTLED AROUND ME LIKE A SHROUD AS I dragged my disappointments across the Ionian Sea to Italy. "Clack, clack, clack, grrrrrrrrrrr, whirrrrrrrrr, clack," went the ailing autopilot. It sounded as bad as I felt, but mine was a sickness of spirit. I was fed up with the life I had created, exhausted by living on the edge, tired of worrying about money and rushing from place to place. At times it did not seem I was any closer to the peace I sought.

Dawn had written from Singapore asking for additional prints for the gallery, but the money to pay for them had not arrived in Lindos or Póros. I had been counting on that money to haul SC out of the water and paint her bottom, and there would be living expenses for September and October and provisions and preparations to cross the Atlantic. My lack of security invaded my thoughts constantly. When I asked myself why I had spent my whole life doing crazy things like this trip instead of finding a way to earn a good income, I had no answer.

"Clack, clack, whirrrrrrr . . . ." Silence. I got up to fix the autopilot, thankful for a temporary distraction. The wind vane did no better. More to pass the time than from any expectation of success, I rigged a sheet-to-tiller steering system. With blocks to transfer the pressure of the wind on the sail to the tiller and bungee cord to maintain the balance, IT WORKED!! Memories of the weary month in the Indian Ocean when I could have tried this mocked me. I had convinced myself then that it couldn't work with the spare parts I had available. Inside the autopilot the power supply connection had failed. With a little solder securing the wires, it ran again.

My momentary sense of satisfaction flickered, then went out, yielding to an enveloping loneliness. I needed to be held by someone. Apart from my brief stop in Trizonia, I'd been alone continuously for six weeks.

After a night at Rocella Ionica, a new partially constructed harbor near the toe of the boot of Italy, I left for Sicily. Mount Aetna stood out against an electric melon sky—not pink nor yellow nor orange, but an indescribable, unpaintable color that lifted my spirits. The artist in me wanted to create one significant thing in my life. I did not need to *be* significant—just to *do* something.

Wild, crazy bodies and faces, patterns and images danced and cavorted in my subconscious, begging to be painted. They played against my eyelids just before sleep arrived and were gone in the morning. There was a door someplace to enter that world of the creative subconscious. I wanted to unlock it and spill the contents onto my paper, to escape the safe and pretty paintings that had been flowing from my brushes.

I returned to Henry Miller's *The Colossus of Maroussi*, which I had been reading. It offered more insights into me than into Greece. To those who envied his lifestyle, he said: "Because nobody can enjoy the experience he desires until he is ready for it. People seldom mean what they say. Anyone who says he's burning to do something other than he is doing or to be somewhere else than he is is lying to himself. To desire is not merely to wish. To desire is to become that which one essentially is." So what was my desire: Sailor, artist, or something else? I just needed to get out of the way and let it happen.

The trip was no longer in my heart. My dream of Greece had coaxed me through five years, and now it was behind me. There was nothing to replace it; no place I wanted to be more than any other and no more curiosity. I had turned this voyage into a job.

In Siracusa, Sicily—Magna Graecia of old and rival to Athens in the eighth century B.C.—I was surrounded by fellow cruisers and learned that Pamela Ashton, a British expat living there, threw a party every Saturday night. It was Saturday; I accepted every hug offered and lost my voice in conversation.

Siracusa warmed me. The city glowed in the early morning light with a golden halo cast up from her ancient stone walls. She drew me down streets so narrow the Baroque balconies on opposite sides of the street nearly touched overhead. Her seventh-century duomo, built around the ancient columns of a temple of Athena, taught an architectural history class as I walked toward the outer walls through layers of developing styles and out onto the piazza in front, surrounded by Baroque palaces.

In the dusk at day's end, families paraded beside the quay. Miniature ponies, the size of large dogs, wore brightly colored plumes and silver-trimmed harnesses as they pulled tiny ornate carts carrying one child each. Lovers sipped coffees at sidewalk cafés, and newlyweds posed for photos in front of our boats.

We left in a flotilla of three for Malta, where I had planned a stop to pick up mail when Tunisia was still on the itinerary as the place to haul my boat. Then Margaret had mentioned that the temperature in Tunis in August would be 110 in the shade. "You'll never be able to work in that heat. The flies'll drive you crazy." Plans had changed, but Malta stayed on the agenda. The mail would be there, along with a replacement Avon (the one from Singapore had a leaky seam) and new gears for the autopilot, and I expected to find all the parts I needed at reasonable prices. In addition, Pamela had provided a contact for a show at the Royal Malta Yacht Club.

Valletta Harbor, at the foot of the medieval walled city, glowed at sunrise with the same golden light that surrounded Siracusa. All the city had been built from soft golden limestone quarried on the dry, rocky island. Seen as critical to the power balance of the Mediterranean, Malta lived under continuous foreign rule from the Phoenicians in 800 B.C. through the Romans, Normans, Arabs, French, Spanish, and finally the British, until independence was declared in 1964.

Eight days after arriving I left Malta more despondent than ever. Dan had sent the copies he offered to make of slides I had taken of my artwork, but not even a note to go with them. I called, and he complained about the place he was living in, about work, about his separation. "Call again soon. Collect."

Nothing was reasonable in Malta. I had spent $600 and only made $135 at my little show. The clubhouse was at the end of a desolate piece of land. The manager insisted I have the show in the evening, from 7 to 11, and put it in the newspaper. Every night I rode my bike down the long, dark stretch of road to visit with the bartender. "I can't understand why you had this at night. I've been here seven years, and no one ever comes then." A few people came— friends I had invited from among the cruisers.

One small load of laundry cost $13.20; a taxi to go one mile was $9; a hamburger was $9; paint that elswhere cost $100 per gallon was $240; a new lightbulb was $15. Diesel fuel was $2 a gallon—better than Italy's $4 price—but the deliveryman waited on the quay with his full tank truck every day, then charged an extra $12 per customer for delivery.

I thanked Navico for the free replacement gears and told them I wanted a new edition of my patched and repaired autopilot. Over the years they had improved the design several times, and I wanted their latest version. They had begun with a plastic housing, then changed to the aluminum one I had replaced; and finally stainless steel. By now the glitches had been resolved.

SC sailed west along the bottom of Sicily to the Egadi Islands. In rough afternoon seas the autopilot broke again. I approached the unlit shore of Levanzo in moonless dark, picking my way foot by foot into the cove without a detailed chart. It was an unplanned stop.

In the morning I sailed through dense fog to Favignana, 3½ miles away, to find an electrical repairman. The autopilot went from bad to worse at the hands of this electrical magician, "Il Mago." He damaged the tiny bronze gear on the motor with a pair of pliers, and the motor still didn't work. In Trapani, a ferry ride away on the west coast of Sicily, the electrical shop fixed the motor for $125, but that wasn't the only problem. Il Mago had blown out an electronic part testing his repair.

Steering sheet to tiller I left in the morning for Sardinia. On a windless sea at 1800 I turned the key. Nothing happened. The starting battery showed dead on the voltmeter. I tried the house batteries. Nothing. *Southern Cross* turned back to Favignana, 30 miles away.

SC reached the rocks outside the harbor as the wind died and the current swept her along. I raced forward to inflate the dinghy, launch it, mount the outboard, and tie it alongside to power *SC* into the anchorage. An hour later I dropped the anchor as curious Sunday sailors stared.

The next morning in Trapani the electrical repairman tested the starter motor and pronounced it very healthy. I sighed with relief. Reinstalling the starter motor I bumped a battery cable, and the voltmeter needle jumped. *Only a loose connection!*

I left again for Sardinia, thinking about the sailmaker in Malta who had fixed my shredded staysail. I had the feeling whatever happened to him he would bounce back—eternally buoyant and upbeat. For most of my life, until I left Turkey in April, I had been that way. Out of bed in the morning with a smile, looking forward to the day. Relishing whatever came my way—a new experience, a chance to learn, a challenge to resolve.

In Malfatano on the southern tip of Sardinia the tree-covered hills invited me to relax, take a hike, unwind. Instead I left for Carloforte with its pastel houses and wrought iron balconies. It was my last Italian stop; I spent the day hunting for ice. "Across the bay in Calasetta you'll find an ice plant."

"Come back at 8:00 tomorrow. We're closed," said a man on the quay.

At 9:00 they gave me half a bag. "Come back later—we don't have any ice for you," a lady said, prodding me in the chest with one of her long fingers.

At 10:00 I returned with the last of my lira, but stopped first at the end of the quay for yogurt and fresh mozzarella—the best thing in Italy. I waited in line for the Sunday morning shoppers ahead of me, my ice bags tucked under my arm.

The man behind the deli counter rushed at me, eyes dilated wide. "*Pesce, pesce, pesce,*" he screamed, waving his arms and holding his nose.

"*No pesce, no pesce, solo ghiaccio, solo ghiaccio.*" No fish, these are only for ice, I tried to reason with him. He shoved me out the door, and I walked down the quay on the edge of tears.

The long-fingered lady handed me a shovel to get my own ice. They had waited on every other customer. I took some, paid her, and left. The man who had sent me away the night before stopped me to talk, and I burst into tears. "I hate this place; I hate Italy."

There were good memories from Italy: the beauty of Siracusa and the fisherman there who gave me a large block of ice, the way the Italians stopped at standup bars for quick, tiny espressos, the beautiful juicy fruit, and the old ladies in Favignana. Every evening when I had walked down the narrow street to the center of town, the three old ladies in cotton housedresses had been visiting. They sat in a row on wooden folding chairs at the side of the street. "*Buona sera,*" they called to me. "*Buona sera,*" I answered. They had smiled and nodded, complimenting me on my Italian.

But there were other images from Italy. More beggars than I had seen since Denpasar, Bali. More litter and less regard for the environment than I had seen anywhere with the exception of Malta. Surly fruit vendors who wouldn't let me touch their fruit to make my choice. The man who said, "You can't sell your artwork here. We have really good painters in Italy. Why would anyone buy yours?" And everywhere I went, fat women in skimpy swimsuits with their pudgy, bare bottoms hanging out from under their T-shirts. I had had enough.

TWO DAYS LATER I TURNED UP THE NARROW CHANNEL past Punta de Felipet, under the watchful guns of the Spanish military, to the small basin at Cala Teulera on Isla Menorca, in the Balearic Islands. As I rounded the final corner, a huge smile crinkled my face. Cruising boats! Friends at last! People waved and called on the radio to welcome me.

They postponed their planned potluck and barbeque to the following night, knowing I was too tired from a sleepless passage to join them that night. I could have swept them into my arms and cried, I was so hungry for companionship.

We gathered around a campfire on the beach to swap stories from the Med and look ahead to the other side of the Atlantic. I heard more navigation advice for the Téhuantepec: "If it's blowing 30 in the Caribbean, it's blowing 90 in the Gulf of Téhuantepec. It's the high in the Caribbean and the low in the gulf that causes it. That low sucks the wind right through the narrow mountain gorges and funnels it down across the gulf."

"Place is full of shrimp boats. If they're workin' their nets, you gotta watch out. They can't see a thing with them deck lights on. If your Spanish's good enough, you can get a weather report from 'em. When they go in, head for port. It's goin' to hit hard."

I filed it away.

Lynn on *Kiwi Star* joined me to sail in tandem to Mallorca—harbor hopping, seeing the sights, sharing dinners, watching videos on *Southern Cross*, and comparing notes on subjects from sailing and travel to grandchildren and life. Lynn was the gutsier sailor, the "let God take down the sails" variety. She could outsail and outdistance me any day. But I was the better mechanic and overall seaperson. We complemented each other nicely. She had been depressed for the past three months in the Mediterranean, too. It was not an easy place to singlehand on a schedule.

A weather window was pushing both of us. I was planning a haulout in September at Almérimar, Spain. In mid-October the steady, dependable winds from Gibraltar to the Canaries would disappear. To avoid hurricane season in the Atlantic I should depart from the Canaries no sooner than early December. And on the other side of the ocean I had a date in February for SailExpo at Atlantic City as the guest of *SAIL* magazine. All the pieces fit carefully together.

From Palma, Mallorca, I sent letters to Mom and Stubby with birthday wishes for his eighty-sixth, to Dayle in New Zealand in appreciation for all she had done—the Blue Penguin had finally sold, and the new owner would not be carrying my prints and miniatures—and to Terri and Glenn, congratulating them on her pregnancy after two years of wishing. The post office attendant handed over the long-awaited check from Dawn and one from *SAIL* for an article.

Dan was in a meeting when I called. I left my name, but there was no number to leave for him to call back. Disappointment and frustration had followed me from phone booth to phone booth across the Med. He could not reach me, and I had no way to know when to call him. Without letters I had no idea what he might be thinking about us. And my own dreams were growing thin.

Navico sent names and fax numbers of dealers who might have my autopilot in stock and the number for a repairman in Palma. A flurry of faxes left and returned without success. They were releasing a new design. My model had been discontinued, and there were no more.

With the autopilot working and our lockers full of provisions, *SC* and *Kiwi Star* sailed to Cala Llonga on Isla de Ibiza, and on to Isla Espalmador with its wild, natural beach. Sand dunes with gray, green, and yellow dune grass fringes stretching along the shore and seabirds wheeling overhead reminded me of the coast south of Santa Cruz. I dove into the light turquoise water to scrub the waterline; it had been months since I had stopped for a swim. Lynn sailed on. After five stops together, we were both ready to be alone again.

I hung "the GALLERY" sign, took flyers to surrounding boats, and settled in the cockpit with Kathleen Norris's *Dakota*. Late afternoon turned the sky pale lavender as gallery customers arrived.

Curly blonde-headed, petite, and all muscle, Teresa Zabell, Spain's gold-medal-winning 470 dinghy sailor from the Barcelona Olympics, was the most famous person to visit *Southern Cross*. She chose a print and signed the guestbook with a drawing of a 470—a light, high-performance racing dinghy requiring both skill and athleticism. The next day I accepted an invitation to visit her on *Boga Boga*. While I signed her guestbook, Teresa called Harbormaster Jorge Haenelt at Benalmádena, near Málaga, to arrange for an exhibition of my art in the lobby of the Capitanía, or port captain's offices. Jorge was a fellow Olympian and close friend. Teresa got off the phone with the news that he would be expecting me when I finished the haulout at Almérimar.

"By the way," I asked, "why does *Boga Boga* fly a British ensign?" Teresa rolled her eyes, describing the stringent requirements for Spanish-flagged boats and the coast guard's enthusiastic enforcement. One day during an Olympic practice session in her 470 in Barcelona Harbor, the coast guard had cited her for sailing without an anchor. In the entire world there were probably as many mountain climbers wearing parachutes as there were 470's carrying anchors! Eventually the matter was dismissed.

SC sailed on to the mainland and into Mar Menor, a 12-mile inland sea on the Spanish mainland northeast of Cartagena, for a Sunday of rest and reading. On Monday at 0800 I approached the swing bridge blocking the exit from the sea. Signs said the bridge opened for the first fifteen minutes of each hour between 0700 and 2200, but it was closed. In the narrow, ¼-mile approach channel with a 2.5-knot current pushing from behind, turning around would be difficult. I drew closer, waiting for the bridge to move; it didn't. At the last moment I threw the tiller over and turned back to deep water.

Calling again and again in Spanish, then English, I reached the edge of tears in frustration. Someone finally answered, "The bridge will open at 0900." I approached again at the appointed time, drawing closer and closer. Nothing. In the tiny basin by the bridge I locked the tiller over, raced below, and grabbed the microphone. "I'm here. Open that bridge."

I drifted forward, blasting the horn continuously. Slowly the bridge opened, and I edged by to freedom.

The port of Almérimar was so close—only 120 miles away on September 4th—but in Mediterranean terms, so far. Seas were calm when I turned toward Cabo de Gata, but by noon they ran to 6 feet high, short and steep, and the wind was over 40 knots. *SC* turned back to shelter behind Cabo de Palos, then left at 0500 in the next morning's calm. In a few hours the wind rose to 30 knots and the seas reached 9 feet, building new ones on top of the old. Mazarrón offered shelter to the northwest; I turned and counted the seconds for two hours, fighting my way past Punta de la Azohia, a rocky outcrop looming as a lee shore in the southwesterly wind. Seas crashed over *Southern Cross*, driving green water over her decks, and I hung on. A tomato jumped out of the basket on the stove; the toolbox dislodged and crashed to the floor, then slid and smashed the tomato; the chart flew off the chart table, landing in the mess; and nectarines rolled across the floor, leaving a trail of sticky juice.

At 1730 I anchored in the protection of the commercial basin and assessed the damage: wet bunk, wet mountings on artwork, salt water filling the bilge and covering the freshwater tanks, the little Singapore TV dripping salt water, and the galley covered in squashed produce. On September 7th at 2200 I left again for Cabo de Gata with a repaired TV and everything dried and cleaned. September 9th *SC* arrived in Almérimar ready for her latest refit.

Despite the upwind battle, my spirits had begun to lift across Spain. Money had eased the weight of insecurity, and companionship had lightened my mood. A pleasant chubby, middle-aged lady on the street in Mazarrón had asked, "Do you like the Spanish?"

"Yes!"

"Then you must dance," she had smiled.

They seemed kinder and more friendly than their neighbors in Italy and Greece. But perhaps it was only my outlook that had changed. *SC* had crossed the Prime Meridian into the Western Hemisphere on September 1st at 1000. The slope of the downhill run tipped a bit sharper now, and the end of the journey moved closer.

Nothing about the fifteen-day haulout at Almérimar resembled the one in Phuket two years before. The boatyard was at one end of the marina complex where friends, mail, phones, fax, bank, and a small chandlery were a short bike ride away. When one of the yard employees realized I was alone, he and his son helped clean *SC*'s bottom and refused payment. There were clean rest rooms and showers with hot water. Just outside the yard gate was a well-stocked supermarket. And there were restaurants. If being hauled out could ever be considered heaven, this was it. And the bill was only $125.

I rode my bike the mile around the basin each day to collect mail, anxiously looking for an envelope with Dan's return address. Months of strained collect calls from pay phones on busy street corners had not satisfied my desire to reach across the space between us. With nothing solid to replace our thirty-one-year-old safety-net relationship, I felt empty.

Rereading his old letters, I found a tone of disappointment, anger, and frustration running through the lines. Life had not been all that he had hoped it would be. Images returned from our times together in Portland and Marmaris. Behind the wheel of a car he had been angry and agitated with other drivers and pedestrians. Our conversations had been of lawsuits and conflicts with clients and unhappiness at home. In my memories of our encounters these were the elements that returned again and again. I wondered if he was ever happy or awoke looking forward to the day.

My spirits had plummeted across the Med, but still those who knew me would have said, "She's always smiling and optimistic." I was usually looking at a cup half full even in the midst of disappointment. Only two happy people could make a happy relationship. Now I doubted Dan would ever be the partner I had imagined. If this were the way he always felt, could I endure such a life of negativity? Why would I choose to?

Three and half years had passed since the letter arrived in Brisbane that sent me down this path. The dreams of a life together that had burned fiercely in my twenties, then drifted in the distance over the years when we fell into a *Same Time Next Year* existence, had grown steadily again after that letter intimated there might be something more. But my image of what that might be included joy and celebration in life, compassion for others, curiosity, and remaining open to change. I couldn't find those desires in Dan's letters of the past few years, our visits, or our phone calls.

Stephen Covey said "love is a verb." You "do love"; it doesn't happen to you. I didn't think either of us could "do love" for the other. Perhaps we didn't know how.

Sadly I tossed the letters away along with dreams I had carried for most of my life. Navico sent a new motor, but they had been unable to find anywhere in the world the autopilot I wanted . I ordered their new model.

A two-day sail carried *SC* to the fairytale harbor at Benalmádena with islands covered in curling Arabian domes that looked like Dairy Queen cones and white walls draped in flowers.

"You're not to pay a penny while you're in our marina," announced the mayor of Benalmádena, after presenting me a hand-painted plate in a "photo op" for the local newspaper. The Capitanía turned into a gallery for two days with the help of Lesley Clements, whom I had met in Almérimar, and her daughters, Zoe and Lucy. The radio station announced at regular intervals that the show would open at 6:00 P.M. Every area newspaper printed photos and interviews, and the television station ran a half-hour show twice on opening day.

The exhibition was a delicious success. I sailed west with $3,600, knowing I would be ready to cross the "pond."

My spirits were buoyant again, maybe because someone had said, "Do you like the Spanish?," and had listened for my response. Or because I had enough money in my pocket to sit at a sidewalk café with a cappuccino, enough time to watch people walk by, and enough ice in the ice box. But more because I had found fellow sailors to visit with.

There was one surprise in my prepassage boat inspection—cracks in the stainless steel supports for the spreaders. There was no shop with equipment to weld stainless steel in Benalmádena or Almérimar. I sailed on to Duquesa, just east of Gibraltar, searching for the welder reported to be there.

The first morning in port I found a copy of *Latitude 38*, the U.S. West Coast renegade sailing magazine—no gloss, just tell it like it is—tied to my bowrail. Over morning coffee I browsed the articles, knowing I was moving closer by the day to those familiar waters. An article on the Papagayo conditions found in Central America carried a report of two boats snapping their anchor chains one night in the fierce winds. I began worrying about the old chain on *SC*.

The stainless steel welder had left for England, but people assured me there would be one in Gibraltar.

Friday the 13th. Whatever possessed me to throw caution to the wind and depart on such a day? Maybe because Lesley's husband, Martin, had insisted on paying my marina bill in Duquesa, and I wanted to save him the cost of an extra day?

Jamie, the skipper on nearby *Cloud Nine*, gave me a hand with the lines. She released the bow on my signal; I dropped the heavy, fat stern line, waited, then engaged the engine in reverse. Easing back into the channel toward an impressive lineup of "gin palace" motor yachts, *SC* came to an abrupt halt and the gear "thunked" back to neutral. The massive stern line had wrapped over, under, and around the propeller.

Two hours later the wrap was off. The folding chairs, where everyone on board the gin palaces had sat to watch the drama unfold, were put away, and I was motoring down the channel with my pride somewhere around my ankles. It helped a little when two old-timers called over, "Never mind, we've done it too—more than once."

I kept thinking about the night I had checked in. The port captain had asked me about yacht insurance. I didn't have any—insurance for voyagers was prohibitively expensive if it could be obtained at all. I had acted indignant and responded, "I've been all the way around the world, and this is the first place anyone's asked me for insurance." He had dropped the subject. What had he been thinking while *SC* sat disabled in front of all those megabuck yachts? He hadn't said a word.

I motored out of the Med, leaving behind five months and 1,800 miles of intensity.

ON A SUNNY FALL DAY I APPROACHED THAT FAMOUS
outcrop, the Rock of Gibraltar. Overhead a large black cloud shrouded the top
of the rock as I searched for the famous view seen in thousands of Prudential
Insurance ads.

Queensway Quay Marina, near the center of town on the west side of the
peninsula, welcomed *Southern Cross*. Navico's Gibraltar dealer handed me an all-
new, totally redesigned autopilot. Accompanying literature announced that the
new, improved model was completely "waterproof"—an important feature
for a device exposed to the weather at all times. But since there had never been
water in the old pilot in any kind of weather or seas, I wondered why they had
made that feature the focus of their advertising.

The black cloud took up residency over the rock, and the winds howled
down the west face of the promontory day and night. Afternoons a sloppy sea
found its way inside the marina, tossing the boats from side to side, their
masts missing each other by inches. I dangled in the bosun's chair midway up
SC's mast for twenty hours over three days, working on the supports for the
spreaders while the boat rocked crazily. Electrolysis had welded the supports'
upper ⅜-inch stainless steel bolt to its aluminum spacer. I tried a hacksaw and
then a cold chisel to remove the head of the bolt. Finally the French sailor
across the dock could stand it no longer. He bounded on board and up the
mast to join me, then took over. Two hours later he triumphed and brought
the parts down.

The welder disappeared with the pieces, and days slipped by.

I saw a dentist and a gynecologist, who doubled as a skin doctor, and
received a clean bill of health. For each two jobs finished a new one developed,
and every one sent me searching from one end of the dingy city to the other.
The former British colonies along my route had possessed an air of tattiness,
and Gibraltar had it more than most. Dirty, unkempt buildings, drab and
dreary colors, were stuck in a bygone time, their gentility faded.

The chandlery said they had the new anchor chain I needed and a new toilet. A sample of the chain fit my windlass perfectly, and the toilet dimensions
were right for the space available. I changed $700 to Gibraltar pounds at what
appeared to be the best rate possible. Four hours later, after filing reports with
the tourist police for unscrupulous money exchange practices and $70 poorer,
I was back at the chandlery. They discovered that the toilet had been sold

before they had shown it to me that morning and the 240 feet of high-test chain were only available in several pieces.

Cold, dark, wet, dirty, and frustrating, the sunny Rock was my final Mediterranean illusion.

The flood tide holding me back in the Mediterranean ended at 2000 just off Tangier, and I slipped out into the Atlantic. I drew in air that had come thousands of miles across the water, cleansing itself as it moved.

In light winds, with ship traffic passing now and then, *SC* ghosted along. I had an entire month ahead in Tenerife to finish the final little jobs, unwind, relax, and play.

SHIP'S DIARY: 28 October 1995, 1100 Zulu, 32°35′N/010°58′W, steering 236M at 6 knots with 12 knots out of NNE and 1-meter seas from NNE. Cloud cover 5–10%, barometer 1022, up 2 mb. 87 miles! It's glorious—like trade winds—sailing wing-and-wing again.

At sea
28 October 1995

Dear Dan,

This has been a very difficult summer. The Med was not what I had hoped it would be, but I know the root of my discontent was an impossible expectation. I wanted to live in sunshine, making art all day and dancing every night. Looking for the illusion stole my real life and left me feeling unhappy and unfulfilled.

But there was a far greater expectation than the Med that also died this summer—the dream of a life with you. I had created a god in my dreams of you. He wore your face and lived in your body with mannerisms and characteristics remembered over the years. But I did not ask you who you were, where your passions lay, or what really mattered in your life. I made my own assumptions. I realize now how unfair this was to both of us. I had not given the real person who got off the plane in Dalaman a chance.

You played a major role in my life, opening doors and windows to the world. The depth of passion I experienced for you showed me how I could feel. There is a great empty hole now. I hope it will fill again someday. I do want a life partner—one who stirs me mentally, emotionally, and physically. I also want a life lived in the world at large, sliding freely across borders on land and water. A life that can give me the peace I am feeling today. The rhythm, the ocean sounds washing over me, the empty time and silence I find at sea. Such a partnership can only work when I look inside for the answers and look to my partner for the chance to share the experience.

No one can make us happy; we must do it for ourselves. We can never intentionally be what someone expects and be true to ourselves too. I have spent the years of this voyage trimming away layer after layer to find what is left at the center—Who I am.

Pat

I cleared old, excess stuff out of lockers and from my mind, making way for what would come next. As *SC* flew along over the Atlantic swells I felt free and wild, full of anticipation, like a kid on the first day of summer vacation from school.

At 0600 on October 31, a large black mass raced toward *Southern Cross*, bringing gale winds of over 50 knots. *SC* heeled sharply. Water crashed over the deck, surged past the toe rail, and poured in everywhere. The familiar knot of tension settled in my stomach, but it was tension these days—not fear.

The next evening as the sun slid behind the mauve clouds along the horizon, one cloud stood out—an unusual perfect, smooth-sided pyramid. I took a compass bearing to plot on the chart; the line led to the volcano Teide, one hundred miles ahead. I had never seen anything that far away before.

I spent the next night at a small anchorage on the east coast of Tenerife and the following day made a leisurely sail into the harbor at Los Cristianos. I was not in a hurry for anything, not even the end of a passage.

_____NOVEMBER 1995

THE CANARY ISLANDS HAD NOT BEEN NAMED FOR the many varieties of canaries present, but the other way around. When Spanish explorers arrived in the fifteenth century they found the small, musical wild birds and carried them home to become pets, naming them after the islands. In the first century B.C., Plinius had documented the islands' discovery and named them for a fierce breed of dogs called canaria (after the Latin *canis*) that lived there.

When Columbus followed my route in 1492, the islands were inhabited by descendants of Berbers from the Atlas Mountains in Morocco. They had come with their domesticated animals and wheat and barley seeds more than 1,500 years before.

Legends surrounding the archipelago passed down through European cultures. They told of the misty, disappearing island of St. Brenddan, dragons turning into trees, the magic golden apples of the Hesperides, and the highest pinnacles of sunken Atlantis creating the island chain.

For the past five hundred years the island group lying 70 miles off the African coast had been an integral part of Spain. Recognized as an autonomous community with their own government, they held the same governance rights as the states of Andalucia and Cataluña.

I stopped at a kiosk on the quay in Los Cristianos where tickets for day charters to watch killer whales were sold. The British woman inside couldn't tell me where to find the port captain's office, but she thought the captain of their thirty-five passenger vessel could help me locate a mechanic, a stainless steel welder, and boat parts for the last of my transatlantic preparations. I left to explore and check for mail.

Angie called out as I passed her kiosk again on the way back to *Southern Cross*, "Stop by the boat at 6:00 o'clock. Luis, our captain, will be expecting you. He's a very special person," she added, with obvious affection.

As I descended the steep gangway to the deck of his boat at the appointed hour, Luis and I came into each other's view slowly, from the feet up. Last came the eyes. His were dark brown and warm. I explained what I needed for my boat, and the whole story followed. Our conversation over cold beers ended with his invitation for coffee in the morning. Over the following week the seeds of a romance were planted in freshly tilled and primed soil.

I don't think either of us began with any intentions. I didn't. It was the beginning of a pleasant romantic interlude—nothing serious, as I wrote to my mother. To my sister I wrote, "I've met a charming charter captain from Uruguay. I think I might like to get charmed." And I did. Day by day Luis began to fill the vacuum left in my heart with the acknowledgment that Dan and I had reached the end. It felt good to be with someone again, to laugh, share secrets, and care for each other. Except for my short one-week "vacation romance" with Peter in Australia, in the more than five years since Fran, I had lived alone, waiting for the impossible with Dan. I was hungry for this companionship and dismissed my usual reservations and guards. Days slid by with Luis showing the whales to the tourists while I did boat work—installing the new toilet bought on shore, rebuilding pumps, and servicing the engine—shopped for parts and supplies, and enjoyed Los Cristianos. I sipped cappuccinos at small outdoor cafés, practiced my budding Spanish in the hardware stores, strolled the pedestrian streets, and checked daily for mail.

Letters carried family news. Terri had been confined to bed rest for the final three months of her pregnancy. Libby was planning to visit me somewhere in the Caribbean. With the cost of a ticket to the States borne by *SAIL* magazine, Mom and Stubby offered a ticket to Bloomington and Santa Cruz following the boat show.

At the end of each day, I listened for the unique thrum of Luis's engines as he came in from his last run. I waved a welcome and jumped in the dinghy to pick him up or join him for an evening in town. He entertained me with preposterous stories of being a spy for Castro, of being in love with a ballerina from the Bolshoi until she put his bags on the doorstep just as several other women had, of being sent to outer space by the Russians as part of an experiment, of burning down his house when his ex-wife complained once too often how cold she was, of advertising himself as a male prostitute when he ran out of money as a young traveler in Barcelona. I took these picaresque tales as elaborate embroideries told, tongue-in-cheek, more to entertain than to reveal. If my instincts were waving flags of warning, I paid no attention.

We both admitted we fell in love quickly, I far more often than he. The life of a solo traveler offered few opportunities to develop deep, lasting relationships, but the desire and need were there nonetheless. We talked about what might lie ahead—after Acapulco—the chance to sail together on *SC*. My departure window drew closer. Less and less I wanted to leave, but I had made a commitment to myself and my family, sponsors, and friends.

When he graduated from a maritime academy in Spain, Luis had passed the examination to be a ship's captain. After several years as an officer, when his employer failed to certify two years of his sea time as needed to secure his captain's license, he had given up on the merchant marine and chose charters instead. Luis was certain his experience would assure him a job anywhere in the world. Within three days of arrival in Tenerife he had been offered his current job, and he hadn't been looking for one.

I found a man at the Sunday market making wrought-iron sculptures and bought one of a basketball player for Shawn's twelfth birthday, then ordered another of a whale jumping with Luis riding on the front and me behind. The sculpture caught our likenesses perfectly . . . both of us with long, curly hair. My curls had come from a bottle in a moment of femininity. His distinctive nose—a gift from his native Uruguayan grandfather—stood out prominently. Other ancestors, immigrants from northern Italy, had given him his light brown hair.

The charter yacht owner respected and liked Luis, as did his crew and the community around the harbor, but Luis was looking at the Caribbean and seeing the possibilities of a new life there. The owner's wife took me aside one day, begging, "Please come back to Los Cristianos when you finish your trip. We don't want to lose Luis." He decided to quit his job and meet me in St. Martin in the spring. If he had not, my leaving would have been far more difficult, but still I would have gone. My mother had discovered and recounted a long-forgotten essay I'd written in the sixth grade declaring my intention to travel around the world. I hadn't mentioned boats; surrounded by cornfields in central Illinois, I had known nothing of sailing. But whatever had sparked that early desire to wander and the absolute determination to go after anything anyone said I could not do had come together in this journey and kept driving me forward. I had come too far alone not to finish the trip that way. I had to be able to say to myself, "You did it, and you did it entirely alone." On this, unlike my artwork, the opinions of others did not matter. Public recognition was secondary. This was a private affair, and my resolve—fueled by some deeply buried drive—was unshakable.

We would meet again on the other side of the Atlantic.

——————— DECEMBER 1995

ON SATURDAY, DECEMBER 9, THE DAY I LEFT TO CROSS the Atlantic, Luis changed his tour route to see me off. Three hours later, still hugging his farewell wave, I went below to log my position and check my course. *Southern Cross* felt empty and far too quiet. March was an eternity away.

The new autopilot steered as Teide grew smaller. The day before I had mounted a new $130 bracket and set the old one aside—just in case. The fuel tanks were full, a gift from Luis. He had also brought me two huge mesh bags of oranges, as big as grapefruit. Everything was ready for the 2,700-mile passage except my heart.

I followed the weather reports from Herb the first few days, aiming well south of the rhumb line course to Barbados. From his base in Canada, Herb offered individual advice to each boat via the marine band—that elusive range of frequencies I could hear but not communicate over. He reported bad weather above 20°N, and on Tuesday the winds picked up. By noon they were 10 to 12 knots from the southwest, by late afternoon 20, and early the next morning over 40. The gale blew directly up my course with 9-foot seas.

Morning dawned through an overcast sky. The winds had dropped to 8 knots from the north-northwest, and the seas were down to 2 meters. The SSB net reported that during the storm a boat in the anchorage at Los Cristianos had washed over the rocks and onto the shore—a total loss. The beautiful mural painted across her stern had greeted me each morning close by *SC*.

Gentle, easy days followed. More than sixty Atlantic Sport dolphins surrounded me in family groups with their babies—jumping and playing. The teenagers raced through the water doing whole-body "high-fives," leaping in the air and crashing together.

Sunday I passed the one-quarter mark and considered the possibilities stored below for a celebration. A craving began in some distant, prehistoric section of my brain that cared nothing for diets and healthy eating. Slowly it crept to the tip of my tongue and finally became an unstoppable, body-wide command, "GO GET THAT JAR OF NUTELLA. YOU'VE HIDDEN IT IN THE STARBOARD LOCKER UNDER YOUR BUNK."

Packages flew as I dug through cans of tuna, corn, carrots, and plums and bottles of mayonnaise, soy sauce, syrup, and vinegar, all carefully labeled and stored with their wrappers removed to protect the bilge pump.

A glimmer shone from the fifth layer down. Relief waited just moments away. But only one spoonful—that jar had to last three more weeks, the rest of the way across the Atlantic.

The smooth, creamy, rich, dark-brown chocolate-and-hazelnut spread slid around my tongue and slowly melted away, leaving a hollow, empty place that cried for more. It would probably stretch for the whole trip at two spoonfuls every three days. I started to note the days on my calendar, but stopped first for one more spoonful. Perhaps I could do three spoonfuls every five days. I gave up on the calendar and washed out the empty Nutella jar to store a half-cup of leftover chopped olives.

SHIP'S DIARY: 18 December 1995, 1300 Zulu, 19°50'N/025°38'W, averaging 1 knot in very light easterlies, barometer at 1019, and 10% cloud cover.

The tenth day out brought the same incredible sense of peace I had experienced on other passages. First came the awareness that my breath and that of the sea had synchronized, then the realization that it was day ten. Only five passages in six and a half years had been long enough for this to happen.

A web of romance wrapped around me, but question marks wandered between the daydreams. Luis's stories tugged at me; what if they were real? I had told him he should be a writer with his imagination. He answered that he had written a book; it was in Menorca, where he had lived before Tenerife. But he offered nothing to deny or confirm the truth of his stories—only that shy smile. On the heels of romantic fantasies came the fears: it had happened too fast; we knew so little of each other.

Thursday, December 21, brought squalls in the night with unending rain. The new autopilot stopped. I reinstalled the old one. The new, "totally water-proof" design had failed—there was water inside and corrosion on the main electronic board. I cleaned, dried, and sprayed a corrosion-resistant coating over the surface. Two days later two overheated electronic parts caused the old autopilot to fail, and the new one went back into service sealed with silicone and wrapped in plastic bags. I cursed Navico for not getting it right before putting it on the market.

If I were going be part of a relationship it had to be based on love, respect, and trust. Luis and I would have to accept each other as we really were and support each other to become our best. And above all we would have to be honest. Did we each know who the other was? His stories surfaced in my thoughts again—why had he told them? Was it only to entertain me?

My needs in life were basic: good health, sufficient food and shelter, my family, a challenge of some kind—not a grandiose struggle, but a way to learn and grow—and an avenue to reach beyond my immediate borders and feel connected to the wider world.

Christmas Eve the BBC interviewed people scrambling to do last-minute shopping. In the middle of the Atlantic, it all sounded strange as they talked about Santa Claus as if he were real. I was completely removed from the activities of a "civilized" Christmas. The motion of a following sea precluded the hanging of decorations, and there would be no presents aboard *SC*. I wondered if it would be worse to have gifts if I had to open them alone.

SHIP'S DIARY: 25 December 1995, 1300 Zulu, 18°13′N/036°12′W, 12 knots out of the east, barometer at 1020 mb, and 20% cloud cover. 108 miles noon to noon. I shouldn't have reefed last night.

A small bottle of wine trailed behind in a mesh bag, chilling in the tepid water. By candlelight that evening I ate baked ham covered in fresh oranges and pineapple, sweet potatoes, and plum pudding. *Southern Cross* slid across the halfway point—a Christmas gift.

Via the net I reached a ham in New England who called my mother. Terri was doing fine and would safely carry her baby full-term. My newest grandchild would arrive in late January. In February I would be holding her in my arms. Mom reported that my brother Stu's wife Karen, in her late forties, had been declared officially blind and was forced to quit her job. This news was totally unexpected and disturbing. Their lives would change in ways I couldn't imagine. Of all the senses, sight seemed most precious to me. She would not see graduations, weddings, grandchildren, and her cherished garden. Tears came as I started a letter, wondering what I could say that would make a difference, what words I could find to wrap her in my arms.

A photo of Dan and me in Turkey fell out of my address book. I tore it into tiny pieces, wanting no more reminders. It seemed that I had been the one to end it when I wrote, but perhaps the absence of letters from him through the Med had been his own subconscious way to close the door. The phone calls after Turkey had sounded almost the same as before, but his missing letters conveyed the real message. I threw the small pieces overboard.

Dan and Luis were polar opposites. Luis, who had little of material value, showed no concern over money issues. But Dan, with all his economic security, always seemed focused on what it could buy, how much of it he had, and who was trying to take it away from him. I was not looking for financial well-being. Emotional richness was what I craved.

On Saturday a pod of thirty True Beaked whales heading southwest crossed paths with *SC*. One dove under *Southern Cross* and rolled onto his back, and I begged him silently not to mistake *SC* for a potential mate. His white tummy slid by and out the other side. We eyed each other momentarily, and the parade continued.

At midnight on New Year's Eve I crossed the three-quarter mark watching *Grumpy Old Men* on the VCR Jim, of *Nepenthe*, had given me in Singapore. According to the net, *Nepenthe* had arrived in Cyprus that fall. Old companions from my more than 30,000 miles of voyaging were strung out around the world. We had lived in tight little communities over the long storm-season stops, sharing our lives, then kept in touch via the radio until we drifted too far apart and others had to pass along the messages. The bond that held us together was an experience we could never fully explain to family and friends at home.

The wind from behind and the long, rolling ocean were giving everyone a miserable ride—a different motion from a Pacific following sea. *SC* continuously wallowed from side to side. That night every movable item clanked, rattled, or clinked. I doused the main and ran up the old genoa unhanked, sheeted to the boom. *Southern Cross* settled into a comfortable rhythm, and I slept.

The end of the voyage approached. I spent my birthday cleaning every inch of the cabin, until *SC* sparkled. The upholstery took on new life, the wood glowed, and lemon oil hung in the air. I listened to the net, hoping someone would think to send a message. Perhaps my mother would call the man in New England. I could say, "Happy Birthday from one Capricorn to all the others." Maybe someone would ask me when my birthday was. Or maybe I'd say, "I have to hurry and take my birthday cake out of the oven." It occurred to me that three holidays alone at sea on one passage were too many.

Winds built from behind as I drew closer to my landfall: 15 knots and a 120-mile day, then 20 knots for 132 miles. *Southern Cross* seemed to be in a hurry, but not me. I savored the last of this easy passage across my final big ocean.

January 6, 1996, at 1630, I tied to the huge, ugly commercial quay at Bridgetown, Barbados. Fellow cruisers who had shared the passage via the radio greeted me with hugs and congratulations. They caught the new twinkle in my eye. "Yes," I admitted, "I'm in love."

——————JANUARY 1996

BARBADOS WAS UNINHABITED WHEN THE BRITISH arrived in 1627. The original Arawak Indians had been wiped out by the Carib Indians, who had in turn been decimated by Spanish slavery, smallpox, and tuberculosis before the Spanish moved on to other islands.

The British lived off wild pigs left by Portuguese explorers, who had named the island after the bearded fig trees they found growing there. Within a few years one percent of England's population immigrated to the island for the free land given to those with good financial and social positions. African slaves were brought to work the sugar plantations, and prosperity for the owners followed. Lying well east of the other Windward Islands—the easternmost string of Caribbean islands curving out into the Atlantic—and with a bold, unprotected shoreline, Barbados escaped the invasions and frequent changes of possession known to the rest of the Caribbean. It had become "Little England."

My first week in the Caribbean was spent waiting in line at the Barbados post office to search for mail I knew would be there. My mother had never missed a mail stop, Tam would have sent my holiday mail, and Dayle's welcome letters were something to count on. But day after day I heard, "No, there's nothing here for you." Finally a notice came to the beach restaurant where we left our dinghies. A package had arrived. This time they couldn't say "no"—I had proof!

A scowling clerk handed over the box and demanded I open it while she watched. She peered inside at the beautifully wrapped gifts from Libby. I longed to escape back to *SC*, pour a glass of wine, and savor each one slowly. "Open them now so I can see what's inside."

A few tears of frustration welled. "Please let me take them home. This is my only Christmas celebration."

"No."

My passport's expiration date—February 10, 1996—was approaching rapidly. I filed a renewal application at the American Embassy. The new photo reflected the transformation wrought by almost seven years of living in fresh air and sunshine, using my body, and finding out who I was and what I could do. With eyes opened wide and willing to see, a relaxed smile, and a mop of wild blondish curls, I looked ready for anything life had in mind for me.

Mom called to wish me a Happy Birthday and Merry Christmas and make plans for my visit to Illinois. She was disappointed to hear that her letters and cards had disappeared. Luis called and we giggled shyly, sharing news of the past month. "I love you," he said.

"I love you, too."

"I can't wait for March."

"Me either."

On Sunday morning, January 14th, *SC* flew out of Bridgetown under twin headsails on flat water with moderate southeasterly winds for a downwind run straight to St. Lucia. Sailing like this was like attending the Met for an opera lover, or the World Series to a baseball fan, or Chez Panisse for a San Francisco foodie.

Old Caribbean hands had extolled the sailing conditions of these waters: "You're always on a beam reach with your destination in view, and you always have wind. Best sailing anywhere." I settled into my favorite corner of the cockpit with a mug of coffee and a new Ludlum thriller, obtained in a book swap with *Baron Rouge*.

The seas picked up out of the shadow of Barbados, but it was a downwind sail and *Southern Cross* slid off the wave fronts gracefully. It took thirty minutes to realize that the huge black mass in the sky ahead was not moving west with the wind. The threatening sky headed straight for *SC*—Mooloolaba, Australia, all over again. I raced to drop the unhanked genie.

As the first wind hit from the northwest, the downed sail billowed up from the deck. I threw myself on top, but the wind squeezed underneath, lifting me with its force. Stretching out on my stomach I fought to gather the edges, wrap the sail ties, and bundle it to the lifelines.

Rain pelted down, and the winds rose to 35 knots. The old hands hadn't mentioned this. By evening the winds had backed to north and eased, then veered northeast again by morning as I rounded the bottom of lush, green St. Lucia.

This northbound trip through the Lesser Antilles was a detour to replenish my budget. From years of chartering in the Caribbean, family friends Dave and Betty Toland had recommended St. Martin. "You'll find plenty of subjects to paint on land and customers on the cruise ships." The arrangements had been made: *Southern Cross* would stay in Ollie's Marina at Oyster Pond on the east side of St. Martin while I flew to the United States. My sister would join me in St. Martin for three weeks in March, and Luis planned to arrive there in early April.

I dropped the hook in Rodney Bay on the northwest side of St. Lucia at 0930. Andy and Sally from *Wand'rin' Star* hurried over to collect their Christmas presents from the Barbados post office—still in their holiday wrappings. "Would you mind taking a 4-horsepower outboard to Antigua since you're already stopping with a sail for *Real Time?*" The informal cruisers' delivery service had often carried packages and mail for me; it was time for the "*Southern Express*" to do her share.

With the new motor, still in its crate, wedged below the table in the main cabin, *SC* left late Wednesday. The sailing was fast, carrying me to rain- and cloud-shrouded Dominica earlier than expected Thursday morning. I pushed on to Deshaies, on the northwest shore of Guadeloupe. Each stop meant port fees and lost time.

At 1525 I passed Basse-Terre, Guadeloupe, wishing I could stop that moment to paint the scene less than two miles away. A quilt of greens dotted with bright red roofs and church steeples undulated across the hills. A baleen whale crossed my wake. If I could hold my speed for twenty miles more, I'd be at Deshaies before dark. Gradually the winds built, then turned fierce, howling down the backside of Guadeloupe's mountains. By 1845, I had been pushed eight miles offshore to leeward. I gave up trying to claw back upwind and changed course for Antigua, to the north.

At daybreak Friday, in 6- to 8-foot seas, I wondered if I could make the 20 remaining miles across the channel before nightfall and wished there were no deliveries to make. But by 1730 *Southern Cross* was anchored behind the protection of Shirley Heights in English Harbor, on the south coast of Antigua.

I checked in, paid for a 90-day cruising permit—for one day of cruising—and found a phone. Answering machine after answering machine picked up the calls until I reached my sister-in-law, Karen. "You're a new grandmother again! Terri had her baby last night, and they are both doing fine. They named her Alissa. She weighed 9 pounds 10 ounces." I tried to imagine Terri, at 5 feet 1 inch and 105 pounds, delivering such a big baby.

Two days later, on the final leg to St. Martin, I found the conditions everyone had raved about, beam reaching from Antigua on an overnight sail. Mid-afternoon on the 22nd, I rounded Witte Kaap into Groot Baai at Philipsburg on the Dutch side of the island. Even at anchor I could see the devastation left in the wake of Luis, the hurricane that had torn through the middle of the island just four months before. It had put nearly a thousand boats on the bottom of the three-and-a-half-mile-long, landlocked lagoon at Simpson Bay.

I checked in and sent the same fax to my folks and Luis. "I'm here. Call Thursday at 0930 (my time). I'll be waiting. Love, Pat"

Southern Cross overflowed with preparations for a movable art show and three weeks of family visits. The settee disappeared under mounted prints and paintings, miniatures, my growing portfolio of news clippings, a portable office to handle sales, and the warmest clothes I could find in the depths of the lockers.

Approaching St. Martin from the east, I had seen the surf pounding against the island on the side toward Oyster Pond and wondered how I would get safely inside the lagoon. The man at Ollie's said, "Don't worry; we'll send someone out to guide you through." But a nightmare in which *SC* tumbled through mountainous rollers into a pounding surf jarred me awake that night. Guide or no guide, I canceled the reservation and went to see the Simpson Bay Yacht Club.

Harold Phillips, an imposing black man, dwarfed the gray metal desk that stood between us in his office at the club. He offered me a seat and I vacillated, thinking I might have a greater presence standing, but he might be more sympathetic if I took the chair. I hated coming hat in hand but had no other reasonable option. I sat.

"Mr. Phillips, I'd like to bring my 31-foot boat into your marina on January 30th while I go to the States for a month. Will you have space?"

"No problem with that. The cost'll be $340 for the month—paid in advance."

"That's something I need to discuss. I'm making a solo trip around the world. I've raised all the funds selling my art as I went, but this past year I've been pushing too fast to make enough money."

"Um, I see."

"*SAIL* magazine invited me to show my art at SailExpo in Atlantic City. They're covering most of the cost—a booth and four days of hotel and meals plus airfare. But there are other expenses too. Right now I have enough to pay for *Southern Cross* and $30 to get from the airport in New York to my hotel in Atlantic City. I've been in the tropics for the past seven years and don't even own any real shoes. I'd like to buy some with the toes enclosed before I leave here. I'll be coming back with money for the balance, if you could just take a portion up front."

"No problem. How much do you feel comfortable paying?" A huge, warm grin said even more than his offer.

"How about $100?"

"Fine. We'll meet you by the bridge around 7:30, just before it opens. Your space'll be ready for you."

Reggae music blared as the bus back to Philipsburg rocked along the road past homes in shambles from Luis. Roofs were scattered across neighboring properties, and blue plastic tarps were stretched everywhere for temporary shelter. Hillsides were stripped of their vegetation. One house might be devastated, while the one next to it had escaped the fickle storm with little damage.

On the 30th I moved into the lagoon as planned, sensing the eerie spirits of the vessels on the bottom of the harbor and the untold lives lost. *Southern Cross* was a maelstrom of action as I packed the show in a cardboard crate and the rest in a $25 suitcase from Marigot, on the French side of the island. I had found it in a shop next to the store where I'd purchased the one inexpensive pair of soft black loafers displayed among sandals and strappy high heels.

I closed *SC*'s seacocks, turned off power and gas, packed the dinghy and chained it to the lifelines, stowed all the removable deck gear below, and locked the sails together on deck. Thievery was a major concern throughout the Caribbean, and I couldn't afford to lose anything. As I left for the airport on the 31st, the guard station not twenty feet from *SC* offered a further sense of security.

The plane touched down at JFK International; I caught the bus to Grand Central and a taxi to my cousin Claire's. In the old days of TWT, every year I had spent a couple of weeks with Claire. She was outspoken, a fast-talking New Yorker from California, and one of my favorite people. She told it like it was, like it or not, and as a rule she was right. And it was usually about my wardrobe, hairdo, or lifestyle, though in those days my wardrobe stood a better chance than the one I brought this time.

I hauled my crates of artwork and supplies up the familiar three flights of creaky wooden stairs to the SoHo loft where she created choreography and rehearsed her troupe, Gotham City Dancers. She hugged me and launched straight into "your towel is here; put your bags over there; my schedule for tomorrow is—I don't wake up before 10; what do you want to eat? your towel and bedding are there; do you want to sleep on a mat on the dance floor or here on the sofa? the sofa is terribly uncomfortable; are you hungry? there's fresh pesto in the frig; I can do pasta and a salad" all delivered like directions to a NYC cabbie, without a breath in between. I staggered under the load of information and questions, attempting to organize myself.

"So what're you going to wear?"

I hauled out a fashionable tan skirt and blouse in heavy cotton—fallish-looking and sort of warm, a black fleece jumpsuit, gray tights and a white tunic sweater, and jeans and a sailing sweater. "That's it?"

" 'Fraid so."

"You can't wear that tan thing in the winter. It's altogether wrong. Is there a cocktail party? What've you got for that?"

She dug through her closet looking for appropriate possibilities that would fit my rounded figure. An elegant periwinkle blue knit dress that just matched my eyes. It was wonderful, and she hated it. I accepted, and we moved on to shoes and the rest of my clothes.

I awoke to the soft, muffled sound of snow—eight inches worth. I couldn't remember the last time I'd seen snow that close.

At the end of the afternoon, in Atlantic City, with my display ready for the opening, I waited in line with twenty others to check in to Trump Towers. Eight days later—four as SAIL's guest and four on my own pocketbook in a cheap hotel down the street—I packed my display and left. I had gained new contacts in the sailing industry, a promise to replace the new autopilot (the first ones built had the wrong size O-ring to make them watertight) and to repair the electronics component in my old model, a moderate stash of money, and a very bad cold with a high fever.

Cousin Claire plunked me into a tub hot enough to cook a lobster and left me marinating with a glass of wine. In the morning I was back at JFK on my way to meet Alissa. I had looked forward to this moment for months. Someday, coming to know Terri's daughter might tell me much about Terri. She had made a commitment to stay at home with her child and not return to work. I applauded her decision and struggled to assure myself it wasn't a condemnation of me for not being there when I took the job at the architect's office.

I met Allisa from behind the protection of a surgical mask; both she and Terri had spent ten days in the hospital with an infection, and I was a walking germ. I held her for a few precious minutes, then reluctantly handed her back to her mother.

Stubby's Kiwanis Club arranged a special luncheon program to hear tales from my voyage, with an invitation to return when the trip was over. A talk at the retirement village where my folks lived followed, and the crowd of two hundred attracted by advance newspaper and radio interviews included several old friends I hadn't seen since childhood.

A family dinner at Stu and Karen's house showed how well she was coping with the challenges of vanishing sight and long hours at home alone. She maneuvered skillfully through the kitchen, fixing a complex dinner. There were handicraft projects in process, new upholstery on the dining room chairs, and new paint on every wall. Stu's delight in his granddaughter, nine-month-old Alex, reminded me of the gentle affection I had seen in grandfathers in Fiji, Tonga, Turkey, and places in between. He and Charlie had a lot in common.

I left Illinois for ten days with Tamara, Kira, and Shawn in Santa Cruz, where the sixth graders' Grandparents' Tea had been rescheduled to match my visit. I swelled with pride as Shawn played the piano, displaying musical skills far beyond his years. He introduced me, saying, "This is my grandmother, Pat, and she's sailing around the world alone."

Kira had moved from belly dancing to theater, staging one-act, one-actress-with-many-roles productions after dinner each night. I stored every moment, touching these beautiful lives that were tied to mine so intimately but with so much distance and time between us.

When my resolve to continue the voyage had wavered from time to time, I had wondered whether I gave them more by my example than I was taking away from all of us by my absence. If so, then it was worthwhile, but how could I measure? We can never go back to capture what has already been lost.

Tam pointed out some of the parts of their new house she had been responsible for building: the exquisite stained-glass door at the entry, the special finishes on the walls, the tile she had set, and her gardens. Her studio was filled with new slumped and fused glasswork and that of her students. But discord in her relationship with Bob strained the smile on her face. My heart ached for her to find the family life she longed to give her children. She could see it so clearly, but she seemed no longer certain that Bob was the partner she could share it with.

When she drove me to the airport in San José, I was certain that the next time we met it would be over.

_____ MARCH 1996

IN 1648 THE SMALL ISLAND OF ST. MARTIN HAD BEEN shared by squabbling Dutch and French settlers, who decided to divide the island in two. Legend said that a Dutchman had set out to the south on a circuit of the island armed with a bottle of gin, and a Frenchman had walked north with a bottle of wine. When they met on the opposite side the Frenchman, being less inebriated, had covered more ground, giving his countrymen the larger share of the island—the green, lush hills of the north. The French and Dutch portions are still divided and administered separately; to eliminate the need for an inner island border, both sides were made duty-free zones. The result is an island-wide modern shoppers' mecca.

Normally prosperous and full of tourists, St. Martin registered the devastating effects of the hurricane in an undercurrent that pulsed through the air, leaving a taste of uncertainty. Opportunities abounded for repair and construction work, but many of the usual tourist jobs had disappeared with the businesses that supplied them. Hotels had shut down, buildings had been destroyed, and public services disrupted. People seemed skittish, shell-shocked, no longer confident.

March inched by, and *Southern Cross* rose out of the water a little more every day as I emptied lockers and tossed with abandon treasures and items I had held onto "just in case." If Luis were coming into my life, I had to make room for him. While we both knew he could not sail with me, we would live together in port.

I painted between the cleaning forays—a misty early morning scene looking over Oyster Pond, the view from the fort over the red roofs of Marigot and beyond to Simpson Bay Lagoon, and the antique-stuffed interior of the old Dutch inn where Queen Juliana had stayed in Philipsburg. The details that filled my paintings had evolved to such a point that a friend said in one of them he could see the dust on the floor near the Oriental carpet.

My sister came, and we enjoyed the best visit we had had in years. Two weeks of good conversation were highlighted by a tour around the island in a car she rented for a day, and meals together on board or in town. Libby was relaxed and full of her usual humor. We skirted the edges of the discord in Thailand but never dug into the meat of it, not wanting to tamper with the pleasant mood.

Going through our father's things she had found a box of photos from my childhood. "There were no photos of me," she said, matter-of-factly. I turned away, stirred by conflicting emotions. I was angry at him, hurting for her, and guilty for having been chosen to fill his box of memories, but pleased that he had cared enough to save them. Unable to find words to forgive what he had done to her, I thanked Libby for bringing them. Neither of us could remember hearing him say, "I'm proud of you." Perhaps he had told her he loved her, but they were words I would never hear. We were bound together by this man but had never enjoyed the link to him that we both craved.

I laughed at Lib's stories of growing up with "D.H.," as we often called our father, and her imitations of him waving his glasses and pontificating on one thing or another, elbows on his knees. He had been a bright man—president of a Fortune 500 company, a guest at the White House, and respected internationally in his industry—but unable to reach out to his two daughters.

Libby flew home, and I focused on *SC*. The Kenwood TS-140S underwent the magic surgery that would give me access to the full marine band and Herb's personal weather advice.

Murmur, a boat that had come down the West Coast the previous spring, showed me a video of their trip. They passed out more advice on the Téhuantepec:

"Yeah, seven boats set out to go straight across; five made it. The others were never seen again. One had a woman captain.

"The only place to take refuge is Salina Cruz. I wouldn't recommend it, but if you have to, you have to. Our anchor got fouled on the bottom. We finally retrieved it, but when we went farther inside, they tried to charge us $100 for agent's fees for one night. Don't go in if you can help it.

"There're two navigation rules to remember about the Téhuantepec: No. 1

is the barking dog rule. If you can't hear the dogs barking on the beach, you're out too far.

"No. 2 is the potato rule. Every so often toss a potato toward land. If you hear a splash, head in. You're too far offshore.

"When you're that close to shore, remember: there're a lot of rivers emptying into the gulf. They'll have shoals off the mouth. Watch ahead for breakers."

My nightmares took on new fantastic images of dogs and potatoes, of dodging the busy fishing fleet trailing their nets, and of mountainous waves as I groped in exhaustion to hold my course with one foot on the beach for two full days and nights. A tourist guide warned that the winds could be so strong that tractor trailers were often blown over. My dreams added colorful semis cascading down on *SC* from the cliffs above the shoreline.

April 9th I raced to the Juliana Airport, looking for the gate where Luis would arrive. Streams of people descended from the plane into the hot tropical air, shedding their cool-weather European clothes, looking pale and winterized. At the tail end I saw Luis and his familiar, slightly shy smile. He seemed shorter than I remembered, smaller. Still sweet and gentle. He felt good in my arms.

On *Southern Cross* he found his place again—the spaces for his things, the familiar feel of her cabin, the cockpit and deck. He brought presents: sandals from Menorca and a patchwork quilt of Indonesian batik. The little sculpture of the two of us riding on a whale's back found a place in a cubbyhole in the main cabin. It represented the life we would share at the end of my trip—just a year away.

I trusted we would pick up where we left off and had given little thought to the possible changing dynamics created by my unusually intense work schedule and heavy correspondence, and the maintenance and repair needs on *Southern Cross*. Nor had I considered how we would negotiate financial arrangements, how Luis would mix with other cruisers, or how we would handle the need for time alone. His easygoing approach to life had drawn me to him, and I hoped his presence would help me "lighten up." Working together, I thought, we would find a way through whatever issues arose.

Luis wanted us to take time off together after the months of separation, but there were paintings to finish and print to fill orders from a local gallery. I did not expect him to pay my way. His own modest funds would last awhile, but as soon as we were located for the hurricane season somewhere south—

Grenada or Venezuela—he would need a job. I was used to living on a tight-fisted budget; he was used to the regular income of a captain's job. When I asked him what the Spanish word for "budget" was, he didn't know.

At last, the package of paintings was shipped off to the printer and boat work took over. I wanted to be ready to go as soon as the prints returned. Hurricane season bore down on the tails of our schedule. I had arranged a ride for Luis with John on *Paradox* en route to Race Week in Antigua and on down through the Antilles to Grenada, so we could travel in tandem.

A chance to do a small architectural concept study arrived, thanks to Harold Phillips, and I jumped at the opportunity to earn a little more money while we waited for the prints. *Paradox* departed without Luis, and the harbor emptied of possible alternative rides. I accepted Luis's reasoning—this leg was not part of my voyage around the world. I was only returning from a side trip over a path I had already singlehanded, and he agreed that Rodney Bay was the limit.

The prints arrived. We moved *Southern Cross* to the clean water outside the bridge, scrubbed the bottom, cooked dinner, and watched the sun set over glasses of Chilean wine.

––––––––––––– MAY 1996

ON MAY 13TH WE SAILED SOUTHEAST TOWARD THE Windward Islands.

The penciled-in rhumb line from St. Martin to Deshaies trailed across the chart with notations in a strange hand, not so neat and tiny as my own strings of fixes. These notes were confident, dark, and quickly jotted by a hand that had done this on countless ships over many years. But I had changed our course to drop between St. Eustatius and St. Kitts for the protection of the islands from the heavier seas on the windward side. The notations along the rhumb line ran off to nowhere.

Luis strolled the small deck, studying the rigging, lines, controls, and sails, investigating all the decisions I had made over seven years alone, anxious to become a part of the operations. I relaxed, knowing that seawise hands and eyes besides my own were sharing the effort. We seemed a happy couple sailing together, like those on almost every boat I had met on my travels. I smiled contentedly and went back to Garcia Marquez's *One Hundred Years of Solitude,*

Luis's gift to me. At 2100 we anchored in the dark at Deshaies, Guadeloupe.

The morning sun sparkled off a colorful little town sprung from the pages of a guidebook—red roofs, magenta bougainvillea, red and yellow hibiscus, lime-green palm trees, and deep green mountains rising behind. I gathered shopping bags, money, and check-in paperwork. At the port captain's office we found an open door, empty desks, a stack of blank forms, and a box for the finished ones. Name of Yacht: *Southern Cross*; Documentation Number: 940065; Owner/Master: *Pat Henry*; Flag: *USA*; Tons: *Net 8, Gross 9*; Home Port: *San Francisco*; Date of Arrival: 15-5-96; Last Port of Call: *Philipsburg, St. Martin*; Next Port of Call: *Marie Gallant, Guadeloupe*; Crew: *Patricia Kay Henry, USA, Captain,* and *Luis Alvarado, Spain, Mate.*

The document told everything they needed to know about us, our boat, and our roles on board. Mine, as captain and owner, included responsibility not only for the vessel but also for the crew member—his well-being, upkeep, to some extent his behavior, and if necessary his repatriation to his home country. Though not something I had given much thought, it would be a recorded fact in each country *Southern Cross* visited with the two of us on board.

We stopped for freshly made coconut ice cream bought from a tiny, white-haired lady who sat in the warm sunshine in front of her home, smiling at each passerby. The sweetness of Deshaies was healing after the raw wounds of hurricane-devastated St. Martin.

While we played and relaxed our way "down island," I kept a running list of projects—a commission to paint; photos to shoot; more paintings to create from the photos; illustrations to propose for the second edition of a book on Caribbean rums, by invitation of the author; a book review to write for *SAIL* magazine; and an article simmering on the back burner about preparing as a couple for the emotional challenges of the cruising life. Until now I had only been an observer.

In our first stop I put all that aside. We snorkeled and fished, hiked, and did small boat jobs, and Luis cooked. He was a "jazz" cook—using no recipes, improvising everything by taste and test. A cake without flour, sugar, or butter? No problem—he used fresh fruit, eggs, and crackers instead. He concocted a delicious pizza crust from a pinch of this and a handful of that while *SC*'s seventeen cookbooks gathered dust. He made fishball soup from the seven small squirrelfish we caught. The galley was a flurry of action every day, while I wrote letters, read, or relaxed.

Not every minute was smooth and perfect, but my years alone had given me patience and new skills for handling conflict. I was amazed to watch myself stop and think before speaking my mind, to weigh consequences and look for middle ground, to stay cool in the middle of the fray.

On shore at Terre de Haut in Îles des Saintes, colors exploded from the plants, the buildings, the clothing, and the fishing boats. The atmosphere was like that of a small Mediterranean town with an overlay of Caribbean spice in the music, food, and ambiance. We sighed, wishing we could stop for months. But this was no place for *Southern Cross* to sit out the hurricane season, and she had to be my first consideration.

Marie Galante, then Dominica came and went, and moments of friction interrupted the good times as Luis grew moody and complained that my painting, letters, and boat work left no time for him. He never tried to talk me out of finishing my voyage solo, but I thought there was a note of resentment in his frequent remark that I was capable of doing anything on the boat alone.

The passage from Martinique to St. Lucia was our last possible sail together. Rodney Bay had marked my departure north to St. Martin. Luis could go no farther on *SC*, but if he had no other boat to sail on and no ticket out of the country, the St. Lucia officials might not permit me to leave without him. Nearby, Paul and Wendy, a charter boat captain and crew for the Moorings, were on a run back to their base in Grenada with an empty boat. They agreed to let Luis join them to Bequia Island.

It was a terrific sail, the knotmeter pegging 7 knots in flat water most of the way, but the opposing current stole 2 to 3 of those knots through most of the day. Luis coached me into Bequia that night via radio, through a dark harbor filled with unlit anchored boats and moorings. He and Paul had been celebrating with a couple of bottles of wine their great sail and a barracuda landed en route. As I finished stowing sailing gear, a membrane of disquiet scented with alcohol dropped between us.

Paul and Wendy's schedule was impossible for me to follow. I could not match their fast daily runs, and without radar could not afford to navigate reef-strewn landfalls after dark. No boats responded to my radio call looking for a ride south for Luis.

Instead, while I sailed south through the Grenadines alone, Luis flew to Canouan, then took the interisland ferry to Unión Island and a 21-foot sailing cargo boat with nine other passengers to Carriacou. He was grinning and waving when I pulled in near the main wharf. After lunch on shore, he caught a bus to Tyrell Bay, and I sailed down to meet him. Only a short hop remained to Grenada.

A new chapter was brewing in our relationship as money diminished for both of us. We needed Grenada to supply Luis with a job, me with opportunities for an exhibition or gallery, and both of us with livable prices and a supportive community.

Luis waited on the town wall in Grenada as I nosed *Southern Cross* in close enough for him to jump aboard. At Secret Harbor on the south side, the Moorings' base location and his number-one hope for work as a charter captain, we anchored to stay for the hurricane season.

But there were no jobs at the Moorings. Luis posted signs and talked to a few people. I prepared his résumé, and he translated it into Spanish. Days moved by and money squirted out sporadically from between our fingers. I painted and wrote and looked for a solution to our financial situation, then set a deadline.

"Luis, I'm taking *Southern Cross* to Venezuela. This isn't working out. There's no work for you, I can't find any viable market for my paintings in the off-season, and I doubt anyone will be here for an exhibition when I'm ready. The cost of living in Venezuela is thirty percent what it is here. You need to find a boat heading south and get a ride. I want to leave before next week."

The deadline came, and still he had not found a ride. I left to search the anchorage. On *bonneAventure* Dick said, "Yes! As soon as my wife Tara returns we'll be sailing to Puerto La Cruz. Luis can ride with us." I assured him that when we arrived in Venezuela, I would take full responsibility for Luis, placing him back on my crew list.

We left at sunset, sailing southwest to Islas los Testigos and the next day to Isla Coche, south of Margarita and just off the Venezuelan coast. As afternoon faded, *SC* screamed across flat seas at 8.3 knots—no current to help, a true 8.3 over the ground. Every nerve in my body rose to the surface as she hummed that happy sound of a boat perfectly trimmed and running with a free rein. *SC* approached the marker for the end of the shoals between the islands, and *bonneAventure* pushed to catch up. I thrilled at beating a larger, faster boat. The marker drew closer, and I planned my jibe.

I would pull the roller-furled sail through the slot between the headstay and the intermediate stay without furling it. I had done it a hundred times without a problem. When the moment came I cranked and eased the sheets in coordination, but the wind snapped the sail forward on the windward side, making multiple wraps around the headstay and leaving a balloon of fabric above and one below the bulk at the middle. The wind tore at the two bulging sections, violently pumping the rig back and forth. I scrambled to get things under control, hardening all the lines. My heart pounded in fear of losing mast, rig, and sails. With the main reefed, I turned upwind. The sail picked up air and the rig thudded and twanged again.

I tightened lines and bashed into the growing head seas. Inch by inch the knotted sail worked free and took off once more in its wild rhythm. I pulled the lines tight again. Two hours vanished while I worked my way in to drop the hook at Isla Coche. Every muscle in my body shook with tension. I realized how close I had put my boat to jeopardy and how little it would take to lose it all.

The following day, sailing southwest together through the islands of Venezuela, *SC* and *bonneAventure* visited a geological museum surrounded by the sea. Just before the final turn to Puerto La Cruz the last island rose out of the water looking like a giant, shiny geode neatly sliced in half. The forms and colors of the islands unveiled a history of the earth's evolution.

I was ready for life in a South American country—a different culture where Luis could speak his native tongue, I could afford the prices, and hopefully where we both could earn money. His was completely gone. All the responsibility for both of us fell on my shoulders.

———————— JULY 1996

WHEN COLUMBUS DISCOVERED THE EASTERN COAST-line of Venezuela in 1498, on his third trip to what he still insisted was Asia, he quickly realized it was more than just another island. The following year explorers sailed west to Lake Maracaibo and named the country Venezuela (Little Venice) after the local fishermen's stilt houses. In 1506, with the founding of Cumaná, the oldest city in Latin America, Spanish colonization began. For three hundred years European bureaucrats and clergy ruled with little opposition, until Simón Bolívar led his successful revolution in 1820. Iberian culture continued to influence Venezuelan language, art, culture, and religion, but a light flavoring of the Caribbean added the spice.

As the world's number-one oil exporter during the Arab oil embargo of the 1970s, Venezuela had reaped the benefit of escalating crude oil prices and become prosperous. At one time it had taken two U.S. dollars to buy one bolívar (the Venezuelan unit of currency), and well-to-do Venezuelans had hopped flights to Miami or New York for little shopping trips. But the vast natural-resource wealth of the country never percolated down to the general population, and poverty was rampant. In 1996 the country still showed the impact of the global recession of the 1980s; laborers' wages were just a dollar or two per day, and the rate of exchange hovered at 455 bolívars to the dollar.

Bahía Redonda Marina Internacional at Puerto La Cruz offered a free day's dockage for check-in, during which we officially transferred Luis from Dick's crew list back to *SC*. At $8 per day, staying at the dock was out of the question; we moved to the anchorage off the center of Puerto La Cruz.

"*Southern Cross, Southern Cross, Angelica* here," Benny's distinct Swedish accent called over the VHF. My friendship with Benny and Elisabeth had begun in Barbados.

Fresh apple cake came out of the oven and the coffee finished brewing just as they arrived. Tiny, blonde Elisabeth climbed up from their dinghy with a huge smile and a black eye patch. "What on earth happened to you?"

"I'm blind in that eye, but don't worry about it. It was a blessing. When we sailed from Trinidad a few months ago, taking out my contact lens I nicked my left eye with my fingernail. In just hours it was badly infected. Antibiotic eye drops made no difference. We returned to port.

"Anyone who wears contacts has this virulent form of bacteria living in their eyes. In only eight hours it destroyed my vision. I stayed in the hospital a long time, but the Trinidadian doctors, nurses, and their families were so good to us that it wasn't too high a price to pay."

Almost anyone else would have been devastated, but Elisabeth and Benny's optimism turned any event to a positive outcome. Encounters with them always made me look at the events in my life from a new angle, searching for the blessings hidden in adversity.

I collected mail and sent a stack of letters with someone flying to the States, letting everyone know we'd sailed on to Venezuela. The pile included an appeal for sponsorship to North Sails. The most critical sails had been replaced, but my twenty-year-old staysail would never handle the anticipated windward passages ahead.

That evening we meandered down the palm-lined paseo along the beach, with the busy city on one side and the anchorage on the other. Along the walkway families sat on wrought-iron benches visiting and eating ice cream, while others strolled, listened to music, watched street artists, and held their collective breaths as youngsters on roller blades dodged through the crowds. The gay, lively atmosphere belied the extreme economic hardships faced by many. With so many wanting for so much, the threat of robbery lurked only feet away in dark alleys.

My search for a gallery brought an invitation for an interview from a local television station, TV1. The lobby receptionist accepted my packet of information for the host of the midday show. "Remember to be here by 10:30, and do wear something nice," she added, eyeing my shorts and T-shirt through heavy-lidded, made-up eyes, with black eyebrows arched high above. She teetered away on spike heels with the little mincing steps permitted by her skintight, short red skirt.

I caught my reflection in the plate glass on the way out, seeing windblown, scraggly long hair with the remnants of a nine-month-old perm, unironed khaki shorts, and a tourist T-shirt from the South Pacific—my standard everyday uniform—augmented for this occasion with sandals and a dash of makeup. No doubt about it—I looked like a yachtie.

The hair salon across Calle Honduras from the television studio caught my eye. I made an appointment for 9:00 the following morning, explaining that I would be on television and wanted a nice style, *suave* and *natural*, piled up off my neck and face.

On board *Southern Cross*, I picked out a ten-year-old navy blue-and-white striped blouse and a pair of navy silk slacks from Singapore. With a few paintings and a map showing the route of my trip, I was ready.

Impatiently I waited outside the locked salon in the morning; 9:15 went by, then 9:20, and at last the owner showed up and began cleaning the shop while I nervously eyed my watch. She spun me around in her chair with my back to the mirror and teased, sprayed, tucked, rolled, and pinned my shaggy locks. At the last minute she whirled me around for a look. The image in the mirror showed a Halloween version of Dolly Parton. Huge curls mounded up four inches above my head in great round tubes, sprayed and pinned in place. It looked and felt like a spun-sugar decoration that would break at a touch. I crossed the street on the verge of tears, feeling as though I were inside the body of a stranger.

Two hours later, back on the street under my mountain of crisp hair, I felt no better. The host had not read the materials in my envelope. He hadn't known who I was or why I was there. Lacking experience at promoting myself in an interview, I had let the moment slip away without ever mentioning the gallery.

At 2:00 Peter York, the manager of Bahía Redonda, welcomed me to discuss a private weekend exhibition. With no time to change and undo the curls, I sat across from him thinking, "He can't believe, looking at me, that

I did these things," as he slowly turned the pages of my portfolio studying each newspaper and magazine article. He smiled his eye-crinkling approval. "Sure you can have a show here next weekend. We have empty commercial space you can use. Why don't you bring your boat over a couple of days before to set up? Actually, bring it in anytime you like to take on water or go to the market.

"When your show's over, don't be in a hurry to leave for the anchorage. I'll let you know when we need the space. You know, I have a partially finished studio apartment in this building that I don't need. That would make a good place for you to paint. Consider it yours. I'll get you a key."

Speechless, I tried to absorb all the good fortune that had just been laid out in a slightly softened British accent. Peter had moved from England to Venezuela twenty years before to open a successful consulting business in marine engineering. London's underground station in the middle of the Thames had come from his drawing board, along with many marinas in the Caribbean, including the handsome condominium and marina development I had just been invited to call home. Bahía Redonda marked the entry to El Morro—the largest earth-moving project in South America—a system of lagoons and canals fronted by estates, parks, golf courses, marinas, and housing complexes.

Over the next few days my hair broke off in handfuls. Everyone said to call Laura, the woman who picked up the yachties' laundry and ran their errands, for help finding someone to cut my hair. Laura recommended her mother's shop.

Ten minutes after arriving, I was in the seat hunting through photo books for a style. The shop hummed with local women. Dryers whirred and spray cans buzzed as elegant, rich black pageboys were fixed in place, perfect for the lush, heavy Venezuelan hair. Laura's mother trimmed and clipped my damaged hair, brushed and dried it, and the result looked wonderful—chin length, silky, and a little golden from the sun and the remains of the old perm. I felt like a new person.

Luis was having no success at finding any kind of work. Discouraged, he came to a complete halt, and sat for days doing nothing. The responsibility of providing for two people and *Southern Cross* was overwhelming. Having lived on the edge taking care of one for so long, I couldn't imagine caring for two. I began advising him on job hunting. He resented the interference.

We moved to the marina and transformed the space Peter had offered into an overnight gallery. Friends and fellow cruisers streamed in all weekend. By

Sunday evening, I had enough money to do a round of prints from my new pieces and feed us for a couple of months.

When I thanked Peter and his staff for their help he handed me another gift. "We need a painting of the marina for our Christmas cards this year. Could you do that?"

"With pleasure."

"You should plan on having a big exhibition here later this fall, with pieces from the area. We'll give you the space and help in any way we can."

Whatever the problems growing between Luis and me, in other respects my path was being smoothed in ways I could never have anticipated.

The new "do" worked well, but only if I used a blow dryer—not a boat-friendly style. I made an appointment for a perm and chose soft ringlets from another big book. Laura's mother papered and rolled every inch of my scalp and doused it with solution. The timer was set, and every so often she tested the results, then neutralized and shampooed my hair. With a slight twinge, I remembered the old admonition not to shampoo a new perm for two days. Oh well, I thought, she knows her business.

"¿Secar?" I nodded for her to dry it. I wanted to look terrific when I walked out the door. She turned on the blow-dryer, rolled the newly permed hair around the brush, pulled with all her might, then stopped to chop a little here and a little there with her tiny haircutting scissors. I walked out with a page-boy—the one hairdo she knew how to do. It began to rain. The perm went limp and frizzy. I'd been FRIED!

For days I could not look in the mirror. Luis assured me I looked fine, but I knew otherwise. Each day was worse than the one before. The women in the office at the marina soothed and advised, "Try hot olive oil." It burned my fingers but made no difference to my hair.

"Try egg, rotten avocado, and mayonnaise." I mashed, stirred, and lathered the mixture on, then covered my head with a large baggie. It oozed out around the bottom and ran down my neck. No amount of shampoo covered the smell. And I still looked bedraggled. The left side hung one inch lower than the right. Large clumps stuck out in all directions as if cut by a lawn mower. I wept and covered my head.

Sunday morning I went to see the former hair stylist on a neighboring boat. "Barbara, is there anything you can do about this mess?" The gorgeous Liz Taylor look-alike from New Zealand studied my hair.

"Ummmm. It's pretty bad, but I think I can trim off the worst of it. At least we can get everything the same length again." Seeing the results in the mirror, I could have kissed her pretty, red-painted toes.

In the studio on the third floor, with a view over *Southern Cross* and the bay, I began to paint in earnest. A bustling Caribbean market full of fruit and fabrics (plaids and flowered prints); the old building in Castries, St. Lucia, where the movie *Rain* was shot in the 1930s; a small bungalow by the coast road in Sam's Gutter, Dominica; the colonial courtyard at the museum in Barcelona— the paintings stacked up. Occasionally in the afternoon Luis brought coffee to the studio, and some of the good feelings returned while we chatted.

Luis spent his days reading, doing part of the cooking and shopping for SC, and now and then announcing on the net that he was looking for a job or a ride north to the Virgin Islands, where he thought he could find charter work. But nothing developed from his efforts.

Tamara's monthly mail packet brought letters from people around the globe. Ty and Helen from *Azura* wrote with information on sailing in the southwestern corner of the Caribbean. They had encountered the worst conditions of their circumnavigation in this region. The pilot charts, showing the historical averages for January, indicated a 40 percent chance of seas running over eight feet for most of the area between Aruba and the Panama Canal.

The envelope with Ty and Helen's letter included a copy of George Day's new publication, *Blue Water Sailing*, with an article explaining the source of the high seas. The strong winter trade winds pushed unhindered across the Atlantic and into the tight little corner by Panama. In front of the winds came the seas, and when they hit the continental shelf off Colombia they mounded up in chaos. The current, following the same route, reached the corner and turned back north, creating even more confusion. They recommended sailing to a point more than 150 miles north of the continental shelf to clear the worst of the seas—three extra days from a direct route. Three big hurdles lay between me and the end of my journey—the Téhuantepec, the Papagayo, and now the coast of Colombia.

Tam's five-year relationship with Bob was over. Though the end had been coming for some time, its arrival saddened me. I wondered if things would be turning out differently for her if I could have shown her what a strong family life felt like, if I could have set an example.

Letters from Rod and Helen, Joe and Kat, Mavis and Will, Harry and Marlys, my folks, my sister, and more said, "When will you end the trip? We'll be there in Acapulco to cheer you in." It was beginning to feel like an accomplishment, something whole and complete. Eight more months and I could tell myself, "I did it. I sailed around the world alone." It was something only ten other woman had done in the history of the world.

An anonymous donor sent $1,000. Then Tom Whidden, the president of North Marine Group, parent company of North Sails, faxed to say they would give me a new staysail. Two pieces of good news in one week was almost too much.

I faxed the measurements to North and chose a selection of prints for their new offices as a thank-you.

Luis existed in the middle of my whirlwind—out of touch and resentful. He could not understand my intensity and dedication. I could not understand his lack of drive and take-things-as-they-come attitude. We were on a collision course. With only five weeks remaining before I had to leave for Panama, I panicked. Luis was on my crew list, and I couldn't leave without him, nor could I leave with him. I threatened, cajoled, and set deadlines, only to back down when nothing happened. His depression hung over the boat like a black cloud. I didn't know how to empathize with someone who waited for things to change. My approach had always been to dive in and fix them.

Details and preparations for the show filled the boat and my hours—calls for sponsorship, publicity, framing, invitations, press packs to assemble, mountings for the unframed work, and a hundred small details to tie down. Hand-carried invitations slowly found their destinations. Venezuela's postal system had a record of unreliability—a letter from the U.S. Embassy in Caracas, 140 miles away, had taken one month to arrive at the marina. Many items never arrived at all. I bused, dinghied, and walked to hand out the four-color cards, while local friends covered their neighborhoods and businesses.

I had hoped to find corporate sponsors to cover most of the $1,500 of expenses for the one-week show. For days I stood at the pay phone outside the marina office, eating up phone cards for long-distance calls. "Did you receive my information packet? It was sent by courier." Each contact ended with the same response: no more budget; too late for this year; call again next year.

Major local newspapers ran articles and did interviews. The *Daily Journal*, a national English-language paper, did a long-distance interview but reported that the exhibition would be on board *Southern Cross*. I taped a half-hour cultural television interview—without the Dolly Parton curls. And I was on the radio.

Wine was donated, and hors d'oeuvres were arranged with the marina restaurant. I bought fans to move the air in the open second-story space. Peter's staff painted the walls and installed a hanging system for the art.

The night before the opening, Luis and I strung fishline and hooks on thirteen new paintings from the Caribbean and Venezuela and thirty prints from earlier stops along my route. At 11:00 P.M. the lights went out, and the emergency lights came on. We worked in the dim glow until 1:00 A.M. The day of the evening opening vanished in a blur, and the lights went on and off repeatedly.

"Peter, do you know anything about the electrical problem we're having today? That could be a disaster. It'll be dark within twenty minutes of the show opening, and we need the PA system for your welcoming speech and my sea stories. People will die without the fans."

"I'll check on it."

I took a shower at 5:30 in flickering light. At 6:00, things were no better. Finally, at 6:30, the lights blared on. A grinning Carlos Reyes, head of marina security, stopped by. "I just called the electricity board and told them we were having a very big function tonight. General So-and-so and General So-and-so would be in attendance. Before I could hang up the lights were on."

One hundred fifty people attended opening night, including a retired U.S. Army colonel, Andy from *Wand'rin' Star*, whose presence lent a little truth to Carlos's story. On the next-to-last day a Frenchman wearing construction workboots and cutoffs came to see the show. His head was wrapped in a T-shirt like a turban, and his bare ribs poked at his skin. I asked if he would care for a glass of wine. He waved me away, studying each piece with his head thrust forward. "I'm an artist," he announced. "Wallpaper, this is just wallpaper. Where's the angst?"

I managed to answer, "I just don't see the world as angst. I see beauty and joy around me, and that's what I paint. We see enough of the great sadness and tragedy in many places. I want to remind people there's another side too." But his words nagged at me. I let them under my skin. Why, I wondered, was it easier to believe his critique than the compliments I'd received from everyone else? Did I not really believe I was an artist?

The last night of the show I locked up and joined Tara from *bonne Aventure* for a celebration dinner. We let our hair down, bared our souls, and returned to our boats at 11:00, feeling great.

Luis was drunk and angry. He reached for the whale sculpture, stormed outside, and threw it overboard, then came below with his shoulders back, chin in the air, piling on verbal abuse.

"I want you out of the cabin," I said. "You can't talk to me like this in here."

He held his ground. I packed his bags and put them on the dock.

"You'll pay for this," he threatened, still refusing to leave.

At 3:00 A.M. I called security and asked for help. It took half an hour of persuasion, but at last Luis climbed down from the bow of *Southern Cross* and left. His departing look of accusation unsettled me, but I kept my resolve as he threatened reprisals. The security officer stood by until Luis left with his bags, then took a seat by the bow of the boat. I breathed easier, wondering about the stories Luis had once told me. Had he really set his house on fire? I moved the red gasoline jerrican out of view and checked once again to be sure the officer was still there.

By 7:00 A.M. Luis had found a boat, and two weeks later he sailed north to the Virgin Islands on their crew list. Slowly I reclaimed my space, spreading my possessions out to fill the gaps where Luis's things had been, changing my diet back to the things I liked, doing what I enjoyed. I was single again.

It would take time to sort out the big issues, such as why I kept making similar choices. Twice I had chosen men from cultural backgrounds totally different from my own. Had I picked the man for himself or for his exotic aura? Three times I had wound up the sole breadwinner for two. I didn't believe it was wrong for a woman to support a man, but each time, in the end, I could not do it forever. Perhaps that was because I never expected anyone to support me. It had been a matter of pride and independence.

I became involved too quickly. Without taking time to know the whole man, I only picked out what I wanted to see and jumped in with both feet. Time tore at the veils of romantic illusion, and I wound up staring in disbelief at the person who had been there all the time. Luis's stories came to mind—the ones I should have questioned at the beginning.

There was a frightening side to the end for Luis and me—the biggest question it left hanging. Would I ever be able to share my life with anyone in an honest, committed, loving relationship? Would such a man look at me as too independent, too confident, too capable, or too involved in my own pursuits to develop a partnership?

Luis had often said that we mirrored each other. I struggled to find myself, reluctantly, in those things about him that I liked the least. But perhaps the things we reflected were our better qualities. In the wreckage of the aftermath, it was hard to let go of the disappointment and remember how we had begun—to see again the warm heart, the mischievous smile, and the considerate acts that had sparked my initial interest.

On the harbor bottom beneath Bahía Redonda Marina lay a small wrought-iron whale with two curly-haired figures riding its back. Bit by bit it was dissolving in the salty water, like dreams wrapped in gauzy veils vanishing from view.

THE FINAL SHOW RECEIPTS—$2,850 INCLUDING TWO last-minute sponsorships—would take *Southern Cross* through the canal, but not to Acapulco. I delivered prints to thank Peter, Bahía Redonda, sponsors, and the friends who had helped make it possible.

The new staysail arrived, and the old one disappeared from the garbage fifteen minutes after I left it. With dollar-a-day wages, nothing in Venezuela was wasted.

Tam's December mail packet brought year-old mail from the Barbados post office—all the mail that had been waiting there when I had arrived. Among the letters was a cashier's check from Dayle that had been mailed back to her while I was still at anchor in Barbados. She had a new one issued at a less favorable exchange rate, paid to cancel the old check, and paid again to issue the new one.

I tackled preparations for departure, pushing to miss the "Christmas winds," as the strong winter trades in this region were called.

On Sunday, while testing a new bungee cord I had installed for furling the mainsail, I reached over to pull the cord under the hook on the side of the boom. It recoiled against the base of my left thumb—the same thumb I had fallen on three months before. It had only been a few weeks since that swelling and bruising had disappeared.

Pain shot up my arm. Certain the thumb was dislocated, I pulled and turned it to seat it back in the joint, and the pain eased. Two days later I stressed it a second time and pulled it again to relocate the bone. Wednesday morning I saw the traumatology specialist at the new clinic on Calle 5 de Mayo.

"I don't think it's broken, but let's take X-rays to be sure."

While they processed the X-rays I worried whether I had enough money. "*Señora, aquí—listo.*" I rejoined the other patients with their collection of casts and crutches in the doctor's small waiting room.

"It's broken. See the crack at the bottom of this last bone in the thumb?"

"How long will it take to heal? I'm sailing to Panama in ten days."

"I don't think so. You need three weeks in the cast and time for physical therapy. We'll see, but I would say six weeks at least before you're ready to go anywhere."

The doctor's receptionist handed me the bill for X-rays, the cast, and all the follow-up visits . . . $60.

I sorted the jobs on *SC* into two lists: "One-handed jobs—do now" and

"Two-handed jobs—is it really necessary?" Meanwhile my internal nag kept up a running harangue: You've got to paint the bottom of the boat. You can't leave without servicing the engine. You'll have to climb the mast and check the rigging.

What did Louise Hay say about thumbs and broken bones in *You Can Heal Your Life*? "Thumb: Represents intellect and worry." Well, my mind had been far from peaceful all fall between Luis, finances, and contemplating the last stage of the voyage.

"Bone problems/Breaks: Rebelling against authority." Maybe the authority I was rebelling against was me: the pressure and stress I created to keep pushing ahead.

I noticed a section on arthritis that I had missed in Australia: "ARTHRITIS is a disease that comes from a constant pattern of criticism. First of all, criticism of the self, and then criticism of other people. . . . They are cursed with 'perfectionism,' the need to be perfect at all times in every situation. . . . Why do we set up standards that say we have to be 'Super Person,' in order to be barely acceptable? It's such a strong expression of 'not being good enough,' and such a heavy burden to carry."

I set an easy pace, rested, and focused on healing both my thumb and the disappointments of the past year. Lists took a backseat. The holidays came and went with celebrations for Christmas, New Year's, and my birthday—this time with friends at hand and a pat of butter on my nose.

The thumb grew stronger; my friends helped with two-handed jobs; for a change, I paid someone to paint the bottom; and *Southern Cross* turned into a sea-ready vessel once again.

The day before my departure, a 60-foot Sundeer pulled in next to me. "Hi, I'm Christian Title. We've heard about you. I'm an artist, too. Why don't you come over for a 'sundowner' and bring some of your work? Say 5:00?"

At 7:00 I returned to *SC* with pages of information on marketing my paintings. But the words that kept replaying in my head were, "This is very professional. I especially like the piece from Castries and the Caribbean market scene. You're ready to put your work out there." Those words sang, they shouted, and they wiped out the Frenchman's critique. Christian was a highly successful artist selling to museums and collectors around the world. He had answered the question at last. "I really am an artist."

GULF OF MEXICO

20°N —

Puerto Vallarta

MEXICO

Acapulco
MAY 5, 1997

LIGHTNING
STORM

GUATEMALA

HONDURAS

GULF OF
TÉHUANTEPEC

EL SALVADOR

GULF OF FONSECA

NICARA

PACIFIC

OCEAN

CO
R

10°N —

GULF OF
PAPAGAYO

|
100°W

|
90°W

CARIBBEAN
SEA

THE CHRISTMAS WINDS

LESSER ANTILLES

Aruba

Curaçao

Bonaire

Aves

Los Roques

Tortuga

ama
anal

Iguana

COLOMBIA

VENEZUELA

Puerto
La Cruz

80°W

70°W

60°W

ALL YEAR THE CARIBBEAN MORNING RADIO NETS HAD carried reports of thefts and aggression toward cruisers and had strongly recommended that no boat travel by itself or anchor in a deserted area. For a month I had been saying good-bye to departing cruisers heading out in groups, but *SC* was leaving too late for company. Except in the Strait of Malacca above Singapore and the waters below India, I hadn't worried about being alone, but now the daily warnings had raised a cloud of anxiety.

On January 10th, Peter, a number of the Bahía Redonda staff, and the few remaining cruisers said their last *adiós* and *bien viaje*'s to *Southern Cross*. "We'll watch the news for your arrival in Acapulco."

Sailing west and north into the Lesser Antilles, *SC* shared anchorages with other cruising boats in Cayo Borracha, Isla la Tortuga, and Cayo de Agua in the Islas Los Roques. Even without visiting, just knowing other sailboats were nearby eased my apprehensions. The tranquil beauty of beaches so white I could not look at the sand in the high noon sun, deep green dune vegetation edging nearby jungle, purples and blues from the coral gardens below, and the opalescent turquoise of lagoon water pulled me back to peaceful, isolated South Pacific coves.

Six days out, well protected behind tiny Isla Palmeras in Ave de Sotavento, *Southern Cross* swayed gently under the noonday sun at the end of her last Venezuelan passage, an overnight sail from the Roques. Only the tip of a mast on the other side of the island kept me company.

Below I stored gear and fixed breakfast, looking forward to a nap, then snorkeling on the reef just off my bow. The tape deck played a favorite old Baez tape while the espresso maker bubbled. Joanie and I singing "Dona, Dona" masked the hum of an approaching outboard until a "thump" on the hull catapulted me out of the cabin. Four men in swimming trunks held onto the side of *Southern Cross* from their long, open fishing boat. We greeted each other in my wary, limited Spanish and their nonexistent English.

"*Guardacosta, guardacosta,*" repeated the guy in navy blue swim trunks. If they were the coast guard, I had no choice but to allow them on board. Their boat showed no official markings, and the men had no uniforms or identification. "*Papeles.*"

Reluctantly, I let two of them on board and into the cockpit and went below for the boat papers: ownership documents, port clearance, passport, and a crew list with one name. They looked from me to the passport and back, then peered inside, searching for the man they knew must be hiding there. Shaking their heads in perplexity they returned the documents and left, and I went back to breakfast preparations a little subdued.

A few hours later, as I toweled dry after my swim, the same boat pulled up again. My apprehensions flared—they already knew my solo status. But the guy in the navy trunks held out a giant two-foot lobster for my dinner, then they motored away with waves, smiles, and good luck wishes.

The next afternoon I picked up a mooring off Kralendijk, Bonaire. With little to offer the colonialists of the nineteenth and early twentieth centuries beyond a wealth of salt, the island of Bonaire above western Venezuela was not a hotly contested prize in the power struggles of the Caribbean. It became an independent territory of the Dutch Antilles, and by the late twentieth century the islanders guarded the crystal-clear water surrounding their island as their most precious commodity. Bonaire, the most environmentally conscientious place *SC* had visited, welcomed water-lovers to dive and snorkel in perhaps the cleanest water in the world.

It didn't take long in the tight little sailing community on shore to meet Laura DeSalvo, editor of *Port Call*, a weekly English-language paper covering events on the waterfront. Almost as quickly, Laura arranged a one-day show at the Harbor Village restaurant, as well as radio and TV appearances. Fortunately the interview wouldn't be in the unique, local Papamientu language—an amalgam of Portuguese, Spanish, Dutch, African, English, French, and Italian.

Locals and foreigners visited my latest impromptu gallery, and some bought. The day's proceeds would carry me to the end of March. But the best reward came at the close of the day from a young Jamaican woman. "Can my husband take a video of you to show my mother what a woman can do? If she doesn't see you she won't believe it's possible. Stand by me; I want her to see how small you are, too."

The next morning a voice floated up to the cockpit from a halo of strawberry-blonde curls in the dinghy below. I was relaxing with a mug of coffee and Gavin Young's *Slow Boats to China*. "We're anchored right next to you— the 60-foot steel boat, *Encanto*. I'm Robin Testa and this is my husband, Serge. I'm sorry we haven't been over before, but we've all been sick with some kind of flu."

Serge Testa was a small, dark, wiry man with a graying beard and heavy eyebrows. He put out his hand, smiling. No trumpets, no fanfare announced the presence of this almost mythological small-boat voyager. I knew something of

Serge Testa, of course, and Laura filled in the details that afternoon. As she talked, I was transported back to Brisbane, Australia, to climb once again the stairs in the science museum for another close look at *Acrohc Australis*. At 11 feet 4 inches long, with turnbuckles the size of my little finger, she had been the smallest boat to sail around the world. I wondered how any human being could exist inside that tiny capsule with all the things needed to survive a long passage at sea. And now the person who had built and sailed that impossible vessel into *The Guinness Book of World Records* was standing in front of me.

Serge was intense, almost fierce-looking in some way. But in reality I saw the confidence of someone who had gone to the edge of life and survived. In Serge there was nothing phony, nothing unnecessary, just like his boat.

I had my heroes, those people I held in my mind when things were difficult and I thought I might not make it. Serge was one, Tania Aebi was another, and there were Beryl Markham, Isabelle Autissier, Katherine Hepburn, Joshua Slocum, and Julia Hazel too—each for different reasons. But the chief characteristic they all shared was courage. My heroes also had their own lists, and I realized that to some people I, too, was a hero. It was difficult to view myself in that light, but accepting the role was part of fulfilling my mission to encourage others to follow their dreams.

Dearest Tamara,   February 1997

I've spent countless hours in the aftermath of Luis thinking about relationships—what makes them work, and what doesn't.

There are messages as old as mankind and reinforced by culture telling us what men and women do and how they act, or should. But many of us are attracted to those who don't follow those traditional paths. Many women seek tender, gentle men who can understand. Men are often drawn to strong, independent, capable women who don't need taking care of. But after the commitment is made, often neither partner has the understanding to make it work.

In the Canaries, when Luis and I were together on land, he was in charge and making decisions; in the Caribbean, on board *Southern Cross*, he looked to me for direction and hated it. His ego chafed. He became unhappy, and held me responsible. The same thing happened to a lesser extent with Fran. The appeal of a woman who sailed her own boat paled when the reality became an everyday life. Luis and Fran pursued dreams instead of a real person, and so did I.

The pressure of a small boat added to the ferment. There was no place to let off steam alone. A sharp break was the only way out, and focusing on the other's foibles the only way to take that exit.

Perhaps my commitment to the trip kept me from fully putting myself into this relationship. Maybe I held something back that would have changed the outcome. If that is true, I am sorry for that. It was unfair to Luis.

And what of love? Did either of us truly love unconditionally? To reach that level of trust and selflessness one must dissolve the ego completely. Neither of us was ready to give away that much control. Of all the men in my life, only Lars may have loved me that much . . . but it did not last.

If I were starting again, I would not build a relationship on dreams, but instead on what we both believe—the foundation that makes us who we are: honesty, empathy, trust, generosity, humor, consideration, the ability to love and laugh.

One divines another's values very slowly by observation, not by conversation. What one lives is more true than what one says. In the beginning, when everything is full of passion, we all dress up for show, then slowly relax into who we are.

I hope someday there will be a partner who can accept me as I am, but it will be a long time before I trust myself again to know I am truly seeing the other person.

With all my love and many hugs,

Mom

From Bonaire to Curaçao to Aruba, I sailed through the so-called ABC Islands, approaching the first hurdle of the voyage's final leg—the notoriously strong winds and heavy seas off the coast of Colombia in the southwest Caribbean. On February 3rd I stopped at Oranjestad, on the southwest coast of Aruba, to call Herb for the weather at 3:00 P.M., check in with officials, prepare for the passage, and rest.

Herb responded, "Yes, this is it. Go now." Conditions were as good as they could be for the passage down the Colombian coast to Panama.

"You'll have 30 knots tonight," Herb reported. In one hour the winds were blowing 35 and the seas had risen to 4 meters. I ducked below at 2200 for a short nap, but while I was asleep, *Southern Cross* lurched sideways. My body hung momentarily suspended above the berth, then slammed against the lee cloth. The fabric gave, and I flew across the cabin and crashed into the table.

The following afternoon winds dropped to 15 to 20 knots, then down to 10 to 12 with leftover lumpy seas. My right side turned red, blue, and black.

On the 9th I anchored in the quiet little backwater bay of Bahía Buenaventura, Panama, and the next afternoon I set the hook in the The Flats outside the Panama Canal Yacht Club in the middle of Carnival. Every office in Cristobal was closed for the Mardi Gras festivities.

The first of the three areas I had spent years worrying about had passed behind, leaving only a few bruises. Two days later a British singlehander arrived. His small boat had been rolled over twice in the same stretch of water *SC* had just come through. I blew a thank-you kiss to the angel hovering over *Southern Cross*, and one to Herb, too.

Days flew by while I stood in lines waiting for telephones to arrange the canal transit, to organize and promote an art show at the U.S. army base at Fort Clayton, and to request permission to stop at Pedro Miguel Boat Club, halfway through the canal. With February 18th as my assigned date for transiting the first portion of the canal, I tackled the required preparations: six large tires wrapped in garbage bags to protect *SC*'s sides from the rough concrete walls of the chambers; four volunteer line handlers; food and beverages for them plus the adviser who would be sent to guide *SC* through the transit; four 200-foot lines (*SC* only carried one); the necessary paperwork; and fuel and ice. After one week in Panama I had spent $850 in preparations and fees.

An hour and a half late on the appointed morning, two young advisers, pilots-in-training, stepped onto the deck of *Southern Cross*, eyeing my four line handlers and me. The one in charge, Hamilton, had a noticeable droop in his shoulders at the sight of an all-woman crew awaiting them.

As I brought up the anchor by hand from the gooey, soft mud bottom 38 feet down, Ham's shoulders sagged more. It took engine power to break the anchor free of the mud's grip, and more time to clean the black sludge from the deck and gear. Ham's shoulders dropped another inch. "I think we're too late to make it," he said.

Hamilton rattled off instructions to me and the four line handlers: Maité, a Spanish friend from Puerto La Cruz; Sandy on *Destiny*, who was bound for the South Pacific with her husband; and Nadine and Shawnie, Australian backpackers looking for an interesting way to cross Panama. Ham gave the impression that he doubted we could handle our duties.

I had requested to lock through "center chamber," meaning *SC* would follow a large ship alone, held in the center of the chamber by the four lines, each controlled by a handler. But Ham asked if I would consider going side-tied to a tugboat. "It really is the safest way to ascend," he said, "and we may be too late to go any other way today." Something prodded at the back of my mind, maybe an article I had read, that said this was a dangerous setup. Ham assured me that after a serious accident some time back they had changed the procedures, and there was no longer a problem.

We drove through a 7-mile dredged channel toward one of the greatest engineering marvels of the twentieth century. First proposed in 1524 to Charles V, Holy Roman emperor and king of Spain, it took 390 years to bring the canal to life. The idea lay dormant until the mid-nineteenth century, when the discovery of gold in California revived it. A canal would cut nearly 8,000 miles from voyages between the Atlantic and Pacific coasts of the United States and as much as 2,000 miles from those between Europe and Asia or Australia, and would circumvent the hazardous waters off Cape Horn. The French began the project in 1879 under international treaty and the leadership of Ferdinand de Lesseps, designer of the Suez Canal, but de Lesseps's plan for a sea-level canal ultimately failed in bankruptcy and scandal. Following the 1903 revolution in which Panama established its independence from Colombia, the United States secured control of the Canal Zone from Panama and bought the 51-mile-long project from France in 1904.

U.S. involvement brought fresh capital, more heavy equipment, and improved health care for workers, and the pace of construction picked up. In 1905 there were 2,600 men working on the canal, but by 1907 they numbered 39,000. The French plan for a sea-level route gave way to the present locked-canal design, which lifts vessels from sea level by stages over the central range of hills on the Isthmus of Panama.

I steered into the first 300-foot-long chamber at the Gatun locks alongside the large tug and behind a freighter. We handed our lines to the tug crew to secure *SC* alongside, and water surged into the lock. The forces in the boiling cauldron passed through the rudder to me. I stood taut and ready. We reached the top, the gates opened, and the ship ahead slipped into gear, sending a shock wave back to *Southern Cross*. Lines were returned, and *SC* maneuvered away from our "buddy" tug.

We passed through one more lock and motored onto Gatun Lake at the top, 100 feet above the Atlantic. Ham ordered, "Raise some sail. We need to go as fast as possible, or we won't make it to Pedro Miguel Boat Club by tonight." If we didn't, it meant that my crew and I would spend a cramped night on *SC* at anchor. Sailors on deck poured on sail and engine while the nonsailors below made tuna sandwiches.

Fed by the abundant rainfall of the surrounding jungle, the lake supplied 52,000,000 gallons of water for each of the 12,000 annual transits through the canal. On the sailboat shortcut to the Culebra Cut we skirted little islands of treetops poking above the water, while jungle birds careened overhead. The 8-mile-long cut had proven the most formidable obstacle to the canal builders. Unstable substrata had collapsed in one landslide after another and still required constant maintenance. The cut was just twice as wide as the Corinth Canal in Greece, but its sides sloped away in loose rocky soil instead of the sheer rock walls of Corinth.

The ship that had come up with us in the Gatun locks arrived at the first descending lock ten minutes ahead of *Southern Cross*. We waited anxiously for Ham to receive permission to enter the chamber, and finally the good news came. We drove alone into the Pedro Miguel Lock for a center chamber descent, and the freighter pulled in behind us, a cluster of sailors leaning over the railing thirty-some feet above to look directly down on us. The water escaped from the chamber, smoothly dropping us 33 feet as it exposed the sculpted cathedral-door-like gates of two-foot-thick metal.

Two of my crew rode back to Cristobal by bus, carrying the heavy lines I had borrowed. Nadine and Shawnie went on to Panama City with stories for their families of going through the "ditch" on a small sailboat.

The grounds at Pedro Miguel Boat Club transported me to a favorite memory from childhood. The large, old, rambling wooden buildings with screens and shutters, the green lawns, and the quiet felt like the old church camp at Lake Geneva, Wisconsin. People gathered in the communal kitchen to cook and eat and in the "library" to read or play games. No one seemed in a hurry.

The next day a reporter from the *Panama Canal Spillway* came for an interview. She brought articles about other singlehanders the paper had covered:

Tania Aebi, Serge Testa, and Margaret Hicks. As when I'd met Serge, it lifted my focus beyond the rails of *Southern Cross* and gave me a bystander's sense that the thing I was doing—by now so much a part of my life—was in fact rare.

The Army base at Fort Clayton had agreed to provide space for a two-day show on March 1st and 2nd. Having read the articles about me, people came to the show or to the boat to visit, bringing with them gifts, dinner invitations, and offers of help. One man, a stranger until the day before the show, drove me from one end of Panama City to the other shopping and running errands.

The day before departure, a fellow cruiser stopped me to say, "There's another woman from the States going around the world solo. You have to hurry to get in first."

"I'm not trying to be first at anything," I told her. "I only want to finish the voyage I set out to make eight years ago. But thanks for telling me." As far as I was concerned, it had already been done by Tania, regardless of the record keepers' opinions.

On March 4th a new crew of line handlers arrived: Annebelle, who was on her way to the South Pacific aboard *Goldenrod*; Jill from *Anza*, also southbound; Brenda Lane, a resident of the Zone; and Dionilka, the niece of canal admeasurer Mickey Donahue, one of the officials who measured boats to determine the fee for a transit. Two advisers followed, both male. (I had looked for a woman to make an all-female transit, but there were none. The only woman pilot in the Zone usually handled nuclear subs, and I knew the Authority would not want to pay her rate for handling my small vessel.) Finally a video camerawoman arrived from the television station. They had scheduled a news special covering my voyage and the transit.

In less than an hour *Southern Cross* had dropped the last 53 feet to the Pacific. Both she and I felt the difference. When I had last been in these waters everything was new, different, and strange. Now seafaring was a way of life, the thing I did every day—second nature.

———————— MARCH 1997

MY LINE HANDLERS JUMPED ON BOARD *ANZA* AS I pulled alongside at the Balboa Yacht Club by the Pacific entrance to the Canal. With one quick photo and a hug for each, our lives split apart, leaving only a thread of memory and some television footage. Jill and Annebelle were beginning their voyages, while I was ending mine. Looking out over the Pacific I could picture the faces and scenes waiting for them and wished I were beginning again, but I wanted this trip to be done. Next time I would share passagemaking with others—my grandchildren, daughter, sister, brother, and friends—to show them what I had written about in my letters. I would do it more slowly, too—that's when I had been the happiest.

I turned toward Isla Taboga for a long night of sleep and a day of relaxation before sailing out of the Gulf of Panama and beginning the trek northwest. Over coffee in the morning I pulled out the Compaq for an overdue letter to Kitty.

Dearest Kitty,

I'm here on the West Coast of the Americas with the end in sight. How precious these last 1,500 miles seem. I'm reminded of singlehander Ann Gash's disaster, when her boat sank less than a hundred miles from Australia at the end of her circumnavigation. My care and diligence will be on extra-high alert.

The weather patterns along this coast are uncertain, but I expect to be in Acapulco no later than May 8th.

The past almost eight years have been the most wonderful gift I could have given myself. Not easy, but worth every hardship for the lessons gained. One you will enjoy hearing: I am an artist now and will always be one. . . . It's a way of seeing and of being, not a job.

What makes one an artist is not the work produced, but the way one experiences the world—sensing the relationships among things in a different way. When the artist lets her spirit flow through her brush, words, dance, lens, or music, it's direct communication from the soul.

At a two-day art show at Fort Clayton in the Canal Zone, a very tall, skinny young soldier on roller blades cruised through looking at my paintings from around the world. He turned to me with a grin totally encased in freckles and shook his head back and forth, "Awesome, really awesome." He rolled on around the room and out the door, saying, "Awesome, man, awesome." Perhaps I lit a small dream for him that day, a desire to see and experience more of the world, to open himself beyond his built-in borders. That's my reward.

I'm so glad to hear how happy you both are in Hawaii. The review of your "broom art" show was well deserved; the pieces are intriguing.

When will we ever see each other again? It's been way too long now, but coming to Hawaii is not in my plans this year. I'll give you an address when I find my new "home" in Mexico in May.

With love and hugs, dear,

Pat

On four hours of sleep, I left for Isla Iguana at 0310.

Rounding the southeast corner of the island at 1700, I searched along the rough shoreline for a safe anchorage. Isla Iguana, less than a mile long in reality and less than ⅜ inch on my chart covering the Gulf of Panama, was listed as a viable stopping place in one of the packets of information other cruisers had passed along to me, but it didn't say where to anchor.

I followed the coast on the west side to a small cove. A few fishing boats were gathered in a corner of the beach. As I angled in toward them the depth sounder began to scream its warning. Rocks loomed just below the bow of *Southern Cross* in the clear water. Turning out to deep water, I waited for the depth sounder to stop its bleating. Farther up the beach I nosed slowly toward shore again, calculating lowest tide depth—seldom a consideration through the Indian Ocean, Red Sea, Mediterranean, and Caribbean—and figuring my level of comfort. Watching a distant line of breakers to the northwest, I dropped the hook in the lee of the point on the north side of the cove.

With the deck organized for an early departure, I went below to fix dinner. A gradual pitching began rocking *Southern Cross* back and forth, and I hurried topside to investigate. The line of breakers was advancing rapidly toward the cove. A fisherman, on his way into shore, motioned for me to get out quickly. I turned the key—nothing. Heart-stopping minutes passed before the engine finally roared into life.

The bowsprit dove underwater, then *Southern Cross* reared back as tumbling surf rolled under her bow. Ankle-deep in seawater, I hauled in chain between the jerks, then ran below for a knife to cut the snubber. As she plunged again I cranked the windlass, then the force of the sea threw the handle into the air and slammed it into my chest.

There was no time to think as I worked and the engine drove SC slowly toward deep water. Every action and reaction had become part of the memory of my body. At last the C.Q.R. anchor cleared the bottom. *Southern Cross* reached deep water once again, and I set a course for Punta Mala, the traffic-filled exit from the Gulf.

The anchorages I passed the following day were filled with southerly swell. Thirty- to thirty-five-knot headwinds hugged the coast, and SC looked for shelter. That evening I pulled into the small bay on the southern tip of Isla Cebaco. The air was still and peaceful under a cloudless night sky, with birdcalls reverberating from the surrounding jungle.

After Panama, the Costa Rican shoreline slid by hidden in pink rain, jungle mist, or star-shadows on moonless nights. In Golfito I picked up a waiting card from Terri and sent a fax to my mother.

Dear Mom,

I'm sorry I don't have answers to your questions regarding the rest of the trip. It's impossible to predict my arrival at Acapulco, still over 1,000 miles away. I may need to wait for parts or weather—who knows? My best guess is "probably no later than May 8th." When I get to Huatulco I can be more precise, but that will only be three or four days from the end.

The emotions surrounding the completion of this voyage are beyond anything I've ever known. After all the time, the hardships, and the struggles, seeing the end just ahead is more than I can begin to explain. I understand why others have turned away just short of a long-sought goal. I think it's a fear of the huge vacuum following the intensity, and knowing life will never be the same again. If SC and I didn't need to regroup, we'd just keep going now. We have grown to love this way of life.

Hugs and kisses,

Pat

At Bahía Ballena, Mom called to say that they would come to visit later, when I was settled somewhere in Mexico. It was too difficult for them to organize a trip on short notice. Tam's budget would not allow her to be there. I began to wonder if anyone would be waiting when I arrived.

On March 26th SC sailed around the Nicoya Peninsula to Playa del Cocos for the last mail stop before Acapulco and the checkout from Costa Rica. In the Costa Rica sailing guide, the address for mail pickup belonged to Maury Gladson, an avid ham operator and friend to passing yachties. After two hours of searching I found his bungalow inside the walled yard of a large home north of town. He invited me in, apologizing for answering the door in his boxer shorts. We talked sailing and radios, and eventually I managed to steer the conversation around to my mail. "Oh, yes. You'll have to go through the mail to look for yours. Could you read some of mine to me while you're at it? I'm turning ninety-two, and I'm blind."

"Where should I look?"

"Well, there's bags of it here on the floor in the corner, and more in my bedroom, and a lot on the table, and on my desk, too." I took in twenty or thirty large, dusty, brown grocery-store bags full of mail and started through the pile on the table, reading a letter to Maury now and then. Most of them he already knew by heart.

I shifted to the desk and then the bags on the floor. The spiders moved aside as I dug down through envelopes dating back to the early 1980s. None of them had my name.

"I gave up that post office box some years back."

"Well, I don't see anything here. I guess my mail's gone astray. Thanks very much anyway. It's been nice to meet you."

"Come anytime. I like the company."

My heart went out to Maury. How would I feel at ninety-two in a foreign country without friends or family? But I also wanted my mail. Why would a 1993 cruising guide have listed Maury as a mail drop? The authors could have said, "There is a delightful old sailor there, go and pay him a visit. It will do your heart good."

After checking out on Monday, I stopped at the post office to send a letter to Lib, and on a long shot asked about my mail. "Oh yeah, it's right here."

Maybe the guidebook authors knew best after all. If I hadn't thought Maury had my mail, I would have missed meeting a wonderful man.

Dear Sis,

These past eight years have given me many opportunities to look at who I am and my relationships with those around me. The recognition of my accomplishments and acceptance of my strengths and talents have been steps to celebrate. Seeing the other side of myself has been humbling.

In Puerto La Cruz, Venezuela, one day I joined a group of yachtie women for their weekly luncheon. A few of us were chatting as we walked down the street to the restaurant. In the course of the conversation I said something about Singapore and Egypt. Later I overheard one of the women saying in a high-pitched, mocking voice, "When I was in Singapore . . . and blah, blah, blah . . . Egypt . . . blah, blah, blah."

It sent a horrible, bitter taste through me. I had never experienced the receiving end of jealousy. It's not the highest form of compliment. It is painful.

Since that day I've thought so often of the jealousy I've harbored toward you, and shuddered at what a destructive emotion it is and the damage it did to our relationship.

I am sorry to have wasted so much of our time together feeding something that could only hurt both of us. Please forgive me.

Love,

Sis

———————— APRIL 1997

I LEFT PLAYA DEL COCOS ON APRIL FOOLS' DAY, TWO years after I had begun to worry about the patch of water ahead. Named for the Golfo del Papagayo on Costa Rica's northern Pacific coast, the Papagayo winds were feared among cruisers for their sudden fury and lack of warning. The blue sky above me was little consolation; Papagayos reportedly came "right out of a blue sky." I had not been able to hear Herb since Panama and had not found an alternate weather source. Again I was at the tail end of the boats heading in my direction, and other cruisers' minds were elsewhere.

The majority of boats going north and south went offshore to make a straight shot between Costa Rica and Mexico, but SC would day-hop, staying close to shore for flatter seas. I wanted to see the countries in the middle of Latin America—Nicaragua, El Salvador, and Guatemala—partially because other boats chose not to. Most feared political unrest.

In light winds, SC motorsailed across the Papagayo to Cabo St. Elena, on the north side of the gulf. At noon a white line of rough water lay ahead to the north-northeast, toward my destination of San Juan del Sur, Nicaragua. The 5-foot short, choppy seas met me with 20- to 25-knot northerly winds, and I bashed slowly toward the harbor.

The 18 miles took eight hours instead of the four I had planned. When SC finally arrived at 2000, the pitch-black harbor—congested with large fishing boats riding to their moorings, empty mooring buoys with trailing pickup lines floating across the surface, and unlit barges everywhere—presented a minefield of obstructions. With shore lights adding still more confusion, I was reluctant to move farther into the bay for shallower water and better protection. I set the hook firmly in 40 feet of water 30 feet ahead and to port of a big, crusty, barnacle-covered buoy holding a large fishing vessel, its crew still at work offloading their catch on the back deck. The wind picked up to 35 knots. I took bearings to points on shore to track my position so I would know if the anchor was dragging, then spent a sleepless night.

In the morning the port captain came to clear *SC* into Nicaragua. The wind eased a little, and I slept. My documents were returned with permission to leave for Corinto. The winds escalated back to 35, and I spent another nervous night.

The next morning, a brilliant sun rose over the mountains backing the small bay. The engine pushed *Southern Cross* slowly forward against 20 knots of wind while I hauled chain up by hand, and every fisherman stopped to watch.

All day in 30- to 35-knot winds, with shortened sail and little sea, *SC* hugged the coastline to make the long pass into Corinto for water, fuel, ice, and oil. There I met *Hanto Yo*, who had just arrived from the north. Traveling farther from the coast than *SC*, she had been battered by 12-foot seas.

Two days later *SC* tucked in at Moneypenny anchorage behind Punta Rosario in the Gulf of Fonseca. El Salvador lay to the northwest, Honduras to the north and east, and Nicaragua to the southeast—my guidebook called it the "Forgotten Middle." I poured a glass of wine, toasted the halfway point to Acapulco, and laughed at myself, the April Fool. The Papagayo winds could be fierce and deadly, but spending two years worrying about them had made no difference. Perhaps it had been luck, or a guardian angel, or maybe I had been too late for the worst of the season, but the Papagayos I'd seen were not the ones of sailors' nightmares.

The Displaced Peoria Ham Net came on as *SC* sailed across the gulf. The seventeen-year-old net of former Peorians had replaced Roxie as my primary contact for the last leg. "KM6DR here. I have a message to pass to my folks. Is there anyone on board from Bloomington-Normal?" Friendly masculine joshing and the exchange of news stopped.

"Go ahead, KM6DR, Dean's on board. He'll relay for you."

"Tell them I'm on my way to La Unión, El Salvador, and all is fine on board. Thanks. And I'll be clear."

The bulk of El Salvador's population had fallen between right- and left-wing powers—landless, in poverty, and without a voice—when the civil war of the 1980s erupted following the assassination of Archbishop Oscar Romero by right-wing extremists. Soviet support of the guerrillas and U.S. support for the right-wing government intensified the conflict, and 75,000 lives—1.5 percent of the population—were lost in the twelve-year bloodbath. A truce had been in place across El Salvador for five years, but visitors were few.

In La Unión, a small town in the northwestern back reaches of the gulf, I found the Immigration officer in a tiny, one-desk room off the street. He towered over me with his bushy mustache and friendly demeanor. After stamping and initialing my passport he added a flourish, giving me permission to stay for ninety days.

Nodding toward my bag of dirty clothes, I asked where I could find a *lavandería*. He assured me he would be very happy to take my laundry home and wash it himself. "No, no, no. I can't let you do that. Isn't there a shop in town where they do laundry?" He shook his head; there was no *lavandería* in La Unión.

As I searched for a woman who would wash my clothes in her home, spirited voices pulled me to a small street stand. A mismatched group of *mariachis* had gathered and were singing with passion to the young women serving Cokes from a cooler. I ordered an orange Fanta, and the musicians warmed up to a new audience. Tall and skinny, short with a beer belly, toothless and frail—a little bit of everything—they made up for their crude instruments with enthusiasm. Their lyrics brought blushes from the young women, who asked if I understood the words and giggled when I shook my head. The men laughed, then left to look for another venue. They were playing for the love of music, not for *colónes* in this poor place. The young women took my laundry with assurances it would be ready the next noon.

Adults, children, and more groups of musicians jostled each other while women with mesh shopping bags bought supplies for dinner—fresh tortillas, pastries, chili peppers, chickens, tomatoes, and mangoes—from the open market that stretched for blocks in all directions.

In the long-distance phone office I took my seat in the front row of the waiting area. A tiny, shriveled old lady in black stopped in front of me, eye-to-eye. Leaning in close, she held my face between her hands, beaming straight into my soul. When she left I wiped away tears for the sights those eyes must have seen, the things that must have touched her family, and for the resilience that let her spread love despite all.

The clean clothes were waiting in the morning for $2.50. Someone gave me directions to the ice factory along the shoreline leaving the harbor.

SC motored down the channel to a dock almost as high as the spreaders, 15 feet or more above deck. A group of men gathered on the high wharf, waving for me to come alongside and hand over my lines. They secured *Southern Cross* to two-foot-high bollards sized for large, commercial fishing vessels. Clutching my two ice bags, I scrambled up the ladder as they gaped.

The crowd passed me from one to another and finally escorted me to the main office, two blocks away, and into the director's private suite. At his request I briefly related the story of my trip, then explained what I needed. "Yes, we have ice," he said. "You can get what you need at the dock. There's one problem, though—we're a large commercial operation for the fishing industry and aren't set up to sell small quantities. Just take what you need. There's no charge."

Only two people had given me ice in eight years—Henrick Hui's girlfriend in Tahiti and the fisherman in Siracusa, Italy. In some places the vendors had even refused to sell it to me. "Thank you so much," I answered. "I really appreciate your help."

The foreman pulled a cord opening an overhead door, and a mountain of crushed ice landed inches away from me. As tall as I, it was the minimum amount they could deliver. They filled my two bags, barely making a dent in the pile, and carried them to the edge of the dock. In moments they had passed down both 70-pound bags and left them in the cockpit.

My icebox overflowed with ice, even with only the most fragile items stored inside, and a nearly full bag remained in the cockpit cooling the rest of the perishable food. A deep orange sun slid down the sky as I inched my way past the islands of the Gulf of Fonseca against a strong, advancing tidal current and heavy afternoon winds.

Traveling north to Acajutla, near the border with Guatemala, *SC* danced between clusters of fishing boats for two long nights. Citing possible obstructions on the bottom and potential exposure to strong winds, my guidebook had discouraged me from stopping at this northernmost port in El Salvador. But at 0640, in front of rows of large fishing boats, *SC* anchored anyway. As a precaution, I set a trip line, providing an alternate way to retrieve the anchor in the event it fouled on the bottom.

The two crisply uniformed navy officers who came to clear *SC* invited me to tie my dinghy to their gunboat when I was ready to go ashore. Even their vessel was dwarfed by the towering freighter docks. I pulled up to their stern, calling for permission to board and wondering what would happen if I tried this on a U.S. Navy vessel. An unconcerned crew member appeared, waved me aboard, and disappeared below.

Small boats bearing young boys anxious to visit circled *Southern Cross* when

I returned. One pointed to the vessel moored on my port side, saying, "*Malo, malo capitán*," and wrinkled his nose.

I watched the "bad" captain with a wary eye, then in alarm saw him climb down to his dinghy and row toward *Southern Cross*. He introduced himself, and I gave a perfunctory, guarded greeting. After more attempts at conversation he held up a large, blue plastic tub full of ice—a gift for me. Influenced by the boys' attitude, I declined. He broke out a big smile, and I realized I had not looked at him through my own eyes.

I emptied the tub into the nearly full icebox and thanked him warmly—not for the ice, but for the lesson.

With gunpowder, steel swords, and horses, the *conquistadores* overwhelmed the lands of Central America in the sixteenth century and claimed them for Spain. Within a century, ninety percent of the indigenous populations in the Americas had been wiped out through war, disease, and slavery, including the Mayans of Guatemala. Their cultured, sophisticated society—including a calendar said to be more accurate than that used by NASA—was in ruins, and the survivors had been turned into slaves in their own land.

But the Mayan community guarded and secretly kept alive the threads of their twenty-three languages and their heritage and religion. Each generation rebelled anew against the yoke of oppression, seeking land and a voice, and for centuries each was crushed. But in 1954 Guatemala's President Arbenz launched his land reform program by turning over a portion of his own family's holdings.

As reparations for property taken from major landholders, the government paid the values the owners had been claiming on their tax documents. But the U.S.-owned United Fruit Company cried foul and appealed to the McCarthy-era U.S. government for help. The resulting U.S.-sponsored coup d'état and military aid launched a civil war that left 200,000 civilians dead and 440 Mayan villages wiped from the map. In the 1990s, Mayans represented eighty percent of the population, but without land and representation they still lived under extreme discrimination, malnourished and illiterate.

Fifty-nine miles up the coast from Acajutla, I anchored in the security of the navy base at Puerto Quetzal, Guatemala—five days for $95. For months I had looked forward to visiting the famous Sunday market in the mountains at Chichicastenango. Photos from friends showed exquisite hand-loomed fabrics and stitchery.

The overloaded bus to the mountain town of Antigua was everything the guidebooks had predicted. Seat cushions were pulled toward the center, allowing more riders to perch in the aisles braced shoulder to shoulder against each other, while the displaced people by the windows hung on by one cheek. Between aisle riders' knees and backs down the center more people stood. Five hours later we pulled into Antigua, the colonial capital full of 200-year-old homes and 400-year-old churches. The very air breathed history, and the sounds of halting Spanish tinged with French, Japanese, Dutch, and Swedish accents drifted everywhere as students from the town's hundred language schools filled the central plaza and strolled the quiet streets.

I checked into the bottom-end Hotel Landivar and scouted for galleries, good food, old buildings, and interesting things to do. A Friday night art opening caught my eye. I showered, changed, and stopped for fresh tomato soup, chips, and guacamole at a popular patio restaurant on the way to the show.

Standing side by side with me at the show, sipping a glass of white wine and surveying the abstract paintings, was a short, plump, fiftyish woman in a navy blue suit and white blouse. She greeted me—"*Buenas tardes. ¿Se gusta?*"— and we chatted, limited by my poor Spanish. I knew no one, and she knew only a few. Anniflores and I left together, strolling toward the main plaza, then stopped to enjoy the cool evening air and the activity around us—students practicing their Spanish, the Mayans selling their handicrafts, and young Antiguans flirting and visiting. As we parted, Anniflores invited me to join her in the morning at 8:00 for tea at a nearby outdoor restaurant. "*Buenas noches.*"

"*Sí, buenas noches. Hasta mañana.*"

A violent attack of food poisoning began at midnight and continued all night. I leapt from bed every fifteen minutes to race for the bathroom. The poisons coming up burned my throat, swelling it closed until I could no longer talk. By 7:30 in the morning I wanted to die. But Anniflores would be waiting, and I needed two prescriptions to stop all the action, so I showered and dragged myself to the restaurant. Anniflores looked at my pale, drawn face in alarm.

We sat a few minutes while I halfheartedly drank a little herbal tea. She talked about her family: her deceased husband and her children in Guatemala City, Mexico, and the United States. I nodded from time to time, my voice a raspy whisper. Anniflores had brought me a gift from her artisans shop—a small painting done by a Mayan teenager.

We stopped at the pharmacy, then she took me back to my room. I climbed into the lumpy bed, pulled the covers, a sarong, and a sweater over me, and shivered, chilled by the morning's effort. In a few hours Anniflores awakened me with a tall glass of thick white liquid. "*Tome, tómelo,*" she ordered. The warm, sweet, cinnamon-flavored drink slid down, soothing my throat and settling my stomach. I climbed back into bed and slept again.

Late in the afternoon, I walked around the block to return the glass to her shop. The little brass bell rang as I opened the door on a space no more than ten feet by ten. To the left stood a counter with small gift items. In the center of the room was a tall, glass-fronted case displaying jewelry, and on the walls were more of the young peoples' colorful *naif* paintings.

In back of the case, behind a flowered cotton curtain, was Anniflores's home. This small corner of her tiny shop held her bed and personal possessions. To my eyes this woman had so little, but in hers she had abundance enough to share with me.

On April 23rd, I sailed across the last international border with my old Mexican flag flying. It was worn and faded but represented a celebration to me. A gray, Mexican Armada gunboat approached from seaward, calling me on VHF channel 16. "What's the name of your vessel? Where're you coming from? How many on board?"—all the usual questions I'd heard in each of the forty countries I had visited.

"*Southern Cross.* Flag: USA. Coming from Puerto Quetzal, Guatemala. One person on board. Nationality: USA."

"But who's the person in the green shirt?"

"That's me!"

They approached, binoculars straining.

The sun set before I reached the entrance to Puerto Madero. I had crashed into short, 5-foot seas for 17 hours. Far too tired to heave-to with potential fishing traffic in the area, and with no place to anchor outside, I reluctantly approached the entry in total darkness. There were no navigation lights marking the edges inside the long channel, but there were leading lights to guide large commercial vessels. I convinced myself that with only a 5-foot, 4-inch draft, *SC* would be fine.

Following the chart, I drove between the markers at the entrance, keeping the two leading lights in line with each other at 39 degrees. Two-thirds of the way down the channel the depth alarm sounded, and *Southern Cross* hit bottom. I turned quickly to starboard and bounced across firm mud back to deeper water.

I sent out a plea over VHF radio to the small gathering of boats visible off the beach: "Does anyone have information on the entry here? Please come back and tell me what's wrong." The crew of *Amadon Light* came by dinghy to escort me in.

Now only the Gulf of Téhuantepec—more than 250 miles wide—stood between me and Acapulco. For more than five years I had worried about the gulf's vicious northeasterlies, which funnel between the mountains of Mexico and Guatemala to harass boats up to 500 miles offshore. But I had no intention of sailing 500 miles out and 500 back to get to the other side; mine would be a coast-hugging passage. I prepared *Southern Cross* as never before—sealing leaky hatches, bagging and securing the dinghy as if for a full ocean crossing, and wedging everything of value into the V-berth under sheets of plastic. I even fixed two days' worth of meals, something I had never done for any passage before. The engine was serviced and ready and the fuel tank full. There was nothing more to do.

Three boats waited with me for a departure window in the weather: *Ocean Sea*, a large power yacht, and *Wind Journey* and *Sanderling*, both small sailboats. We conferred and talked daily to the port captain, but each day Herb, who was back in radio range, warned me to hold off a little longer. On April 26th, with a high in the Pacific and a low over the Caribbean, an on-shore south westerly was blowing; it was time to leave. Herb advised, "It looks good. Go for it."

At 1410 the convoy motored out, our hearts thumping almost as loudly as our engines as we passed down the mismarked channel. Winds were light and perfect for off-wind sailing. We set a schedule of radio contacts every two hours. *Ocean Sea* steamed out ahead of us and fired back reports of good conditions as she approached the boundary of strong winds. Encouraged, I edged away from the shoreline to shorten the distance around the gulf. Offshore I could at least grab catnaps.

The seas were empty. The entire fishing fleet had left the day before to spend hurricane season in Mazatlán, far to the north. Positive reports came in from my companion boats every two hours. Winds moved from southwest to east and back again with the rising and setting sun.

On the second night *Ocean Sea* reported being hammered by rough winds and seas on the far side of the gulf. I angled in toward the lee of the shore. *Wind Journey* called to say they were proceeding under sail only. The mounting bolt for their alternator had sheared, and they had no way to repair it. I offered easy outs when we reached Huatulco.

The second morning dawned with perfect conditions along the western coast. Swarms of small bees descended on *Southern Cross*. Maybe the sweet taste of success I was feeling brought them out. I sang and laughed. The five years of my life spent worrying about these last two days had been another waste of time. When would I ever remember that fear is worse than the event . . . always?

Exactly forty-eight hours after my departure, I anchored in Puerto Huatulco, ready to jump overboard and celebrate. In the pan beneath the engine I found a large bolt. It belonged in the gaping hole in the starboard forward engine mount. The mount had swiveled out of line, with only one bolt securing it. *SC*'s guardian angel had been on duty again.

In a one-desk, long-distance telephone office at the top of a narrow concrete stairway, I sent faxes: one to Mom and Stubby telling them I had crossed the Téhuantepec safely and would arrive in Acapulco on May 4th or 5th; one to the Acapulco Marina asking if they could give me a slip for a week at no charge; one to Juan Lans, a friend from Mexico City, asking if he could be in Acapulco to help me celebrate; and one to Amy Ullrich at *SAIL*, informing her that I was about to finish my circumnavigation, the second American woman and probably the oldest woman in the world to do so. "Do you know anyone in the media who might be interested?"

Amy faxed back that I would be the *first* American woman, since Tania's trip had been disallowed. I found this news uncomfortable to accept—Tania remained first in my heart—but the bandwagon was off and running, and I was on for the ride. A fax arrived from Barbara Lloyd of the *New York Times* with questions about me and my trip. I left my responses at the fax office and went shopping at the central market.

In an open courtyard surrounded by soft turquoise walls and cascades of flowers in brightly colored buckets, my painter's eye came back to life. The market thronged with colorful people surrounded by local fruits, herbs, and vegetables in an abundance and variety I hadn't seen in months. I shot rolls of photos, thinking ahead to life after the trip—painting and living somewhere in Mexico—then shopped, explored, and people-watched for a day.

Towering, muscular Dan Wellbery, the hired captain of a large motor vessel stranded inside the port, shifted my motor mount back in place, then looked for more jobs on *SC*. Dan reminded me of so many others who had helped, keeping a little piece of my journey for themselves.

On May 2nd, at 2050, I made my last departure with 260 miles to go. The next night I moved closer to the coastline, out of the shipping traffic off the Oaxaca coast. Between the Río Verde and the Laguna de Alotengo, lightning erupted over the land, extending as far as I could see up and down the coast.

The powerful, intense display crackled and boomed, breaking the night sky into shards of black. Slowly it began to walk toward the sea. Closer and closer it came, and *SC*'s mast was the tallest object in its path.

I knew of boats that had been hit and lost all their electronics. But could lightning also travel down the rigging and through grounded through-hulls to blow a hole in the bottom of a boat? No matter how much reading I had done or how many people I had talked to, I had never been able to convince myself that *SC* was ready to handle a strike.

Silver and gold flashes advanced across the beach. I pulled 30 feet of stern-anchor chain forward, wrapped it around the turnbuckle of the upper shroud, and draped the balance overboard to drag in the sea, making an easy exit path for the discharge. The storm surrounded *Southern Cross* on every side while she sat in the middle of a pocket of clear air with stars overhead, safe from the crackling bolts.

The same power that had provided everything I needed for eight years, had kept an angel on board when the trip was beyond my strength, and had shown me how to find beauty and joy in the darkest moments was still present. So much had been given to me. Now I could accept it without expecting it and not wonder if I was worthy. If friends came with a basket of food, I could say thank you and enjoy the gift.

I had changed by small increments over the eight years of my trip. Like a jeweler reshaping a piece of precious metal by hundreds of small taps from her forging hammer, the events of eight years had slowly shifted the way I viewed myself, responded to events, and related to those around me. I had found forgiveness for myself and acceptance of the past life that had pushed me out across the Pacific.

Ship's diary: 5 May 1997, 0135 Local, 16°49′N/099°51′W. Anchored at Marques Bay by Acapulco.

The Displaced Peorians were listening for my call in the morning: "Net Control, KM6DR here. I've arrived. Tell Mom I'll call by phone in a couple of hours." Congratulations fired back from hams all over the country. It was my first rush of success.

At 1000, I weighed anchor and sailed across the bay seaward of Isla Roqueta to tie the knot on my circumnavigation. Crossing my invisible outbound line, I waited for the emotion to hit. Nothing happened. I drew the route in my mind, stretching it west to the Marquesas and on and on around the world, trying to make it real. It was the line a frightened, desperate woman had made westward as she slowly became a whole person. Faces, landfalls, and moments from the past eight years and one day flooded my memory. The moment of arrival became real, but still without emotion.

"This is *Southern Cross*. I'll be at the dock in twenty minutes. Can you have someone there to take my lines, please?"

I worked my way through the marina. The dark-skinned, smiling dockmaster in his khaki uniform reached out for my lines and tied me off in the first slip inside the dock gate. I stepped off to check in at the office. Gisela, the office manager who had answered my fax from Huatulco, waited with a handful of messages from family and friends congratulating me on my accomplishment and a huge bouquet of flowers from the marina staff.

Mom and Stubby were both on the line when I called collect. They sent loving praise and good wishes. I walked back to my partner, *Southern Cross*, and thanked her for being a reliable, seaworthy vessel. We had seen so much together.

Below I sat down on the settee, and finally, from deep inside, came an explosion of emotion. I shouted, "There, now did I do enough?" I was looking upward toward the companionway. There was no one standing there, but I knew inside the power I felt was the specter of my father—the man I was never good enough for. I hadn't mattered enough when I was five for him to fight to keep me. I hadn't mattered enough when the adoption was pending. And I hadn't mattered enough when I asked for help to go to college. It seemed I hadn't ever been worthy of his effort.

Until this moment I had had no idea to what extent his role in my life had influenced not only this voyage, but my constant push "to measure up," "to reach higher and higher." I saw the incredible impact that his abandonment and rejection had had on me. Now it was over; I had done it and could accept that I was "good enough." Perhaps he had not been worthy of me. I let the tears come.

A bottle of champagne from Panama was waiting in the icebox. Looking for someone to share my celebration with, I saw four cruisers visiting on the terrace. "I just finished a solo circumnavigation," I told them. "Would you like to help me celebrate?"

They all stared for a minute, then broke out in congratulations. *Photon, Adagio*, and *Southern Cross* toasted with plastic cups of champagne.

As we finished the bottle, Juan arrived. He took me to dinner and listened to my sea stories, but I could not yet share the layers of self-discovery enmeshed in the homecoming. They would unfold over time.

BARBARA LLOYD'S ARTICLE IN THE MAY 6TH *NEW York Times* set off a flurry of activity. Calls and faxes arrived by the hour, requesting interviews and asking questions. Fox TV scheduled a telephone interview on my trip for their Sunday morning show. Lloyd asked me to call the Associated Press and have them shoot a photo for her article in *Cruising World*. The Mexico City office responded, "Your timing's really bad. President Clinton's here. We don't have anyone to send." Two days later an AP photographer and reporter arrived. When their article flashed across the country more calls and faxes arrived. At moments I was glad to be south of the border, a little out of reach of the flurry. After years alone, the sudden celebrity was almost too much to handle.

The largest television system in the world, Televisa, based in Mexico but covering all of the Americas, sent a crew for an interview. People looked at me differently on the street and in shops. At times I seemed to be floating in a bubble, somewhere between reality and the "busy-ness" around me. The attention was flattering but at the same time unreal.

I sailed north to Puerto Vallarta, looking for a new home for *Southern Cross* and me. The following month the major U. S. sailing magazines all carried articles about "the first American woman" to complete a solo circumnavigation.

In July, Terri and my mother hosted a surprise celebration in Bloomington, where I was surrounded by family and friends who could share my moment in the spotlight. A one-day art show at a local mall brought out hundreds of well-wishers. One special moment from that day stood out: an attractive woman in her early forties approached, saying she had been following my trip in the local news. That spring she had convinced herself that "if Pat Henry can do what she did, you can ride your motorcycle to Florida for a vacation," and she did. We hugged in mutual congratulations, shedding tears of understanding and success. This was exactly what I had hoped my trip would accomplish.

In September Libby threw a party for me in Portland, and Tam planned another in Santa Cruz. I enjoyed one more month of visiting and celebrations. Both trips—Illinois and the West Coast—let me share the accomplishment with those who had helped make it possible by shopping, handling mail, gathering information, sending gifts of money and gear, and cheering me on when I was down.

In January I moved *Southern Cross* from the marina in Puerto Vallarta to a small private housing complex on the water—quieter and less expensive. There

I was surrounded by towering palms and pink, red, magenta and yellow tropical flowers. To the soft hum of gardeners, nearby sounds of boat work, Latin music, and Spanish conversations, my brushes laid down the colors of Mexico while my mind turned over the pieces of eight years, pulling them together to make a whole. I had found peace within and with most of those around me. The only gap I could not fill separated me from my daughter. But we both had to reach across the abyss, and she was not ready.

Dear Terri,

Everyone is asking where home will be now that the trip is over. When I went to church with Mom and Stubby last summer, I wrote "the World" in the address blank on the visitors' list.

If I were dropped from an airplane somewhere above the earth, wherever I landed I would be at "home." It is something inside—not a place, nor a building, but a state of being.

My travels taught me that we are all made of the same things at the core. In different proportions certainly, but love, anger, passion, weariness, fear, joy, boredom, and more all fill the lives of people around the world. To experience this has been one of the greatest gifts of the past eight years.

On the bus yesterday, a young woman stood next to my seat. Her heart was breaking. The sound of her crying raised memories of pain in my life, and I could feel myself inside her skin. We had no common words, but I reached out and took her hand for just a moment. We were not strangers.

But I still do not know my own daughter. Our interactions are only on the surface. The cord that connects us is so thin.

Mom came to see me in Santa Cruz once when I desperately needed to talk with her. Each morning we took out some memory, some idea, put it on the table between us and talked about it . . . without accusations, without defenses, just as we saw it then and how it felt. I pray that someday you and I can have such a time together.

I love you, dear, with all my heart,

Mom

As time went on, controversy developed around my use of the Suez and Panama Canals; the former had required a pilot, and the latter, line handlers and an adviser. Meanwhile Karen Thorndike was battling through the gale-ridden southern oceans, south of the world's great capes, to finish the voyage she had begun in 1996. The following summer the sailing magazines all carried articles congratulating her on being the first American woman to complete a solo circumnavigation. Her route had stayed in open ocean and did not require that anyone come on board.

When Karen pulled in at the end of her voyage, the first question one reporter asked her was, "What do you think of Pat Henry?" The press seemed more interested in stirring controversy than in reporting what Karen had achieved. The title—the chance to enter the record books—became the focus, not our respective accomplishments. Friends and supporters on both sides wrote letters defending each of us.

I sent a congratulatory e-mail. A year later Karen wrote back to say she had just received it and wanted to call me. One Sunday evening, the phone rang. "This is Karen Thorndike." We visited for half an hour, and when we hung up, I knew this was a woman I would like to have for a friend. Together with Tania and the other women singlehanders, we had a message to share about women and our potential to meet challenges, to set incredible goals, to shoot for the stars, and to find ourselves in the rare atmosphere of success.

Karen called the Joshua Slocum Society, an organization of shorthanded and solo sailors from around the world, to nominate me for the same award she had received only months before, the Golden Circle Award. Hers was the spirit of sportsmanship I had found in New Zealand during the Whitbread in 1990, a spirit that made everyone a winner.

In the spring of 2000, the *Guinness* record-keepers sent a certificate to Karen declaring, "A U.S. record was set by Karen Thorndike, who became the first American woman to sail solo around the world in a sloop, *Amelia*, from 4 August 1996–18 August 1998, starting and finishing at San Diego, California, USA."

It wasn't easy to have been given a title and then have it taken away, but making a record had never been my intent. It was for my own sake, and no one else's, that I'd kept my voyage solo. The best and most meaningful awards are the ones we give ourselves. Even had I learned in Singapore that the canals would disqualify me, I would not have changed my route to go around the capes, but I would still have done the rest alone.

With the grace I found in my voyage, I could let the title go, knowing life was taking me in other directions. I had paintings to create, new art forms to discover, flute lessons to take, Spanish to learn, dancing to do, and more places to visit and people to meet. I had sailed away from an old life, and a new one was just beginning. There were new dreams to take the place of the one just fulfilled.

Sail and Boat Plans

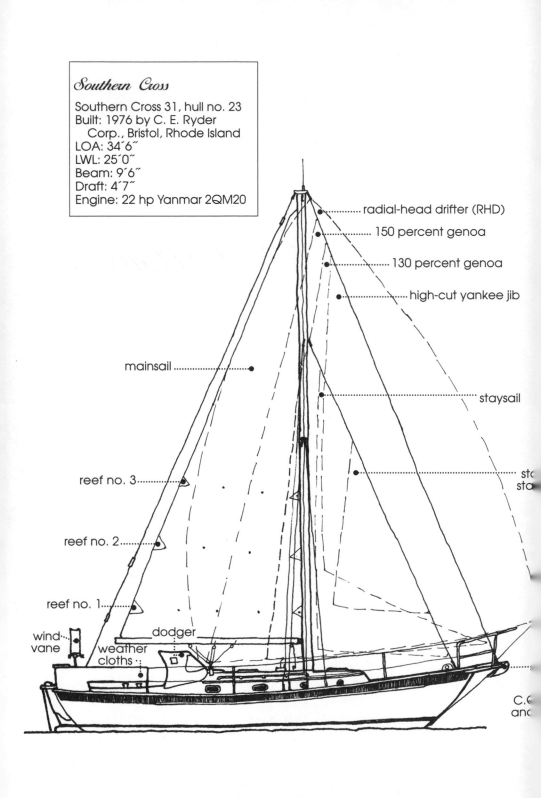

Southern Cross

Southern Cross 31, hull no. 23
Built: 1976 by C. E. Ryder
  Corp., Bristol, Rhode Island
LOA: 34´6˝
LWL: 25´0˝
Beam: 9´6˝
Draft: 4´7˝
Engine: 22 hp Yanmar 2QM20

radial-head drifter (RHD)

150 percent genoa

130 percent genoa

high-cut yankee jib

mainsail

staysail

reef no. 3

sta
sta

reef no. 2

reef no. 1

wind
vane

dodger

weather
cloths

C.6
and

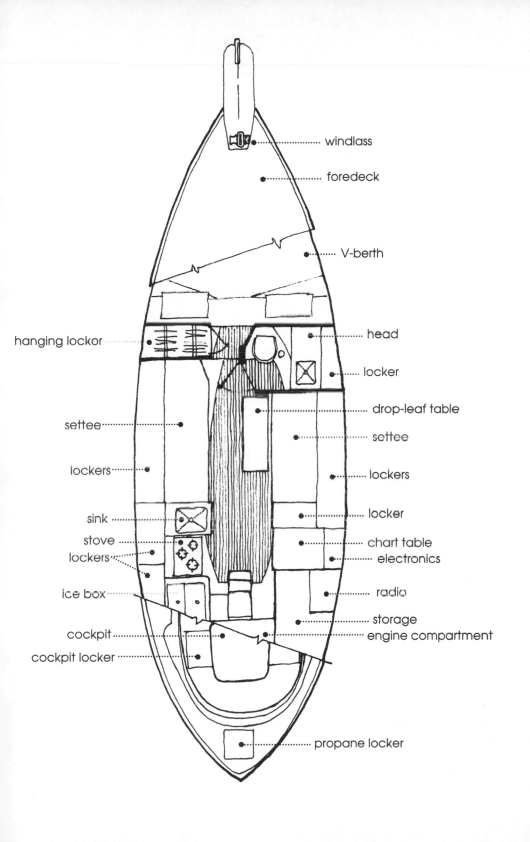

- windlass
- foredeck
- V-berth
- hanging locker
- head
- locker
- drop-leaf table
- settee
- settee
- lockers
- lockers
- sink
- locker
- stove
- chart table
- lockers
- electronics
- ice box
- radio
- cockpit
- storage
- cockpit locker
- engine compartment
- propane locker

Acknowledgments

The writing of this book, the voyage and the lessons gained en route would not have happened without the encouragement, assistance, and participation of many. Some did only so much as smile when it was needed while others gave in major material ways, but each one has a thank you from my heart. You are remembered, even if your moment in my life is not found among the stories I chose to share.

I thank . . .

My family: Mom and Stubby; Tamara, Shawn, and Kira; Terri, Glenn, Alissa, and Krista; Stu and his family; and Libby for the laughter, errands, letters, visits, gifts, prayers, and faith in me.

Lesa for your abiding love and help and afternoon cappuccinos and listening to every chapter four times.

Elizabeth for the beautiful home in Puerto Vallarta where "Grace" came to life.

Sally for reading, encouraging, and advising. I would have given up but for you.

Adene for your guiding light through the maze.

Sam for persevering past closed doors.

Kitty for art lessons through life.

Sarah for the gift of her poetry.

Terry and Evelyn for reading the sailing passages.

Joe and Kat for being there always on the trip and after.

To the cruising community who became my family away from home for friendship, encouragement, and support.

To the ham nets and the weather volunteers who kept me in touch and informed.

To shoreside friends in countries around the world who provided a wider view of humanity and our interconnectedness.

To my sponsors Profurl, Compaq, and North Sails for the equipment they supplied.

To those who came to exhibitions of my art and encouraged me to continue.

And to those who read this book and find in it a message that touches their lives.

About the Author

Born in Chicago, Illinois, in 1941, Pat Henry grew up in the small-town Midwest. Her quest for adventure began with a solo after-noon journey at the age of three to search for the "pot of gold at the end of the rainbow," and has never ended.

Henry began sailing in 1976 at the age of thirty-five when a friend with a 50-foot trimaran invited her on a Christmas voyage from the San Francisco Bay area to Mexico. She eventually crewed for 40,000 miles on various boats, primarily as navigator. She bought her first sailboat, a 24-foot MacGregor day-sailer, in 1985. She bought her present boat, *Southern Cross*, in 1988 and has sailed it more than 40,000 miles. For her solo circumnavigation, Henry received the Joshua Slocum Society International's Golden Circle Award in 1999.

In Puerto Vallarta, Mexico, at the beginning of her grand adventure, she began painting watercolors to finance her travels. Painting became not only the means to an end but her key to experiencing the forty countries her circum-navigation aboard *Southern Cross* took her to. An accomplished artist, Henry has exhibited in galleries around the world.

She is the mother of two daughters and has four grandchildren. Her pro-fessional credits include architect, university professor, and importer. Today her home is in Puerto Vallarta, Mexico, with *Southern Cross* waiting nearby for her next adventure. She can be contacted through her Web site (www.wright printing.com/pathenry/index.html).